Electrical Installations

3rd edition

Electrical Installations

3rd edition

Christopher
Shelton

First published in 1993 by:
Pearson Education Limited
Second edition 1996

Third edition published in 2004 by:
Nelson Thornes Ltd
Delta Place
27 Bath Road
CHELTENHAM
GL53 7TH
United Kingdom

04 05 06 07 08 / 10 9 8 7 6 5 4 3 2 1

A catalogue record for this book is available from the British Library

ISBN 0 7487 7979 5

Page make-up by Saxon Graphics Ltd, Derby

Printed in Great Britain by The Cromwell Press Ltd, Trowbridge, Wiltshire

Contents

Dedication

**To our grandchildren:
may you all have
long and happy lives**

Acknowledgements

We would like to thank the following people for their help and time given in the preparation of this book: Andrea King for the loan of a decent camera and my wife Shirley who helped in every way possible. Finally, I would like to say 'thank you' to Stephen Hearn of SGB Youngman for his help and advice when writing about freestanding access towers.

A special thanks to City and Guilds of London for their time spent in reviewing the manuscript and illustrative works that serve this book.

I would also like to say a big 'thank you' to the following companies for their help in providing photographs or giving permission to reproduce copyright material: AEI Cables Ltd.; Robin Electronics Ltd.; Salisbury College; Arena-Walsall Ltd.; Wiltshire Fire Brigade; RS Components (UK) Ltd.; Wylex Ltd. and the Marshall Tufflex Company of Hastings Ltd.

Extracts from BSEN 60617 are reproduced with the permission of British Standards Institute (BSI). Complete copies of this standard can be obtained by post from BSI Customer Service, 389 Chiswick High Road, London W4 4AL (telephone 0181 996 7000).

Finally I would like to say 'thank you' to the Further Education staff at Nelson Thornes Limited for their hard work and for making this third edition of *Electrical Installations* possible.

Chris Shelton
June 2004

Preface

This book, designed to accompany the *City and Guild 2330* award scheme and incorporating the optional unit, *Buildings and Structures,* is for candidates who are in an apprenticeship and wish to forward their career in the electrical service industry.

The *Level 2 Electrotechology Award* has been fashioned to offer an opportunity for candidates to add official approval for the work they have carried out and completed throughout their course.

This book will help to contribute towards knowledge requirements and technical understanding for the *2330 NVQ Level 2* course in electrical installation engineering. *Electrical Installations* reflects the scope of the *National Occupational Standards* – some smaller topics are deliberately absent but the college workshop will provide for these under the many practical activities which accompany this course.

Welcome to the third edition of *Electrical Installations*! The design and much of the content of this book has changed from the first and second editions to meet the requirements of the new *National Vocational Standards* at *Level 2* in electrical installation work and the students who read it.

Each chapter will start with a brief summary of what you will be expected to know or demonstrate in order to obtain the award you are studying.

This third edition has been carefully written, taking on board the requirements of *BS 7671:2001,* which, on occasions, will be referred to as *The Wiring Regulations.*

Graphical symbols used throughout the book are from *BSEN 60617.* Where I needed to make things clearer, I have used *pictograms* instead.

I hope you benefit from reading this new edition: there is a lot more in it than you might think – and good luck with your studies.

Chris Shelton
June 2004

1 Maintaining a safe and healthy system of working

Introduction

The contents of this chapter have been taken from the Level 2 (2330 Scheme) syllabus, which seeks to ensure the health and safety of people like you within the workplace. It has also been written to protect others against risks arising from your day-to-day working activities.

How to obtain your Level 2 Certificate

In order to obtain your certificate you will have to achieve the following:

- Pass the three compulsory core units.
- Choose and pass one occupational unit (the occupational unit serving this book is *Buildings and Structures*).
- Take a written multiple-choice examination and demonstrate to your assessor that you can carry out the following practical activities:

1 Make a list of the ways required to work safely and effectively.
2 Identify safety equipment within the workplace.
3 Identify safe working practices.
4 Check that warning notices and barriers are sited and installed correctly.
5 Confirm that your worksite conditions are safe for work to continue.
6 Ensure that all work equipment is in a safe workable condition.
7 Make sure that, on completion of work, all tools, equipment and material items are removed from the workplace and securely stored.

You will find that some of these requirements might overlap throughout the book. The assignments you carry out are a formal assessment of your skills but are not designed as a recognised teaching aid.

Health and safety in the workplace

Your legal duties

There are three sets of safety regulations, with which you must try to become familiar during your NVQ study course:

- The Health and Safety at Work Act (HASAWA) [1974]
- The Electricity at Work Regulations [1989]
- The Wiring Regulations, now known as BS 7671.

Further reading

The Electricity at Work Regulations is a *legal* framework that covers all aspects of your electrical work and the equipment to be used. You must abide by this set of rules or prosecution could follow.

More details may be found in the following publications, which you should be able to find in a public reference library or your own college library:

- A guide to the HASAWA [1974]
- The Essentials of the Health and Safety at Work Act

Your responsibilities as an apprentice

1 If you sense a health and safety problem exists in your workplace get in touch with your *site manager* or *safety officer*. If it is a serious health problem and you feel no one will listen, telephone your local *Health and Safety Executive Employment Medical Advisory Service* and listen to his or her advice.

2 Try to cooperate fully with all factors concerning health and safety. If you have an accident, make sure that you fill out your company accident book (Figure 1.1). This is very important – keep a record!

3 When you are at work, you are responsible for your own health but, if you are the appointed *jobholder,* you are then answerable for the health and safety of others under your control that are affected by any decision you make. It is quite a responsibility! As an example, it would be very foolish to ask an apprentice to carry out a job in a biohazardous area without first getting formal clearance from others. Figure 1.2 illustrates the type of sign used where there is some sort of biohazard.

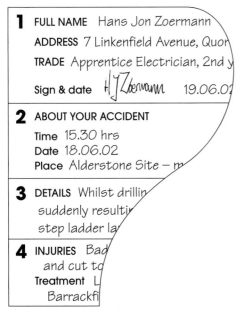

1 FULL NAME Hans Jon Zoermann

ADDRESS 7 Linkenfield Avenue, Quor

TRADE Apprentice Electrician, 2nd y

Sign & date H J Zoermann   19.06.0

2 ABOUT YOUR ACCIDENT

Time 15.30 hrs
Date 18.06.02
Place Alderstone Site – m

3 DETAILS Whilst drillin
suddenly resulti
step ladder la

4 INJURIES Bad
and cut to
Treatment L
Barrackfi

Figure 1.1 *– A page from your accident book – make sure you log all details.*

BIOLOGICAL
RISK

Figure 1.2 *– Biohazard warning sign.*

Hazards inside the workplace

I am sure that the vast majority of work-related accidents are avoidable. The cause is lack of care and unawareness of the hidden dangers that lie in wait within our workplace. When a major accident takes place, the job slowly stops – there are many person-hours lost. It is important to put into operation a risk assessment procedure before any work commences. There are five main stages to consider:

1 Identifying your workplace hazards.

2 Weighing up the risks involved.

3 Putting in writing what you find.

4 Organising and putting into practice a plan of action.

5 Reviewing at regular intervals what you have found.

Consider the following:

- Any obvious dangers should be checked out.

- Morning-after hangovers should be avoided as they often lead to misjudgement.

- A friendly eye should be kept on less experienced workmates.

- Safety signs should not be ignored – they are there for a purpose! (Figure 1.3 illustrates a selection)

- In older properties, rotten or unstable flooring, holes and pits, disused wells and sudden changes in the direction of stairwells are common. They can be a big problem if you are not expecting them.

MANDATORY SIGNS　　　　WARNING SIGNS　　　　PROHIBITION SIGNS

Figure 1.3 – *A selection of site warning signs.*

New faces

Try to provide suitable guidance and direction to new workmates. Avoid putting pressure on them, as this can generate stress. Stress can lead to getting things wrong and this in itself could cause an accident, as Figure 1.4 shows. Give them time to settle in before you make any judgement.

Health and safety risks in your own job role

Be honest with yourself – do you have any personal health risks in your present job role? For example, are you possibly diabetic or even colour blind to some degree? Are you prone to attacks of epilepsy, back pains or migraine? Any of these problems could contribute towards an accident in the workplace.

You must control all health and safety hazards within your job responsibilities. If you are unable to do this, you must get help and advice from someone who knows about these matters.

Think whether the job you are about to carry out could cause any potential harm within the workplace – storing a large amount of old-fashioned ionisation smoke detectors removed from a disused installation, for example.

Evacuation plan – in case of an emergency

You must talk over and agree to an emergency evacuation plan and check out the positions of all fire exits before work starts. In the event of a site emergency, it is essential that you *stick to the rules,* follow an agreed procedure and make your way to the nearest assembly point. Keeping to the rules saves lives!

Remaining alert
Asbestos

Keep an eye open for potential hazards within your workplace. Asbestos is a *long-term killer* and is often present in older houses. If you come across this deadly material, get it removed by professional people who are equipped with the

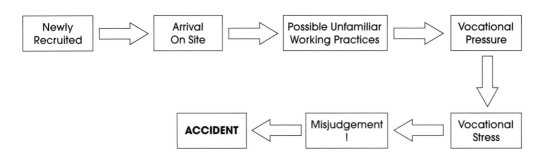

Figure 1.4 – *Stress can lead to misjudgement that could cause an accident.*

protective clothing and equipment to deal with this lethal substance.

Over 3000 people die in the UK from diseases directly caused from breathing in particles of asbestos and this figure is expected to grow to over 10 000 by the year 2011. People at risk are those who work in the building trade, such as carpenters, electricians and plumbers. In addition, this risk applies to computer network installers, television aerial technicians and telephone cabling engineers. Asbestos can be coloured blue, white or grey but, whatever its colour, keep well away from it!

Petrochemical sites

In plants that make or contain vast quantities of petrol, by the very nature of the businesses, there is always a risk of fire or explosion. This type of site is always a high-risk area – so obey the rules! Please remember that NO SMOKING really does mean *no* smoking – it could just keep you out of hospital!

Working at heights and near to water

If you have to work near to deep water, it is important to wear a properly fitted lifejacket. If there are just one or two of you, discuss an emergency plan in case one of you gets into difficulty and falls into the deep water.

When working at heights, choose your means of access carefully. For example, it would be very unwise to access a tall round-bodied street light using a ladder with fixed rungs, no matter how safe you think it is. Safe site access will be discussed within Chapter 2, page 31.

Escape routes

Well-organised sites have escape route directions posted onto the construction walls. This is most important, especially if you are working in a block of flats or a complicated building. Fire security measures are important, so you must decide what to do long before work commences. If it is possible to put this in writing – then do so. Figure 1.5 illustrates a site exit route using purpose-made signs.

Just because you are a small company carrying out minor electrical work, it does not mean you can ignore these regulations. Keep safe and live to work another day!

Site evacuation procedures

Emergency evacuation notices must be word-processed in clear, readable text. Place this information in convenient positions where people can read it comfortably. Figure 1.6 illustrates how such a notice might look.

Keep material and equipment out of passageways. These could cause enormous problems for anyone in a panic and trying to leave the building like a 'headless chicken'.

When the emergency bells start to ring

- Stop all work promptly.
- If it's safe, isolate all power tools from the site's temporary supply.
- Switch off the main 230 V supply serving the site if it is safe to do so.

Make your way out of the building quickly but do not run. Gather at the nearest *assembly point*

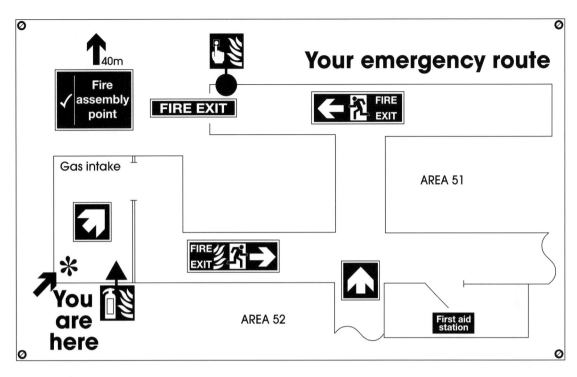

Figure 1.5 – *A site evacuation route using purpose-made signs.*

TARA ELECTRICAL PLC

Procedure in the event of an emergency

- On discovering a fire
- Sound the alarm
- Try to extinguish the flames
- Do not put yourself at risk
- If the fire cannot be put out quickly make your way out of the builiding by the QUICKEST AND SAFEST approved escape route
- Routes are identified
- Make your way to assembly point 'A', Chestnut Close
- Report to your foreman

A. Zimmerman
Site Safety Officer

Figure 1.6 – *Site evacuation instructions must be in readable text.*

and, if you are in charge of the job (*the jobholder*), check that all your staff and any visitors you might have had are safe.

Damage to property

Fire is destructive. If you are unfortunate enough to have a fire, you have a duty to list all damaged items and to pass on all relevant information to an appropriate person – keep a copy yourself. This is important.

Your list should include:

1 Site address, together with the time and the date of the fire.

2 Where the fire started.

3 Possible reason for the fire.

4 Details of any action which you took to extinguish the fire.

5 Your list of damaged company and personal items.

Injured persons

Your first aider will treat any minor cuts and bruises but, for cases that are more serious, you must call the emergency services by dialing 999 or 112 on your mobile telephone or by using the nearest landline public phone box. Please be precise when giving information to the emergency services – lives might depend on it.

How to report health and safety problems

You must report a health and safety problem within your workplace to the person on site who is responsible for these matters. This could be your site manager or jobholder on smaller jobs, or your resident safety officer on larger installations.

Always report an accident and record the details clearly within your site accident book (refer back to Figure 1.1 for details). Accident books vary in style but generally you must provide details about the following:

- The date and time of the accident together with your name and trade.
- Your accident and the type of injury you had.
- Where it happened.
- Whether plant or equipment was involved?
- Whether you had first aid or to went to the A & E department of your local hospital?
- Whether you had to have time off from work and, if so, how long?

Your legal requirements

Sometimes we have legally enforced health and safety matters within the workplace, when certain specified accidents occur. The four most important incidents are:

1 Death.
2 Where two or more days have to be taken off from work.
3 An accident where you have to go into hospital.

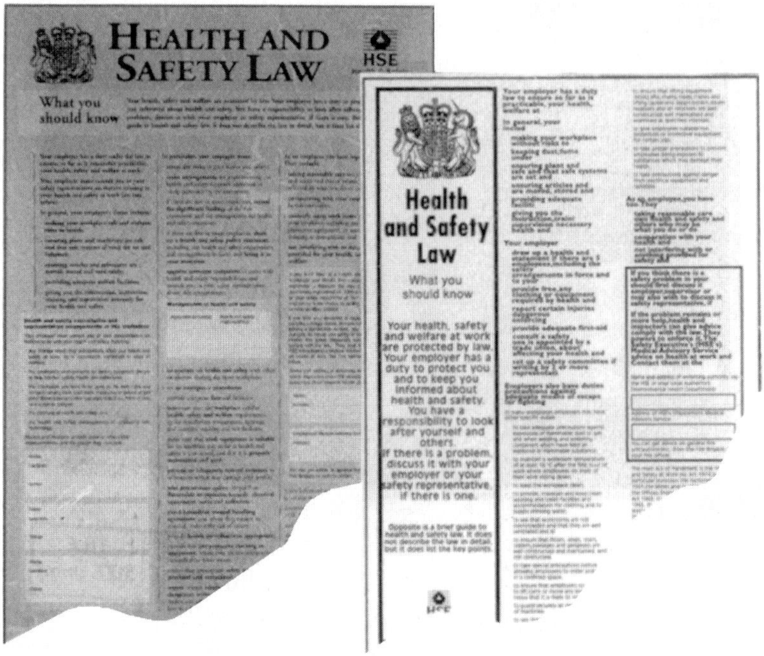

Figure 1.7 – *A poster showing Health and Safety Law must be put on view within the workplace.*

4 Where blame for the accident is traced to faulty plant or equipment.

You will have to report clear details of how and where the accident happened to the Health and Safety Executive as soon as possible. Their address will be handwritten on your site's Health and Safety poster, similar to the one illustrated in Figure 1.7.

The terms '*accident*' and '*emergency*' explained

Accident: a mishap, a disaster or an unforeseen event – such as breaking your ankle.

Emergency: an unexpected happening – such as a chemical store explosion or part of a building collapsing.

Remember to use the correct terms if you have to phone for professional help. List building or small installation site emergencies as either:

- Fire.
- Explosion.
- Toxic atmosphere.

Summary so far...

1 Record all accidents in your site/company accident book.

2 Keep a friendly eye on less experienced workmates.

3 Control all health and safety hazards within your job responsibilities.

4 Keep escape routes free from obstructions.

5 Give correct information to the emergency services.

6 An accident is a *mishap* or an *unforeseen event*. An emergency is an *unexpected happening*.

Review questions

1 Suggest three hazards you might find in the workplace.

2 How could red/green colour blindness cause an accident in the workplace?

3 Describe what you would do if you found quantities of asbestos where you were working.

4 What type of personal protective equipment would you wear when working near to deep water?

5 What would be the first thing you would do as a *jobholder* if you were to withdraw from your site due to an emergency?

6 You can call the police by dialing 999. What other number can you use?

7 Name two types of accident that, by law, must be reported to the HSE.

8 Please explain in your own words the term, *accident*.

9 List two types of construction/installation site emergencies.

10 To whom would you refer if you have a health and safety problem that is being ignored?

11 Fatigue caused by lack of sleep often leads to one of the following:
a better awareness
b tiredness
c misjudgement
d blissfulness.

12 Your site evacuation plan must be drawn up:
a any time during the first week of work
b before the start of any site or installation work
c by discussion, during the first site meeting
d any time this is convenient.

13 To whom would you report a health and safety problem on a large construction site?

14 Explain the term *emergency*.

15 There are three sets of safety regulations. List two of them.

1 Extended overtime causes tiredness and fatigue.

2 Carelessness causes accidents.

3 Keep your first aid box well stocked.

4 The CE mark found on electrical equipment, Figure 1.8, means that the product complies with the EC Electromagnetic Compatibility Directive (1996). This guarantees that the product will not interfere with any other electrotechnical equipment and will withstand any electromagnetic induction emitted from any other apparatus.

5 All fire extinguishers in the UK are *red* and a secondary colour enables quick recognition. For example, a carbon dioxide extinguisher has a *black* band painted on the red base colour.

6 Divide your bathroom installations into four *zones* (zones 0, 1, 2 and 3). Check the requirements by reading Amendment 3 of BS 7671 (The Wiring Regulations).

Figure 1.8 – *The CE mark means that the product complies with the EC Electromagnetic Compatibility Directive of 1996.*

Carelessness

This is one of the major causes of accidents in our industry today. It is often brought about by daydreaming or worrying about personal concerns through to more serious problems such as lack of sleep or the after-effects of too much ale the night before. Sometimes we get upset because of harsh and often unnecessary words from our management team and this alone can bring about an offhand attitude to the work that you are carrying out and cause you problems.

Lack of knowledge

Young apprentices who are told to carry out jobs about which they know nothing are often subject to this type of accident. An employer in the name of cost-effectiveness and profit often places pressure on young people, irrespective of how experienced they are.

Extended working hours (human limitations)

We are inclined to believe we are capable of far greater physical achievements than we really are and it is only later that we become aware that all is not quite as it should be. Strains and muscular problems are responsible for many person-hours lost.

Fatigue and listlessness

Long hours, weekend working and lack of good sleep are the major causes of fatigue and listlessness. Without doubt, this leads to silly mistakes. Silly mistakes will lead to big mistakes and big mistakes will lead to accidents!
Try to divide your day into both work and play. This will reduce your stress and tiredness factors that accompany extended overtime.

Your guide to common causes of accidents

There are many reasons why accidents happen, the most common of which are:

1 Carelessness.

2 Lack of knowledge.

3 Extended working hours.

4 Fatigue and listlessness.

5 Horseplay and improper behaviour.

7 Badly lit workplace.

8 Dirty/untidy/greasy place of work.

9 Not enough ventilation.

10 Faulty or unguarded machinery.

Horseplay

The workplace is not the place to carry out high jinks and practical jokes – it is too dangerous a place! This sort of behaviour often happens when site discipline is too relaxed and when the general working conditions are unpleasant or boring. Wise leadership, together with a clean tidy site, will help to provide a happier and more favourable workplace. You still may hate what you are doing but at least you will be free from harm and live to work another day.

The importance of a tidy site

It is in your interest to keep all working areas free from clutter and general litter. Remove all off-cuts from the floor and place them in a suitable container. Place material that could possibly cause or add to the seriousness of a fire in the site skip as soon as possible. In passageways, leave a gap as *wide as an exit door* that is free from tools and material items so evacuation may take place in the event of an emergency occurring. You do not want your workmate to trip over your gear and injure him- or herself when trying to escape from the building in a panicked state!

Protective clothing

I have noticed that there seems to be a growing trend amongst electrical workers to remove their overalls during the milder seasons. An overall not only protects your everyday working clothes from unnecessary wear and contamination but also provides you with a reasonable degree of safety from the many hazards we come across during our working day.

Be dressed for the occasion – it makes good common sense!

(Personal protective equipment may be found on page 159 of this book.)

Basic do's and don'ts: your responsibilities

DO:

1 Report to your supervisor any faulty electrical tools or plant.

2 Report any faulty safety equipment to an appropriate person.

3 Wear safety boots or shoes to EN 345 specification whilst in the workplace, Figure 1.9. Unprotected trainers are a lot more fashionable but they will not provide the protection required when working under site conditions.

4 Watch out for other trades working overhead. Always wear a hard hat and high visibility Day-Glo clothing.

5 Check your ladder for damage. Position your ladder correctly, as shown in Figure 1.10. Lash both the top and bottom rungs, if possible, and clean any grease or mud from your shoes before climbing.

6 Take care when carrying high objects near to overhead, low-strung power lines.

7 Remember to wear your ear protection when working in noisy surroundings.

8 Have plenty of light when working in fading daylight.

Figure 1.9 – *Always wear high-performance safety footwear meeting the requirements of EN 345 in the workplace. (Reproduced by kind permission of RS Components Limited.)*

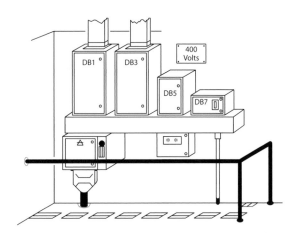

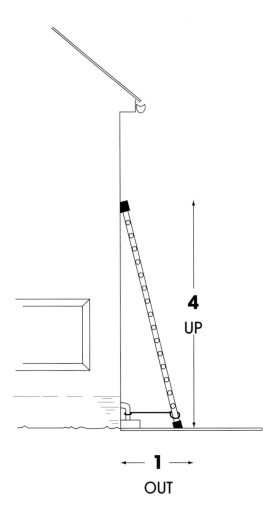

Figure 1.11 – *The area in front of electrical mains must be kept free from rubbish.*

Figure 1.12 – *Avoid overloading multisocket adaptors.*

Figure 1.10 – *The basic safety rule for ladders: four up and one out and always lash the bottom of your ladder before use.*

DON'T:

1 Attempt to repair electrical equipment unless you are experienced to do it.

2 Obstruct areas in front of electrical mains positions. Figure 1.11 illustrates how it should look.

3 Use silver paper in place of a cartridge fuse.

4 Assume that a conductor is 'dead'. Check first by use of a suitable voltmeter. Avoid using a flexed lamp holder and a small wattage lamp, a volt-stick or a LED voltage indicator. Be professional – use a voltmeter!

5 Overload multi-socket adaptors. Try to avoid using them if possible. Figure 1.12 illustrates this.

6 Allow temporary flexible cables to become part of your installation.

7 Short out or tamper with the switching action of a faulty residual current device (RCD).

8 Grease conductors as an aid when drawing through steel or a PVCu conduit. Use only *French chalk* or a *wire pulling lubricant*.

Handy hints

- Always replace damaged flexible cable serving electrical power tools and equipment. Remember, *red cable* to serve 400 V portable equipment, *blue* for 230 V appliances and *yellow* for portable power equipment served with 110 V.
- Regularly inspect plugs connected to power tools for loose or disconnected conductors. Carry out a portable appliance test every three months under site conditions and check over your battery-operated drills for damage and fault conditions.
- Faulty or damaged appliances can be responsible for fire, injury or death.
- Never use portable 230 V powered tools on site. Stick to 110 V tools – it's far safer!

A few installation guidelines

There are many but space will only allow for ten:

1 Where plant, equipment and life are exposed to hazardous conditions, always install a 30 mA (tripping rated) *RCD*: Regulation 412-06-01 applies.

2 Think ahead and check out any potential problems.

3 Mechanically shield your installation wherever necessary. Protect your cable runs by using a small length of 25 mm steel conduit as illustrated in Figure 1.13.

4 A warning to us all! The Control of Pollution Act (1974) prohibits the burning of PVC and rubber insulated cables on an open fire out of doors. Harmful chemical compounds and corrosive or toxic fumes are thrown into the atmosphere and can add to environmental problems. If you have to burn, then be *green* – use an incinerator designed for the purpose!

5 Always draw up a route plan after laying a cable directly in the ground. Give a copy to your client and keep one within your company as a record. Figure 1.14 is an

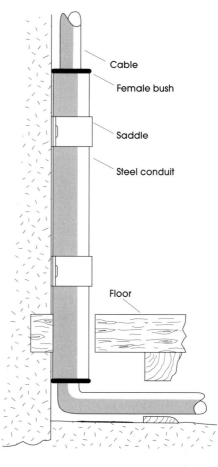

Figure 1.13 – *Protect cables from mechanical damage with a short section of steel conduit.*

example which Regulation 712-01-03 (xvii) confirms.

6 Capacitance can often be stored in very long runs of cable. To avoid an unnecessary and unexpected shock after insulation testing, short-circuit all current-carrying conductors to the circuit protective conductor (CPC) with a large test/discharge resistor. This will discharge any capacitance within the conductors. If fluorescent fittings have to be bench tested with an insulation tester, discharge any built-up capacitance by short-circuiting the internal phase and neutral conductors after each test. Use a suitably insulated discharge resistor as illustrated in Figure 1.15.

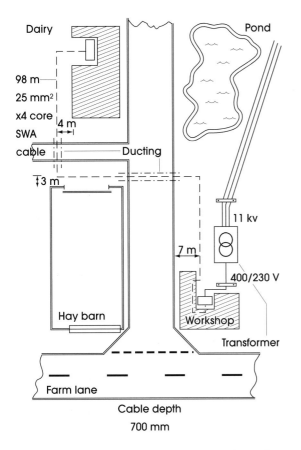

Dairy

98 m
25 mm²
x4 core
4 m
SWA
cable

Ducting

3 m

Pond

11 kv

7 m

400/230 V

Hay barn

Workshop

Transformer

Farm lane

Cable depth
700 mm

Figure 1.14 – *An as-fitted route plan will indicate the exact position of your buried cable.*

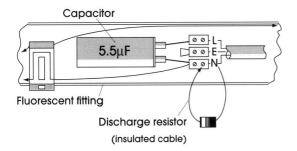

Capacitor

5.5μF

L
E
N

Fluorescent fitting

Discharge resistor
(insulated cable)

Figure 1.15 – *Discharge the capacitance generated after each test.*

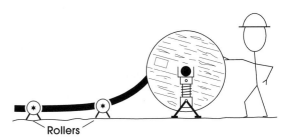

Rollers

Figure 1.16 – *Dispense your cable from the top of the drum – it's easier and safer.*

7 Sometimes, masonry nails serving cable clips will snap on impact and fly apart, causing physical harm. Avoid damage to the eyes by wearing suitable eye protection.

8 Always man large wooden cable drums when rolling off cable. To create easier and safer working conditions, draw from the top as Figure 1.16 shows. Watch out for splinters, nails and sharp obstacles. Wear well-fitting industrial gloves.

9 A greased cable drum spindle will enable you to have far more control over the cable you are giving out. Use cable rollers to manhandle the cable through the site.

10 Cables must suit the environmental conditions. You would not, for example, lay PVC insulated and sheathed cable within a trench to serve a field sited water pump.

Authoritative bodies serving the electrical industry

The type of installation work you do will depend where you are. Compulsory and legal requirements covering many classes of work are published and can be obtained as photocopies from many public libraries. A small fee is always charged.

Listed in Table 1.1 are selections of publications covering a wide range of installation work practices. Some you will be familiar with – others, you will be less familiar with.

Table 1.1 – *A selection of legal and advisory regulations serving the electrical industry.*

Item	Title of publication	Web site	Issuing body
1*	The Wiring Regulations (BS 7671: (2001))	www.iee.org/	The Institution of Electrical Engineers
2	Quarries (Electrical) Regulations (1956)		Health & Safety Commission
3	Electricity Supply Regulations (1937)		Secretary of State for Energy
4	Agricultural Regulations (1959)		Agricultural Regulations
5	Factories Act (1908 and 1944)		Health & Safety Commission
6	Cinematograph Regulations		Home Office
7	Coal & Other Mines (Electricity) Regulations (1956)		Health & Safety Commission
8	Electricity at Work Regulations (1989)		Secretary of State for Energy
9	Guidance on the Electricity at Work Regulations		Secretary of State for Energy
10	The Deposit of Poisonous Waste Act (1972)		UK Parliament

*BS7671 is an advisory regulation.

Professional bodies serving our industry

There are many, but here are a few well known organisations that have become household words and listed in a way which people recognise them best:

- The British Standards Institute (BSI).
- City and Guilds of London.
- The Electrical and Plumbers Trade Union.
- The National Electrotechnical Training Organisation (NETO).
- The Institution of Electrical Engineers.
- National Inspection Council for Electrical Installation Contracting (NICEIC).
- Electrical Contractors Association (ECA).

Handy hints

- Avoid using hand-held electrical equipment in the rain.
- To prevent overheating, extension leads must be fully unwound from the reel.
- Fit a plug-in-type *RCD* to protect against electric shock when using an extension lead.

Agricultural installations: avoiding accidents

Be cautious when carrying out agricultural installations. By practising carefulness and lots of concern, many accidents need not happen. Listed are a few tips and important safety features that you should bear in mind.

1 Current leakages to earth from storm-soaked connections, via wet and contaminated line taps and insulators, through to rain-saturated wooden distribution poles will give electric shocks if touched. Figure 1.17 illustrates this point further. An animal standing in a field close to a power distribution pole could receive a lethal shock, as shown in Figure 1.18.

2 Take extreme care when carrying long metal ladders across the path of a privately owned overhead distribution system. Some older installations use a network of *bare hardened copper conductors*. Figure 1.19 illustrates this.

3 Thoroughly bond milking parlours and dairies. Check that protection for the installation is by means of a 30 mA RCD. Livestock can suffer lethal or disabling shocks from as low as 25 V.

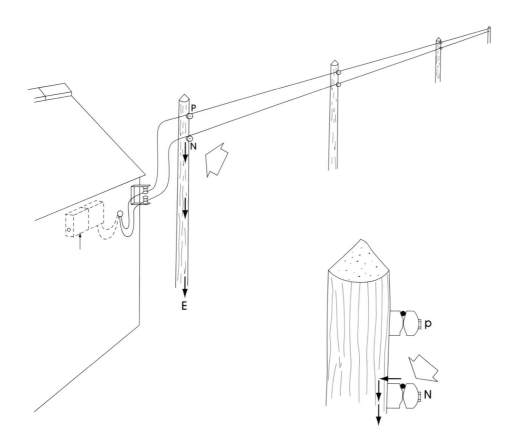

Figure 1.17 – *The first three poles illustrated have phase to earth insulation values of 2000, 2500 and 50 000 ohms, respectively. The total current leakage to earth, when served with 230 volts, would amount to 211.6 mA.*

4   Make sure, if you remove guards from electrical machinery, that the guards are firmly replaced.

5   Large amounts of water are used to wash down and clean milking parlours and dairies. Never use an in-line block connector to serve equipment such as milk paddle motors. Always use a waterproof snap-on connection unit. This will provide greater safety.

6   Wear all necessary personal protective equipment – *farms are dangerous*!

7   Wash your hands thoroughly before eating. Look after your health!

8   It is important to wear a suitable face mask when working in a grain storage silo,

poultry farm or piggery. The dust created within grain storage bays has the effect of restricting your windpipe, causing breathing problems.

Handy hints

- Be extra careful when you are doing agricultural installation work.
- Never fool around with charged capacitors.
- Do not use open-fronted quartz halogen temporary lighting in barns containing straw or in thatched roof spaces.

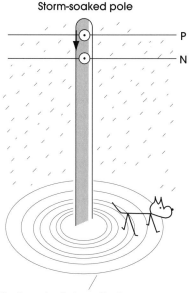

Storm-soaked pole

P

N

Electropotential gradient

Figure 1.18 – *Surface voltage gradients can produce lethal or crippling shocks in many animals.*

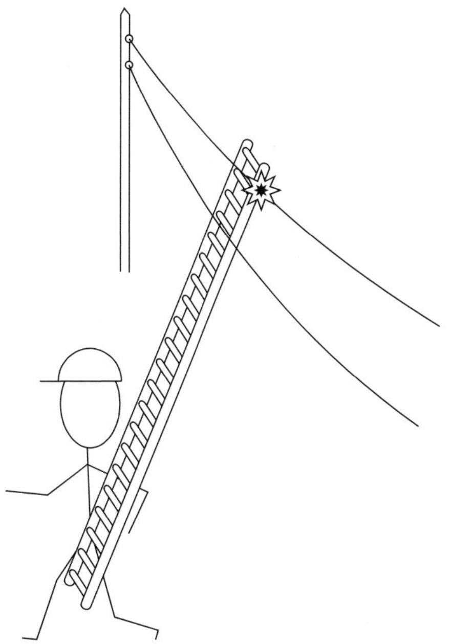

Safe working with batteries

If you are not used to handling primary and secondary cells, you are at risk from many potential hazards.

Provided you carry out sensible precautions the risk of an accident is reduced. Listed is a random selection of the more important safety aspects that you should bear in mind when you work with batteries.

Primary cells (non-rechargeable)

1 Once exhausted (worn out), always remove the battery from the equipment it serves.

2 Never throw a used battery on a fire. It could explode.

3 Keep a leaking battery away from your skin – they contain very nasty ingredients.

4 Never try to recharge a battery that has not been designed for that purpose.

5 Dispose of your unwanted batteries sensibly. Never give them to children to play with.

6 Some batteries contain toxic material such as cadmium (Cd) and mercury (Hg). Please be very careful.

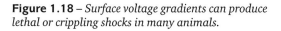

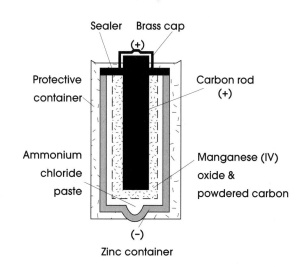

Sealer   Brass cap
(+)

Protective container

Carbon rod (+)

Ammonium chloride paste

Manganese (IV) oxide & powdered carbon

(–)

Zinc container

Figure 1.19 – *Take care not to touch low overhead, privately owned conductors when carrying metal ladders or lengths of steel conduit when working on farms.*

Figure 1.20 – *A Leclanché cell – output up to 1.45 volts.*

Primary cells vary in internal design; they are not all the same. Figure 1.20 illustrates the basic component parts of a typical 1.5 V primary cell.

Secondary cells (batteries you can recharge)

1 Protective clothing and eye protection are very necessary.

2 Before charging, unscrew the battery breather caps to allow ventilation.

3 Never smoke or use a naked flame where batteries are charging. A hydrogen (H_2) and oxygen (O_2) mix is formed. Hydrogen is highly inflammable.

4 Ventilate your battery charging room to prevent a build-up of hydrogen.

5 Since the weight of sulfuric acid is greater than an equal amount of water, splashing will occur if you add the water to the acid. Either add the acid to the water or use a vessel with an extended spout, as shown in Figure 1.21. This will avoid splashing.

6 Never apply a load or short circuit to the terminals of a battery under charge. Hydrogen formed from the plates could ignite from the resulting spark. If the total hydrogen content of your battery charging room exceeds 4%, an explosive atmosphere will exist.

7 Take care when you use a hydrometer for testing the specific gravity of the acid/water mix. Allow the top of the rubber dispensing tube to rest on the battery ventilation port. This will avoid unnecessary spillage, as illustrated in Figure 1.22.

8 Remove conductive objects, such as rings and watches, from your hands and wrists before using metallic tools on secondary cells. They could cause flesh burns if in circuit with the battery.

9 Dispose of unwanted acid in accordance with The Deposit of Poisonous Waste Act (1972). If in doubt, contact your local authority.

10 To prevent terminal arcing and conductors heating up, check your load is securely clamped to the battery lugs. The voltage may be low but the current can often be high. Figure 1.23 illustrates the basic component parts of a typical secondary cell.

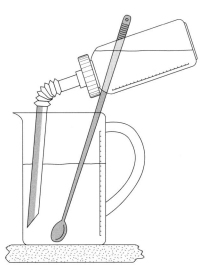

Figure 1.21 – *Add distilled water to your acid as illustrated. This will avoid splashing.*

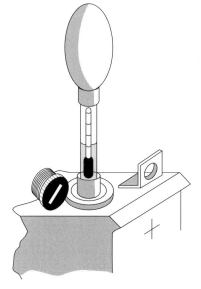

Figure 1.22 – *Rest the hydrometer within the ventilation port to avoid spillage.*

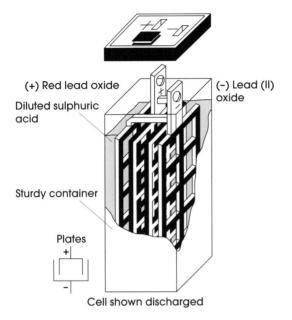

(+) Red lead oxide

(–) Lead (II) oxide

Diluted sulphuric acid

Sturdy container

Plates

Cell shown discharged

Figure 1.23 – *The internal construction of a lead acid cell shown in simplified form.*

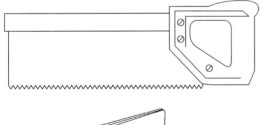

Figure 1.24 – *Plastic oval conduit cut lengthways will form a reliable hand-saw blade protector.*

Handy hints

- Bricks used for night storage heaters (refractory bricks) contain iron filings. Take care when handling to avoid cuts and scratches.

- Select your fixing methods relative to your on-site material. Wall plugs, for example, in a plasterboard ceiling would not be appropriate!

- Static voltage can be stored within your body when the weather is very dry. Nylon carpets and synthetic rubber-soled footwear can cause this to happen. If it is a nuisance when you are working, discharge yourself to earth through a neon test screwdriver every now and again.

- Oval plastic conduit cut lengthways can make a very cheap blade shield for handsaws and wood chisels. Figure 1.24 illustrates this.

- Avoid push/pulling a prefabricated access tower across rough ground. It can be very unstable.

- Steel conduit is best stored *under cover* during frosty weather. Freezing temperatures will cause *frost burn* when the conduit is manhandled.

Disconnection procedure
A flow chart to make it easy to remember

An initial routine check of the circuit you will be working on will minimise accidental direct contact with live conductive parts. Figure 1.25 shows how you can do this in a very practical way using an algorithm – a flow chart to you and me.

Fire hazards

Accidents involving fire caused by power tools or equipment are often caused by the people who are using them. Keep an eye on your power tools – prevention is better than cure as lives and

17

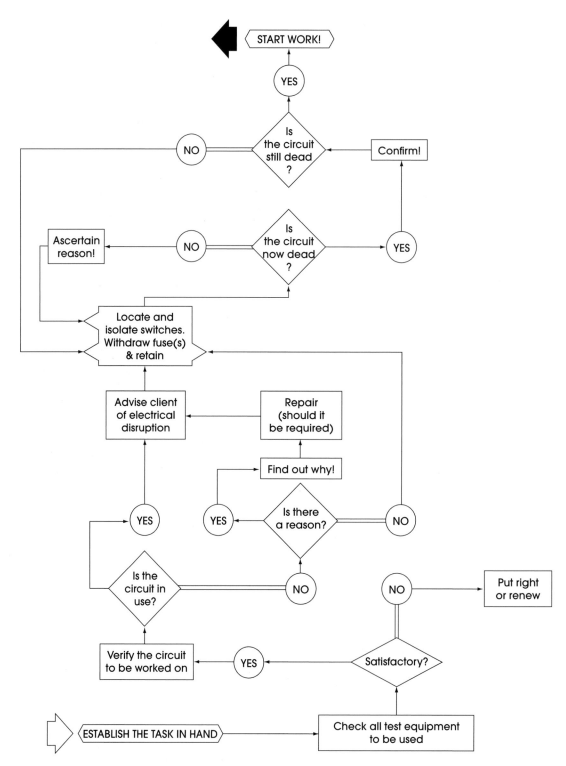

Figure 1.25 – *Disconnection procedure.*

property are at risk when fire strikes. Listed are a few important safety measures that you should take:

1 Check what action you should take in case of fire. This you can read from the Health and Safety posters dotted around your site. If you are working on a small site have a word with your jobholder.

2 Large sites will be provided with temporary fire 'call-points', extinguishers and emergency exits. Get to know where they are for your own sake and those of others.

3 On discovering a fire:
   a sound the alarm,
   b try to put the fire out but do not take risks,
   c if you are unable to put the fire out, get out of the building – fast.

4 Respect NO SMOKING areas and never smoke near a thatched roof.

5 Avoid overloading the temporary installation you have installed.

6 If you have to use halogen floodlighting, make sure that it is properly secured and is not open-fronted.

7 Make sure all terminals serving your temporary power and lighting are tight and secure. Arcing generates heat – heat can cause fire!

8 Never install current-consuming equipment in a loft that has a thatched roof, such as a television amplifier or a non-enclosed lighting fitting. It is very risky.

9 Have regular fire drills so you will know what to do if fire ever strikes.

Fire extinguishers

In the UK, fire extinguishers are colour-coded *red* and a secondary colour in the form of a band is applied to the extinguisher to help recognition. A *blue* band indicates that the extinguisher has dry powder content.

Be very careful when using Halon 1211 (BCF): please refer to Table 1.2. If you use it in a restricted space, the fumes given off can be dangerous if inhaled – a point to remember!

Handy hints

- Place a hand-held fire extinguisher where you can get to it quickly.

- Never risk personal injury to fight a fire. Put your own and your workmates' safety first. If in doubt – *get out*.

- Never allow a fire to come between you and safety.

- Use water-based fire extinguishers to tackle an electrical fire *only* if the electricity has been *turned off* at the mains. If in doubt – *do not!*

- Tackle a fire in its earliest stages: never wait until it gets out of hand.

Table 1.2 – *A list of five commonly used extinguishers, together with their respective voltage ranges and operational usage.*

Secondary colour	Type of extinguisher	To use on	Voltage range (V)
Black	Carbon dioxide	Flammable liquids	+ 1000
Blue	Dry powder	Flammable liquids	Up to 1000
Cream	Aqueous foam	Flammable liquids and solids	Unsafe – do not use on electrical fires
Green	Halon 1211 (BCF)	Flammable liquids and solids	+ 1000
Red (completely red)	Water	Solids, paper, cloth and wood	Unsafe – do not use on electrical fires

Lifting techniques – ways to stop personal injury

Lifting and moving heavy electrical equipment is one of the biggest single causes of personal injury. If the load is too heavy, get help, or if you are able, use a mechanical means to carry out your job.

Loads over 20 kg (approximately 44 pounds) need to be handled with power-lifting equipment. If you are unable to manage, *get help*. It is better to lose a little pride than time off from work recovering from a strained back or a hernia operation.

Using available help

If several of you have to move a large load, for example a factory-assembled mains control panel, choose somebody to provide the instructions. This will avoid confusion and prevent an accident occurring.

If trained to operate mechanical lifting aids – take advantage and use them. Nobody enjoys unnecessary hard work. Check your load for sharp or ragged edges and do not forget to wear protective clothing and footwear. Take a couple of minutes to plan your route ahead, making sure it is free from obstacles and obstructions. Finally, check in advance that there is sufficient room to set down your load with safety.

Try to remember these points

1 Chin in and back straight.

2 Elbows tucked into your body and knees bent.

Handy hints

■ Keep bolsters and cold chisels trimmed and sharpened (Figure 1.26). Overhang around the impact area can shear off, causing injury, and the sharp edges can often cause skin damage to the palm of your hand.

■ It is dangerous to ride on a mechanical hoist designed only to carry plant or material items.

■ Make sure you can see over your load.

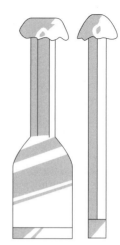

Figure 1.26 – *Trim your bolsters and hand chisels around the impact area to avoid damage to your hands.*

3 Grip your load firmly but do not just use your fingertips.

4 Position one foot in front of the other close to the load and lift by using your leg muscles.

First aid

First aid will provide a short-term stopgap of medical care until a doctor or trained paramedic arrives.

You owe it to yourself to acquire a *basic knowledge* of first aid so you will know what action to take should an emergency arise.

Workplace conditions throw up many unexpected medical hazards, often resulting in skin damage in the form of cuts, scratches, bruises and abrasions. Infection could set in, if left unattended. It is wise to consider a course of tetanus immunisation that you can receive from your local health clinic or doctor's surgery. This is very advisable, especially if your work takes you to farms and horticultural businesses. Look after your health.

First aid points to remember

1 Get to know your first aider. If you are working on a small site, keep a well-stocked first aid box.

2 Qualified medical staff must always treat eye injuries, crushed limbs and problems with foreign bodies in the nose.

3 Wash off with clean water any battery acid or chemical contamination. Seek medical advice as soon as possible.

4 A dressing soaked in clean cold water and rung out will help to relieve pain and swelling caused by severe bruising and sprains.

5 Never force liquid into an unconscious workmate's mouth – your patient could choke.

6 Cotton wool applied directly to a wound will stick. Always dress a wound using sterile lint.

Dealing with electric shock

When dealing with electric shock there are a few important points to remember. They might save your workmate's life!

- Switch off the electrical supply.

- If this is not practical, push/pull the victim away from the source of the current with something dry like a wooden broom, a chair or a length of dry hosepipe.

- Only touch the victim with uninsulated hands when he/she is removed from the live conductive parts.

- If the victim is unconscious, but breathing and severely burnt, call the emergency services and seek advice. If you decide it is quicker to take him/her to your local emergency centre – get someone to help you.

Coping with an emergency: mouth-to-mouth resuscitation

It is very important to remember that, when breathing stops, caused by direct contact with electricity, brain damage will probably occur within three minutes. A sobering thought! It is therefore vital that air is forced into their lungs until breathing starts normally again. If ever you have to give mouth-to-mouth resuscitation, please remember these few points.

1 Lay your casualty on their back. Check the casualty's level of response. Is the casualty conscious? Open the casualty's airway by placing one hand on their forehead and tilting back their head. Remove material from their mouth that should not be there. Figure 1.27 illustrates this.

2 Tilt the head back again and lift the chin. This 'sniffing the morning air' position will provide a clear airway passage to the lungs (Figure 1.28). Check for signs of breathing.

3 If the casualty is unconscious and not breathing, ask someone to call an ambulance. In the meantime, commence CPR. If circulation is present but the casualty is not breathing, you will have to breathe for them. Apply a little upward pressure to the chin. Pinch the nostrils together and blow two steady breaths by covering your casualty's mouth with your own (Figure 1.29).

4 After the second ventilation, check that their chest rises and falls. If not, then blow through the victim's nose, closing their mouth with your hand.

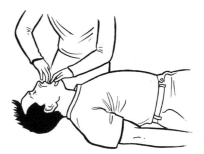

Figure 1.27 – *Remove any obvious obstructions from the mouth.*

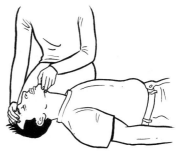

Figure 1.28 – *Place the casualty's head fully backwards in order to open the air passage.*

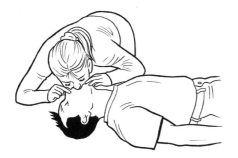

Figure 1.29 – *Pinch the casualty's nostrils together and blow two steady breaths into the victims's mouth.*

Figure 1.30 – *Place in the recovery position once breathing has started.*

5 Continue in the way described, monitoring the rise and fall of their chest each time you inflate it.

6 When your patient is breathing normally, place them in the *recovery position*, as Figure 1.30 illustrates. This prevents their tongue from blocking the entrance of the windpipe.

7 Call the ambulance and stay with your patient until medical help arrives.

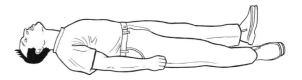

Figure 1.31 – *Lay the casualty on his/her back with both legs raised.*

When the heart has stopped

These next few items are guidelines – an insight of what to do in a dire emergency. Spend time to get further advice and to understand the procedure well. Practice leads to perfection and somebody's life might depend on you!

When your workmate's heart has stopped due to an electric shock, be calm, be efficient but, above all, *do not panic*, for he/she will depend on you remembering what to do!

- Lay the casualty flat on their back. Tilt the victim's head and lift the chin. Remove anything from their mouth that should not be there (Figure 1.31).

- Give 2 effective rescue breaths out of 5 attempts and assess for signs of circulation.

- Check that the pulse is not present at the neck. Locate the bottom of the ribcage – then at a distance of two fingers up from this mid-point position, place one hand on top of the other (Figure 1.32), linking the fingers of both hands. Apply regular pressure using the

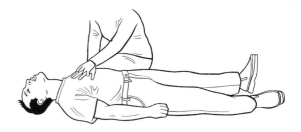

Figure 1.32 – *Apply regular and smooth pressure using the heel of your hand.*

heel of your hand. The ribs in this area are flexible to allow up to 30 mm of movement.

- Compress the chest 15 times. The frequency should be 100 times per minute. Each compression should last just under a second in time.

- Alternate 15 chest compressions with 2 rescue breaths.

- Continue CPR until emergency help takes over; the casualty takes a breath; or you are too exhausted to continue.

- Check out the pulse in the neck artery once every *three minutes*. If a pulse has been established continue CPR until the patient is breathing again. Place in the recovery position and call the ambulance.

Handy hints

- Never become a minor monument to carelessness!

Final thoughts

Health and safety at work is the responsibility of every one of us. Through education and example, we can all help each other to attain a far healthier and safer workplace.

Chapter 1 offered a straightforward introduction to cover the more general aspects of safety through the eyes of an apprentice. This

Summary so far...

1 Accidents are caused by carelessness, lack of knowledge, working extra-long hours, fatigue and horseplay.

2 Obtain professional advice when dealing with asbestos.

3 Never obstruct passageways: they could be used for emergency exit routes.

4 Do not try to recharge batteries not designed for that purpose. It is dangerous!

5 Get to know what to do in case of a fire. Check out your escape routes before it is too late.

6 Replace items that have been used from your first aid box. Enter all accidents in your company's accident book.

Review questions

1 Name three common causes of accidents.

2 Voltage used in the workplace has one of the following values: 240 V, 110 V, 230 V, 400 V.

3 Why is it best not to burn PVC or rubber insulated cables on site?

4 Why is it unwise to wear a wristwatch, bracelet or rings whilst working on 'live' equipment?

5 Who is responsible for The Electricity at Work Regulations (1989)?

6 Why is it essential for milking parlours to be thoroughly bonded?

7 What is the voltage output of a Leclanché dry cell?

8 Why should you never smoke or use a naked flame in a room where batteries are being recharged?

9 State the reason for storing steel conduit under cover during frosty weather.

10 Describe what action you would take on discovering a small fire.

11 It is recommended that loads over a certain weight need to be handled with power-lifting equipment. Which of the following is recommended: (a) 25 kg, (b) 40 kg, (c) 45 kg or (d) 20 kg?

12 Describe the treatment for a badly sprained ankle.

13 How would you remove a victim of electric shock away from the live conductive part?

14 Describe, using your own words, the position you would place a victim of electric shock in when giving mouth-to-mouth resuscitation.

15 How often must you check for a pulse in the neck artery when you suspect your casualty's heart has stopped?

chapter is not a complete work, but I hope it has provided an important insight into the many potential dangers and hazards that seem to lurk around every corner whenever we do our electrical work.

Safety is a shared concern. Spend time to get to know the health and safety rules for this will help to create a good and safe atmosphere within your workplace – this we should all try to accomplish. After all, in the end the people who will benefit will be the likes of you and your workmates.

Handy hints

- A pulsating magnetic 'growl' coming from a three-phase motor often indicates that a phase is missing. This condition is known as *single phasing*.

- A loose terminal connection is sufficient to cause a three-phase motor to '*single-phase*' and trigger the overload protection circuit.

- A 'chattering' starter serving an electric motor will, if left unattended, cause the coil to burn out. Often an over-sensitive probe or temperature control working on a narrow degree of difference is to blame.

- As a precaution against electric shock, you must wear rubber gloves when obtaining earth resistance values.

- Be security minded and remove personal belongings and power tools from your company vehicles each night.

- Check that your first fix accessory boxes are not plastered over. Refer to your site installation drawing if you are unable to find them.

2 Safe site working practices

Introduction

This chapter will explain how to make your workplace safe and free from hazards. We will also be discussing the safe positioning and operating of access equipment.

To obtain this unit you will have to sit a written multiple-choice examination and demonstrate to your assessor that you can carry out the following practical activities:

- Make a list of what it takes to work both safely and successfully within the workplace.
- Identify safety equipment in the workplace.
- Carry out safe working practices.
- Check all warning notices and barriers are both sited and installed correctly.
- Monitor equipment and safe working conditions throughout your task.
- Inspect all your work equipment and maintain in a safe working condition.
- Ensure that, when your job is complete, all tools, equipment and materials are removed from your task area and are stored both safely and securely.
- List the five main stages in the processes of risk assessment.

Before you start work

Find out from your site manager or the electrician in charge that your site is safe and free from hazards. If there are hazards, find out where and what they are for your own sake.

Real-life hazards

There are many dangers you might come across when working on site. Old houses seem to be the worst for obvious reasons. Here are some examples:

- rotten flooring
- dead animals
- tripping hazards
- unstable timbers, walls and ceilings
- holes, pits and covered disused wells
- oil, chemical spillage, etc.

It is best to fully cover yourself and record all hazards in your site's day diary so that others who follow are aware of the dangers. *Remain alert and keep alive!* Do not underrate the responsibility – your life and those of your workmates depend on it.

Risk assessment

There are five main stages of a risk assessment process:

1. First, identify hazards in the workplace.
2. Evaluate the risks involved.
3. Keep a record of your findings in your site diary.
4. Prepare and put into action a practical plan.
5. Check out your findings every now and again.

Your site security

If the company you work for is the main contractor, then they will be responsible for site security.

You must decide a suitable way to stop unauthorised entry to your site. Consider the following options:

■ Anti-child perimeter fencing which is strong.

■ Lockable access gates for site traffic.

■ Lockable storm-proof enclosure for your temporary lighting and power switchgear and distribution centre.

■ Security lighting and an intruder alarm for high-risk areas.

■ Perimeter notices attached to the perimeter fence (see Figure 2.1) and warning notices for traffic leaving the site onto a busy main road, as illustrated in Figure 2.2.

Figure 2.1 – *Notices such as these might be attached to the outside of the site boundary fence.*

Figure 2.2 – *Warning notices positioned on site, warning drivers of hazards ahead.*

Site key holders

It is best to have two key holders to gain access to your site. One set of keys should be held by the person charged with running the job, with the other set being kept by a senior electrician. Both people should give their names and telephone numbers to the local police in case an emergency arises during out-of-work hours. It really is best to cover yourself when you have the responsibility of running a job.

How you stand regarding the law

When you are in a position of managing a job for your company, as many of you will one day, you are legally responsible for the health and safety of all who visit your site – whether invited or uninvited. Your company will be legally responsible for anyone who is injured inside your boundary – at any time of the day or night.

Before you start work – working to a programme

It is a good idea to check with your supervisor that the work you are to do is both safe and practical. For example:

■ The type of work you are to do, storage arrangements and accessing equipment.

■ Check your drawings are up to date and that you will have a working programme in the form of a bar chart, as in Figure 2.3.

■ Finally, discuss procedures for dealing with emergencies and matters of site security.

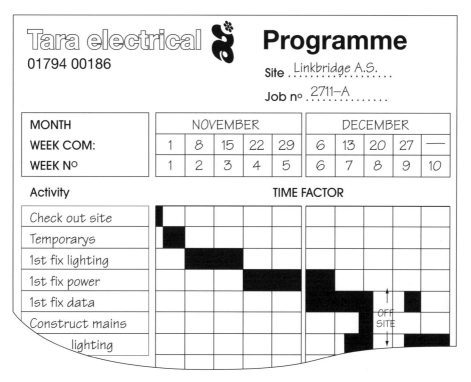

Figure 2.3 – *A site working programme designed in the form of a bar chart.*

Storage matters

Try to be security minded. Before you go home, gather together all your material items and tools and store them in a windowless lockup. A purpose-made steel container or a lockable room would be ideal.

If conditions are damp, add in a thermostatically controlled electric heater. This will help to prevent damage from condensation and mildew.

Heavy and breakable items

It is best not to pile breakable items on top of each other – you could have a disaster on your hands! Bending vices and heavy tools must always be stored on the floor. Try to separate your steel and plastic conduit into site-made racks – place their accessories in plastic bins.

Cable reels can be positioned on a lower shelf in size/type order. Keep electrical accessories in their original cardboard boxes – this will provide you with easy product recognition and hopefully minimise breakages.

A few other points to consider

Listed are a few common-sense points to consider when you have to create a site store:

1 Remove rubbish to lessen the risk of fuelling a fire and install a smoke alarm.

2 Keep an all-purpose fire extinguisher near the door.

3 A good level of lighting is essential – an intruder alarm is optional, Figure 2.4.

4 Avoid fitting a 'Mickey Mouse' lock – get a reliable one.

5 Remember that you must store substances covered by COSHH in a separate and secure ventilated compound with a spill-proof floor for liquids.

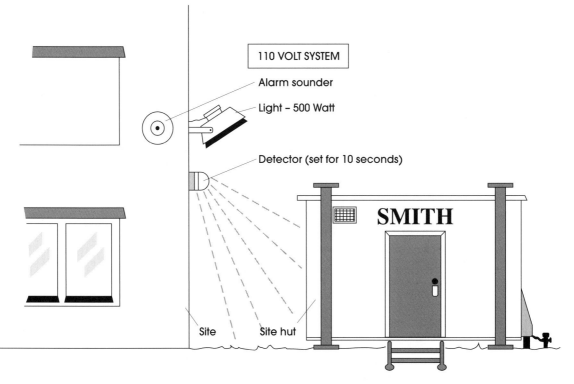

Figure 2.4 – *A simple intruder alarm can be installed to serve your site material store.*

Starting work

When it is time to start your job, please consider the following points:

■ Check out your new workplace is free from personal hazards.

■ Confirm that your plans check out with your specification.

■ Alterations to the specification must be reported to your company as soon as possible.

■ Make sure the material you have been given is suitable for the task you have been asked to do.

■ All site tools and appliances must be portable appliance tested.

■ Never use technical jargon when in conversation with a non-technical visitor. They will not understand what you are saying.

■ If you have to work on equipment you think might be 'live', check using a suitable voltmeter as illustrated in Figure 2.5.

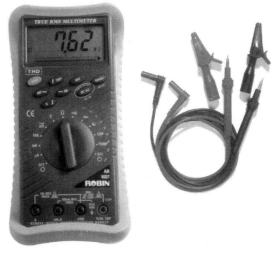

Figure 2.5 – *A voltmeter will confirm that a supply is not present. (Reproduced by kind permission of Robin Electronics Ltd.)*

Your installation drawings

Before work is started, site-working drawings (an example is Figure 2.6), charts and schedules must be studied and understood. Any problem areas can then be put right. Check for mistakes – you would be surprised how many you can find. Use a scale rule to transfer the measurements from your drawing to *real time* measurements. Check the scale on your rule is the same as your drawing scale or you will make mistakes.

Your in-house paperwork

1. Time sheets

Complete your time sheets accurately on a day-to-day basis. Never leave it to the end of the week – it is easy to forget where you have been and what you have done. You may be asked to complete the following information:

- The name and address of your client.
- Your job number.

- Description of the work you carried out.
- Time and materials.
- The time spent having lunch (not paid for by your customer).

This information will allow your office to pay you and to calculate the profit made.

2. Job sheets and day work sheets

A job sheet provides information about the work you have been asked to do. Typically, it will contain the following information:

- Your company's job number.
- The name and address of your customer and possibly a photocopied map of your route.
- A description of the work – whether it is a *priced* or a *time and materials* job.
- A list of materials.
- Special instructions. For example: 'Our clients are of a religious order which does not permit

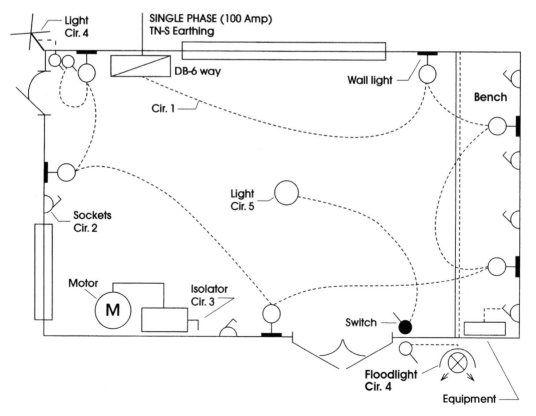

Figure 2.6 – *An example of a site working drawing (a small workshop).*

the use of radios or mobile telephones. Please respect their wishes.'

When you are doing *price work*, any additional work you have done will be treated as *day work*. This will then be charged to your customer at a standard day work rate. This is usually time, materials and a margin for profit.

Safe keeping of your installation drawings

It is best to keep two sets of working drawings. Keep one set in your site office: the other will be given to the electricians who are doing the installation work. If one set is accidentally damaged a replacement copy can be issued right away.

Preparing a material list

Use a scale rule to measure the amount of conduit, trunking, cable tray, etc., you require for your job. Remember to consider the depth. An electrical location drawing is only two-dimensional and you can miss out a lot of material if you measure directly off the drawing. Figure 2.7 illustrates a small selection of graphical location symbols.

When you have to provide information to your customer

There are many ways to communicate – but do so in a language your customer can understand. You can do the following:

- Provide a written report; if possible by word processing.
- Send an e-mail.
- Use a drawing – but please use BS or BSEN standard symbols.
- Telephone – but be both clear and precise.
- Send a fax message to your customer – keep it short and to the point.
- Use site drawings and diagrams.
- Use microfilm and microfiche viewing devices.
- Use computers and the internet.
- Use video tapes or DVDs – these are a great way to provide information for your customer.

Name of component/accessory	Graphical symbol
Main control (distribution centre)	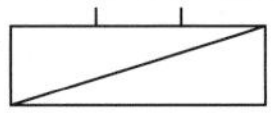
Wall-mounted lighting point	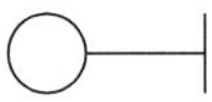
Heating element	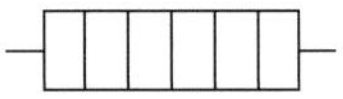
Thermostat	 $t°$
Voltmeter	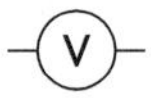 V
Ammeter	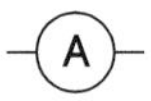 A
Resistor	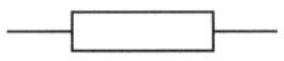
Horn	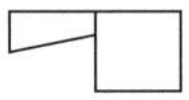
Floodlight	
Time switch	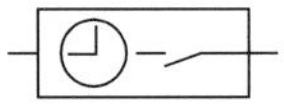
Alternating current (AC) relay	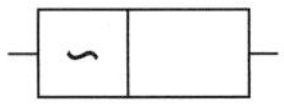
Electric motor (general symbol)	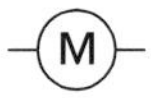 M
One-way switch (general symbol)	
Wiring (general symbol)	
Battery	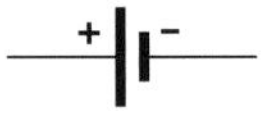 + –
Indicator lamp	

Figure 2.7 – *A selection of graphical symbols used in electrical location drawings.*

When your job is finished

Remove from the site all plant, equipment and unused materials. Make a list of all items that have not been used before returning them to your company store. Keep a copy for yourself just in case it is ever required.

Summary so far...

1 Check your new site for hazards before work is started.
2 Agree which procedures to follow in case of an emergency.
3 If you are a jobholder, you are legally responsible for the health and safety of anyone entering your site.
4 Store your materials in a secure windowless shelter. Provide a fire extinguisher and a battery-operated smoke detector.
5 Keep two sets of working drawings.
6 When your job has been completed, remove all plant and equipment from the site.
7 Remove any rubbish and hand over your site both clean and tidy.

A few guidance points to consider

Return all paperwork to your company office. Check the power tools you have used are free from damage before you hand them back and take '*off hire*' any equipment that you have rented out.

Other things to consider are:

- Arranging for temporary services to be disconnected.
- Repairing any damaged fabric, property or equipment.
- Checking that your site is free from rubbish and in a satisfactory condition to be handed back to your client.

Using the correct type of access equipment

Use the correct type of access equipment – your safety could depend on it. It would be silly to go to the trouble of erecting an aluminium tower when a ladder or a pair of steps would be safe to use.

The types of access equipment we use as electricians include the following:

- modular aluminium access tower (Figure 2.8)

Handy hints

- Do not have your meals in the site office. If your drink is knocked over, paperwork will be spoilt in seconds.
- Always cover yourself by listing serious hazards found in your workplace and inform an appropriate person (part of your risk assessment plan).
- Make sure you have an up-to-date drawing before acting on it.
- Site perimeter notices must be of the correct type – remember, your company is legally responsible if something went wrong.
- Remember to inform your customer in good time if you are to switch off the power and lighting. Check out before throwing the switch – computers and other IT equipment could still be on-line.

- steps
- trestles
- hydraulic scissor platform (training is needed to operate this)
- mast-supported platform (training is needed to operate this)
- power hoist (used for plant and equipment only)
- traditional steel scaffolding (erected by others).

Often the high cost of hiring mechanised access equipment is justified when compared to the time involved in providing traditional scaffolding arrangements.

A review of two of the most common types of access equipment follows.

Extending ladder

This type of ladder, more commonly known as an extension ladder, must be checked for problems before use. This will ensure that it is OK to use and suitable for the structure to be accessed. For

Figure 2.8 – *Modular aluminium access tower. (Reproduced by kind permission of SGB Youngman Limited.)*

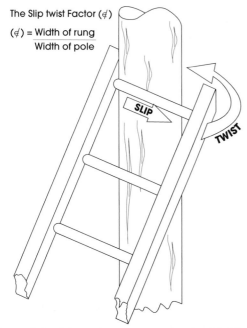

The Slip twist Factor ($\not\subset$)

$$(\not\subset) = \frac{\text{Width of rung}}{\text{Width of pole}}$$

SLIP

TWIST

Figure 2.9 – *It is unwise to use a conventional ladder to access a round wooden pole.*

example, it would be foolish to use a traditional ladder to access a round wooden pole. The rung resting on the curvature of the pole would cause the ladder to become very wobbly when you were climbing up the rungs, as shown in Figure 2.9.

Looking for problems – or how keep out of hospital!

- Check the wooden rungs and sides are not split or rotten.
- Examine for unevenness, which could make your ladder wobble.
- Avoid fully painted ladders – they hide many defects.
- Position your ladder so that its height is four times greater than the distance it is from the structure you are to access. Figure 2.10 illustrates this.

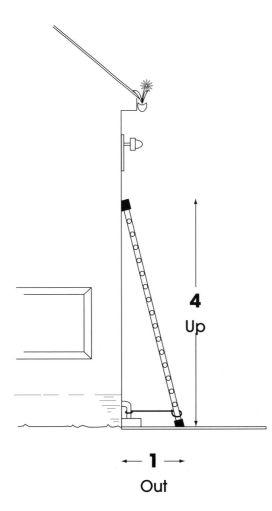

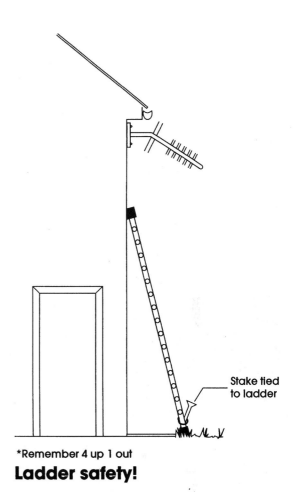

Figure 2.10 – *The height of your ladder must be four times greater than the distance the ladder is from the structure you wish to access. Remember: four up – one out.*

Figure 2.11 – *Tie the bottom of your ladder to a secure fixture. A stake is ideal.*

- Tie the top and the bottom rungs to a secure fixing, as shown in Figure 2.11, and try to extend the top of your ladder by at least one metre above the top of the landing area.
- Clean any mud or grease from the soles of your shoes before you step onto the rungs of the ladder.
- It is dangerous to use a ladder to access the topmost platform of a mobile tower – the tower could move.

Stepladder

We are all very familiar with the humble stepladder but unfortunately it is often ill-treated. I am sure we are all guilty of this at some time or another. Please remember these safety guidelines when using your stepladder:

- It is best to wear flat bottomed, firm-soled shoes – *not* trainers.
- Your stepladder must be tall enough for your requirements.
- Check for stability and use on firm ground.
- Work with both feet on the steps and never over-reach.

- Do not stand on the top handrail to gain additional height.

- Standing on the rear cross tube will cause it to buckle.

- Only allow one person on your stepladder at a time – 95 kg is the maximum load for domestic-type steps.

- Check for potential obstacles when carrying steps under your arm. This is very important when you are working in someone's house.

Many accidents have been caused by the misuse of stepladders: some have been caused by people applying a sideways pressure whilst drilling a wall. Always drill *facing the front of the steps* and never try to get round this rule by using your steps in a closed position – slipping could occur. Finally, if your stepladder has a handrail, please keep a firm grip when carrying material items up or down. Make sure both ropes or the tie bar is fully extended, as shown in Figure 2.11a.

Proprietary unit scaffolding (access towers)

This type of scaffolding, known as prefabricated aluminium tower scaffolding, has been fashioned to be put together on site, in a DIY manner. Its purpose is to support access platforms at various heights to enable you to work safely.

The components are generally either of the *slot-in* type or *spring clipped* in design and are fitted without the use of tools.

The following list describes a few of the more important components:

- End frame (1.3 or 0.75 m wide, Figure 2.12).

- Adjustable legs with wheels or base plates, Figure 2.13.

- Horizontal and diagonal braces (installed every fourth vertical metre).

- Safety guardrails and toe boards. The uppermost guardrail, positioned between 1.0

Figure 2.12 – *Access towers and frames – check your end sections are level before you start putting them together. (Reproduced by kind permission of SGB Youngman Limited.)*

Figure 2.11a – *Always open your stepladder fully and, if you have tie-bars, they must be locked into place.*

Figure 2.13 – *Castors (wheels) lock independently of the weight of the completed tower. (Reproduced by kind permission of SGB Youngman Limited.)*

Figure 2.14 – *An access platform must have a hinged hatch. (Reproduced by kind permission of SGB Youngman Limited.)*

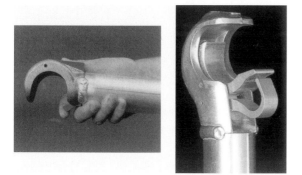

Figure 2.15 – *An automatic self-priming brace hook. (Reproduced by kind permission of SGB Youngman Limited.)*

and 1.5 m from the working surface. Guardrails and toe boards must also be fitted at this point.

■ A vertical ladder, as illustrated in Figure 2.19.

■ Locking wheels, which should be locked when working on the tower. Never be tempted to hitch a ride when it is being moved. When your tower has to be moved, always push–pull it – never move the tower by mechanical means.

■ Hinged hatch access platforms, Figure 2.14.

■ Snap-on components, as shown in Figure 2.15.

■ Warning notices.

Building your access tower

Please consider these simple guidelines whenever you are assembling a mobile scaffolding tower. Check your components are damage-free and are of the same design. For outside use, your maximum height will be three times the minimum base measurement. Used

inside, the maximum height allowed is three and a half times the minimum base measurement.

1 Use base plates standing on planks when using on soft soil. Save your wheels for concrete areas and indoor use.

2 Always follow the installation instructions – this is important.

3 Tie your tower to a nearby structure for stability or spike it to the ground – or you can use ballast weights (Figure 2.16).

4 Always secure when you are using out of doors.

5 Tools dropped from a height can do much damage to a person below!

6 Slot components into each other carefully – never use a hammer (Figure 2.17)!

7 Fit an intermediate rest platform every fourth vertical metre (Figure 2.18).

8 Install a fixed internal ladder on your tower as illustrated in Figure 2.19.

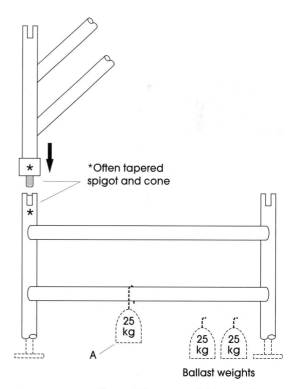

Figure 2.16 – *Ballast weights are available in 25 kg units. They are used to stabilize the tower.*

35

Figure 2.17 – *Slot one section into another with care. (Reproduced by kind permission of SGB Youngman Limited.)*

Figure 2.19 – *A fixed vertical tower ladder is used to gain access to the topmost platform. (Reproduced by kind permission of SGB Youngman Limited.)*

Taking down your access tower

This done in the reverse of the erecting procedure – you start at the top and work your way down. Never attempt to dismantle on your own; always work in pairs and with someone who is used to working with mobile towers. Always wear your hardhat, safety footwear and high visibility jacket wherever you are working. You must look after yourself!

The following points are common-sense guidelines you should keep in mind when you are dismantling your tower:

- Dismantle one section at a time, starting from the topmost handrails.
- Tie each section you have released to a nylon rope and lower it to the ground. Untie and stack.
- Your tower will collapse under its own weight if the diagonal braces are removed before it is safe to do so.
- Keep your work area clean and tidy.

Keep in mind the following safety points:

- Read your instruction manual and check your components.

Figure 2.18 – *An intermediate rest platform with a hinged hatch must be placed every 4 vertical metres. (Reproduced by kind permission of SGB Youngman Limited.)*

- Assemble on a firm base.
- Secure your tower to a nearby structure.
- Fit guard rails and toe boards to platforms.
- Always *lock your wheels* when working from the tower.
- Never use your tower outside during high wind.
- Do not use a stepladder on a working platform.
- Leave a warning notice on the platform if it is structurally incomplete.

Other means of access

Other means of access, which you may have seen, such as hydraulic mast-supported platforms, cherry pickers or lattice scissor platforms, are often expensive to hire. However, the cost is often justified when high or difficult positions have to be accessed – also it is a lot quicker than hiring traditional steel scaffolding.

If your company decides to hire a mechanical means of access, you will be given a short training course showing you how to use the controls. As part of the hiring agreement, an instruction manual is provided.

Power hoists for plant and equipment

This type of hoist is used for carrying both plant and material requirements to the upper floors of a partly constructed building. Each floor has its own staging point for the delivery of equipment. You should never be tempted to hitch a ride – however attractive it might appear. It is very dangerous! The building contractor is responsible for the maintenance and control of the hoist but a standard warning notice has to be

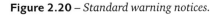

Figure 2.20 – *Standard warning notices.*

displayed and easily seen, as shown in Figure 2.20.

The Electricity at Work Regulations

More legal requirements – this set of regulations affects both *you* and your *employer*. Should anyone break these rules they could be heavily fined or end up in prison. Somebody who offends must legally prove that reasonable measures had been taken to prevent the breaking of these rules. Unlike our wiring requirements (BS 7671), the Electricity at Work Regulations is a set of legal rules laid down by Parliament.

I have chosen four of these regulations which will fit well within your own workplace:

Regulation 4 – Protective equipment. Protective equipment provided by an employer must be used properly, suitably maintained and relevant for the use intended.

Regulation 10 – Connections. Cable joints and connections must be mechanically and electrically suited for the job intended and relevant to the installation.

Regulation 11 – Protection against excess current. All circuits are to be protected against excess current and short circuit conditions.

Regulation 13 – Working on equipment made 'dead'. You must take measures to stop previously made '*dead*' equipment becoming '*live*' again, if this would cause a dangerous situation.

I have purposely shortened and rephrased these regulations in order to make it easier and less boring to read – it is difficult!

Your safety and welfare arrangements

Practice care and caution within the workplace and this will help to prevent an accident occurring. Sometimes you will have to think for others who want to treat your workplace as though it were a sports field!

There follow a few points which you should try to take on board – it might just keep you out of hospital:

- The first point to remember is very important. When a person is involved in an accident, *people are more important than property*.
- On a large site, always know who your first aider is.
- Never use an open-fronted halogen light (Figure 2.21) in thatched roof spaces.
- Allow a jigsaw to stop before removing. It could shatter.
- Work accompanied on live main equipment.
- It is safer to remove your wristwatch, bracelets and rings when the equipment you are working on is 'live'.
- Look after your lungs! Wear your face mask (Figure 2.22) in the following places:
  - in roof spaces decked out with fibre glass.
  - near asbestos lining or decaying water pipe insulation
  - on poultry or pig farms
  - when you are using a masonry disc wall chasing machine.
- Remember to wear your personal protective clothing to protect your head, ears, face, lungs, hands, knees and feet. Wear overalls –

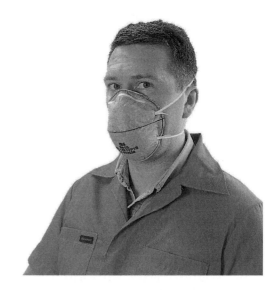

Figure 2.22 – *Protecting your lungs from dust. (Reproduced by kind permission of RS Components Ltd.)*

Figure 2.23 – *Goggles or other forms of eye protection must be worn when using equipment such as grinders, power tools, etc. (Reproduced by kind permission of RS Components Ltd.)*

this will give protection to your body and goggles will look after your eyes, as illustrated in Figure 2.23.

- Think before lifting your load. Page 20 of this book will provide you with details of how best to avoid back injury within the workplace.
- Trim any metallic overhang around the impact area of masonry tools as shown in Figure 2.24.

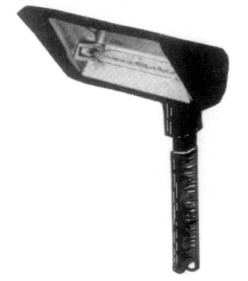

Figure 2.21 – *An open-fronted halogen light must not be used as a temporary light.*

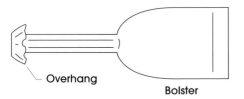

Figure 2.24 – *Impact overhang can be dislodged and cause damage to your hand.*

Your temporary accommodation

Before erecting temporary site accommodation, clear the area of rubbish and rubble. This will provide a safer workplace for everyone involved. A clean site will also provide secure access for delivery vehicles without fear of damage caused by sharp obstacles and scattered debris. A tidy site helps to make a safe site – download and remember!

Try to provide for the following temporary buildings. This decision will be the responsibility of your management:

- An office (a wood shed, a caravan or a Rollalong® cabin).
- A mess room (heating, table, chairs and a means to boil water).
- A materials store (lockable and windowless).

Toilets, first aid posts and drying rooms are the responsibility of the main contractor. They might even allow you to use their works canteen! However, if your company is the main contractor, they will be obliged to provide all health and welfare facilities. Your employer always provides first aid equipment. Keep safely in a wall-mounted container clearly marked FIRST AID, as illustrated in Figure 2.25.

The importance of good housekeeping

I am sure none of us is too fond of site housekeeping – but it is important if we are to maintain a clean and secure workplace free from rubbish. This will provide a safer place for everyone. Remember the following points:

Figure 2.25 – *First aid equipment must be clearly marked and placed where all can see. (Reproduced by kind permission of RS Components Ltd.)*

- Keep your access and through routes clear of obstacles.
- Pick up cable and conduit off-cuts from the floor.
- Store your flammable liquids in a locked container.
- Clean any spillages of grease and oil from the ground.
- Keep your mess room as clean and tidy as your kitchen at home.
- Stack your material items sensibly.
- Never rely on others to tidy up for you – your company will be charged for this service by the main contractor!

The benefits gained

There are benefits which in the long run will help to produce a far happier workforce:

- Potential fire hazards are removed.
- Efficiency and morale are improved within the workplace.
- The Health and Safety people are kept happy.
- Minor accidents will be reduced.
- Good impressions are created.
- Quarrelsome incidents are reduced.

Table 2.1 – *On-site damage to property.*

Situation	Potential damage to property
Glue spillage on a domestic carpet.	Carpet ruined by contamination (see Figure 2.26).
Removing ceiling tiles for wiring purposes, etc.	Chipped or broken ceiling tiles. Dirty hands or fingermarks.
Domestic installation	Damage moving ladders or stepladders.
Gaining access to a house	Carpets/floor covering spoilt by dirty shoes (see Figure 2.27).
Domestic installation (occupied)	Damage caused by lifting floor coverings and fitted carpets.
Domestic and commercial	Damage in the form of split and shattered tongue and grooved floorboards.
All types of installation	Damage caused to copper pipes and other hidden services.
Home gardens (occupied – see Figure 2.28)	Damage to plants and shrubs caused by the legs of access equipment.
Industrial lighting arrangements	Accidental damage caused by impact whilst moving mobile scaffolding.
Industrial buildings	Damage caused to structures or fabrics by carelessly placed equipment whilst in transit on a powered hoist.
Finished paintwork/decoration	Scuffed or chipped paintwork due to connecting electrical accessories. Plaster damage while trimming round pressed steel accessory boxes or fitting extra low voltage ceiling lights.
General – all types of installations (occupied/construction)	Damage caused by the over-use of wide tipped permanent marker pens. Light emulsion colours are unable to cover this with just two coats of paint.
Farms – hay barns (see Figure 2.29)	Burning of fabric/hay, caused by the careless positioning of floodlights.
Décor lighting in stately homes	Hot luminaries too near to flammable fabric.

Table 2.2 – *Suggested remedies to site-damaged fabrics.*

Damage	Suggested remedy
Damaged caused to plaster	Make good by replastering.
Torn carpet	Professionally repair or replace.
Broken or damaged ceiling tiles	Replace with the original design.
Dirty foot or hand prints	Clean dirty areas to acceptance.
Broken or split floorboards	Replace floorboards by screwing.
Data loss caused by isolating computer circuits	Inform your company for advice.
Breakage in a customer's home or place of work	Inform your company for advice. Provide a written apology.
Plant or shrub damage caused by outside installation work	Tidy up – replace damaged plants.
Foot through your customer's ceiling whilst working in the roof space	Arrange for the ceiling to be made good. Provide a written apology.

Avoiding damage to property

We are all guilty of accidentally damaging property from time to time. Often breakages and scratches happen by the careless use of access equipment such as stepladders and hop-ups. Table 2.1 describes some real-life cases, whilst Table 2.2 suggests some practical on-site remedies.

Figure 2.26 – *Spillage of industrial solvents when carrying out a domestic installation can prove costly.*

Figure 2.27 – *Floor covering will be soiled by contaminated footwear which in turn will strain the relationship between your customer and your company.*

Figure 2.28 – *Garden borders will be ruined through careless positioning of access equipment.*

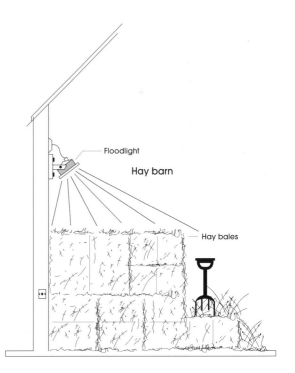

Figure 2.29 – *Halogen lights are very hot when illuminated – careless positioning causes fires!*

The Control of Substances Hazardous to Health Regulations

Keep under lock and key substances which are hazardous to health and only issue them in *need-to-have* circumstances. If you are the jobholder, ask for a signature each time material is issued – this will cover you.

Please remember these points – they might be useful to you one day:

- Separate your liquid and solid material stock from each other. Liquid materials will be stored in a spill-proof room.

- Clearly label all your hazardous stock. You will be provided with information about the type of materials you have in store (re. COSHH Regulation 12).

- Figure 2.30 illustrates warning signs of hazardous materials.

- There are four classifications of risk (see also Table 2.3):
  - toxic/very toxic (e.g. ionisation type smoke detectors),
  - corrosive (e.g. battery acid),
  - harmful (e.g. PVCu adhesive),
  - irritant (e.g. the insulation of MI cables).

- Other harmful materials you will come across include the following: dry asbestos, liquid mercury, the phosphorus coating inside a fluorescent tube and the fumes given off by lead solder. Also harmful to health are loose fibres from fibreglass insulation and liquid epoxy resin used to insulate underground steel wire armour joints.

Getting familiar with COSHH safety signs

Table 2.3 describes the meaning of four principal hazardous safety signs and provides a few common-sense precautions.

Other hazard signs

Table 2.4 lists and illustrates other hazard signs that might be seen in your workplace. It is unlikely that you will come across these signs within a new development but these are more likely to appear if you are working in an occupied business where they are handling such substances. It is good to know!

Summary so far...

1 Follow safe site working procedures and make sure you are able to operate different types of access equipment correctly.

2 Before work begins, check that your programme is both safe and practical.

3 Study your plans and schedules. Ask questions if you are not sure.

4 Keep strictly to BS7671 and the Electricity at Work Regulations.

5 There are many benefits from good housekeeping – keep your workplace free from rubbish and rubble.

6 Try to avoid damage to property whilst doing your job.

7 Remember the four principal hazardous substance signs:
  - toxic/very toxic (could cause death)
  - corrosive (can destroy living tissue)
  - harmful (can damage your health)
  - irritant (can cause inflammation to the skin).

Figure 2.30 – *Safety warning signs for hazardous materials.*

Table 2.3 *Definitions of harmful substances.*

The meaning	The sign used (orange backing, black logo)	Precautions to take
Toxic/very toxic – Substances which can cause death or badly damage your health.	 **Toxic** **Figure 2.31** – *Hazardous substance symbol – toxic/very toxic.*	Wear suitable protection. Wash off with water if in contact with your skin.
Corrosive – Substances in the form of gas, liquid or solid which may destroy living tissue.	 **Acid** **Corrosive** **Figure 2.32** – *Hazardous substance symbol – corrosive.*	Wear suitable gloves and face protection.
Harmful – Substances that may cause chronic damage to your health if swallowed, inhaled or absorbed through your skin.	 **Harmful** **Figure 2.33** – *Hazardous substance symbol – harmful.*	Use a suitable face mask. Wash before you eat. Use in well ventilated areas.
Irritant – Non-corrosive substance which may cause irritation to the skin or to the linings of the nose and lungs.	 **Irritant** **Figure 2.34** – *Hazardous substance symbol – irritant.*	Avoid breathing in and contact with the eyes and skin. Wash thoroughly if contaminated. Seek advice if necessary.

Table 2.4 – *Hazard signs within the workplace.*

Hazard	Sign used	Colours of the sign
Danger of death	 **Figure 2.35** – *Warning safety sign – danger of death.*	Yellow backing. Black boarding, logo and lettering.
Flammable liquid	 **Figure 2.36** – *Warning safety sign – flammable liquid.*	Yellow backing. Black boarding, logo and lettering.
Biological hazard	 **Figure 2.37** – *Warning safety sign – biological hazard.*	Yellow backing. Black boarding, logo and lettering.
Acid	 **Figure 2.38** – *Warning safety sign – acid.*	Yellow backing. Black boarding, logo and lettering.
Radioactive substance	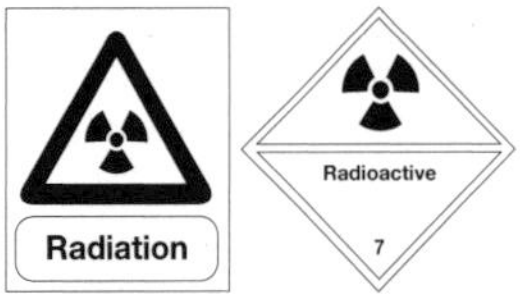 **Figure 2.39** – *Warning safety sign – radioactive substance.*	Yellow backing. Black boarding, logo and lettering.
Explosive material	 **Figure 2.40** – *Hazardous substance symbol – explosive.*	Orange backing. Black logo. Can also appear as a yellow triangle, black boarding and logo.
Dangerous to the environment	 **Figure 2.41** – *Hazardous substance symbol – dangerous to the environment (e.g. chlorofluorocarbon gas – CFC).*	Orange backing. Black logo.

Review questions

1 List three dangers you might discover whilst surveying your site.

2 Describe where material items and personal tools should be stored.

3 Name four different types of access equipment.

4 Is it true or false that guardrails and toe boards must be fitted to all access platforms above two metres from the ground?

5 Face masks must be worn (please indicate the line you feel is correct):
   - in uninsulated roof spaces
   - when hammering home masonry nails
   - when working in a grain silo
   - when working above 5 metres in windy conditions.

6 List five items of personal protective clothing that are worn within the workplace.

7 Name four input services you would expect to find when surveying a building site that is due for redevelopment.

8 What are the benefits of good housekeeping?

9 Describe briefly how potential damage can be done to property.

10 When you are working with battery acid, there are four classifications of risk. Choose from the following the correct option:
   - irritant
   - corrosive
   - toxic
   - harmful?

11 How would you describe the term *toxic*?

12 Illustrate or describe the hazard warning sign, *Danger of Death*.

13 Why is it best to be careful when using a well used fully painted ladder for the first time?

14 Describe how you would prevent an adjustable leg of a mobile scaffolding from sinking into soft soil.

15 Suggest three ways which would help make your site secure from unauthorised entry during off duty hours.

Handy hints

- Use the correct personal protective equipment when drilling or power-chopping masonry. Flying masonry can hurt and is potentially dangerous!
- To help prevent corrosion setting in, smear fixing devices with a little grease.
- Take care when carrying steps during windy weather. Both your steps and fixed platform will act as a sail and control can be quickly lost.
- Never be tempted to use faulty electrical tools – people are far more important than profit!
- Remember to use dustsheets when chasing or drilling walls in an occupied building. Think *customer relations*!
- Never stand on the top of the handrail serving a stepladder in order to gain extra height. It is dangerous.
- It is best not to speak in technical terms to a domestic customer. Adjust your language to the level of their understanding.
- Try to build good working relationships with co-contractors, workmates and customers. It will pay off in the end.
- You may need a licence from the HSE if you have to work with or handle asbestos. (Example: old ducting covers serving service risers.)

The structure of a company

Structure 2.1 summarises the internal structure of a middle-sized electrical engineering company from ownership/shareholders and management to the people who create the wealth of the company – people like you and the electricians with whom you work.

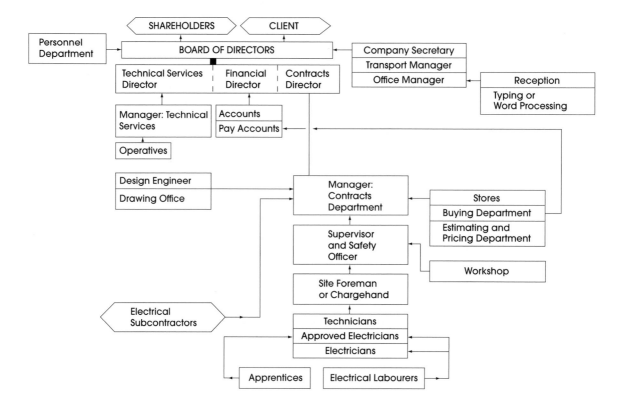

The roles and responsibilities of company members

Structure 2.2 describes the roles and responsibilities of members of the same middle-sized company, from the directors downwards. Not all companies will be so well organised but many will.

Department or rank of employee	Role	Responsibilities/duties	Status (approx)
Board of Directors	Managing the day-to-day affairs of the company. Advisors, decision and policy makers	To remain solvent, create wealth, to protect the interests of the shareholders and client. To maintain good working relationships	1
Company secretary	Legal and financial	Legal studies. May sign documents on behalf of the company. Maintains company financial interests	1.1
Personnel department	Dealing with staff appointments and the welfare of all employees	Serving the welfare and addressing the problems of all company employees. Arranging interviews and appointments. Spokesperson for company announcements. Responsible to the Board of Directors	2
Vehicle transport manager	Supplying and maintaining company transport. Dealing with insurance matters and legal transport requirements	Ensuring that all vehicles are road worthy, are taxed, insured and Ministry of Transport tested. Responsible to the Board of Directors	2
Office manager	Department head. Provides all clerical and administrative requirements	Administrative records. Letter writing. Providing requested information from computer or files. Responsible to the office manager	2
Reception	Receiving clients and visitors. Queries. Introductions. Telephone duties	Welcoming clients and visitors and to see their immediate requirements. Often telephone and typing duties are called for. Responsible to the office manager	2.1
Word-processing department	Word processing or copy typing company documents and letters	Copy typing or word processing duties which include letters, documents, accounts and promotional information. Responsible to the office manager	—
Accounts	Financial matters	To inspect and maintain company accounts. Keeping records. Invoicing customers. Settling suppliers accounts. Responsible to the financial director	2
Pay accounts	Wages, salaries and expenses	Ensuring that wages, salaries and expenses are paid and that other personal financial requirements such as sick pay are attended to. Responsible to the financial director	2
Contracts manager or engineer	To coordinate the needs of the client and act as a link between senior management and the workforce; to advise	Managing the contracts department and monitoring progress. To maintain agreed budget lines. To advise and recommend. Control of subordinates. Attending meetings with clients or potential clients or potential clients. Maintaining the policy of the company. Responsible to the contracts director	2

Department or rank of employee	Role	Responsibilities/duties	Status (approx)
Supervisor	Supervising site progress. Liaison officer between management and the workforce	Regular site visits to oversee progress of work. To discipline. To advise and inform and cater for site material requirements. General administrative duties. Responsible to the contracts manager	2.1
Site foreman	Maintaining progress and harmony at site level. Company site representative	Responsible, at site level, for all electrical work undertaken. Coordinator and technical advisor. Will liaise at site level with the architect and other companies' representatives. Responsible to the supervisor	2.2
Chargehand	Responsible for a small number of operatives of mixed grades	In charge of a small team of operatives. Non policy decisions can be made and advise given. Will maintain production and liaise with the site foreman. Often a chargehand is responsible for his/her team's work sheets. Responsible to the site foreman	2.3
Technician	Technical overseer	Similar responsibilities as carried out by the chargehand. Can make technical decisions at a local level. Responsible to the site foreman	2.3
Approved electrician	A mature and fully experienced operative who is fully qualified	Carrying out tasks of a technical nature and must be thoroughly conversant with electrical installation engineering practices and problems Responsible to the chargehand or technician	2.4
Electrician	Supplemental to an approved electrician. Often recently qualified in electrical practices	To assist and carry out tasks of which he/she is technically competent. Responsible to the chargehand or technician	2.5
Apprentice	To study and learn through hands on experience and by watching others carry out electrical installation work. Attainment of NVQ, Levels 2 and 3	To develop and build on existing skills in order to qualify as an electrician. To carry out supervised work according to his/her technical ability and experience	2.6
Electrical labourer	Supervised non-technical electrical work. Assisting where required	General duties usually of a non-technical nature. Example: chasing walls threading and cutting steel conduit. Drilling holes, etc.	2.7
Electrical subcontractor	Electrical duties according to grade	To assist and carry out electrical duties of which he/she is technically competent. Responsible to the contracts manager/engineer but usually, in practice, to the site foreman	—
Design engineer/drawing office	To produce a working drawing from an idea or scheme submitted by a client	Meeting with client. Site visits. Production of draft proposals in keeping with the writing regulations. Advising, and answering the site foremans queries in relation to the working drawings. At times the design engineer may be asked to attend a site meeting if considered necessary Responsible to the contracts manager	2.1
Stores	Issuing of material items such as cable, plant and accessories on production of a stores requisition order	Supplying material items for the job. Stock taking. Administrative duties and ordering. Responsible to the contracts manager	2.1

Department or rank of employee	Role	Responsibilities/duties	Status (approx)
Estimating/pricing department	Pricing enquires relating to potential assignments or undertakings	Pricing from site visits and customer's provisional drawings or sketches. A possible formal meeting with the customer. Administrative work. Responsible to the contracts manager	2.1
Buying department	To seek to obtain the best possible price for material items needed for a contract. To order material items	To negotiate preferential discount prices with wholesalers. To keep within the budget of the proposed installation. Responsible to the contracts manager and the accounts department	2.1
Workshop	Site built assemblies, etc. access to fixed power tools. A means to carry out repairs of a delicate nature	All power tools and fixed machine tools must be maintained and inspected regularly. The workshop should be kept clean and tidy at all times and exit and formal escape route is kept free from all obstructions. Often responsibility for the workshop is given to an electrical supervisor	2.2
Technical services department	Electrical maintenance, small works. Electrical breakdowns	Usually a 24-hour seven-day week service. Operative must be competent in electrical fault finding. Usually given to approved electricians or technicians	2
Client	Customer	To provide data and relative information to produce a fair and reasonable price accompanied by accurate working drawings	—

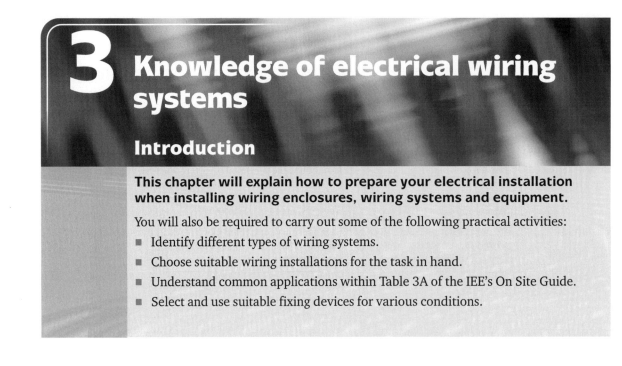

3 Knowledge of electrical wiring systems

Introduction

This chapter will explain how to prepare your electrical installation when installing wiring enclosures, wiring systems and equipment.

You will also be required to carry out some of the following practical activities:

- Identify different types of wiring systems.
- Choose suitable wiring installations for the task in hand.
- Understand common applications within Table 3A of the IEE's On Site Guide.
- Select and use suitable fixing devices for various conditions.

Starting work

Before you start your job, check with your contracts manager or boss that it is okay to do so and that your site is free from hazards as previously discussed in Chapter 2.

Useful points to bear in mind

- When you work on a small site, check that your tools are powered by 110 V.
- Check that your battery-operated tools and mobile telephone are in good working order.
- Do you have the correct *personal protective equipment* to do your job?
- Have your power tools and any appliances you might have been *portable appliance tested* recently?
- Do the drawings meet with the specifications?
- Is there any other information you should know: site working hours, whether radios or mobile phones are permitted or the times when noise is forbidden?
- Do you feel that your management's programme of work is practical within the time allowed to do your job? If not, now is the time to speak up!

Plans and drawings

It is usual to receive two sets of drawings if the job is of some size but only one if the work is only to last a couple of weeks or so. Whatever the job, make sure your working drawings are up to date. Revised drawings will be marked with a capital letter of the alphabet followed by the date of the revision within the title block, as illustrated in Figure 3.1.

Since not all installation plans are accompanied by a legend (this is a key which tells you the meaning of the various electrical symbols) it is wise to become familiar with them. Page 30 provides a few examples of electrical location symbols and their meaning. Studying these will help you to interpret electrical drawings and provide you with a little more confidence. When reworking your own drawings always used the correct symbols – never design your own. It could be very confusing for those who follow.

Preparing a material list

Prepare a handwritten list of all the material needs for your job. This will include lighting and power cables, accessories and maybe appliances, etc. Your list can be presented in many different ways but please not on the back of a cigarette

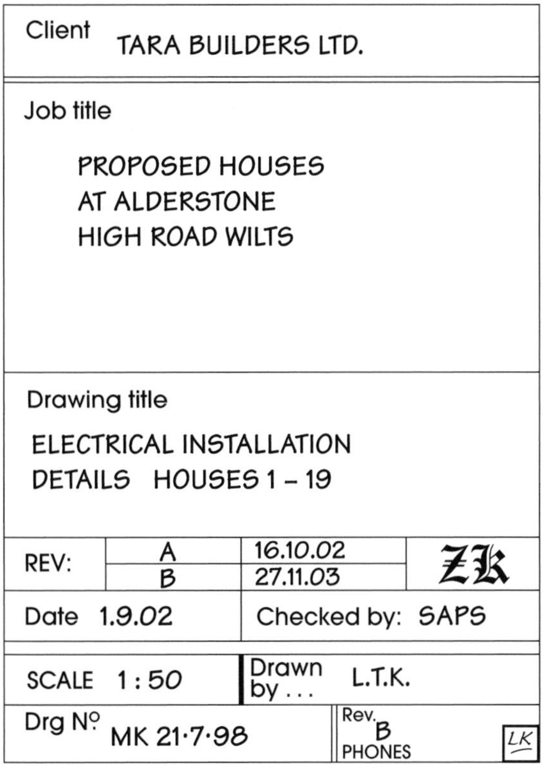

Client	TARA BUILDERS LTD.

Job title

PROPOSED HOUSES
AT ALDERSTONE
HIGH ROAD WILTS

Drawing title

ELECTRICAL INSTALLATION
DETAILS   HOUSES 1 – 19

REV:	A	16.10.02	ZK
	B	27.11.03	

Date 1.9.02	Checked by: SAPS

SCALE 1 : 50	Drawn by . . . L.T.K.

Drg No. MK 21·7·98	Rev. B PHONES	LK

Figure 3.1 – *Check your drawing is up to date.*

packet – it is just not professional! Many companies these days have printed requisition duplicating books in which you can place a formal order. This is an ideal way to get your message across as the carbon copy can be kept as an all-time reference.

As an example, you could write a list in the style shown in Table 3.1 – again this is far better that using the back of a fag packet. A list drawn up this way is both practical and helpful. It is easy to read and reduces the possibility of error and confusion occurring.

A quick way of preparing a materials list

I cannot guarantee that this will work – but it is well worth a try! Instead of listing each material item from your working drawing, ask your company estimator to supply a computer printout of all the materials priced for the installation. This request may not be welcomed, as estimators are often very busy people – but it is worth a try.

When you receive your order

Check all the materials you have ordered through your wholesaler or company stores as soon as they arrive on site. If you do not and

Table 3.1 – *An example of a stores requisition form often used by well established companies.*

Tara Electrical Installations Ltd.	Jobholder's name. Zimmer P.Y.
	Site...Whiteparish (Stage3)
Site material requirements	Job number... KL 3421
■ *Please list clearly*	Required on... 17th September
3...7 PIR security lights	Smith Cat. # SLO 01
2 metre.Tuf-Strut channel support	MT – CC1
14... Bulkhead lights	Coughtrie BH 18 – 2 x PL9
14... BC (pearl) 100 watt lamps	Any make will do
5... Industrial luminaries 150 watt SON-T	Osram HR 150X
20-metre heavy gauge welded steel conduit	Any make will do.

Special instructions: Please deliver before 10 a.m. at the Common Road side entrance.

Signed Zimmerman [Peter]   **Date**. 15th September

there is something missing, they will tell you that it was included – it happens all the time. Sign for the delivery and keep the despatch note in a safe place. If the delivery is from your own company it is best to make a note in your site day diary. Always record deficiencies or damaged goods both promptly and accurately – never rely on your memory.

Materials used as electrical conductors and insulators

Table 3.2 lists, in random order, materials that we use for conductors and insulators. Pure silver ranks as one of the very best conductors of electricity whereas tap water can be described as a poor conductor of electricity.

What type of wiring system is required?

If you alone have to decide the type of wiring system to install, then you need to choose wiring methods that will suit the conditions your installation has to operate under. It would be silly to install plastic conduit and accessories within a constantly warm atmosphere such as a boiler house or to use untreated mild steel trunking out-of-doors to face the weather.

Table 3.3 outlines the general requirements for seven different types of installation.

Table 3.2 – *Conductors and insulators of electricity.*

Good conductors	Good insulators	Poor insulators/conductors
Silver (used for contacts)	Mica (a rock-forming mineral)	Cotton (from a plant)
Platinum (used for contacts)	Paraffin wax	Germanium*
Copper (cables and bus bars)	PVC material	Selenium*
Gold (used for contacts)	Plastic	Dry paper
Aluminium (used for cables)	Porcelain	Silicon*
Brass (bolts/nuts)	Quartz (a rock-forming mineral)	Wood
Lead (batteries)	Shellac	Wool
Tungsten (lamp filaments)	Sulfur	–
Carbon (brushes and batteries)	Pure rubber	–
Tin (a component of solder)	Man-made rubber	–
Zinc (battery electrodes)	Polythene	–
Steel (conduit and switches)	Magnesia (used in MI cable)	–
Stainless steel (cable carriers)	90°C thermosetting	–
Nickel (electrical accessories)	Bakelite®	–
Invar (temperature probes)	Ceramic	–
Impure iron (switchgear)	Transformer oil	–
Bronze (electrical accessories)	Glass	–

* Materials used in electronics.

Table 3.3 – *General requirements for installations.*

Type of installation	Suggested cable to use	Recommended carrier
Boiler house	Mineral Insulated®, Fire-Tuff® FP200/LSOH® Any other fire-resistant cable	Cable tray (steel)
Houses	PVC insulated and sheathed cable	Laid direct or mini-trunking
Fuel refinery	PVC insulated, double steel wire armoured with or without a lead bedding sheath	Steel cable tray or ladder
Farm	Stranded single PVC insulated cables	PVC conduit and accessories
Industrial	PVC insulated single cables, MI cable, steel wire armoured cables and specialised cables	Steel conduit, trunking and cable tray and cable ladder
Commercial	Single PVC insulated cables. Fire-resistant cables, steel wire armoured and MI® cables where required	All types of cable carriers
Data transmission	Braided screened/PVC insulated cable and fibre optic cable	PVC trunking and mini-trunking, sometimes laid in screened PVCu trunking and modular flush data boxes as illustrated in Figure 3.2

Figure 3.2 – *Screened PVCu trunking. (Reproduced by kind permission of Marshall Tufflex Limited.)*

Fixing methods

You must install cable carriers and enclosures such as conduit, trunking and cable tray precisely and in agreement with your electrical specification. Please remember all cables must be routed clear of other electromagnetic services such as intruder and fire alarm circuits – it could cause problems.

If you find it difficult to fix within an installation that stipulates defined routes and methods to use, you must get permission for an approved alternative method to carry out your work.

It is important to know the type of material you are using to fix your accessories. Never fix to asbestos without obtaining specialised advice: the dust created could cause you serious problems in future years. Avoid fixing to soft fabric board unless you can provide a suitable backing in order to strengthen the board.

Table 3.4 provides a selection of common fixing devices and how we use them. Do not use standard wall plugs (Rawlplugs®) for fixing an accessory to a ceiling – your fixing within the plasterboard is just not strong enough to hold the weight of the electrical accessory. Aluminium spiral fixings are better for this application but they are not reliable for fixing to damp plasterboard.

It is difficult to estimate the number of fixing devices you will need for your job but try not to under-estimate. If necessary ask for a complete box – hand back any left over or they will always come in useful for your next job!

Table 3.4 – *Fixing methods.*

Supplementary support device	Made from	Fixed by	Site application
Site assembled brackets	Mild steel/painted	Woodscrews; wall bolts or coach bolts	Trunking, cable tray installations
Cable clips	PVCu	Hardened nails	Securing sheathed cables
Cable strapping	Coated aluminium or copper strip	Brass nuts and bolts and brass woodscrews	MI cables on cable tray
Cable ties (Figure 3.3)	Nylon, PVC or stainless steel	Self-fixing	Securing bunched cables
Channel support	Mild steel, PVCu or polyester (reinforced)	Woodscrews, wall bolts or coach bolts	Cable trunking and tray, sometimes ladder packing installations
Cable cleats	PVC, aluminium or glass reinforced nylon	Threaded stud, woodscrews, wall bolts or coach bolts	Securing SWA cables
Pipe hook or crampit, see Figure 3.4	Mild steel	Self-fixing by impact	For securing conduit to soft building fabric
Saddles	Steel or PVC	Woodscrews	To support conduit
Self-adhesive cable clips	Mild steel and plastic coated	Self fixing	Lightweight, extra low voltage cables and telecom cables
Spiral fixings	Aluminium	Self-fixing plus a wood screw	Accessories on plasterboard surfaces
Strapping (round holed)	Mild steel/galvanised or nylon	Bolts, studding or coach bolts	Used to support cable on large cable tray
Racking support	Mild steel or aluminium	Bolts, studding or coach bolts	Cable ladder, trunking or tray systems and sometimes used with cable basket systems

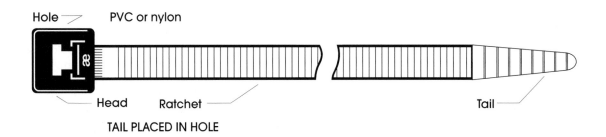

Figure 3.3 – *Nylon cable ties.*

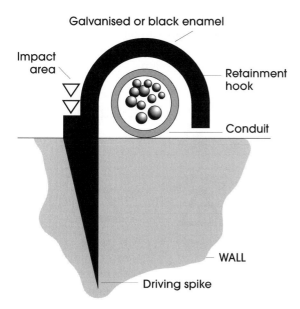

Figure 3.4 – *Pipe hook – also known as a crampit.*

Things you should know about health and safety

More regulations, I am afraid! In summary, this section includes the following:

1 Control of Substances Hazardous to Health.
2 First Aid at Work Regulations.
3 Safety signs and signals.
4 Manual handling of loads and equipment.
5 Personal protective equipment (known as PPE).

Control of Substances Hazardous to Health (COSHH)

This regulation places a legal duty on your employer to protect you from hazardous substances within the workplace that could be a risk to your health.

- There must be an assessment of any health risk associated with the work you are to carry out that involves the use of hazardous substances. Figure 3.5 is an example of a warning sign indicating hazardous substances.

- Your boss must apply controls to limit the risk of contamination to his workforce such as providing facemasks, rubber gloves, etc.

- Your employer must monitor and check on the effectiveness of all measures taken.

Oxidizing   Toxic

Figure 3.5 – *Hazardous substance warning signs.*

First aid at work regulations

The person you work for must provide first aid requirements within the workplace. In general, he/she must provide the following:

- The appointment of trained first aiders within the workplace. In practice, this seldom works for every site.

- First aid equipment, including eye wash services.

- An appointed person to take charge if there is any need for first aid within the workplace but not intended to take the place of a trained first aider.

Get to know your first aider. Check out the location of your nearest first aid station or A & E unit – it could prove very helpful! If you have an accident at work, no matter how small, it is important to record it in your company's accident book.

Safety signs and signals

This regulation is to advise on health and safety information by the use of coloured signs and logos. It also takes on board illuminated signs such as FIRE EXIT and signals in the form of sound waves such as alarm bells, sirens, etc. Get to know the type of sound you will hear – it could just save your life!

55

The five types you will come across

Mandatory – these are used to inform you. Examples include: 'you must wear protective clothing', 'this is a safety helmet area', 'all drivers must report to the site office'. Figure 3.6 illustrates this type of sign.

Figure 3.6 – *A mandatory warning sign will tell you what to do and is coloured blue with a white logo.*

Prohibitive – this is shown to tell you not to carry out a particular activity, such as no smoking or do not ride on the mechanical hoist. Figure 3.7 illustrates this.

Figure 3.7 – *A prohibitive sign is bordered red and has a black logo on a white background.*

Safe condition – this type of sign is to provide you with safety information such as the location of first aid posts and fire exits, etc. Figure 3.8 illustrates this.

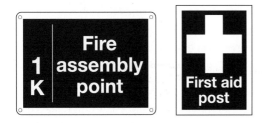

Figure 3.8 – *A safe condition sign has a green backdrop with a white logo.*

Warning – this type of sign is to warn people a risk or hazard exists. Examples are danger, caution, harmful material, etc. Figure 3.9 illustrates this type of sign.

Figure 3.9 – *A warning sign has a yellow backdrop with a black logo and triangular border.*

Fire fighting equipment – as the name suggests this is all to do with fire fighting equipment. These signs are either square or oblong with a red backdrop on which there is white wording and a logo. They show the location of fire fighting equipment. Examples include: fire alarm control, do not use on electrical fires and fire alarm do not switch off! Figure 3.10 provides examples of this type of sign.

Figure 3.10 – *Signs for fire safety messages are red and support white logos and lettering.*

Manual handling – or how to avoid a hernia!

This is another legal requirement for you to download. It has been designed to reduce the risk of personal injury resulting from pushing, pulling, lifting and carrying.

When taken on-board it will, with any luck, reduce the danger from the following injuries:

- cuts
- tendon damage
- hernia
- muscular/ligament damage
- bruises and fractures
- nerve damage through crushing.

Chapter 4 has a formal lifting plan but before then let us preview the following points:

1 Seek advice if you are not sure.
2 Wear protective clothing.
3 A firm grip is necessary.
4 Ask for help if your load is too heavy – do not try to be macho!
5 Back straight, knees bent and chin in before you lift.
6 Keep your arms close to your body and make good use of your weight wherever possible.
7 When carrying, remember the size, shape and weight of your load.
8 When two or more of you are moving a load, always ask one person to provide you with instructions.

One last point – if you injury yourself outside your workplace and it affects your ability to lift you could worsen your condition by ignoring your injury. Look after yourself!

Personal Protective Equipment (PPE)

PPE is worn in the workplace and your employer has a legal duty to provide this equipment so your job can be carried out in safety. PPE should:

- Be appropriate for the risk. Example – high visibility clothing for site use.
- Be appropriate for a person's needs. Example – providing larger size protective footwear for an apprentice who would normally take a smaller fitting would be against this regulation.
- Be adjustable, to fit the wearer without undue comfort. Example – if you have to alter the adjustment of your hard hat, it must feel comfortable and not fall below your ears!
- Not add to the risk factor. Example – scratched or semi-clear eye protection would add to the risk factor.
- Bear the CE mark (see p.8).

Examples of PPE

1 Safety footwear, safety harness for working at heights.
2 Work gloves, thermal clothing, environmental suites, overalls.
3 Ear and eye protection.
4 Safety helmets (hardhats).
5 Face masks (see Figure 3.11) or fresh air hose equipment.
6 Overalls and high visibility clothing.
7 Knee protection, and harness belt when working at heights.
8 Bump caps.
9 Hair nets.
10 Other items can include sou'westers, gauntlets, mitts, wrist cuffs, armlets, gaiters, leggings, etc.

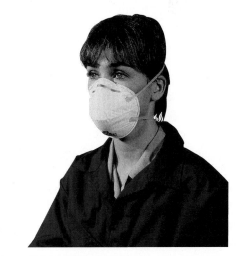

Figure 3.11 – *PPE equipment to protect your lungs. (Reproduced by kind permission of RS Components Limited.)*

The Health and Safety law in brief

- Cooperate with your employer on all aspects of health and safety.

- Report a safety problem within the workplace.

- Never interfere with anything to do with health, safety or welfare.

- You must be accountable for your own health and those of your workmates by activities carried out by you.

- Record all accidents in your company accident book.

The legal duties and responsibilities of your employer

There are many, I am afraid, but it is the requirement of this scheme that you have the opportunity to familiarise yourself with them. I will try to be brief!

1 If there are more than five employees, your boss must prepare a written health and safety policy for all to see.

2 Your workplace must be safe and without risk to your health.

3 All protective clothing will be provided free of charge.

4 A safety committee will be formed if requested by two or more people.

5 Fire fighting equipment to be provided together with means of escape.

6 Guards and barriers have to be provided on all workshop machinery.

7 You must receive training if you are to use dangerous machinery or tools.

8 An employer must provide suitable welfare facilities.

9 Good levels of lighting and warmth must be offered in company workshops.

10 First aid equipment must be provided by your employer.

11 Injuries or certain diseases must be reported to the enforcing agency.

12 Maintenance of ladders, etc., has to be carried out by your boss.

13 Mechanical handling aids must be available for heavy goods.

14 Your employer has to maintain all floors, stairs and passageways within his premises.

15 Clear labelling of dangerous materials is the responsibility of your employer.

16 Your boss is responsible for keeping your workplace free from noise, dust and fumes.

17 An employer must show his/her Liability Certificate.

Other useful legal documents

These include: Management of Health and Safety Regulations (1992), Provision and Use of Work Equipment Regulations (1992) and the Personal Protective Equipment [PPE] Regulations (1992).

Handy hints

- Think safe, work safe – your family needs you!

- Do not be shy to report matters that you consider unsafe.

- It is not a good idea to wear a pullover whilst working – wool will snag on almost anything.

- Remove your twist drill from your battery-operated drill and lock the switching mode if you are carrying it.

Wiring systems – choosing the right cable

It is important to select the correct type of cable for each particular wiring task. There are many considerations and a selection of these follows:

- Situation – *industrial, commercial, domestic, etc.*?

- Environmental – *inside, outside or below the ground*?

- Fauna – *cattle, rodents or domestic animals etc?*
- Flora – *plants, shrubs, trees and root formation?*
- The temperature – *hot, cold or moderate?*
- The applied voltage – *high, low or extra low?*
- The design current of your circuit – *milliamp or amps?*
- Use – *motor circuit, data transmission, power or lighting?*
- The wetness factor – *saturated, wet, moist or humid?*
- Trench depth – *for underground cabling.*
- Explosive situation factor – *gas, battery room or fuel oil, etc?*

Practical wiring examples

1 Steel wire armoured cables (SWA), Figure 3.12, may be used for:
   - general industrial wiring uses; the distribution of temporary power to serve new building sites.
   - above and below ground power distribution systems.
   - industrial, commercial and agricultural control circuits.
2 Mineral-insulated (MI) cables and FP 200 Gold® and Fire Tuff® may be used:
   - where it is very hot
   - for fire alarms and central battery emergency lighting circuits
   - in corrosive and radioactive atmospheres.
3 PVC insulated and sheathed cable may be used:
   - in domestic installations
   - in commercial installations

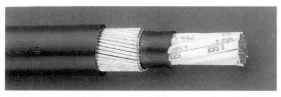

Figure 3.12 – *Steel wire armoured cable. (Reproduced by kind permission of Walsall Conduits Limited.)*

- for lighting and power requirements for schools and colleges.
4 SY-flexible cable may be used:
   - for trailing leads in workshops.
5 PVC single-insulated cable may be used:
   - in steel and PVCu conduit installations
   - in steel and PVCu trunking and mini-trunking installations.
6 Arctic grade cable is used:
   - in very cold places
   - inside low temperature (cold) rooms.

Choosing the size of your cable

There are a few points to consider when choosing the size of the cable you wish to use for your circuit. It is not good enough to say by rule of thumb that 2.5 mm² will support *x* amps – other considerations must be taken into account. In summary, these are:

- The surrounding temperature.
- Will your cables be grouped together (this is called bunching)?
- The current you expect to flow through the circuit.
- The type of installation method you intend to use. Example: enclosed in conduit, laid in trunking or clipped the surface of the wall, etc.
- What type and size of current device you want to use.
- Is there any possibility of a large voltage drop within your cable?
- Do you need to apply *correction factors*? If you have not come across this term before, then briefly correction factors are used to determine the correct size of cable to use in your installation. There are four categories:
   - C_g cable grouping (when cables are grouped or bunched),
   - C_a ambient temperature (the surrounding temperature),
   - C_i thermal insulation (if only one side of your cable is placed in contact with the insulation the factor is 0.75 but if your cable is surrounded then it will be 0.5).

- C_f the type of fuse serving your circuit. If it is semi-enclosed a factor of 0.75 is applied but not if your circuit is to be wired using mineral insulated cable (MI).

An example of how to apply correction factors

A 230 V, 3000 W fixed wall heater circuit will be installed using single PVC insulated copper conductors and protected by a 15 A semi-enclosed fuse. The installation will be installed in an area where the maximum temperature is 35°C. The circuit will be alongside two other single-phase circuits – steel conduit will be used as a cable carrier. Each circuit will carry about the same load to the proposed wall heater circuit as illustrated in Figure 3.13.

Find out the minimum size conductor that you will use to comply with our wiring regulations.

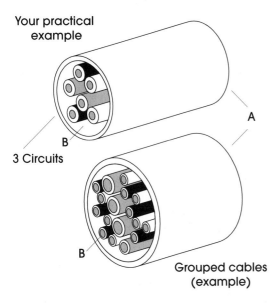

Your practical example

A

B

3 Circuits

B

Grouped cables (example)

Figure 3.13 – *Each circuit within the conduit installation has identical loads.*

Solution – a step-by-step approach

a) Calculate the value of the design current (I_b) of the circuit:

$$I_b = 3000 \text{ watt}/230 \text{ volt} = 13 \text{ amp.} \quad (3.1)$$

b) Next, find the correction factor for an ambient temperature (C_a) of 35°C. The wiring regulations supply a factor of 0.94.

c) Now, find the grouping factor (C_g) for single core PVC insulated cable enclosed in conduit. The factor provided by the regulations is 0.7.

d) Finally apply the correction factor for a semi-enclosed fuse (C_f) which is 0.725.

e) As there is no thermal insulation to consider the correction factor (C_i) will not apply to our calculation.

Now work out the value of the minimum current carrying capacity of the cable. This is known as I_z:

$$I_z = \frac{\text{Rating of the protective device in amps}}{\text{temperature} \times \text{grouping} \times \text{fuse factors}}$$

$$= \frac{I_n}{C_a C_g C_f} \quad (3.2)$$

Substituting for our known values:

$$I_z = \frac{15}{0.94 \times 0.7 \times 0.725} = \frac{15}{0.477} = 31.4 \text{ A}$$

BS 7671 – The Wiring Regulations will recommend a minimum size cable. Now select a suitable cable from BS 7671 under Installation method 3. This will show that a 4 mm² conductor with a current carrying capacity of 32 A would be a suitable size to use.

Considering voltage drop

Regulation 525-01-02 states that the voltage drop between the incoming supply terminals and a fixed current consuming appliance must not be more than 4% of the nominal voltage U_0 of the supply. The term 'nominal voltage' refers to the *declared* voltage of the supply; for example, 230 V.

Calculate the voltage drop by using the following expression:

$$\text{Permissible voltage drop} = U_0 \times 0.04 \quad (3.3)$$

where U_0 is the *nominal* voltage and 0.04 is a factor of the volt drop permitted. BS 7671 shows a selection of voltage drop values in the form of easy-to-read tables. If the voltage drop is greater than 4%, you will have to consider using a heavier size cable.

How can I calculate the maximum number of conductors that can be placed within conduit or trunking installations?

Single-core PVC insulated cables

First, obtain a cable factor from Table 3.5 for each cable you place within your conduit. Add them all together and compare the figure you get with the conduit factors given in Table 3.6. Remember to take into account the length of your conduit run and the number of bends and sets that you will form. The minimum size conduit is that size having a cable factor either equal or greater than the sum of the cable factors. If you are not sure of this, please read this paragraph again.

A practical example

A 10 metre run of conduit, served by one right angle bend, has to accommodate the following single-core PVC insulated cables:

- four 2.5 mm² cables
- two 1.5 mm² cables
- five 1.0 mm² cables.

Table 3.5 – *Cable factors used in conduit incorporating bends.*

Type of conductor	Cross-sectional area of the conductor in mm²	Cable factor
Stranded or solid copper, PVC insulated	1	16
	1.5	22
	2.5	30
	4.0	43
	6.0	58
	10.0	105
	16.0	145
	25.0	217

Table 3.6 – *Selecting the correct size of conduit by means of cable factors.*

	Straight run of conduit				Conduit with one bend			
Conduit diameter (mm)	16	20	25	32	16	20	25	32
Length of conduit (m)								
3.5	179	290	521	911	162	263	475	837
4.0	177	286	514	900	158	256	463	818
4.5	174	282	507	899	154	250	452	800
5.0	171	278	500	878	150	244	442	783
6.0	167	270	487	857	143	233	422	250
7.0	162	263	475	837	136	222	404	720
8.0	158	256	463	818	130	213	388	692
9.0	154	250	452	800	125	204	373	997
10.0	150	244	442	783	120	196	358	643

Work out, by using the above tables, the size of conduit needed:

1 First, refer to Table 3.5.

2 The cable factor for 2.5 is 30, for which there are four cables = 120

3 The cable factor for 1.5 is 22, for which there are two cables = 44

4 The cable factor for 1.0 is 16, for which there are five cables = 80

5 Now add up all your cable factors: 120 + 44 + 80 = **244**

6 Next, refer to Table 3.6 and cast your eye along the row of figures serving the 10 metre run with one bend. The nearest factor greater than your calculated figure of 244 is 358.

7 Look at the topmost figure of this column and you will see a 25 mm diameter conduit will be required for your installation.

This is a just a brief example of how conduit sizes are calculated. A more detailed table will be found in the IEE's On-Site Guide.

What size cable trunking will I need for my installation?

The way to calculate the size of cable trunking you will need for your installation is much the same as finding the correct size of conduit you

Table 3.7 – *Cable factors for steel trunking.*

Type of single-core conductor	Cross-section of conductor	BS 6004 PVC cable factor	BS 7211 Thermosetting cable factor
Stranded	1.5	8.6	9.6
	2.5	12.6	13.9
	4.0	16.6	18.1
	6.0	21.2	22.9
	10.0	35.3	36.3
	16.0	47.8	50.3
	25.0	73.9	75.4
Solid	1.5	8.0	8.6
	2.5	11.9	11.9

Table 3.8 – *Calculating the size of trunking from the total sum of your cable factors.*

Unit factor (sometimes known as 'the term')	Minimum size of trunking you need (mm), space factor taken into account
738	25 × 75
993	25 × 100
1037	50 × 50
1555	50 × 75
2091	50 × 100
2371	75 × 75
3189	75 × 100
4252	100 × 100
4743	75 × 150
17429	200 × 200
39428	300 × 300

would require, the difference being that the numbers are smaller.

1 Find the appropriate cable factor from Table 3.7.

2 Add your factors together to obtain a *total cable factor.*

3 The minimum size required can be taken from Table 3.8 and its size will have a cable factor either *equal to* or *greater than* your total cable factor.

This will be the size – but please consider whether you will have to install additional cables in the future. If the answer to this is 'Yes' then think about increasing the size.

Table 3.8 is a just a guide: a more detailed table will be found in the IEE's On-Site Guide.

Fixing to unknown building material

The effect of fixing to an unknown building fabric could have terrible costs and could cause damage. It would be very unwise to fix a heavy electrical appliance using wall plugs and screws to a soft thermal block wall. Aluminium spiral fixings are very useful but must never be used in a building fabric that would soften or weaken when damp. The weight of your accessory would dislodge the fixing from the fabric into which it was screwed!

Table 3.9 – *Building fabrics and safe methods of fixing.*

Fabric	Method of fixing	Example	Common mistakes
House bricks	Wall plugs, pin plugs, expansion bolts, coach bolts, cable clips	Electrical accessories, lights, switches, etc.	Hole too big. Wrong fixing device.
Ceiling tiles	Timber fillet placed above the tile. Appliance then fixed with screws	Smoke detector or a light fitting	Using wall plugs and screws or just screws.
Standard concrete	Expansion bolts, wall plugs and screws. Threaded studding with nuts and washers	Switchgear, cable supports and accessories	Incorrect depth of hole and careless positioning.
Damp-proof treated walls	Industrial adhesive or self-adhesive cable clips	Areas built below ground Old houses	Drilling and fixing by the usual method.
Flintstone with mortar	Wall plugs and screws positioned in the mortar	Outside walls with lighting	Attempting to drill the flintstone.
Lightweight thermal block	Wall plugs and screws, expansion bolts, threaded studding, nuts, and washers	Switchgear and general accessories. Knock out boxes.	The wrong size hole and fixing device.
Plasterboard	Aluminium/plastic spiral fixings, toggle bolts, soft metal compression devices or plastic 'butterfly' fixing devices	Ceiling/wall lights, general accessories	Using wall plugs and screws.
Plastic finishes	Self-adhesive clips. Self-tapping screws with washers	Cables and general accessories	Using the wrong type of glue.
Steel	Clamps, sprung steel fixing devices Drilling/nuts and bolts, drilling and tapping Stud work and brackets	Industrial applications	Often undersized fixing devices.
Timber	Wood screws, coach bolts, threaded stud and cable clips	Cable and equipment	Often undersized.

Your health is at risk if you fix to asbestos sheeting. If in doubt seek advice from someone who knows – better still, completely avoid this type of old building fabric.

Table 3.9 lists a few common building fabrics and suggested methods of fixing.

How to position accurately

Marking the position for an accessory then drilling a hole may seem reasonably straightforward. Usually it is – providing the fabric is moderately soft. However, when a marked hole has to be drilled in concrete, your reference will be erased when your drill bit hits the concrete. It is then free to wander from its original point without you being fully aware of what is happening.

To avoid this problem, draw a small cross where your hole will be, as illustrated in Figure 3.14. Apply gentle pressure (drill – don't vibrate) in the centre of your cross to form a small depression in the concrete. If your drill wanders, it can be quickly corrected.

If you do this as described, it will guarantee that all your holes will line up squarely with your accessory. Poor positioning is not good workmanship!

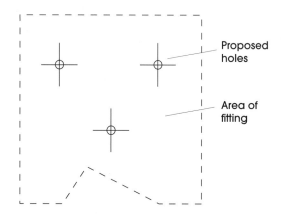
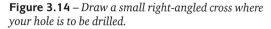

Proposed holes

Area of fitting

Figure 3.14 – *Draw a small right-angled cross where your hole is to be drilled.*

Communicating with the appropriate people

Keep in mind a simple code of practice when dealing with customers or potential clients. A good image, coupled with professionalism, is essential! Good manners and a few social graces will often be enough to create the necessary self-assurance to win a customer over to form a good working relationship.

Consider the following:

- Personal appearance – *dress for the job.*
- Attitude – *good manners, be pleasant and helpful.*
- Personal hygiene – *body odours are offensive; never smell like a dustbin!*
- Tact – *avoid gossiping about common business relationships.*
- Safety – *respect your customer's rules relating to safety.*
- Information – *respond promptly.*
- Strained relationships – *find an independent go-between.*
- Communication – *avoid jargon; they will find it difficult to understand you.*
- Names – *remember names; if you find it difficult, write it down.*
- Technical awareness – *check out your client's body language; you will know if they understand what you are saying.*

It is good to keep a good relationship with your customer and workmates. A happy site or workplace is often a safe one – keep this in mind!

When variations to your job are required

Always request that variations or alterations to your job be instructed in writing. An appropriate person will then sign them. Your works orders can be delivered to you in several ways:

1 Architect.
2 Customer.
3 Electrical designer.

Figure 3.15 – *A site variation order – sometimes called a site instruction.*

4 Main contractor or a sub-contractor.

5 Site manager/agent.

These requests, known as architect's instructions, variation orders or site instructions, all mean much the same thing. Somebody wants you to carry out some additional work. An example is shown as Figure 3.15.

Log variations given by word of mouth in your site diary but do *not* carry out any new work until you get official notification. Your company will find it difficult to receive any payment if you do not have the paperwork to back up what you have done. Please remember – if at all possible, photocopy the original orders before you hand them into your office every week.

On completion of your new work

When you have completed your new work, record the details on your time sheet and pass it to an appropriate person. The style might be similar to the following example:

- The 'last year' apprentice who did the job – *Andrea King*.
- The materials used – *50 metre of 2.5 mm² sheathed twin and earth cable*.
- The time taken – *2 hours*.

- Where the work was carried out – *Whiteparish Hall, north wing*.
- The date – *Wednesday 16th October*.
- Brief description of the work – *Rewire damaged cable*.
- Travelling time/expenses – *None*.

Remember to keep a copy for yourself. The people who work in your office are quite capable of losing or mislaying documents.

A quick word concerning manufacturers' instructions

Place aside any manufacturer's instruction leaflets you come across. They are useful for the following reasons:

- Collectively they can be brought together and processed into a customer's instruction manual. Often a manufacturer will provide a list of spares and addresses where servicing is carried out.
- For reference regarding assembly, fitting and wiring interconnections as with the case of a central heating control circuit.
- As a personal reference in case you are asked back later to do corrective or snagging work. It is impossible to keep everything in memory – after all, that is the reason for textbooks!
- They make life a little easier for everyone. Do not bin them!

Other sources of technical information

- British Standards Institute (BSI).
- BSEN Harmonisation Standards.
- The IEE (Electrical Regulations and Guidance Notes).
- Codes of Practice (available from libraries).
- Libraries.
- Manufacturers' catalogues, manuals, CD-ROMs and floppy discs.
- The internet.

Get into the habit of reading your instructions!

Site paperwork is often the least appealing duty if you are the jobholder of an installation. Try to avoid saying to yourself that *if all else fails – read the instructions*. I have – and have lived to regret it! Reading the directions and advice provided will help you to gain a working understanding of what you have to do. Guessing can cause many problems and has a knock-on effect for others who follow you. Be professional – do not guess!

Site paperwork

Paperwork can either make or break a job. It is important to keep this in mind – for many of us it is just one big bore. We find electrical installation work far more interesting to do.

Insist you have *two* up-to-date copies of the installation drawings. Use one as an on-going working drawing, whilst filing the other away for more formal use. A current edition of BS 7671 is handy for formal reference whilst a copy of the IEE's On-Site Guide provides on-the-spot guidance for most electrical installation problems and queries associated with our regulations. Your company must supply these two publications.

Using a day diary

If you are the jobholder, ask your boss or manager for a *day diary*. This will be a useful addition to your paper tool kit. Record regularly comments and notes on a daily basis – it could get you out of trouble. Figure 3.16 illustrates this. Your entries could include the following:

- People who should be at work but are not.
- Accidents.
- Damage – deliberate or accidental.
- Deliveries of materials and items not delivered.
- Site/job meetings – dates and times.
- Occurrences – fire, theft, disruption, explosion.
- Progress and delays.
- Unwritten variations orders.
- Site visits from senior members of staff.
- Bad weather – when relevant to work.

Figure 3.16 – *It is useful to place regular comments and job notes in your day diary.*

A word concerning site meetings

Before you start your job, you could be asked to attend regular site meetings to represent your company. Do not worry; this will only happen when you have made it to an approved electrician!

Weekly or fortnightly meetings are essential if smooth progress is to be maintained. Generally, the larger the site the more formal the meetings. At times, it is difficult to stay interested when other trade problems are discussed but you must, because discussion can often lead to an agreed joint working programme. Information is then delivered to your customer, which will help to generate and maintain goodwill.

Regular meetings benefit everyone. They can prevent several trades being in the same place at once. Imagine an electrician, plumber, tiler and a snagging decorator trying to work together in a small bathroom!

The recorded notes (these are known as *minutes*) from your site meeting are published and sent to all interested parties, usually within 48 hours. When you receive your copy of the minutes, please read them and file them away in a safe place. Figure 3.17 shows a typical example.

Minutes GHY LTD page 1 of 3

Meeting at: Site office, Newton Pl.

Re: Development of 200 houses Ph.1

Date (time) 23rd March, 2004 (09.15)

Those present M.H. King (Ghy Ltd)
N. Parker (KTE Ltd)
L.R. Sang (DL Ltd)

*1 Minutes of last meeting read.
2 An extension of 1 week agreed.
3 Additional smoke heads asked for by Ghy Ltd.
4 Phase 2 to be brought forward by three weeks.
5 Complaints from Super Deal Ltd.
6 Problems sorted out.
7 Sort

Figure 3.17 – *The notes, known as* minutes, *from a recent site meeting are sent to all interested parties within a couple of days.*

Summary so far...

1 Before you start work – check that your site is free from hazards.

2 Lift wisely – get help if your load is too heavy.

3 Report dangerous happenings and injuries or certain diseases.

4 Use cable factors to find the conduit or trunking size you require.

5 Keep up good business relationships with your customer and co-contractors.

6 Keep a works day diary to record incidents, etc.

Review questions

1 Explain the meaning of the initials PPE.

2 Identify three good *conductors* of electricity.

3 What type of cable would you install within an oil refinery?

4 State the meaning of the initials COSHH.

5 List five examples of *personal protective equipment*.

6 Propose an area or type of environment suitable for mineral insulated cable.

7 Name four types of *correction factor* used to determine the size of a conductor.

8 State the percentage voltage drop, which BS 7671 allows, when measured between the incoming supply terminals and a fixed current consuming appliance.

9 Why should you avoid using aluminium spiral fixings in damp plasterboard?

10 Recommend a means of fixing heavy switchgear to a concrete wall.

11 Advise a way to fit a smoke detector to a soft ceiling tile.

12 Describe how you would mark out a concrete wall to allow precise drilling to take place.

13 Why must you avoid speaking jargon to customers who are technically unaware?

14 Give details of why we use variation orders.

15 Put forward a reason why it is important to keep manufacturers' instructions leaflets.

Handy hints

- Keep augers sharp and in good condition to avoid extra load on your battery drill.

- Be impartial and objective when given the task as a *jobholder* – no favouritism.

- Cut steel channelling with tin-snips. A junior hacksaw can be troublesome.

- Never over-reach whilst using a pair of steps – you could lose your balance!

- A couple of 6 mm holes drilled at the base of an outside length of vertical trunking will provide a means of drainage for accumulated condensation.

- In the workplace, cooperation is better than conflict.

4 Methods of installing wiring systems, wiring enclosures and equipment

Introduction

This chapter will show you how to install electrical wiring systems; wiring enclosures; cable carriers and equipment; and why you must follow the correct procedures and instructions that you are given.

You will also have to explain to your assessor that you are able to do the following:

- Identify different types of installation.
- Select the most suitable wiring and cable carriers for your installation.
- Identify different types of earthing arrangements.
- Understand the applications and limitations of different cables.

Cable basket systems

You will probably not come across this type of installation unless you get to work on a very large site. A cable basket is a good cost-effective way of managing medium size bulky cables such as steel wire armoured and large multi-core cables insulated with PVC, XLPE or LSF materials.

Made from strong galvanised steel wire in the form of a 50 × 50 mm square mesh, a cable basket is in widths from 100 to 400 mm. A 50 mm mesh wall stops the cables from falling off and helps to strengthen the system. Figure 4.1 illustrates an example of a cable basket.

Installation methods

Attach a length of cable basket to the next by means of a purpose-made coupler. These couplers come with an earth continuity-bonding link, as illustrated in Figure 4.1a. Cable basket accessories, such as tee units, crossovers, right angles or slow bends, could be constructed on site but it is difficult and it is far better to use the purpose-made fittings, as illustrated in Figure 4.1.

Figure 4.1 – *Cable basket. (Reproduced by kind permission of Marshall Tufflex Limited.)*

Cutting

You can cut cable basket with a hacksaw but it is far easier to use good quality bolt cutters. It saves time and effort! Remember to paint the cut ends of the basket with a cold galvanising finish such as Galvafroid® or a similar product. This will prevent rust from setting in.

You may lay cable basket on the ground or support it by means of brackets. Your brackets can be site made and painted or obtained purpose-made. Basket finishes include stainless steel, hot dipped galvanised and polyester coatings in a small range of colours.

Additional information

Listed are a few additional points for you to consider:

- It can to used to support modern fire alarm cables.
- If you use polyester finished cable basket, remove the coating to ensure a good earth bonding to adjoining lengths.
- By snapping on a purpose-made coloured trim to the edge of the basket you can quickly identify the cables installed within.
- Fit conduit adaptor to your cable basket if required (see Figure 4.1a).

Cable ladder systems

Cable ladder systems are also known as *ladder packing* or *cable racking* and are used to manage heavy power cables. As its name suggests, it is formed in a way similar to a heavy aluminium ladder with rungs placed every 400 mm or so. Supplied in 3-metre lengths it comes complete with coupling pieces and fixing bolts. Figure 4.2 illustrates a selection of accessories. Cable ladder is available in *galvanised steel* (heavy) or in *glass reinforced polyester*, with two types being available for each product:

- heavy and medium duty
- two finishes – painted or galvanised.

A small gap of about 1 or 2 mm must be allowed between each length of cable ladder to allow for natural expansion. If not, it will buckle.

Cables lie along the length of the ladder system whilst PVCu clamps, reinforced cable ties or purpose-made saddles secure them.

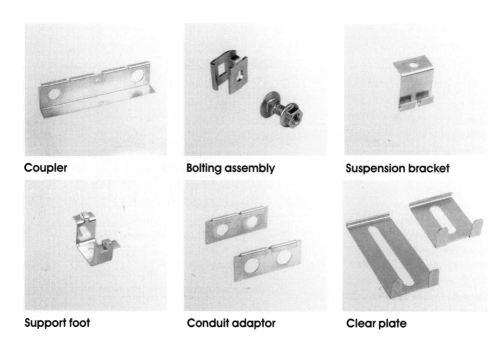

| Coupler | Bolting assembly | Suspension bracket |
| Support foot | Conduit adaptor | Clear plate |

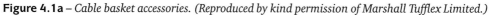

Figure 4.1a – *Cable basket accessories. (Reproduced by kind permission of Marshall Tufflex Limited.)*

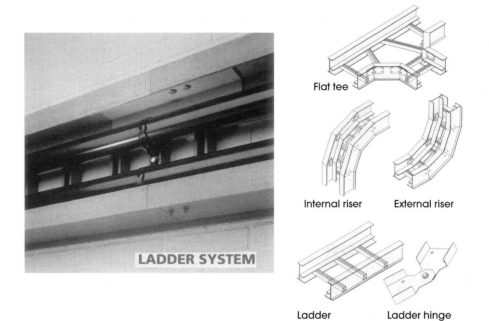

Flat tee

Internal riser   External riser

Ladder   Ladder hinge

Figure 4.2 – *Cable ladder. (Reproduced by kind permission of Marshall Tufflex Limited.)*

Accessories

Optional extras are available to suit most installations:

- fixing brackets
- intersections
- left hand reducers
- inside bends (Figure 4.3)

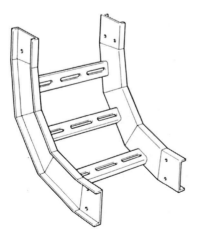

Figure 4.3 – *Cable ladder – the inside bend is also referred to as a riser.*

- centre reducers
- tin and copper bonding/continuity links – for steel cable ladder.

Installations serving large commercial and industrial complexes are designed with cable ladder in mind. It is strong and ideal for the job it has to do – the management of large cables.

Means of cutting cable ladder

Cut *steel* cable ladder either with a hacksaw (which is very hard work) or with the use of a power assisted tool. This is a far easier method but you must take extra care when cutting by this means. It is advisable to use a tungsten carbide tipped heavy-duty saw when cutting or shaping reinforced polyester ladder systems. The polyester edges will then be dressed using a fine file or suitable glass paper.

A word of warning – Please observe all health and safety rules and insist that you have training before using this type of power cutting tool. Use eye protection and industrial gloves when cutting this type of material.

Before you start work on your cable ladder, securely fit your fixing brackets and decide the positioning of accessories.

Cable trunking installations

This is a cable carrier ideally suited to singly insulated cables. Made from high impact, self-extinguishing plastic or mild steel, trunking is obtainable in 3-, 4- and 6-metre lengths.

The cover serving mild steel trunking is fitted with fixing screws, turnbuckles or hinges. Snap-lock plastic covers into position but you will require a wide bladed screwdriver to release them again. Obtain single-, twin- or multi-compartmental trunking to suit the needs of your installation. Figure 4.4 illustrates this.

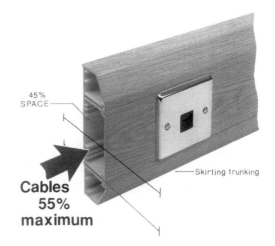

Figure 4.5 – A space factor of 45% is required. (Reproduced by kind permission of Marshall Tufflex Limited.)

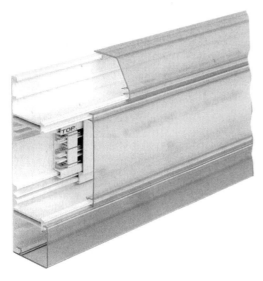

Figure 4.4 – Trunking can be obtained to suit the needs of your installation. (Reproduced by kind permission of Marshall Tufflex Limited.)

Planning your route

Listed are a few installation points that will be useful to you:

1 Work out the size of the trunking you will need for your installation. Keep in mind that a space factor of 45% is required (see Figure 4.5).

2 Mark out your route, making notes of the positions of your in-line accessories.

3 Drill the back of your trunking and fix using pan-headed screws. Fix securely – keep in mind the weight of the cables.

4 Remember to fit copper continuity links onto each section of steel trunking.

5 Assemble your trunking installation before cables are installed – Regulation 522-08-2.

6 To maintain trunking straightness throughout your installation, just stretch and flick a chalk line. Work to the line.

7 Use only factory-produced couplers when putting together your cable trunking run.

8 The IEE's On-Site Guide will provide you with all the information you wish to know about the spacing for supports used for the trunking run.

Design and application

Table 4.1 describes in general terms how various types of trunking are used.

Table 4.1 – *The design of modern trunking and where it is used.*

Trunking type	Material	Design	Application
Bench	Steel/PVC	Triangular or delta	Workshops and laboratory benches
Bus bar	Steel	Rectangular	Rising mains for industrial use and cavity floor
Bus bar	PVC	Skirting profile	Domestic and commercial use
Cornice	PVC	Concave or triangular	Domestic (used with mini-trunking)
Dado	PVC	Rectangular	Domestic and commercial
Floor trunking	Steel	Rectangular	Industrial and commercial
General purpose trunking	Steel or PVC	Square or rectangular	General purpose (industrial and commercial installations)
Lighting trunking	Steel	Square	Industrial lighting installations
Mini-trunking	PVC	Square or rectangular	Commercial and industrial installations
Skirting	Steel or PVC	Rectangular	Industrial, commercial and domestic
Under floor	Steel	Rectangular	Industrial installations. Inspection boxes are fitted where required
Under slab	Steel	Rectangular	Installed beneath the construction slab of a building. Inspection boxes fixed to the floor above. Cables routes from the main trunking run through pre-cast openings to the inspection boxes

What to do about expansion and contraction

If you do not consider thermal expansion, trunking systems made from plastic will buckle. To remedy this, please bear in mind the following:

- Form two elongated holes; one above the other, on every third length of trunking you install. The fixing screws you place in them will be pan-headed with a suitable washer but do not over tighten.

- Leave a small gap of about a couple of millimetres between the lengths of trunking you install.

- Mini-trunking is best fitted with an expansion coupler to combat thermal expansion (see Figure 4.6). One end of the coupler is PVC glued whilst the other end is coated with non-hardening plastic cement. Expansion couplers are fitted every third length of trunking.

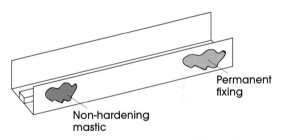

Figure 4.6 – *Mini-trunking – an internal expansion coupler.*

Why do we need a space factor within cable trunking?

If cable trunking is full to capacity and on load, the cables will become very warm to the touch and will create a potential fire risk or damage to the plastic insulation on the conductors. It is therefore important to allow a space factor of at least 45% at the design stage of your installation. This means that, when you have drawn in all your cables, there will be 45% of space left within your trunking (see Figure 4.5). Manufacturers' tables showing you the size of trunking you will require are obtainable through catalogues. Alternatively, look through the pages of the IEE's On-Site Guide.

Tools you will need for the job

There is no need to buy specialised tools for building trunking systems. The following is a list of essential equipment that will help to make your job a little easier:

- A chalk line (a dark colour is practical).
- An electric drill kit (110 V within the workplace).
- A flat and round file (medium cut).
- A jigsaw (this is a machine fretsaw).
- Two sizes of hacksaw.
- A mitre block (this will help to cut material at 45° and 90° angles).
- A soft pencil and retractable tape measure.
- An adjustable set square.
- A selection of hole cutters.
- Your screwdriver kit.
- A 300 or 600 mm water level.

Practical installation points

- Accessories and trunking lengths must match.
- Mark out your work exactly – never guess.
- Cut to the waste side of your pencil guideline.
- Complete your system *before* you draw your cables and fire barriers in.
- Fix with pan-headed screws.
- Use cable straps for vertical trunking runs.
- Take care when you fit your lid. It is easy to pinch cables.
- Use purpose-made accessories – they are far smarter.
- Allow a good radius on cables when they change direction.
- Do not forget bonding links across each section of steel trunking.
- Avoid trunking stretching under its own weight after the cabling. (Please refer to Regulation 522-08-06.)

Site-built steel trunking accessories

A simple 90° bend

- Select a short workable length of trunking. Halfway along the length of the trunking, draw a line around the body of the trunking, as shown in Figure 4.7.
- Check the exact diameter of your work piece and transfer this measurement to the top left or right hand side of your datum line and mark this point, as shown in Figure 4.8. Draw a pencil mark from the marked trunking to the bottom of the datum line, as shown in Figure 4.9. Repeat on the opposite side.
- You will now have a right-angled triangle drawn on each outer side of your trunking. Cut out the two triangles and file off the ragged edge. The trunking will now appear as shown in Figure 4.10.
- Find a piece of hard timber with a square edge and cut it to the width of the internal diameter of your trunking. Place the wood bordering the *vertically cut side* as shown in Figure 4.11.
- Hold the timber firmly (the square edge next to the bending point). With your other hand, push up the side of the trunking adjoining the angled cut. Allow the vertically cut sides to be sandwiched between the angled trunking sides, as in Figure 4.12.
- When completed, dress the bend with a hammer and strengthen with pop rivets.

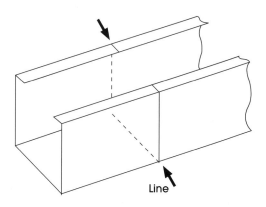

Figure 4.7 – *Draw a line around the body of the trunking using a set square.*

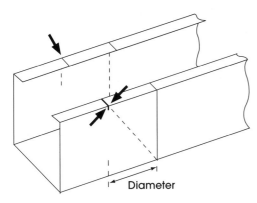

Figure 4.8 – *Transfer the diameter of the workpiece to the top left- or right-hand side of the central datum line.*

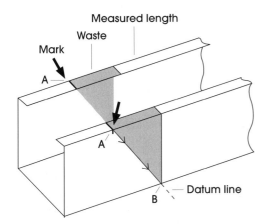

Figure 4.9 – *Draw a line from the marked trunking to the bottom of the central datum line (A, marked trunking; B, bottom of datum).*

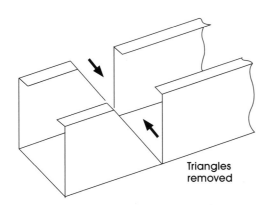

Figure 4.10 – *Remove the two triangles.*

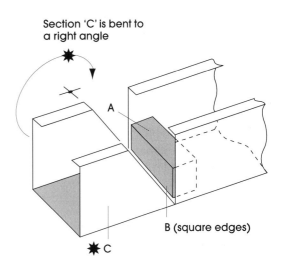

Figure 4.11 – *Place the shaped timber to the side adjacent to the vertically cut side. A, wooden template; B, square edge of timber; C, steel trunking.*

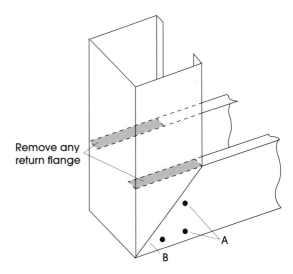

Figure 4.12 – *Bend into shape. Check for squareness and support the sides with pop rivets. A, pop rivets; B, angled cut.*

Trunking sets and return sets

Make this accessory (see Figure 4.13), in a similar way to a right-angled bend – but you will have to be precise or your measurements will be way out!

Select the length of trunking you require. Draw a datum line around three sides of the trunking as shown in Figure 4.14.

- Check the diameter of your work piece and transfer *half* of this measurement to the top left or right hand side of the centre datum line drawn on your trunking with a mark. Now draw a line to the bottom of the *vertical* datum, as shown in Figure 4.15. Repeat this on the opposite side to produce a pair of 22.5° right-angled triangles.

- Cut out the triangular shapes and file the rough edges. Your trunking will now look similar to Figure 4.16. Cut a piece of timber with a good square edge that fits across the internal diameter of your trunking. Place the timber on the side next to the vertically cut datum line as shown in Figure 4.17. Hold the timber firmly with one hand whilst gently bending the other half of your work piece until you construct a 45° set. You will now find your vertically cut sides are sandwiched between the angled trunking sides.

- Check the angle and strengthen with pop rivets (Figure 4.18).

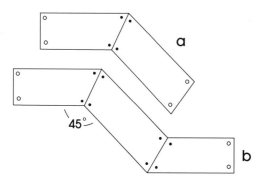

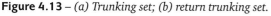

Figure 4.13 – *(a) Trunking set; (b) return trunking set.*

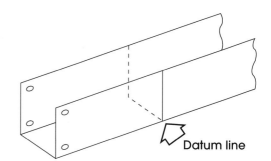

Figure 4.14 – *Draw a datum line with a soft pencil – be guided by a set square around the three sides of the trunking.*

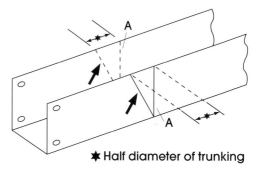

Figure 4.15 – *Measure the diameter of the trunking and transfer half of this measurement to the top left- or right-hand side of the datum line. Draw a line from this mark to the base of the datum line, A.*

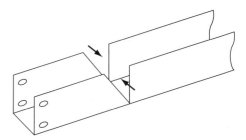

Figure 4.16 – *Cut both pencilled triangular shapes from each side of the trunking.*

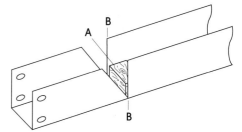

Figure 4.17 – *Place the wooden shape by the vertically cut trunking. A, wood in trunking; B, vertically cut trunking.*

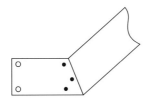

Figure 4.18 – *Bend into shape. Strengthen with pop rivets.*

Building a return set

- Draw a straight line on a flat surface and place the *shortest* section of your set on the line as shown in Figure 4.19.

- Measure the depth of the set you want and mark your trunking. This is the bending point to form a return set.

- Prepare your trunking as shown in Figure 4.20.

- Cut out the complete left-hand side of the centre line. This consists of two trunking side triangles, bridged by a rectangular base section. The trunking lid must remain unbroken – this will help with electrical continuity.

- Cut a 2 mm diameter **'V'** shape along both sides of the bottom edge of the trunking from the vertical centre line to the angled dotted line, as shown in Figure 4.21. This will act as a supplementary lip and help steady the return set when assembled.

- Bend your work piece to unite both sections, allowing the vertically cut edge (which once formed the centre line) to be sandwiched between the angled sides of the trunking, as illustrated in Figure 4.22.

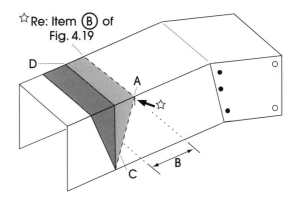

Figure 4.20 – *Preparing the return set. A, depth of the required set; B, this measurement is the same diameter as the trunking; C reference line; D, centre line.*

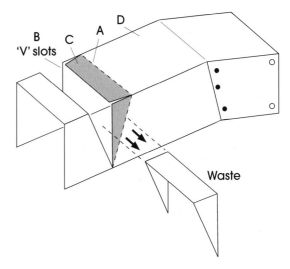

Figure 4.21 – *A small 'V' must be cut along both edges of the trunking from the vertical centre line to the angled dotted line. A, depth of set mark; B, 'V' slots; C, supplementary lip; D, bottom of trunking.*

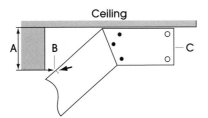

Figure 4.19 – *Measuring the depth of the required set. A, required depth of set; B, point of set; C, shortest leg.*

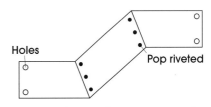

Figure 4.22 – *A side view of a site-constructed return set.*

Now check your angle is correct and the depth of your set is how you want it. Secure and strengthen with pop rivets. Depending on how careful you have been, you might have to dress the supplementary lip to accommodate changed angles. The more careful you have been, the better your site-made return set will be. Remember to fit your earth bonding links where necessary.

The way to practise within the comfort of your home

Find a manageable length of lightweight cardboard and form an accurate trunking profile as shown in Figure 4.23. Use a pair of scissors or a safety razor to cut out the shape as shown in Figure 4.24. This method helped me many years ago – it might help you!

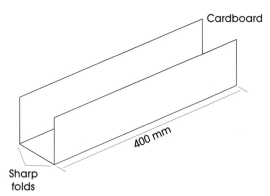

Figure 4.23 – *A model trunking profile can be formed from cardboard at 160 g/m².*

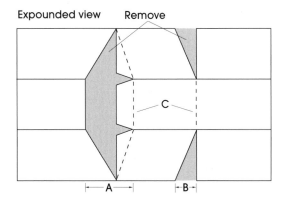

Figure 4.24 – *Cut to shape with a pair of scissors or safety razor. A, diameter of trunking; B, half the diameter of trunking; C, bend points.*

The way to cut rectangular holes in steel trunking

Figure 4.25 illustrates a typical metal-clad distribution centre used to serve an industrial installation.

The centre is butted to the top side of steel trunking by way of nuts, bolts and spacers. It is okay to remove a section of trunking provided the depth of your distribution board is wider than your trunking, when measured horizontally. This is better than drilling a series of holes in both the distribution centre and cable trunking. Cutting holes is time-consuming and costly. Male type brass bushes, and steel locking rings (see Figure 4.26) have to be added to protect the conductors.

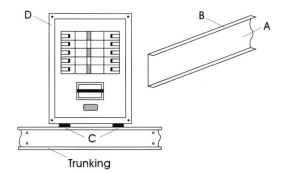

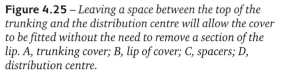

Figure 4.25 – *Leaving a space between the top of the trunking and the distribution centre will allow the cover to be fitted without the need to remove a section of the lip. A, trunking cover; B, lip of cover; C, spacers; D, distribution centre.*

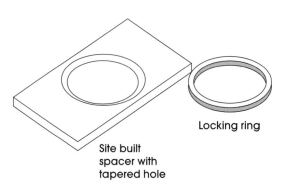

Figure 4.26 – *Spacers can be either designer-made or a 20 mm steel locking ring may be used.*

Removing a section of trunking

Distribution centres have removable end plates screwed to both top and bottom. Most have weakened '*knockouts*' to create holes of various sizes – some have not. Remove the plate you wish to modify – keeping in mind its length. The section of steel you plan to remove from your trunking will be *smaller* in length than the length of the modified bottom plate, as you will have to bolt your distribution centre to the trunking to aid earth continuity. Decide on the length of your cable entry hole, draw two parallel lines from the front to the rear of your trunking, as outlined in Figure 4.27, and cut to your lines on the back of the trunking. Using a good medium cut file, rasp along the back right-angled edge of your trunking from cut to cut. When you have removed about 50%, snap off the worked section by bending it backwards and forwards. Use a file on the rough edges and dress with a suitable plastic edging strip. Bolt the distribution centre to the top of the steel trunking with the modified bottom plate acting as a through route for cables from the point of distribution to the trunking system.

To provide additional earth continuity, clamp an earthing lead from the earthing bar serving your distribution centre to the side of the steel trunking using a compression lug, bolt and washer.

Trunking slots – an alternative to removing a side section of trunking

Use the following guidelines to form slots within the top of your trunking to provide a path for your cables.

1 First, decide on the shape of your slot and mark your trunking accordingly, as shown in Figure 4.28.

2 For a square-sided slot, drill two sets of 6 mm diameter holes in opposite corners of your template, as Figure 4.29 illustrates.

3 Realign the blade in your hacksaw to 90° to the frame to remove the waste from your pencilled template. Figure 4.30 shows you how.

4 Carefully cut the shape you require, adjusting the alignment of the hacksaw whenever necessary.

5 Alternatively, drill two 32 mm holes at either end of your proposed slot and cut between them using a metal-bladed jigsaw. This is the easiest option provided you have the use of a jigsaw.

6 Dress the freshly cut edges with a file and apply plastic edging strip to finish off. The edging strip can be stuck if required.

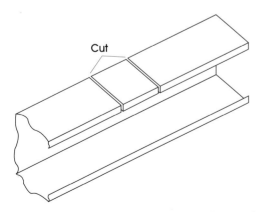

Figure 4.27 – *Draw two measured parallel lines and cut with a hacksaw to the top rear of the trunking.*

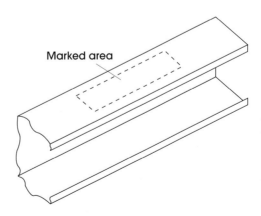

Figure 4.28 – *Decide on the shape of the slot required and mark accordingly.*

79

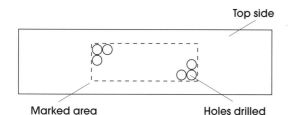

Figure 4.29 – *Drill two or three sets of holes in opposite corners of your workpiece.*

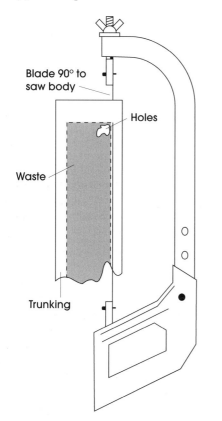

Figure 4.30 – *Align the blade of your hacksaw to accommodate the prepared elongated holes and carefully cut the required shape.*

Constructing a cable trunking tee-section

These are easy to make and can be produced to an acceptable standard in a reasonable time.

- Select a section of trunking to represent the horizontal component of your proposed tee. Now draw two parallel lines from a mid-point position to match the diameter of the vertical section of your fitting.

- Cut these two parallel lines to the bottom of the trunking. Now file deeply along the *bottom right-angled edge* from cut to cut. Snap off the waste by bending when you are about halfway through.

- Finally, construct a flanged section from a short length of trunking as shown in Figure 4.31b. You can do this by cutting the back right-angled edge of your work piece to a depth of about 10 mm. After removing the two 10 mm sections of lip, bend both sides to a right angle to form a flange as shown in the last illustration.

- When completed, square up your work, drill and pop rivet to strengthen. Drill additional fixing holes where needed.

- Remember your earth continuity bonding links!

Cable trunking and BS 7671

Vertical runs (reference is made to Section 422)

Provide internal heat barriers within vertical lengths of trunking to prevent heat building up at the top of the trunking. As a guide, place every 3 m or between each junction of floor and ceiling.

Holes made in floors and ceilings associated with your trunking runs are filled and sealed. The material you choose has to have the same quality of fire resistance as the original.

Observance of British Standards (reference to Regulation 521-05-01)

Trunking has to meet the terms of BS 4678 or, alternatively, be constructed from an insulating material with combustibility factor 'P' as recommended in British Standards 476 Directive – Part 5. You will be able to buy this publication as a photocopy from most public lending libraries. It is not expensive.

Exposure to water (Regulation 522-03-01 to 03)

When exposed to water or moisture, steel trunking must be non-corrosive and never placed in contact with other dissimilar metals. This will avoid any possibility of an electrolytic effect occurring between the two surfaces.

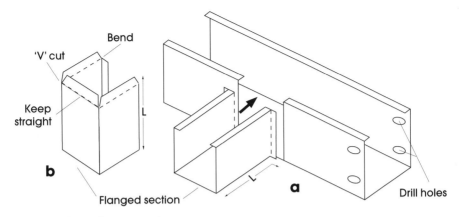

Figure 4.31 – *A site-made trunking tee section.*

You will have to select a trunking system to suit the conditions of your surroundings – and that will require a great deal of thought on your behalf. Place holes serving conduit on the *underside* of the trunking. It is then advisable to seal around the entry point with a suitable external sealant.

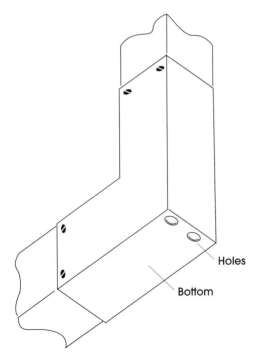

Figure 4.32 – *As a precaution against accumulated condensation, two or three small holes can be drilled in the lowest point of the trunking.*

As a precaution against accumulated condensation, drill two or three 6 mm holes at the bottom lowest point of your trunking as shown in Figure 4.32. Regulation 522-03-02 confirms this.

Cables laid in trunking (Regulation 522-08)

Take great care with the cables you draw into trunking. Never pull a group of cables around a right-angled bend as cable burn and snagging could occur and go unnoticed until you switch on.

BS 7671 will allow up to four 5 or 6 amp circuits bunched within trunking when protected by a semi-enclosed (re-wireable) fuse. Up to six circuits are permitted when a high breaking capacity fuse (BS 88) or a cartridge fuse to BS 1361 protects your circuit. Alternatively, use a miniature circuit breaker – BS 60898.

If you have installed more than the minimum number of bunched cables then correction factors will apply. You will find tables within the current edition of the IEE's On-Site Guide very useful when determining the size of conductors you will require for your installation.

How it works – A *cable factor*, in the form of a number, represents each conductor. When *added* together the resulting figure is matched up to a three or four figured number known as a *unit factor*. The size of your trunking will have a unit factor equal to, or larger than, the sum of the collective cable factors. Please see Table 3.8 on page 62 for details.

Space factor

After installing all your circuits in your trunking you must have a space factor of at least 45%. Never be tempted to cram as many cables as you can into your trunking – it is dangerous. Your cables will get warm on load. I must stress that it is important you keep to the spirit of BS 7671 – it will save many future problems caused by over-heating and insulation breakdown.

BS 7671 calls for 'Adequate means of drawing cables in and out'. Regulation 522-08-02 confirms this.

Supports for cable trunking

Adequately support your trunking to avoid mechanical stress and damage to the insulated conductors. Steel trunking must be secured every 3 metres both horizontally and vertically when the cross-sectional area exceeds 5000 m². When plastic trunking is used, the horizontal fixing distances are every 1.75 metres and every 2 metres for vertical runs. For more information, please consult your On-Site Guide.

Fire barriers

When walls or floors are fire barriers you must seal the holes you have made before the installation of your trunking – Regulation 527-02-01 confirms this. An additional fire-resistant barrier must be provided when the cross-sectional area of your trunking goes beyond 710 m² (see Figure 4.33). Your fire barrier will take the form of glass wool. Place the glass wool within the trunking but leave a little proud, as it will compress when you secure the lid and

Figure 4.33 – A trunking fire barrier. (Reproduced by kind permission of Walsall Conduits Limited.)

provide sufficient protection against the spread of both fire and heat.

Partitioned trunking (Regulation 528-01)

Low voltage systems (that is, 230 V, AC), telecomm cables and fire alarm circuits (Bands 2, 1 and 3 in that order) must be kept apart from each other by electrically earthed partitions which are continuous to any common outlet serving the trunking. If you find it difficult to do this, then wire all circuits using a 600 V grade cable. Regulation 528-01-01 confirms this.

However, there is an exception to the rule! You are permitted to mix Band 1 and 2 voltages when included within a multi-core mineral insulated cable; as BS 7671, Regulation 528-01-01 bears out.

Band 3 circuits, which include *fire detection/ alarm systems* and *emergency lighting* (central battery system only), require separating from other bands. I refer to Regulation 528-01-04 and BS 6701. For an example of three compartmental trunkings, please refer to Figure 4.34.

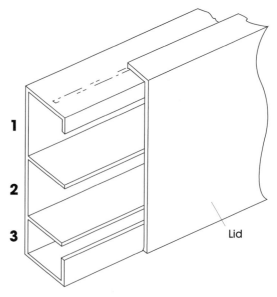

Figure 4.34 – *Three-way compartmental trunking.*

Switching within steel trunking

The electrical regulations demand that there is *no switching device* or break incorporated within your steel trunking installation. It must be continuous. Only incorporate *removable joints* for testing earth/bonding continuity values. Never use steel trunking as a PEN conductor, that is, Phase plus Earth/Neutral combined as Regulation 543-02-10 will confirm.

Sockets in or served by steel trunking

Please remember this small point – it is often misunderstood. If you install a socket outlet within your steel trunking system, an independent circuit protective conductor must connect when the trunking also acts as the *circuit protective conductor* (cpc). In practice, a green/yellow insulated flexible/stranded fly lead links the earthing terminal serving the socket outlet and the back or side of the associated metal accessory box. Alternatively it may be bonded to the main body of your steel trunking.

Jointing couplers (Regulation 543-03)

When you rely solely on the steel trunking as a *circuit protective conductor* you must be very sure that each trunking coupler and copper continuity link is secure. Joints in your system need not be within reach for inspection – therefore they have to be very tight. When routed through a damp location, try to protect from the possible effects of *electrolytic action*. To reduce this type of contamination apply a suitable coating of paint over your copper bonding links after you have installed them throughout your trunking run. It works!

Mini-trunking

Most of you will be familiar with mini-trunking – we use it a lot these days. This type of cable carrier, made from high-impact *unplasticised polyvinyl chloride*, is similar in design to its commercial opposite number. Mini-trunking is available in progressive sizes from 16 × 10 mm to 75 × 16 mm in cross-sectional area, as illustrated in Figure 4.35. Multi-compartmental styles are available in larger sizes (see Figure 4.36), many of which are available with self-adhesive backing.

Figure 4.36 – *Four-way PVCu multi-compartmental trunking. (Reproduced by kind permission of Marshall Tufflex Limited.)*

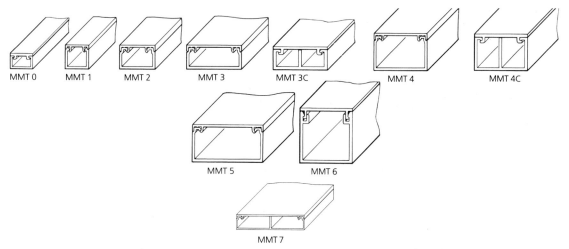

MMT 0   MMT 1   MMT 2   MMT 3   MMT 3C   MMT 4   MMT 4C

MMT 5   MMT 6

MMT 7

Figure 4.35 – *Mini-trunking sizes. (Reproduced by kind permission of Marshal Tufflex Limited.)*

The standard colour is white although brown, beige and charcoal are available to order. Red is readily obtainable for fire alarm installations.

'Snap on' your lid once wiring has been completed – it is as easy as that. To remove, ease the lid off from the main body of the mini-trunking aided by a flat screwdriver. Once you have a few centimetres in your hand you can pull the remainder off with ease. This type of trunking system is ideal for domestic and commercial installations where additional or restoration work is required.

Installation techniques

As with most installation tasks, first consider route planning and decision-making. After deciding on the quantity and size of trunking you require, mark out your proposed route, noting, for example, the future positioning of your tees, right angles and stop-end accessories.

Drill your mini-trunking and then fix with *pan-headed screws* at about 400 mm between each fixing. On the other hand, you can use self-adhesive trunking – but *do* secure with screws after you have positioned it. Do not rely on the adhesive, especially in a warm environment. Sticky-backed mini-trunking will not bond to damp or dirty surfaces – nor will it attach to flaky paint.

You must be accurate when working with this type of trunking. Correctly position and align, for once offered to a good bonding surface it is often difficult to remove if you make a mistake. For additional strength, glue in-line components (couplers, etc.) using a suitable liquid weld. Figure 4.37 illustrates a selection of moulded snap-on mini-trunking fittings that will not have to be glued.

Thermal expansion

Drill two lengthened holes, one above the other and positioned about 100 mm from the end of each length of trunking. This is in addition to your regular fixing points throughout the length of trunking, as Figure 4.38 shows. Fix lightly with pan-headed screws and washers but please do not over-tighten. This will allow freedom for expansion and greatly reduce the risk of buckling the mini-trunking during hot or warm weather.

Make all your butted joints secure with an internal coupling. These are either snapped or stuck on, depending on the make and design of the trunking. On very long straight runs, it is wise to install an expansion coupler between every other length of trunking fitted as described in Figure 4.39. This is simply done by cementing one end of the expansion coupler whilst the other end is coated with *non-hardening mastic*.

Figure 4.38 – *Drilling elongated holes will allow your trunking to expand.*

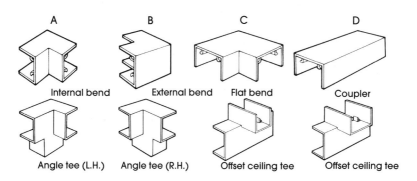

Figure 4.37 – *Mini-trunking fittings. (Reproduced by kind permission of Marshal Tufflex Limited.)*

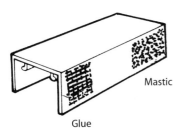

Mastic

Glue

Figure 4.39 – *A mini-trunking expansion coupler.*

Cornice trunking

This style of trunking has been designed to harmonise at the point where ceiling and wall meet. Providing your measurements are exact

and not repeated in the cutting process, installation work is usually straightforward. All fittings slightly overlap at the joints, making it possible to work to a high standard.

Cornice trunking manufacturers, such as Marshall Tufflex®, design their product to be compatible with the smaller sizes of mini-trunking. This is an advantage when fitting switches and ceiling-mounted accessories. Figure 4.40 illustrates a typical cornice trunking arrangement. On long runs, it is wise to leave a small gap between the 3-metre lengths to allow for expansion. Once the lid and external couplings are in place, the expansion gap will be completely out of sight.

Figure 4.40 – *Cornice trunking. (Reproduced by kind permission of Marshall Tufflex Limited.)*

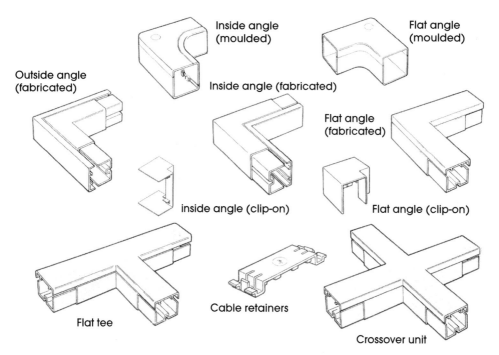

Figure 4.41 – *PVCu cable trunking fittings. (Reproduced by kind permission of Marshal Tufflex Limited.)*

High-impact plastic trunking

This type of system is used to provide a safe and sensible cable management arrangement for light industrial and commercial installations where it might be impractical to use conduit as a means of distribution. Plastic trunking has many practical advantages over its steel counterpart. Here are a few to consider:

- Light, easy to handle – quicker to install.
- The risk of a major personal injury reduced.
- Plenty of sizes and can be selected with internal dividers.
- Many trunking accessories, illustrated in Figure 4.41.
- Lids designed to be snapped on or screwed.
- Aluminium screening may be fitted to protect sensitive circuits.
- Accessories are designed to be either stuck or pinned together with purpose-made rivets.
- Manufactured in a variety of profiles – square, rectangular, delta-shaped, etc.

Busbar trunking

Floor trunking

This is a useful way to distribute power when, for practical or artistic reasons, an overhead system would not be suitable. Available to serve single- or three-phase and neutral supply, a typical floor busbar arrangement supplies 63 amps of power. The copper busbars within the steel trunking are on insulated pads. The system will allow fused tap-off points wherever required throughout the installation.

Methods of installation

Lengths of busbar trunking are '*handed*'. This means *they will only fit one way*. This is to ensure that the proper polarity (phase and neutral connection) is correct throughout the installation. Fitting one-way means all component parts are correctly installed.

Laying floor trunking will require the cooperation of your site manager to provide a series of *datum lines* (lines that indicate the level of the finished floor). You will also require from

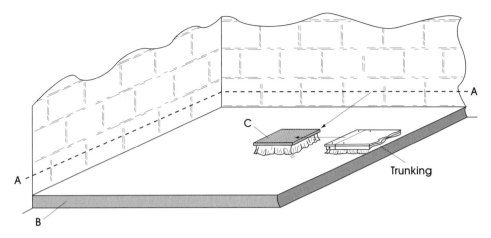

Figure 4.42 – *Concrete mounds (dunes) and datum lines are supplied and created by the building contractor. A, finished-floor datum line; B, construction floor level; C, concrete dune capped with a slate.*

him an arrangement of light-mix concrete *dunes* (several level mounds, topped with slate, that will indicate the finished floor level). Figure 4.42 illustrates this idea more clearly.

To get started you will need a 3-metre long builder's level and a reasonably long water level/laser level so you can line up your trunking with the builder's final floor screed.

It is an advantage to have many datum lines and points of reference within your working area – it is a lot easier this way. Putting your installation together is similar to working with steel box trunking but you will find there is more cutting to do. A retractable rule, soft pencil or a fine-tipped marker pen, a large set square and means of cutting (by hand or an electric power saw) are all the tools you will require. Once measured, cut and drill for a coupling, if needed, then install your *track interconnection unit* for busbar continuity. Handed floor busbar systems make it impossible to connect lengths the wrong way round. You will have to decide how to secure your floor trunking – possibly using small, but strong, adjustable steel brackets would be your answer – but whatever you decide, your system *must be secure* and free from movement as floor screed will be laid beneath and around it. When terminating your trunking, you will have to install a track stop-end box that is similar in design to the one in Figure 4.43.

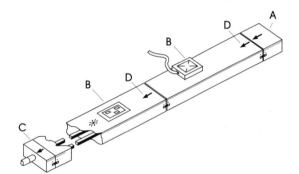

Figure 4.43 – *A track stop-end is always fitted when your floor trunking ends. A, track stop-end; B, power tap-off point; C, supply termination unit; D, polarity arrow marking.*

When you have completed your floor trunking arrangement, supply with a suitable size cable in steel conduit or under-screed cable trunking – 25 mm² conductors would be ideal when the maximum demand is under 100 A per phase.

On completion

Ask your site manager to inspect the level of the trunking to verify that it is okay in relation to the proposed finished floor. It is no good him/her complaining after the finished floor has been laid.

It is best to check all your screws are tight and your *copper* (tinned coated) *bonding/continuity links* are secure and in place. It is a wise move to screw down all the trunking cover plates and cover the heads of the screws with a small length of PVC insulation tape. This is to stop the floor screen from getting into and round the counter-sunk fixing screws. Floor trunking lids have a protective *PVC film overlay* to shield the lid from scratches during the installation process. Remove only when advised to by your site manager – not before.

Finally, you must *impedance test* your floor trunking installation. Use a *conduit/trunking continuity and impedance tester* switched to the ohms or milliohms scale. If the values you obtain are high (say, several ohms), you *must check* your installation again for loose couplers and bonding links. A further test will be necessary once you have completed your corrective work. Ideally your impedance value should be between 0.05 and 0.8 Ω.

Industrial busbar trunking

Use steel busbar systems in factories as a means of distributing power to serve machinery. In high-rise commercial buildings, this system provides a straightforward means of delivering power to each floor; see Figure 4.44. The busbars are copper but occasionally aluminium is used. Busbar trunking, as with other types, is *handed* – this is to avoid polarity mistakes. Always consider protective measures appropriate to any external influences (wet, hot, cold, animals, etc.) – this is important.

There are many finishes to choose from, including *stove enamel, galvanised* or *totally insulated*, to meet the conditions and external influences of your installation. Accessories are readily obtainable and include *angles, bends, tees* and *tap-off boxes*. The rating of this trunking is up to 300 amps, in lengths of 1.5 and 1.7 metres. Fit fused tap-off units wherever necessary to provide general power and lighting arrangements; see also Regulation 523-03-01.

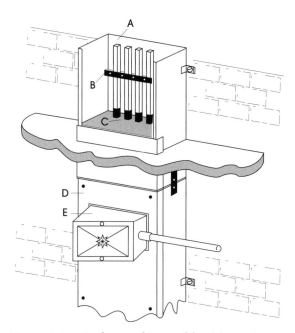

Figure 4.44 – *Busbar trunking used for rising main power distribution. A, copper busbars; B, insulated busbar supports; C, busbar insulated sleeving; D, removable cover; E, power tap-off box.*

Using steel trunking as a protective conductor

As with all steel trunking arrangements, your butted joints must be secure and *copper bonding/continuity links* placed across each mechanical intersection.

Regulation 543-01 requires the cross-section of a steel trunking arrangement, which acts as a protective conductor, to be equivalent to that resulting from the application of the following expression:

$$S = \sqrt{\frac{I^2 t}{K}} \qquad (4.1)$$

where S is the cross-sectional area in mm², I is the value of the fault current in amps which would flow through your fuse or MCB, t is the operating time in seconds for your fuse or MCB to disconnect the supply (e.g. 0.4 or 5 seconds, etc.) and K is a factor dependent on the material composition of the protective conductor; its initial and final temperatures and the type of insulation surrounding the protective conductor.

Finding the value of I

The most practical way is to measure the value of the earth loop impedance at the source of the supply (the mains position). If the earthing arrangements are TN-CS or TN-S then you can expect a low value of around 0.02 to 0.67 Ω. If the earthing arrangements are TT (overhead phase and neutral wires) then the value can be anything from about 0.9 to 7.0 Ω or even in double figures – depending on how damp the soil and sub-soil is. In the winter it is usually low, but will be high in the summer months if there is not much rain about.

Uncovering the value of t

You can obtain this information by checking out the technical characteristics printed on the side of your protective device. If not, telephone the maker's technical service line – they will help.

Solving the value of K

You can find values of K in Table 43a of BS 7671. Briefly, this requires that the electrical resistance offered does not exceed 0.005 ohm per metre.

Listed in Table 4.2 is a selection of helpful nominal cross-sectional areas for steel trunking. These reflect approved sizes published in BS 4678. Table 4.3 shows values for general-purpose cables up to a disconnection time of 5 seconds.

Table 4.2 – *Cross-sectional area of steel trunking. Refer to BS 4678.*

Steel trunking sizes (mm)	Cross-section (mm²)
50 x 37.5	125
50 x 50	150
75 x 50	225
75 x 75	285
100 x 50	260
100 x 75	320
100 x 100	440
150 x 50	380

Testing the impedance of your trunking system

As a guide to the value in ohms you should expect from your test, consider the following expression:

$$R = mKr \qquad (4.2)$$

where R is the resistance of your trunking in ohms, m is the total length in metres of the trunking under test and Kr is the factor 0.005 ohm per metre taken from BS 4568.

As a hands-on example, consider Figure 4.45 and the following:

A 52.5-metre length of 100×50 mm steel trunking is to be tested. Given that the maximum resistance of the trunking conforms to BS 4568, that is, 0.005 ohm per metre, calculate the maximum practical value you can expect.

Table 4.3 – *Calculating the effects of a fault current and values of K for general-purpose cables (for disconnection times up to 5 seconds).*

Type of cable	Insulating material	Initial and assumed temperature (°C)	Value of K
Copper conductors up to 300 mm²	PVC @ 70°C PVC @ 85°C Rubber @ 60°C	70/160 85/160 60/200	115 104 141
MI, plastic covered	Magnesium oxide	70/160	115
Aluminium conductors up to 300 mm²	PVC @ 70°C PVC @ 85°C	70/160 85/160	76 69

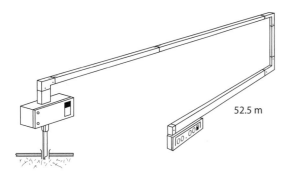

Figure 4.45 – A 52.5 metre, 100 mm × 50 mm, steel trunking installation offered for test.

First, back to Expression (4.2): resistance = length in metres × a factor. Substituting for known values, then resistance = 52.5 × 0.005. Thus the total expected resistance = 0.2625 Ω.

Lighting busbar trunking

Plug-in busbar trunking for general lighting arrangements is used in commercial, industrial and agricultural buildings where the need to have many control switches is limited.

For current rated between 25 and 40 amps, plug-in busbar trunking is available with two to six conductors. The metal housing acts as a protective conductor. You can obtain it in either 3 or 5 metre lengths. It is both lightweight and easy to handle.

Assemble your lengths only when your fixing brackets are firmly in place – Figure 4.46 illustrates this.

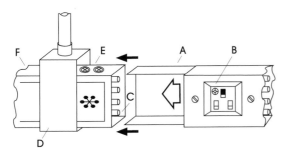

Figure 4.46 – Lengths of busbar trunking may be mechanically and electrically joined with a single action and secured with captive screws. A, trunking coupler; B, socket point; C, busbars; D, trunking support attached to the ceiling; E, captive screws; F, lighting trunking.

Connect the integral busbars by snapping each length into position and securing with captive screws. The electrical connection to the lighting fitting is by use of a standard 13 amp plug. Remember to fuse correctly!

Skirting and dado busbar trunking

These trunking arrangements serve hospitals, schools and offices. Your own college will probably have such a system. Made from PVCu, this type of trunking is generally multi-compartmental, each compartment supporting its own independent lid. Figure 4.47 illustrates a cutaway section of *Sterling Busbar Trunking*®. One of the thoughtful safety features is an internal busbar cover to prevent accidental direct contact with live conductive parts.

A good range of electrical accessories and trunking components are available, enabling you to produce a good standard of work.

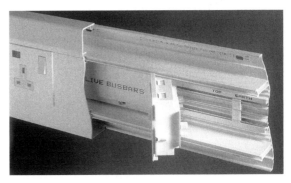

Figure 4.47 – Sterling busbar trunking. (Reproduced by kind permission of Marshal Tufflex Limited.)

Cable tray work

A cable tray installation will take the place of a trunking or ladder packing arrangement where medium-sized grouped cables share a common route. Defined as a shallow semi-enclosure with not less than 30% of its surface made up from perforated holes, this type of cable carrier is ideal for petrochemical, cement manufacturing and agricultural installations. It is used above false ceilings and within boiler houses. It has many uses!

Materials from which cable tray is made – a quick list

- Glass-reinforced polyester – for heavy cables and high operating temperatures.
- Lower smoke, zero halogen – used where sensitive equipment is used.
- Mild steel – used in industry and as a general purpose cable carrier.
- PVCu – used in the textile and food industries. Found in mines and the petrochemical and nuclear industries.
- Stainless steel – used throughout the food industry.

Finishes in mild steel include the following:

- Epoxy resin finish.
- Galvanised.
- PVC coated.
- Red oxide painted.
- Yellow chromate primed.

Two types of steel tray are available: light gauge and heavy gauge. They come in 2.5 and 3 metre lengths varying from 50 to 915 mm in width. Figure 4.48 illustrates the heavier type.

Working with cable tray

Check your route first for potential problem areas. Mark the positions of your take-off points and where you intend to place your accessories

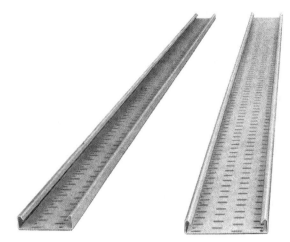

Figure 4.48 – *Heavy-duty return flange cable tray. (Reproduced by kind permission of Marshal Tufflex Limited.)*

such as tees, crossover points, etc. Your brackets must then fit along the route you wish to take.

Measure, cut and assemble your lengths of trunking to your brackets using 6 mm diameter bolts, nuts and washers. You will achieve a better standard if you use factory-made accessories but site-constructed ones can be easily made.

How to choose the required width of cable tray

As with cable trunking installations, you must allow a space factor of *45%* – this is important.

Use this straightforward expression to determine the width you will require:

$$T_\emptyset = (D1 + D2 + D3 + \ldots) \times (\% \text{ space factor}) + D_t \qquad (4.3)$$

Table 4.4 – *Approximate overall diameters for PVC steel wire armoured cables in millimetres.*

PVC/SWA/PVC conductor size (mm²)	Number of cores and diameter		
	Two cores	Three cores	Four cores
1.5	11.7	12.3	13.0
2.5	13.1	13.6	14.5
4.0	15.1	15.8	17.7
6.0	16.5	18.1	19.2
10.0	20.1	21.2	22.8
16.0	21.4	23.1	26.3
35.0	24.5	26.9	30.1

where $T_\emptyset$ is the required width of the cable tray in millimetres. *D1, D2, D3*, etc., are the *overall diameters* of the individual cables and D_t is the sum of the overall diameters of the cables.

Table 4.4 provides approximate overall diameters for PVC steel wire armoured cables from 1.5 to 120 mm².

Quick installation points

- Allow time to mark out your route and target where accessories and fixing brackets have to go.
- If your route takes you through a closed environment or if your tray has a *cover* attached to it, increase your space factor to *60%*.
- Do not expose your support brackets to mechanical stress.
- Each length of your cable tray should overlap by about 100 mm, as Figure 4.49 shows.
- Fit tinned copper *bonding/continuity links* to bridge each section of mild steel cable tray. Rub down to bare metal if the tray is painted or coated with plastic.

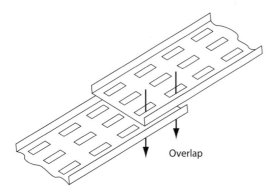

Figure 4.49 – *Lightweight steel cable tray is bolted together by lapping one section of tray to the other.*

Cable tray accessories

Examples of factory-produced cable tray accessories include:

- External 90° riser bend.
- Non-metallic external riser up to 90° (Figure 4.50).
- Unequal and equal tees.
- Bonding/continuity links.
- Flat bends at 30°, 45° and 60°.
- Angles at 30°, 45° and 60°.

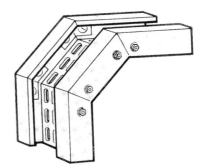

Figure 4.50 – *External cable tray riser bend. (Reproduced by kind permission of Marshall Tufflex Limited.)*

Site-built cable tray accessories

Internal bends at 90° – Figure 4.51 shows how a 90° internal bend is made from a section of cable tray.

By cutting two 45° 'V' slots in the sidewall of your cable tray, you will be able to bend to form a 90° right angle. When formed, site weld and paint the wall of your tray work with cold galvanising and support by mechanical means.

Equal tees – Construct your equal tee with the radius of your largest cable in mind. Apply a factor of 6 to the overall diameter of your largest SWA cable to determine the minimum internal radius when you form your cable into a right

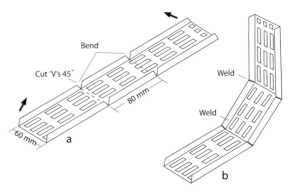

Figure 4.51 – *A site-built 90° internal bend.*

angle. An example: a twin 1.5 mm² SWA cable has an overall cross-sectional diameter of about 11.7 mm. If you multiply this number by the factor 6, it will provide you with a minimum internal radius of 70.2 mm, as illustrated in Figure 4.52.

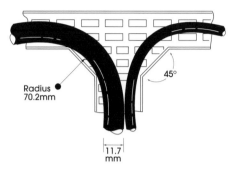

Figure 4.52 – Design your cable tray junctions to accommodate the radius of your largest cable.

A way of reducing your cable tray – Decide the amount you wish to reduce your cable tray, and then cut the tray at an angle of about *10°* to the opposite wall of your workpiece, making sure the wall is untouched and left complete. Bend the flexible angled portion inward to meet the required width. Secure with 6 mm diameter bolts, washers and nuts – see Figure 4.53 for details.

Cable exit holes – A hole formed on the surface of your tray will provide a neat through route for a

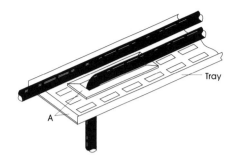

Figure 4.54 – Cut a hole in your tray to suit the size of the cable to be re-routed. Dress around the hole with lead flashing or a heavy PVC edging strip.

cable leaving it. Place a length of heavy plastic edging strip around the hole to protect the cable, as illustrated in Figure 4.54.

Cable supports

You have five to choose from, depending on the size of your cable and the type of installation it serves:

1 Plastic/nylon ratchet straps – for *small* steel wire armoured cable on tray work.

2 Cable cleats – for *heavy* steel wire armoured cables fitted directly to a surface.

3 Galvanised mild steel cable strapping – for *heavy cables* on cable tray.

4 PVC-coated copper strapping – for *grouped mineral-insulated cables.*

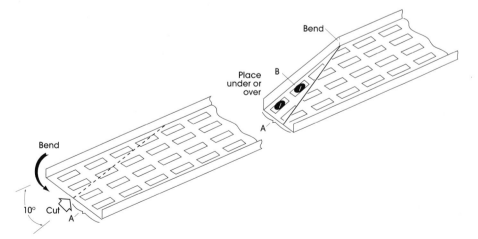

Figure 4.53 – A simple site-built cable tray reducer. A, the new width you wish to create; B, once cut, bend the flap under the main body of the cable tray and secure with 6 mm diameter bolts and nuts.

5 Site-assembled/purpose-formed clamps – *for very large supply cables.*

Working with non-metallic cable tray

Three groups are ideal for harsh or corrosive atmospheres:

- Glass-reinforced polyester
- Lower smoke zero halogen
- PVCu, illustrated in Figure 4.55.

Do not over-tighten plastic products such as bolts, washers and nuts used to assemble the non-metallic cable tray. Assembly is similar to its mild steel counterpart and some systems come with an optional heavy-duty snap-on lid. Glass-reinforced polyester brackets are available to support the installation.

It is wise to leave a small gap between the lengths installed to allow for thermal expansion, otherwise buckling will occur during hot weather.

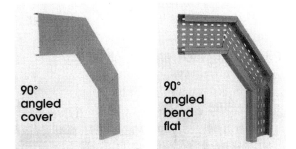

Figure 4.55 – *PVCu cable tray. (Reproduced by kind permission of Marshal Tufflex Limited.)*

The advantages

- Easy to use – lightweight yet strong.
- Many accessories.
- Continuity bonding not required.
- Ideal for damp situations and sensitive circuits.
- Polyester cable tray can be used in high surrounding temperatures.
- It can easily be dressed using a file or glass paper.

- Practically chemical resistant but please refer to 'The disadvantages'.
- Cable tray made from low smoke, zero halogen has a very good temperature range [– 40 to +130°C]
- Cable separators for extra-low voltage circuits are available.

The disadvantages

- Obtain guidance from the manufacturer before you install a PVCu cable tray. It is not suitable in temperatures above 42°C.
- It has poor chemical resistance to nitric acid and ammonia.
- It will buckle at high temperatures if you have not allowed for expansion.
- This type of cable carrier will not tolerate site-constructed accessories.

Mineral-insulated (MI) cables

A highly reliable cable that is able to operate in temperatures up to 1000°C for short durations. Conductors of solid drawn copper are inlaid into compressed powdered *magnesium oxide* insulation. This is included within a soft copper sheath as Figure 4.56 illustrates. Tests have shown that it can be thoroughly flattened yet continue to function. The copper sheath provides for both screening and mechanical protection as well as a *circuit protective conductor*.

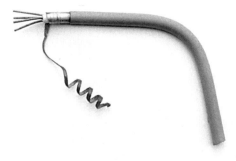

Figure 4.56 – *Four-core MI cable with a plastic sheath.*

Grades and sizes

There are three choices:

- Bare copper (at one time the sheath was made from aluminium).
- PVC covered – many colours are available.
- LSF covered – low smoke and fumes.

There are only two grades to choose from:

- Light duty – for voltages up to 500 volts and available in four sizes, 1.0, 1.5, 2.5 and 4 mm^2 and in the choice of two-, three-, four- or seven-core cable (4 mm^2 cable is usually only available with two conductors).
- Heavy duty – for voltages up to 750 volts and available in sizes from 1.5 mm^2 to 240 mm^2. Wide selections of cores are available but not all are present within the 15 conductor sizes.

Where do I use MI cable?

MI cable is ideally suited for wiring tasks demanding a high degree of reliability. Here are a few suggestions for you to consider:

- Boiler house installations.
- Fire detection and alarm circuits.
- Central battery emergency lighting arrangements.
- Commercial kitchen canopy wiring.
- Hazardous installations.
- Plant rooms.

There are many more that we could list if space permitted – are you able to provide a few additional items?

Preparing a cable end for termination

To terminate your cable a special *brass gland* and *screw-on pot* is fitted to the outer sheath of the cable – see Figure 4.57. Once secured, fill the pot with a soft plastic sealing compound and mechanically seal by means of a plastic cap.

Special tools will be required to prepare your cable gland:

- Junior hacksaw.
- Rotary cable stripper.

- Ringing tool – to score an indent around the copper sheath to terminate stripping (not needed when a rotary stripper is used).
- Pliers – to use with your rotary stripper.
- Pot wrench – to enable the pot to be screwed onto the copper sheath.
- Crimper – for crimping the seal to the filled pot.
- Cable bender – used to form and bend larger sizes of MI.
- Cable straightener – for ironing out bent or crinkled cable.
- An insulation tester.

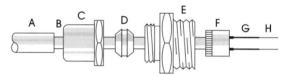

Figure 4.57 – *MI cable termination. A, PVC outer sheath; B, protective copper cable sheath; C, compression gland; D, compression olive; E, gland housing; F, brass screw-on pot to accommodate the plastic compound and sealing cap; G, push-on sleeving for the copper conductors; H, copper conductors.*

Cable termination techniques

Remember: practice contributes to confidence – self-assurance leads to greater skill.

1 Trim the end of your cable with a junior hacksaw, then calculate the amount of sheathing you want to remove.

2 Place the *rotary stripper* on the end of your cable and turn in a *clockwise* fashion, slightly pushing in the first instance. This action will remove the copper sheath as if you were removing the skin from an apple with a knife.

3 When you have removed enough copper, clamp a pair of pliers around the cable sheath and *continue to turn* your rotary stripper. This will shed the copper waste and provide a square edge for the next stage.

4 Slide the plastic shroud and brass gland onto the copper sheath.

5 Place the pot squarely on the end of the prepared cable and screw the pot-wrench on

to the gland. At this stage, the pot will be sandwiched between the *gland* and *pot-wrench* as shown in Figure 4.58. Remove the wrench and clear any contamination in the form of copper swarf from inside the pot.

6 Slide the plastic *sealing cap* onto the conductors, see Figure 4.59, and insert the *plastic compound* from *one* side of the pot. This will stop air pockets forming.

7 Next, use your *hand-crimping tool* to seal the brass pot but first, press the *seal* towards the pot and remove any surplus compound. Do not rotate the pot.

8 Once crimped, remove the tool and surplus compound, cut your insulating sleeving to the required length and push them home into the seal assembly unit.

9 Next, you must insulation test. A value of 0.5 MΩ is acceptable using a test voltage of 500 volt DC. It is wise to accept a far higher value for individual terminations when considering the value of the complete installation. Remember: $1/Rt = 1/R1 + 1/R2$ means a reduced value for the installation.

10 Lastly, identify each conductor using a continuity meter (Regulation 712 -01-03 (ii) confirms this).

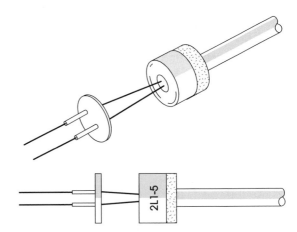

Figure 4.59 – *Thread the copper conductors through the holes in the plastic seal until about 30 mm from the leading edge of the pot.*

A quicker way of terminating your cable end

BICC Pyrontex® makes an all-in-one seal pot for use with their brand of MI cable. It does away with using the potter and hand crimper.

To fit the seal, remove the outer copper sheath in the way described previously. An all-insulated

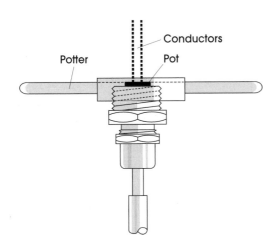

Figure 4.58 – *Pot ready to be screwed onto the copper cable sheath.*

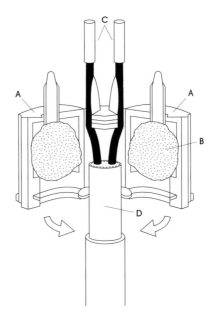

Figure 4.60 – *An alternative method of terminating MI cable. A, seal pot with built-in plastic compound; B, compound; C, insulated sleeving for your conductors; D, the copper cable sheath.*

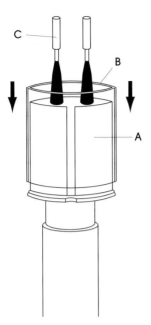

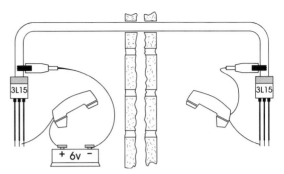

Figure 4.62 – *An easy way to establish core/conductor identification with MI cable. Use two telephone handsets and a 6 volt battery.*

Figure 4.61 – *A clear plastic tight-fitting sleeve is placed over the snap-lock moulded pot for added security. A, fitted seal pot; B, security shroud; C, insulated sleeving for the copper conductors.*

moulded-hinged seal pot with built-in sealing compound clamps to the cable, as described in Figure 4.60, and is snap-locked into position. A small plastic sleeve placed over the moulded pot, illustrated in Figure 4.61, secures your work piece. A choice of coloured sleeving is available to slide over your conductors.

Core identification over long runs

You can use a *continuity meter* but this is both tiresome and time-consuming. Use two *telephone handsets* wired in series formation and powered by a 6 volt battery as an alternative. Place your battery in series with the master handset and the copper sheath of the MI cable under test. Select conductors at random until you hear your workmate's voice at the other end of the line, as graphically illustrated in Figure 4.62.

MI installation techniques

In practice, it is more convenient to terminate either one, or sometimes both, ends of your cable before securing your work piece to the wall

or ceiling. Clip your cable with purpose-made copper clips or plastic coated copper strips when you have several cables to run. Be accurate when bending or setting copper sheathed cable – it hardens the more you play around with it and if you try bending it too much it will snap off. Getting it correct first time avoids wasting your time!

Check out both the size and the number of conductors you will need for any given run of cable. It is best to think ahead – you will not run into any trouble that way.

Older and imperial size cables

Moisture-resistant MI cable arrived in the UK in 1985 – before then it used to absorb moisture from the air at quite an alarming rate.

When you have to re-terminate pre-1985 cables, it is advisable to do the repair well away from any source of water. On critical circuits such as fire detection and alarm systems, it is very necessary that you have a high insulation resistance. This will avoid fault conditions.

High-temperature seals

When surrounding temperatures exceed 105°C, for example within a commercial kitchen canopy, you will have to use a different type of sealing agent that will allow your circuit to operate up to 150°C. If the ambient temperature is even higher and reaches 250°C then you can use a specialised seal. Be precise if you have to use this type of seal – it can cause a lot of trouble if you get it wrong!

When you have completed your work, take a good look at what you have done and, if okay, carry out an insulation resistance test.

Insulation testing

- Close all switches and circuit breakers (switch them to 'ON').
- If you are using fuses, these must be wire and installed.
- Remove all lamps.
- Isolate all fixed equipment.

Connect your *phase and neutral* conductors physically together and test between these and the *circuit protective conductor* – the copper sheath of the cable. Figure 4.63 illustrates this. Your tester must be set at twice the working voltage of your installation – in practice, 500 volts. Now, take a further test between the phase and neutral conductors, as shown in Figure 4.64.

The test values you obtain must not be less than 0.5 MΩ (that is, 500 000 Ω). Regulation 713-04-04 confirms this.

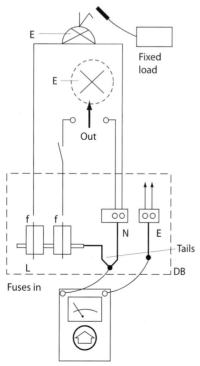

Figure 4.63 – *Test the insulation between the phase/neutral and the circuit protective conductor.*

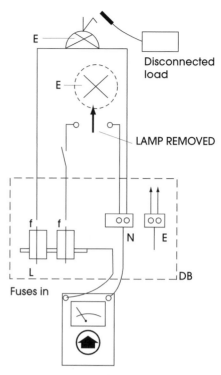

Figure 4.64 – *Now, test the insulation of your conductors between the phase and neutral conductors.*

Testing a three-phase and neutral installation

Figure 4.65 shows a systematic way in which you can test a *three*-phase and *neutral* installation. The minimum acceptable insulation resistance is 0.5 MΩ.

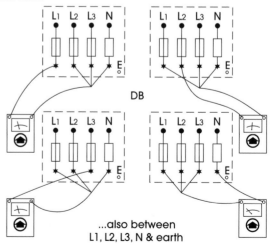

Figure 4.65 – *Insulation testing a three-phase and neutral installation.*

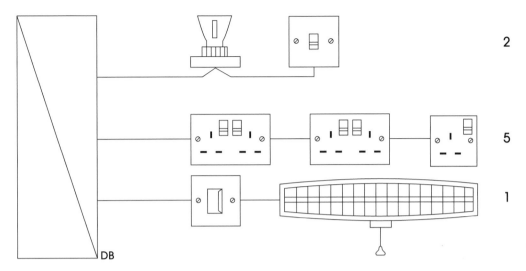

Figure 4.66 – *Two twin and a single socket would be regarded as five outlets whereas a heater served by a fused connection unit is just one.*

On larger installations, subdivide the system into sections of no less than 50 points just for testing. This will help to increase the basic value of your system and will avoid disappointingly low insulation results. Figure 4.66 describes the term 'points' in graphical form. Each *switch, socket outlet* and *light* you install is regarded as a point. Any accessories that have a fitted switch also count as a single point.

Armoured PVC insulated cables

These are tough and robust cables suited for power transmission and industrial control circuits. Purpose-made cleats made from plastic and aluminium secures the cable or, when grouped, metal or nylon strapping is used. Alternatively, lay directly into the ground (Figure 4.67). If required, you can draw your cable into a 'below-floor' ducting system.

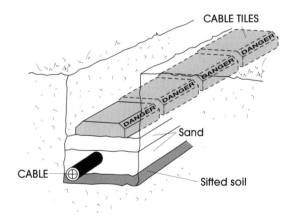

Figure 4.67 – *Steel wire armoured cables can be laid directly in the ground. Protect with cable ties or yellow "cable buried below" plastic warning ribbon.*

How to terminate your armoured cable

Cable ends are terminated with a purpose-made gland that acts as an anchorage point for the steel wire sandwiched between its housing. We will look at this later.

Smaller cables are sized from 1.5 mm^2 to 16 mm^2 in a selection of between 2 and 40 cores. Not all cores are represented in each of the conductors' sizes. Larger cables come in a choice of 2, 3 and 4 cores with cross-sectional areas from 25 to 400 mm.

Copper cable is made using stranded conductors covered with plain black (numbered) or coloured plastic insulation. A thin bedding sheath is wrapped or moulded around the conductors and provides support for a single layer of galvanised steel wire armouring. The *steel protective covering* can also act as a *circuit protective conductor (CPC)* if required. Alternatively, if you have a spare core it can be colour coded *green and yellow* with oversleeving and used as a CPC. Finally the armouring is protected with a thick moulding of PVC, which acts as an outer sheath as shown in Figure 4.68.

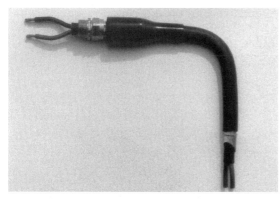

Figure 4.68 – *A glanded steel wire armoured, PVC insulated cable.*

Installation tips

It is best to pull your cable off from the *top* of your cable drum aided by a couple of *cable jacks*, a *solid steel spindle* and a few *cable rollers*. Raise your wooden cable drum about 90 mm above the ground as shown in Figure 4.69. Never leave it unattended and free to rotate – this is dangerous!

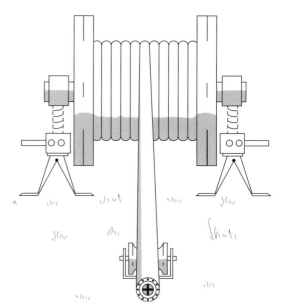

Figure 4.69 – *Dispense your cable from the top of the drum – it is safer.*

Manhandling your drum, whilst others pull with you, will make it far easier and safer. It often helps to smear a little *grease* on the *steel axle* to reduce the resistance generated by the weight of the cable.

Making cable pulling easy

To avoid having to pull a vast amount of heavy cable in one go, it is best to 'snake' your cable as illustrated in Figure 4.70. This way only a small amount of your total length is being pulled at a time. Another way is to position your drum at a mid-point location and pull one half in at a time. Remove remaining cable from your drum and place in a snaked formation as shown in Figures 4.71 and 4.70 – but you will need plenty of room to do this successfully.

Avoiding cable kinks

Through manhandling it can be easy to obtain kinks and bends lying opposite to the natural twist of your cable armouring. Keep your eyes on the cable when you are changing direction, making sure your cable lies as intended – this will avoid extra work at a later date. As an additional aid, use cable rollers on long straight runs.

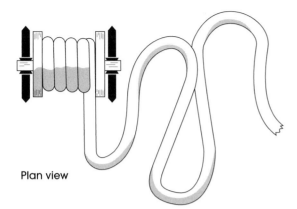

Plan view

Figure 4.70 – *Try 'snaking' your cable to make your task easier.*

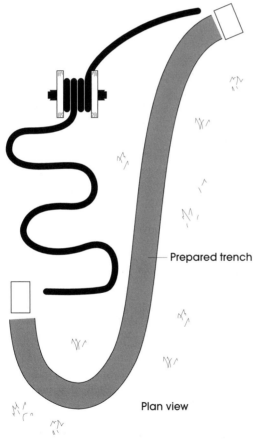

— Prepared trench

Plan view

Figure 4.71 – *Another way to reduce the weight of the cable pulled is to position your cable drum at a mid-point position.*

Heavy vehicles and construction plant must be discouraged from driving over your armoured cable, especially over rough or unfinished surfaces. Flintstone forced into your cable can do a lot of damage!

Attaching your cable to a catenary wire

Use a catenary wire that will accommodate the weight of your suspended cable. It is best to attach your cable to the catenary with heavy-duty nylon cable ties, placed at a distance of about 250 mm apart, as illustrated in Figure 4.72. Fitting the nylon ties is best carried out whilst the cable is on the ground but lifting could be a bit of a problem. If your cable is too heavy then mechanical assistance will be required. Securely anchor it to ceramic insulators when both ends of your catenary wire is in position. Adjust your straining wire with a mechanical catenary adjuster – this will make your catenary tighter and your finished work more professional.

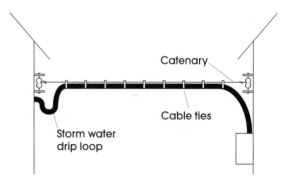

Catenary

Cable ties

Storm water
drip loop

Figure 4.72 – *Catenary suspension: steel wire armoured cable.*

All about tools and terminations

You will not need special tools to prepare a cable termination:

- A strong sharp knife.
- Two adjustable spanners or equivalent tools.
- A hacksaw (about 32 teeth per 25 mm).

Unless you use the wrong size gland, steel wire armoured cable terminations are straightforward. The following list provides a few easy-to-follow guidelines:

1 Measure the amount of armouring you want removed.

2 Saw around the outside edge of your cable at your chosen position, cutting the outer PVC sheath and about 50% of the armouring beneath it.

3 Remove the outer PVC sheath with a sharp knife from the point of termination.

4 Remove the armouring – it is best to take off about five or six strands at a time.

5 Cut the *pointed section* of your plastic shroud to match the *outside* diameter of your cable, then slide the shroud (smallest diameter first) onto the cable, to be temporarily parked beyond the point of termination.

6 Next, cut off sufficient outer sheath of your cable for the armouring to be contained within the tapered section of your brass gland (Figure 4.73).

7 Slide the *curved gland nut* section onto the cable parking just below the shroud.

8 Splay open, in conical fashion, the short length of exposed armouring as described in item 6 and Figure 4.74.

9 Offer the second half of the gland (the *conical section*) into the *splayed armouring* – glance again at Figure 4.74.

10 Reunite the two parts of your gland and tighten.

11 Remove the inner bedding sheath starting about 20 mm from the face of the gland. Be careful, as cutting too deep will destroy the insulation serving the conductors! Place the shroud over the gland and insulation test your termination as described in previous paragraphs.

12 Fit a brass earth/bonding tag on the end of your finished gland. This will be sandwiched between the gland face and the side of the cabinet your termination will serve. Make secure with a steel locking ring. Fit a supplementary bonding conductor to the brass tag with a small bolt and nut and connect to the earthing terminal.

Bedding sheath   Armouring   Shroud

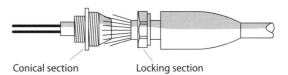

Figure 4.73 – *Exposing the wire armouring.*

Conical section   Locking section

Figure 4.74 – *Marry the two component parts of the gland after the splayed armouring has been offered the conical section of your gland.*

Summary so far...

1 MI cable is obtainable in two grades – light duty for voltages up to 500 volts and heavy duty up to 750 volts.

2 Make your terminations by removing the copper sheath and applying a purpose-made gland and pot. The pot is sealed once plastic compound is added.

3 Rubber oversleeving is placed over the bare conductors. It is then wedged onto the sealing cap. Test once complete. The minimum test value must not be less than 0.5 MΩ. Three choices of seals are available to suit your temperature range.

4 On larger installations, subdivide into divisions of no less than 50 points for testing.

5 Connect your phase and neutral conductors together and test between the grouped pair and the copper sheath of the MI cable. A further test between each current carrying conductor is applied.

6 Armoured PVC insulated cable is suited to power transmission and industrial control circuits and general factory installation work.

7 Measure the amount of armouring you wish to remove. Once prepared, offer the cable to the gland and tighten.

Handy hints

- Terminating PVC insulated steel wire armoured cable in the winter can be difficult. Gently warm up the outer sheath of your cable with a hot air blower but do not allow heat to build up in one place. This will allow for safer cutting.
- Keep batteries serving portable electric drills in peak performance – you never know when you will want to use them without warning.
- Identify your tools with coloured plastic tape. This will not stop them from being stolen but it will provide you with a means of recognition if you leave them hanging around or if they are accidentally placed in someone else's toolbox!
- If you have to connect a UK landline telephone, wire as follows: pin 1 – GREEN/white, pin 2 – BLUE/white, pin 3 – ORANGE/white, pin 4 – WHITE/orange, pin 5 – WHITE/blue, pin 6 – WHITE/green. Colours in capital letters indicate the base colour of the wire. For example, there will be more GREEN coloured insulation on the conductor than white, so green is the base colour.

Steel and PVCu conduit

Steel conduit

There are two types of conduit used today:

- solid drawn – heavy gauge
- heavy gauge – welded steel.

Produced in many dimensions, both types are in four metric sizes (see Regulation 521-04-01 I to iii): 16, 20, 25 and 32 mm outside diameters. For specialised installation work, three imperial sizes are available: 1½, 2 and 2½-inch diameter conduit. An imperial inch is about 25.4 mm.

Steel conduit is obtainable in a choice of three finishes:

- Stove black enamelled – for dry situations.

- Hot dipped galvanised – for damp or external use.
- Stainless steel – for food preparation and special projects.

A wide selections of fittings is available: examples range from *reducing sockets* and *couplings* to *locking rings* and *adaptors*. Malleable (soft) cast iron and screwed circular *inspection boxes* are available in a wide choice of design and include the following:

- terminal box
- right angle
- through
- tee box
- 'Y' box
- four-way box.

Figure 4.75 illustrates a few of those most commonly used.

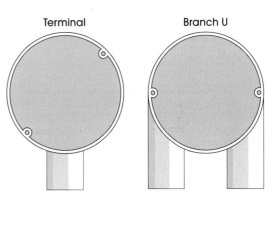

Also available

Figure 4.75 – *Standard conduit inspection boxes.*

PVCu conduit – a brief introduction

PVCu stands for *unplasticised polyvinyl chloride*. This type of conduit is available in five metric sizes: 16, 20, 25, 32 and 50 mm outside diameters. Finishes are generally in black or white. Order other colours direct from the factory via your electrical wholesaler. As with steel conduit, there are two gauges available:

- Light gauge, suited for underfloor screeds or concealed work.
- Heavy gauge/high impact, reserved for exposed situations.

Use the accessories provided for either gauge of conduit. Apply a PVC solvent to glue your accessory to your work piece. We will discuss PVCu conduit installations more fully later in this chapter.

Introducing oval conduit

Oval conduit is not used as a means of forming an installation but is ideally suited as an inexpensive method of providing a way of drawing your cable in and out of an installation buried within a plastered wall. It also serves to supply a little protection to your cable during the plastering phase but offers no protection against screws or nails.

You have a choice of five metric sizes in 3- metre lengths: 13, 16, 20, 25 and 32 mm outside diameter.

Points concerning steel conduit installations

There are advantages and disadvantages in choosing steel conduit as a cable carrier. The advantages are:

- Rewiring and additional work is possible.
- Steel conduit provides an excellent protective conductor.
- Three types to select to suit where your installation is located.
- You can employ a mixed variety of conductor sizes.
- Mixed sizes of conduit are possible within the same installation.

The disadvantages are:

- High material and labour costs.
- Careless or defective joints can cause large current drains should a fault condition to earth occur.
- Maintenance is required.
- If broken, steel conduit can be less effective as a protective conductor.
- Stove enamelled conduit will corrode gradually if not properly maintained.
- A high skill level is required.
- Many tools are required if your job is to be done properly.

Pre-installation thoughts

Long before you start your job, check out the number and sizes of cable you will require. Look at Regulation 522-08-02, which recommends that there must be sufficient means for drawing cables both in and out. Remember, also, to allow for future additional wiring and give a little thought to *voltage drop* and correction factors for

Handy hints

- PVC solvent is harmful – keep away from the fumes and never smoke whilst using it, as it is very flammable.
- Keep the lid on a PVC solvent tin firmly ON when not in use and when in use, stand the container on a spill-proof tray.
- If you have to install a dedicated supply to an outhouse or garage containing, amongst other things, a freezer unit and an incandescent lamp (household bulb), it might be wise to protect your supply circuit with either a *re-wireable fuse* or a *Type C* or *D miniature circuit breaker*. This will stop the MCB from switching itself OFF when the bulb comes to the end of its life and blows. Check also the earth loop impedance of this circuit is correct in relationship to the characteristics of your chosen protective device.

cables grouped within a conduit. Regulation 525-01-01 advises on this.

The tools you will need

You will require quite a few tools in order to carry out your conduit installation efficiently. Please consider the following:

- Stocks and dies for making threads on your prepared conduit.
- Conduit bender and pipe vice.
- Conduit formers of various size to suit your installation.
- A hand-held tapering reamer to clear jagged inside edges.
- A large hacksaw to cut and form your conduit.
- A flat, medium cut file.
- A retractable rule for general measurements.
- Soft-lead pencil.
- Adjustable pipe-grips or Footprints®.
- A 110 volt drill and a reliable battery drill with good sharp drill bits.
- Nylon draw-in tape.
- French chalk or wire lubrication gel.
- A small paintbrush and touch-up paint.

Keep your *pipe vice* in good order. Worn jaws will allow your conduit to slip when you are threading your work piece. If this happens, remove the damage with a flat file and paint to prevent corrosion from setting in later – then change your worn jaws.

Planning your route

Decide on the size you will require for the work you have to do and then take a little time to plan your route ahead. Drill holes needed through ceilings and walls and then made good after your work is completed. Check there is nothing in the way of your proposed conduit route – if there is, move it if possible or route around.

Mark out where you intend to site your conduit boxes and other accessories then drill and fit your conduit saddles to support your conduit run. The On-Site Guide will supply all the information you need to know about spacing

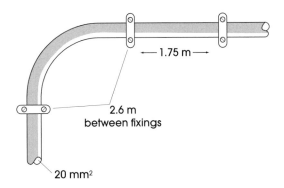

Figure 4.76 – *Additional supports are often required in conduit installations.*

distances for supports to serve your steel conduit. Often supplementary fixings will be required, as Figure 4.76 demonstrates. Please refer to Regulation 588-08-05.

Working with conduit

It is always a good point to recut the manufacturer's original thread – it often becomes damaged. It is important to keep a good sharp set of dies – this way you will always cut threads that are up to standard. Dull or damaged dies will tear your conduit threads to pieces and produce poor workmanship.

To obtain the best results, you must use a cutting compound. First, fit your stocks and die on your work piece, then push whilst rotating two and a half turns in a clockwise direction. To clear accumulated swarf, stop and rotate a couple of times counter-clockwise. Keep threading the pipe in this manner until you see three threads beyond the viewable face of your die.

Unwind and remove your stocks and dies and file across the face of your conduit. Next, reamer or file out the inside edge. This will prevent cable damage when you wire.

It is better to screw inspection boxes, etc., to your conduit when it is within the jaws of your pipe vice – it is a lot easier this way.

The importance of inspection boxes

It could be tempting to install length after length of straight conduit without giving any thought to how it might be wired! Good practice is to fit an inspection box after about every *8 metres* in order to make it easier for wiring. Your inspection box must be secured to the wall or ceiling with two fixing screws. This will prevent the box from turning when adding the next length of conduit. A conduit installation with plenty of inspection boxes is easy to wire and problems will be minimised.

Site-formed angles and sets

If you incorporated too many formed bends and sets within your installation without regard to inspection boxes, you would have a massive headache on your hands – wiring would be impossible. Please take account of the following:

- The sum of the total angles must not exceed 180° before you install an inspection box.
- An inspection box should be added after the following (see Figure 4.77):
  - two return sets
  - an assortment of two 45° sets and one right angle
  - after every second right angle.

As a final word, do not underestimate the value of inspection boxes – especially when you use tight knuckle bends and sets within your installation.

Think ahead – wiring will be far easier and less troublesome in the end.

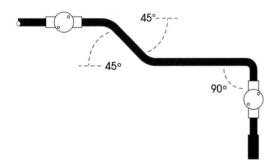

Figure 4.77 – *Sets and angles incorporated within a conduit installation must not exceed 180° before an inspection box is installed.*

Bending and setting conduit – getting it right first time

It is difficult to make quality bends and sets on anything other than a bending machine – although some of us try at times.

Figure 4.78 shows how two simple steel conduit templates will allow you to produce accurately measured right angles and return sets when working under site conditions. To make your pattern, just bend two short pieces of conduit, one to form a perfect right angle, the other a 45° set. Permanently mark your formed shape, in line with the back of the bending former – best done with a hacksaw, as a line drawn with a pencil will eventually rub off.

Look at Figure 4.79. It shows two opposing right angles drawn from one length of conduit sprawling across a small passageway. To do this, offer your right-angle template to each corner as illustrated in Figure 4.80 and follow these straightforward guidelines:

1 First, arrange your *right-angled template* with the marked section uppermost as shown in the illustration.

2 Mark the ceiling adjacent to the hacksaw scratch on your template in each corner.

3 Measure, very accurately, between each ceiling pencil mark.

4 Transfer this measurement, accurately, to a suitable length of conduit. Mark accordingly.

5 Bring this mark into line with the rear of your bending former and use your machine to bend two perfect right angles. You might get it wrong a few times. I did, but keep trying – you will get it eventually!

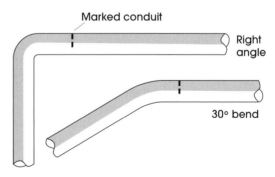

Figure 4.78 – *Working templates for steel conduit.*

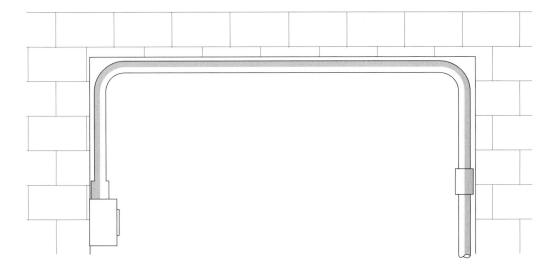

Figure 4.79 – *Forming two right-angles from one length of conduit.*

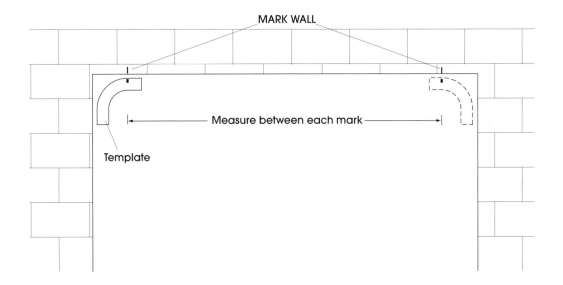

Figure 4.80 – *Offer the template to each corner. Lightly mark the wall next to the mark on the template. Measure between each mark.*

Sets and angles

These may be formed in a similar way but you must be accurate. Your formed angle must be the exact angle of your template or your set will be wrong. As a guide, please check out the following:

1 First, mark your conduit at a position adjacent to the rear of the former and bend to match the angle of the template.

2 Remove your work piece from the bending machine and position the template directly above it as though impersonating the finished set (Figure 4.81). Do this by laying the unfinished work on a flat surface, such as a floor.

3 Use the template to adjust the required depth of set and mark your work piece as shown in the last illustration.

4 Place the newly marked conduit to the rear of the bending former. It is important to line your mark up with the rear of your former. Keep your angles straight with each other – then bend to the *exact* angle of your template.

Practice and determination will achieve a good standard of workmanship.

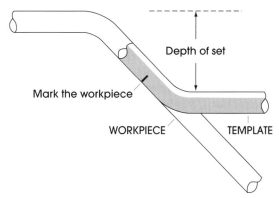

Figure 4.81 – *Forming a return set using your conduit template.*

A few thoughts concerning galvanised conduit

For exterior installations, we use galvanised conduit. It is also laid in floor screeds, cast *in situ* – which means that cement is poured over it and it is buried within fabric forming walls and ceilings.

If your installation is *in situ*, pull all your bends and sets with generous radii for ease of wiring. If you do not, your work will be set hard within the cement and you won't be able to do anything about it.

Pack all your inspection boxes and socket boxes with dry paper, with lids securely fixed to prevent concrete contamination filtering into the conduit. It is best to install your conduit using galvanised *loop-in* boxes. Loop your conduit from box to box terminating in short vertical right angles. Fix your ceiling boxes to the construction shuttering timber with nails and light gauge fencing wire. Snap off any nails poking out of the ceiling when the concrete shuttering comes down – see Figure 4.82.

Wear industrial gloves when working with conduit that has been stored outside in sub-zero temperatures. This will prevent damage to your bare hand through sticking to the frozen steel. Frost burn can be very uncomfortable.

Place rubber gaskets behind box coverlids serving as inspection boxes. The fixing screws must be short to prevent the route of the screw from scuffing or biting into your conductors. A

Handy hints

- A wheel-type cutter (the type plumbers use) is suitable for plastic and steel conduit.

- Screw-in, extendable cable rods are a useful addition to your tool kit. You can use them to get to places where it is hard to get otherwise. Just secure your cable to the rod with plastic tape and pull the rod to where your cable needs to be.

- Use heavy draw-in tapes to find your way around larger imperial size conduits. The smaller size ones often cause problems and you will wish you had never used them!

- An enclosed glass-fronted halogen light is a good friend during the cold winter months but never use the open-fronted type for temporary lighting when your work takes you to a farm.

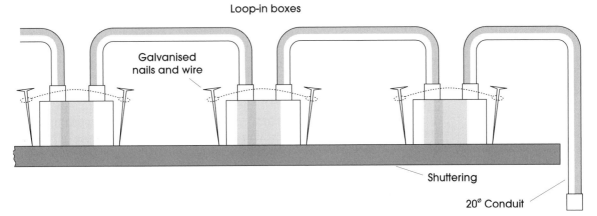

Figure 4.82 – *Preparing conduit when cast* in situ.

smear of grease on your screw will prevent the steel lugs from corroding.

An introduction to plastic conduit

One of the main disadvantages of using steel conduit is the high cost of materials that are used and the many person-hours needed to complete the installation. Plastic conduit offers an alternative method, reducing both material and labour costs.

PVCu conduit has many practical advantages over its steel cousin. Fewer tools are required; it is easier and lighter to install and a junior hacksaw can often take the place of a large one.

Your tools and equipment

Basic tools and equipment required for this type of work include:

- Junior hacksaw or wheel cutter.
- Hand-held reamer.
- Retractable rule.
- A good battery drill, hole-cutters, etc., and screwdriver bits.
- Nylon draw-in tape.
- Bending springs (20 and 25 mm diameter).

Bending and setting is by pushing a moulded spring attached to a length of 2.5 mm² cable into your workpiece and forming the bend over your knee. Once bent, pull out your spring using the attached cable. You will need to form larger sizes of conduit (32 mm diameter) within a bending machine – but *you will still have to use a moulded spring.* It is important to keep your springs in excellent condition. A damaged spring will damage your bend or set.

Thinking about your installation

Select the size of conduit you will need for your job and prepare the route as described in the sections for steel conduit.

If exposed to heat, plastic conduit will sag. It is best to increase the frequency of your fixings to about one saddle every 900 mm if you have to route your installation opposite a skylight or through a warm area. Avoid fixing heavy accessories to PVCu inspection boxes as the brass lugs pull away from the moulding of the inspection box when the temperature is high. Warm weather brings other problems, especially on long lengths of conduit. Thermal expansion causes it to bend and buckle. To avoid this, fit an expansion coupler every other length of conduit or no less than 8 metres apart. Figure 4.83 illustrates this type of fitting. Apply solvent only to the smallest section. The larger of the two sections is used solely as a guide, so conduit which has expanded can move freely within the coupling and avoid buckling. Please refer to Regulation 522-07-01.

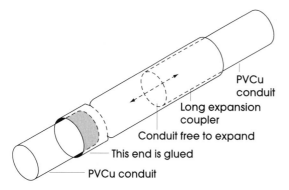

Figure 4.83 – *A PVCu expansion coupler.*

The effects of low temperature on bends and sets

Extremely low temperatures will cause plastic conduit to snap when formed. To overcome this problem, gently bring the temperature of the conduit to an acceptable level by playing an industrial hot air blower or other heat source on the area you wish formed. Take it easy and do not overdo it or you will end up with a far worse problem you originally had.

Gluing problems

Before you apply solvent to your work piece, clean off any contamination that might weaken the joint when you bond the two surfaces together. Apply solvent to both surfaces and twist your work piece to spread the glue evenly. Get into the habit of returning the lid to your solvent container after each use. It will topple over if you leave it off and that could prove a very costly mistake! Please be very careful using PVC solvent if you have plastic lenses in your glasses. Accidental splashes can ruin them in seconds. If you are concerned, wear additional eye protection.

Overcoming wiring difficulties

If you follow the rules concerning the number of bends and sets recommended before adding an inspection box, then wiring will be reasonably straightforward.

If you are installing only three or four lighting cables then one of the easiest methods is to push them through the empty conduit. If more, then thread a *nylon draw-in tape* into your conduit

first. If problems arise getting around tight bends, try feeding a *hooked stranded cable* through the opposite end of your conduit. When (by measurement) both your draw-in tape and hooked conductor are next to each other (Figure 4.84), *rotate your hooked conductor* several times whilst gently removing it from the conduit. This is best done working in pairs – one pushing the draw-in tape whilst the other pulls the hooked conductor. You might have a couple of disappointments but keep trying and you will be successful.

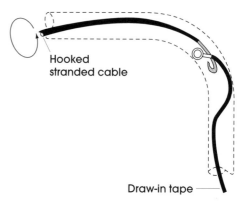

Figure 4.84 – *Drawn-in tape recovery technique.*

Preparing your cables

Careless or ham-fisted methods of attaching your single cables to your draw-in tape is a way to failure, especially when long runs are involved. A well-tried method is to bunch your cables together in a straight and staggered arrangement. To prepare, remove about 80 mm of insulation from the end of each cable and twist the bare conductors around each other to form a spearhead of staggered cables. Wrapping a layer of insulation tape around the spearhead will help to prevent snagging from strands when the cables are fed through your conduit. Attach the spearhead to the eye of your draw-in tape by way of the leading conductor.

Drawing your cables into your conduit

Place your cable drums on a suitable cable dispenser. If all else fails, use a section of steel conduit clamped into your pipe vice. It is best to wire in pairs – one pulling whilst the other feeds the cables into the conduit. Feed your cables as straight as possible but, if you experience problems, sprinkle *French chalk* or *smear gel* over your cables as they enter the system. You must pull and push/feed in harmony – if you lose this rhythm you will get into difficulties. Take time and do not rush as if there were no tomorrow – that is the secret.

Wire one section of your installation at a time when your runs are long or complicated. Allow the maximum radius for all cables routed through right-angled and multi-way inspection boxes, as illustrated in Figure 4.85. Laying tight to the edge of the inspection box will only add difficulties if additional wiring is done.

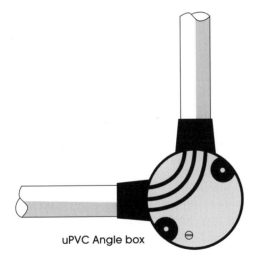

uPVC Angle box

Figure 4.85 – *Allow a good radius for your cables to change direction.*

Flying leads

Provide a supplementary circuit protective fly-lead on all sockets installed using steel conduit. Attach a *green/yellow* cable to the earth terminal point on the socket outlet and connect the other end to the earthing terminal point on the back of the accessory box. With plastic conduit, this practice is not necessary.

Types of cutting tools

Listed at random are selections of more familiar tools we use in our industry. I apologise for the length of the list – I will be brief:

- *Large and junior hacksaws* – this is an ideal cutting tool for steel and plastic enclosures and accessories.

- *Jigsaw* – used for forming oddly shaped holes in material where conventional methods would prove difficult.

- *Hole saws* – for cutting holes in steel or plastic. Clearance sizes: 16, 20, 25, 32, 38 and 50 mm in diameter at 10 teeth per 25 mm.

- *Files* – used to provide a finish for steel and plastic work pieces. Files remove burrs through cutting. Many shapes and various sizes are obtainable.

- *Hand-held reamer* – a tool which will enlarge the bore of a hole or it can be used to remove the burrs around the edge of a freshly cut hole.

- *Stocks and dies* – used to cut threads on steel conduit with a suitable cutting paste. Die sizes are: 16, 20, 25 and 32 mm external diameter. Two imperial sizes are also available: 1½ and 2 inches.

- *Taps* – use these to cut internal threads in holes bored slightly smaller in diameter than the diameter of the tap. Ideal for re-tapping threaded lugs within steel accessory boxes.

- *Pad saw* – a disposal flexible steel blade fitted into a permanent handle. Ideal for cutting holes in dry-lining walls when installing recessed sockets and switches.

- *Knife* – a retractable bladed tool ideally suited for cutting or stripping the insulation from cables. As an example: Stanley Knife®.

- *Wire cutters/compression tool* – sometimes known as *service pliers*. The tool is for manual operation to remove the insulation and cut conductors up to 6 mm², shear small electrical screws or compress pre-insulated cable terminations. Figure 4.86 illustrates this.

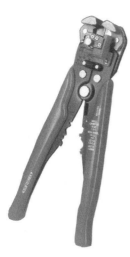

Figure 4.86 – *Service pliers. (Reproduced by kind permission of Walsall Conduits Limited.)*

The importance of cutting accurately

A hole wrongly placed represents wasted time and causes additional work. Trunking will appear amateurish to the professional eye if badly cut and will require extra work on your behalf to put it right.

The way to gain precision in your work is by *exact measurement*. Before you drill your hole, measure the position of the precise centre and draw a pencilled cross where you are to cut. You can then instantly correct your drill if it wanders from this target area.

When you cut trunking, it is important to cut from the *unwanted side* of your work piece. Accurate measurement and correct cutting techniques together are a good team and will always guarantee good results. Never be tempted to guess!

Summary so far...

1   Installation techniques overlap in many areas when PVCu or steel conduit is used. PVCu conduit sizes are 16, 20, 25 and 32 mm outside diameter in both light and heavy gauge.

2   Before starting your job, check out both the size and type of conduit you will need for your installation.

3   Plan your route and where you are to install your inspection boxes and accessories, then fit your saddles to suit.

4   Use a steel conduit template to assist with the formation of difficult bends and sets.

5   Wire in pairs – one feeding cable into the conduit whilst the other pulls in harmony. Maintain this rhythm whilst wiring.

6   *Cable pulling gel* or *French chalk* will help you to install your cables if difficulties arise.

7   A flexible fly-lead attached from an accessory's earthing terminal to an earthing point within the accessory box socket must accompany all steel conduit installations.

8   Place a cross on your target area to drill a hole with precision.

Handy hints

- Drilling a small hole at the base of a low positioned inspection box forming part of an outside installation will control condensation problems. Please refer to Regulation 522-03-02.
- Place an orange band around conduit installed in a multi-service duct for instant recognition. Regulation 514-02-01 and BS 1710: 1984 (1989) apply to this.
- Metal clad switches or sockets forming part of an outside installation could indicate storm water contamination within the accessory if warm to the touch. Once checked, drill a small hole at the base to allow future storm water or condensed water to drain away freely. Please refer to Regulation 522-03-02.
- It is important to isolate the supply before working on live circuits – for your own sake and for the safety of others.
- Look out for *easy-strip* sheathed cable. It saves a lot of time and is far safer than using a knife.
- With the use of very sharp dies, it is possible to thread heavy gauge plastic conduit. No cutting paste will be required.

Introducing cable duct

Cable duct is useful as it forms part of the infrastructure (the floors and walls) of a modern building. Often you will see it shaped to contain a rising main from an electrical control room to the uppermost floor of a commercial building.

Some cable ducts are big enough to allow technical staff to walk through whilst others are formed below removable flooring, permitting power cables to be drawn in and out. Fit smaller cables to the side of cable ducts and lay very large power cables directly onto the floor.

Ventilation is important within cable ducts to allow the passage of cool air to pass over the cables. This will remove any build-up of heat within the duct.

Cable ducting

Cable ducting is a site-built or manufactured enclosure in which to lay cables. Made from metal or an insulating material, which is not conduit or trunking, cable ducting does not form any part of the building structure. As a brief example, use a 152 mm diameter storm water pipe to protect special circuits routed through a roof space or basement area of a commercial building.

Input services to buildings

British Standards directive 1710:1984 (1989) provides the means for identifying pipeline and service conduits installed in buildings and on board UK registered ships.

Each service has a basic colour. This provides a means of identification and is fashioned as a band of sticky tape some 150 mm wide which is stuck to the wall or cladding of the service pipe. If it is essential to know the exact contents of the pipe, a safety or reference coloured band about 100 mm in width is sandwiched between two 150 mm printed vinyl-based coloured bands as illustrated in Figure 4.87.

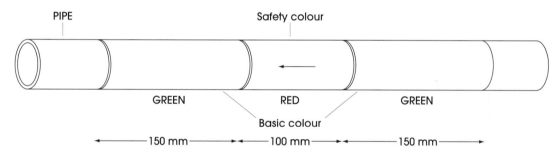

Figure 4.87 – *The contents of this water pipe are used for fire-fighting.*

Table 4.5 – *Services to buildings – means of identification.*

Services – contents of the pipe	Basic colour code	BS colour reference number
Acids and alkalis	Violet	22 C 37
Air	Light blue	20 E 51
Electricity	Orange	06 E 51
Fresh water	Auxiliary blue	18 E 53
Fuel oil	Brown	06 C 39
Gas	Yellow ochre	08 C 35
Other liquids	Black	00 E 53
Steam	Silver grey	10 A 03
Vacuum	Light blue	20 E 51

Table 4.6 – *Service pipe information – contents advice.*

Information or usage	Safety colour	BS colour reference number
Warning	Yellow	08 E 51
Danger	Yellow and black stripes	Yellow 1
Water for firefighting	Red	04 E 53

Conduit containing low voltage electrical mains is coloured *orange*. This is BS colour reference number 06 E 51, as demanded by Regulation 514-02-01.

Table 4.5 provides a selection of typical services found in industry today, while Table 4.6 offers helpful details of the service pipe concerned.

Lighting and power circuits

Polyvinyl chloride insulated cables – PVC

Conductor sizes ranging from 1.0 to 400 mm² are able to operate in temperatures up to 70°C. A choice of cores are offered, the most common being *twin* and *three core*. All cables carry a bare *circuit protective conductor* (cpc).

This type of cable presents a wide choice of wiring methods to your installation. Each has its merits and disadvantages, and these we will weigh up next. Figure 4.88 shows the basic requirements for a typical one-way lighting circuit.

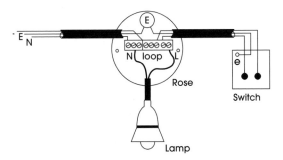

Figure 4.88 – *The loop-in method of wiring a one-way lighting circuit.*

Wiring for a simple lighting circuit

It is usual to wire your lighting circuit in either 1.0 or 1.5 mm² twin PVC insulated and sheathed cable.

Route your cable, securing with cable clips, from your distribution centre to your first ceiling rose. The rose has three independent sections where the conductors are connected but not electrically linked with each other. The incoming and outgoing red phase conductors (the *live conductors*) are connected to the middle of the three sections whilst the neutral (the *blue wire*) is ranged and connected within the left-hand section where you will find a blue flexible conductor leading to the lamp holder as Figure 4.89 shows.

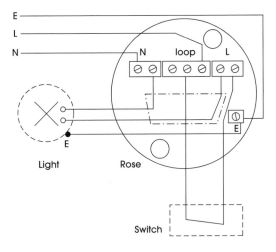

Figure 4.89 – *The supply neutral is common with the blue flexible neutral serving the lamp holder.*

The next step – wiring to your switch

Clip or place a second cable from your ceiling rose to your switch. Connect both the conductors and the cpc at this point. The blue conductor, now the switch-wire, must be *phase coloured brown* at both ends of the cable as a means of identification. Use either brown PVC tape or *brown plastic sleeving*. Please refer to Regulation Table 51A. A 'one-way' lighting switch has two termination points. Connect the *all brown* conductors to the bottom termination and the blue, *colour-coded with brown*, to the top.

Place *green/yellow* oversleeving over the bare cpc and connect to the earthing terminal on your accessory box.

Connections at the ceiling rose (from the cable serving the switch)

Place the *all-brown switch feed* with the incoming *brown* phase conductor. Connections are within the *middle section* of the ceiling rose. Connect the blue, *colour-coded brown*, conductor (the switch-wire) to the *right* of the middle section. In this section there will also be a *brown flexible wire* leading to the lamp holder. Finally, place *green/yellow* oversleeving over your bare CPC and connect to the earthing terminal within the ceiling rose.

Other ways of wiring lighting circuits

There are about seven ways of wiring a lighting circuit. Some you will be familiar with – others not:

- The joint box method.
- The loop-in method.
- Central joint box system.
- Double pole switch method.
- Steel or plastic conduit system.
- Final lighting ring circuit method.
- Fused connection unit method.

Before you start work on an existing wiring system, make sure the supply is not present by using a reliable test meter and set to the correct scale. Alternatively, use a dependable *approved* light emitting diode (LED) test lamp.

The joint box method

Figure 4.90 shows you how to wire a simple lighting circuit using a four-terminal joint box – Regulation 130-02-05.

Take a supply from your distribution centre using 1.0 or 1.5 mm² twin cable to a round four-terminal joint box. The cables you will put in or route away from this box will provide you with the means of control or delivery. The advantage of this system is cables can be laid and connected

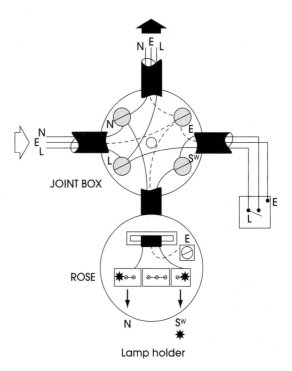

Figure 4.90 – *A single point lighting installation using the joint box method.*

during the first fix stage of the installation. This method is quicker and easier to connect accessories, as there are only one or two cables present – the majority are within the joint box at an earlier stage of the installation. The disadvantages will show up after the installation is finished. It can be difficult to trace faults or carry out cable tests when, for example, a chipboard floor has been laid. Another weakness is the practical ease of access to all the joint boxes. Ideally, marked traps cut and fitted directly over the joint box during the construction stage would provide a way out of this problem. Figure 4.91 illustrates how to make a small inspection trap within traditional flooring.

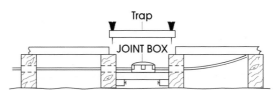

Figure 4.91 – *Providing a route to your 'below floor' joint box.*

The loop-in method

This is one of the most widely used methods of wiring within the electrical installation industry. A PVC sheathed cable (phase-neutral and cpc) supplies each ceiling outlet point on your lighting circuit. From each point, another cable provides electricity to each control switch. All connections are at the ceiling rose or switch, as shown in Figure 4.92.

There are many advantages using this method:

- Ease of wiring – all connections are made from one level.
- Easy to fault find – no flooring or inspection traps to lift.
- Can be added to without prior knowledge of where joint boxes are placed.

The only disadvantage is that other trades may accidentally pull out cables during the first-fix period. This is fine if you are the only person around but if there is any danger of this happening, tie or twist your cables together so they provide support for each other.

Marking your cables

Always identify your cables clearly, when installed. Use a *fine lined permanent marker pen* to recognize the role of each cable. Example: feed, switch-wire, looped feed and loop to next light. It is tempting to place crosses and nicks on the cable sheath. This method is fine providing you are to see the job through to the end but it can become confusing if someone else takes your place.

Points concerning your ceiling outlets

Prepare your switch wire first and attach a length of *brown sleeving* onto the *blue conductor* as Figure 4.93 illustrates. This will help to ensure you have a correct connection – an important point if your light is to work as intended.

It is tempting to overload one particular ceiling point with *looped supply cables* when situated in a handy place. This will cause cable crowding and you will regret doing it. Restrict yourself to one cable to serve the ceiling outlet with electricity, one to loop on as a *looped feed* to the next light and a cable to serve your switch. Sometimes there may be more if, for example, the same switch, as illustrated in Figure 4.94, controls two or more lights.

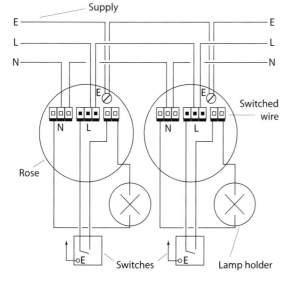

Figure 4.92 – *Lighting installation: loop-in method.*

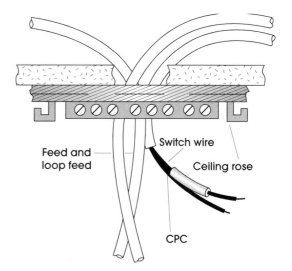

Figure 4.93 – *Prepare and colour code your switch wire first.*

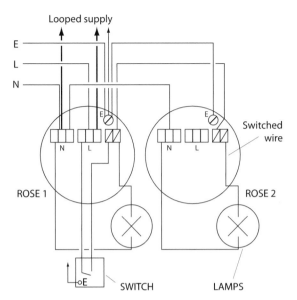

Figure 4.94 – *Two lighting points controlled by a single switch.*

Cable crowding can happen when wiring wall lights. Too many can create a practical difficulty when you are fitting a slim or small wall light.

Outdoor fittings

It is best not to use the loop-in method of wiring outdoor lighting fittings if a residual current device protects your installation. It is sensible to fit a *double-pole switch* as both the phase and neutral conductors are isolated from the supply whenever the switch is in the OFF position. Figure 4.95 illustrates this point in schematic form.

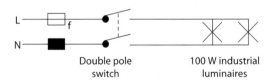

Figure 4.95 – *A double-pole switch can be used to control an outside lighting installation.*

Central joint box system

First, supply your central joint box with a lighting circuit from your distribution centre. Your central joint box will take the form of an *adaptable box* made from plastic and measuring about 100 × 100 mm by 25 mm in depth. Connect your supply cable into a 15 amp block connector strip and secure it to the base of your box with small cable ties (there are usually hooks or holes for this purpose). You can add additional circuits, supplied from the *same phase*, to your connector block, if you wish. Figure 4.96 outlines this way of wiring.

The advantage of this arrangement is that the majority of major interconnections you make will just be at one or two points within your installation. For example, you can make plans for a central joint box within the roof space to serve the top floor and one within the floor space to provide for the floor beneath – but do not forget your floor trap! This wiring method is simple, *providing all your joint box related cables are marked.* As you only use one cable to serve either a lighting point or a switch from your central joint box, you can easily prevent cable crowding.

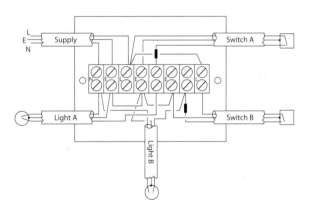

Figure 4.96 – *The central joint box method of wiring a lighting installation.*

Industrial use

Central joint box wiring is ideally suited for lighting installations wired using MI cable. You would then exchange your plastic joint box, used for PVC sheathed cables, for a pressed steel adaptable box to maintain your earth continuity throughout the installation.

Double-pole switch method

The double-pole switch is used in two ways:

- As a means of control – to switch your light 'on' and 'off'.

- To connect and terminate your incoming and outgoing supply cables throughout your circuit, as Figure 4.97 illustrates.

Use this method for wiring volumetric portable accommodation where it could be impractical to wire in any other way. You will find it very easy to test, so fault-finding is both simpler and quicker. As with the loop-in wiring method, all cable/conductor termination points are on the same level and mistakes can be minimised. This method is very useful as only one or two cables will be present at a lighting point, while there will be two or three at a switch position. It is best to choose switch boxes that are a *little deeper* to accommodate the additional cables. Wire two-way and intermediate switching arrangements in the usual method.

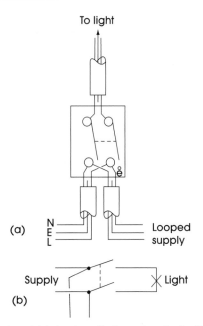

Figure 4.97 – *Lighting installation using the double-pole switch method (a) and shown in schematic detail (b).*

Using conduit as a cable carrier

This is a good way to deliver your circuits when wiring takes place in an industrial setting. Extending an installation is straightforward – but you must take care not to damage the original circuits by *cable burn*. This happens when you pull additional cables through a conduit that is close to its capacity. Apply *wiring gel* or *French chalk* to your new cables to reduce the effects of friction when drawing cables through the conduit.

Support to your conduit installation is by way of saddles. Make sure there are sufficient when you add more cables to the original installation. Conduit can be pulled from the wall or ceiling when reworked!

A BESA box is the collective name given to your screw-on, round accessory box. The initials stand for British Electrical Standards Accessory and Figure 4.98 illustrates a selection that are most commonly used today.

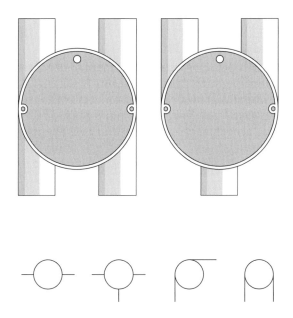

Figure 4.98 – *Inspection boxes. From left to right, top row: twin through way, branch three way; bottom row: through way, three way, angle tangent and branch 'U'.*

Wiring your lighting circuit in conduit

Draw your wiring cables through the electrical conduit with the aid of a *nylon draw-in tape*. Strip about 75 mm of insulation from the end of each cable and twist them around each other in a staggered fashion to create a spearhead of cables. Figure 4.99 will help to explain this procedure. By tying your cables onto your draw-in tape, as illustrated in Figure 4.100, you will find it difficult finding your way around all your bends and sets – this is the wrong way to do it! Wrap a single layer of PVC insulating tape around your *spearhead* of cables to prevent snagging taking place and, if you feel it is required, place a splodge of *cable gel* on the leading point to make it easier for yourself.

Progression is sometimes brought to a standstill when your draw-in tape snags on the inner wall of a coupler. When this happens, try tapping the conduit with a hammer whilst a workmate pushes the nylon tape. If this fails, try pushing a hooked length of cable from the other end of the troublesome conduit (this might be the nearest inspection box) and try to pass the head of the nylon draw-in tape twisting your back-up cable as you go. The aim is to twist the cable around the draw-in tape and *gently* pull the nylon tape through the conduit by use of the auxiliary cable. This is a four-handed job, one person pushing the nylon tape whilst the other smoothly pulls the hooked support cable. Figure 4.101 will help to make this clearer. By installing sufficient inspection boxes, problems with seized draw-in tapes will be minimised.

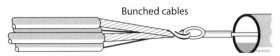

Figure 4.100 – *This is not the way to group your cables together for drawing into conduit.*

Figure 4.101 – *A single conductor, purposely bent into a hook at the leading end, will help free a snagged nylon drawn-in tape. Once contact has been made, rotate your hooked conductor.*

Starting your wiring

Let us assume that your installation cable carrier is steel and you will be using the metal conduit as a CPC.

Draw in a *brown phase* and *blue neutral* conductor from your distribution centre to a point where each colour cable will go their separate ways (blue to your lighting point and brown to the switch position). Direct the *brown* feed conductor to the switch whilst drawing the blue neutral to the lighting point. To complete your circuit draw in a *brown cable* (the switch-wire) from the switch position to where the lighting point is. It is best not to draw cables in one at a time for fear of cable burn, so think ahead when you are wiring – it will help.

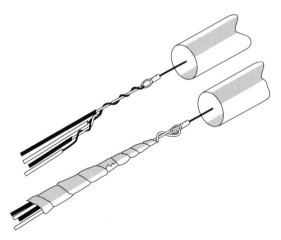

Figure 4.99 – *Preparing cables to be drawn into conduit. To avoid snagging the cables can be lightly taped as illustrated.*

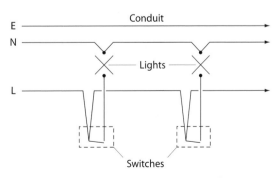

Figure 4.102 – *A single cable lighting installation using steel conduit as a carrier.*

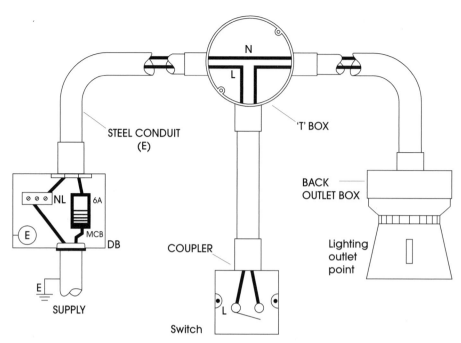

Figure 4.103 – *A lighting installation carried out using steel conduit shown graphically.*

Loop the blue and brown unswitched *supply cables* if there is any need to continue the lighting supply to another area within the installation (Figure 4.102). The looped blue *neutral* will originate from your lighting point, whilst the looped brown *phase* conductor will stem directly from your switch position. It is wise to place a small nick on the end of your switch wire (the brown wire that serves the light from the switch) so there will be no mistakes when you second fix your installation. This is the basic method to use when wiring a lighting circuit within a steel conduit system. Figure 4.103 summarises this pictorially.

To recap the advantages and disadvantages

The advantages of choosing conduit as a cable carrier include the following:

- Easy to rewire or add to.
- Power and lighting circuits can be housed within one conduit.
- Can be used in hazardous locations.
- Strong; will withstand mechanical damage.

- Different sized conduits can be used within the same installation.
- Can be installed indoors and outdoors.
- Different coloured cables can be used to suit the needs of the installation.
- Can be cast in concrete.
- A good choice of screw-on accessories.

Some disadvantages are:

- High installation costs and a high level of skill required.
- Relies on the system for earth continuity (Regulation 543-02-04).
- Plastic conduit is not flame-proof and will sag in direct sunlight.
- Can be over-accommodated with cables (Regulations 522-08-02 and 06).
- Black enamel conduit will rust if placed outside.
- Plastic conduit requires a CPC. The colour must be *green/yellow*. You *must not* use plain green; Regulation 514-06-02 refers.

The best way to wire without getting into difficulties – summary

You must draw *all* your cables into your conduit together to reduce the risk of cable burn. Mixed voltages may be included within the same conduit, providing the value of the insulation is the *same* as the highest voltage conductor. Wiring requires two people: one to pull the draw-in tape whilst the other feeds the cable into the conduit. Each cable within your cable bunch must be *parallel* with the others to reduce friction and snagging around your bends and sets. Pull and push your cables *simultaneously* – this way you will not experience too much trouble.

Long cable runs

Never attempt to pull too much cable into your conduit at one time. Form loops of cable at well-located inspection boxes and feed one loop of cable into your conduit at a time. You will be able to manage your wiring task far better this way, as Figure 4.104 shows.

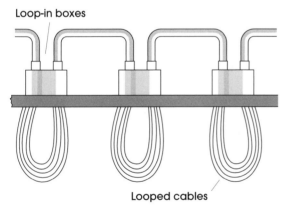

Figure 4.104 – *Create loops of cable for ease of wiring when wiring in conduit.*

Wiring your switch

Place small nicks at the end of your switch-wires. This will identify where they are to be placed within the switch. Keep your feed and loop feeds unmarked. The role of each cable will then be clearly recognized when you come to connect your switch. This technique is very handy for multi-gang switches but remember your marking code.

Connecting aluminium conductors to switches

Take care! Being softer than copper, aluminium conductors are easily compressed from the pressure from the terminal screw when tightened. Too much pressure will cause the conductor to shear off unnoticed. This will cause problems during the testing period of your work.

Voltage drop in conduit systems

Be wary of lengthy cable runs serving inductive lighting loads (fluorescent and sodium/mercury vapour lighting, etc.). If the cable size you have used is too small or marginal, the load high and the circuit long, then both cable and conduit will gradually increase in temperature and cause damage to the installation over time. If you have any doubt, wire with a larger conductor. Better still, calculate the voltage drop mathematically. Please consider cable *correction factors* – it matters a great deal.

Lighting final ring circuit method

Some telephone exchanges adopt this lighting arrangement method but it is not common in the UK. Figure 4.105 illustrates in schematic form how this circuit is constructed.

You can apply this technique to a variety of installations. In a domestic situation, a final lighting ring circuit can supply lighting to individual rooms. *Un-switched fused connection*

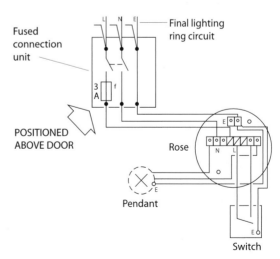

Figure 4.105 – *Lighting installation: final ring circuit method.*

121

units form a ring circuit using 1.5 mm² cable. The units are above each door or at a high level near to the door. From this point onwards, conventional wiring takes over but a 3 amp cartridge fuse replaces heavier ones. The size of the breaker protecting your lighting final ring circuit will be 10 or 16 amps, serving between 20 and 30 lamps.

The advantage of this system is if there is a problem, only the room or area served by the fuse connection unit will be in trouble – the problem can then be quickly resolved.

Fused connection unit – final ring circuit method

A lighting point can originate from a power circuit by way of an *un-switched fused connection unit* forming part of a *final ring circuit*. Take as an example a remotely located area previously wired for power only, where it would prove time-consuming and costly to install additional cabling for a single lighting circuit. This system is the ideal answer. Figure 4.106 explains in more detail. Protect your new lighting circuit with a 2 or 3 amp fuse fitted within the fused connection unit. Remove the original 13 amp fuse – it is far too large.

Take a lighting cable from the fused connection unit and terminate at your ceiling rose. From this point, please wire using the loop-in method.

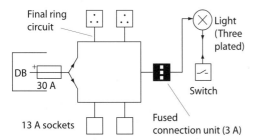

Figure 4.106 – *Lighting installation – from your final ring circuit (power) method.*

Wiring a two-way switch

Arrange your cabling using *twin* and *three-core* PVC insulated and sheathed cable connected

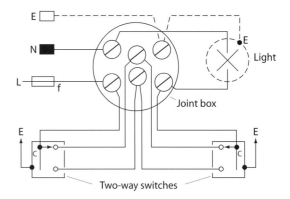

Figure 4.107 – *A two-way lighting circuit using a six-terminal joint box.*

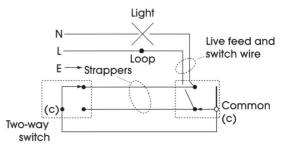

Figure 4.108 – *A basic one-way lighting circuit converted to a two-way arrangement.*

into a six-terminal, 20 amp joint box as shown in Figure 4.107. A popular way is to wire without the use of a joint box as shown in Figure 4.108. This is the *conversion method* and has the advantage of having all cable terminations at hand on one level.

Intermediate switching

Intermediate switching is a method of control when three or more switches are required to serve a lighting arrangement – wire in as many as you wish. It is impossible to install this type of switch alone.

Interconnect the *three-core cable* that links your *two two-way switches*. Only the *black* and *grey* conductors are used; leave the *brown* conductor whole. Place the two brown conductors within a connector if you decide to cut the three-core cable to make it easier for yourself; Figure 4.109 illustrates this.

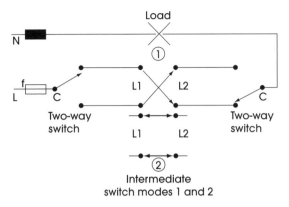

Figure 4.109 – *A basic two-way/intermediate switching arrangement shown schematically.*

Connecting your conductors

Preparing for termination

Use a sharp knife, a pair of wire cutters/cable strippers and be guided by these few points:

1 Cut your cable to the length you need to connect into your switch or joint box.

2 Score the cable vertically with your knife and pull apart the sheathing to expose the coloured conductors.

3 Next run your knife around the top of the split sheathing but take care not to cut into any of the coloured conductors or yourself.

4 Tug off the unwanted sheath with a sharp pull to expose your conductors together with a bare CPC.

5 Remove about 8 mm of insulation from the end of each conductor with an adjustable wire stripper.

6 Do not cut, nick, dent or damage in any way the exposed copper conductor.

Clamping your conductor at the point of termination

Your conductors must be both electrically and mechanically sound. A connection which is loose will give you trouble when current is drawn as *arcing* will occur (arcing is a luminous discharge of electrical energy across a tiny gap between two conductors) and the terminal will be

destroyed by heat – it is only a matter of time. The bond between the jointed conductors must not exceed 0.05 Ω. Over-tightening can be as bad – it can cause the screw to shear off or rotate in on itself, making it impossible to tighten the termination.

Another practical mistake is to leave too much copper exposed at the point of your termination, as shown in Figure 4.110. When you terminate to a joint box, measure the complete length of the conductor you will need to serve your chosen terminal. Wire *neatly* and make sure the outer sheath of your cable has entered your joint box by some 5 or 6 mm. Lay each conductor carefully, making sure unnecessary surplus conductors are minimised. After you have completed your work, *label* your joint box appropriately.

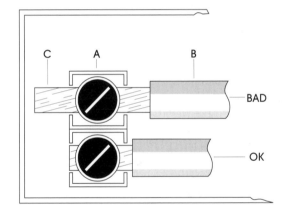

Figure 4.110 – *It is wrong to leave too much copper showing at the point of termination.*

Handy hints

- Mark/identify your cables as you lay them during the first fix stage of your installation. Describe in plain English – avoid using marks and signs. You will know what they mean but will others who follow you?

- Two of your most cherished tools are your battery drill set and mobile phone – look after them or others will!

Wiring domestic power circuits

Please remember the acronym 'STRAW': *Stop, Think, Review, And Work*'. Mistakes cost time, money and often pride. Get it right first time by starting at the highest point and work down. In a typical three-bedroom house this will probably be the roof space. It is often better to install your *first* floor final ring circuit from a position within the loft – alternatively you can wire from the floor space on the *first floor* but allow for additional time if you decide to wire this way. Route your cables down the first floor walls under the protection of channelling to the power point accessory boxes beneath. Never install cables unclipped in a roof space – it is best to fix them about every 600 mm or so. Others can easily damage them if you lay them on top of the roofing timbers. Clipping looks far more professional. Smoothing the insulated sheath of the cable for a couple of metres and securing with an anchor clip on the *side* of the joist will keep your cabling straight. Once you are happy with your work, clip between the anchor clips. This is a simple way to make your job look good.

Providing you meet certain conditions, you can have as many sockets as you like to form your final ring circuit. These conditions involve the *size* and *type* of cable and the form of *over-current protection* you choose. Chapter 8 – Electrical Science will provide additional information. In the meantime, final ring circuits are summarised in Figure 4.111.

The way ahead

In summary, the best method of installing your final ring circuit is:

- Prepare the wall to accommodate your accessory boxes – known as 'boxing out'.
- Fix the boxes firmly with screws and wall plugs and place rubber grommets in the holes provided for your cables. Check your box is square with a miniature level.
- Drop your cables down the wall passing your box by some 100 mm.
- Place your cables within your box, via the rubber grommets.
- Manage your cables, routed down the wall, so they appear both straight and flat.

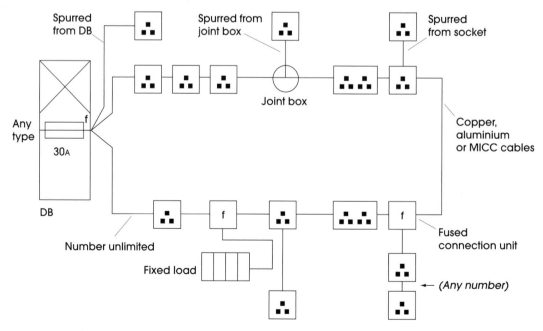

Figure 4.111 – *Final ring circuit. Maximum floor area of 100 m². PVC insulated at 2.5 mm² or MI cables at 1.5 mm² may be used.*

- Cover them with plastic or steel channelling, and secure with masonry nails every 300 mm or so. There is no hard and fast rule.

An alternative way

Another way is to use the *wall cavity* as a means of delivering your cables to your accessory box. If you decide on this method please remember that *correction factors* will apply if the cavity is to be filled with insulation. This might require you to increase the size of your cable.

If the cavity wall method appeals to you, punch a hole in the wall at the back of your accessory box. This will provide a route through to the wall from the space behind. Next, push

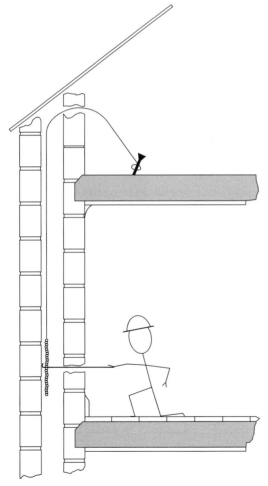

Figure 4.112 – *Uninsulated cavity wall wiring techniques using a weighted draw wire.*

your plumb line or a length of nylon cord with a jack chain attached to it down the cavity. This method is easier when there is no ceiling as you can work from one level and target the accessory box beneath. If there is a ceiling, made a small locating hole in the plasterboard at a point directly below your accessory box. This will help you to position your plumb line in the right place. The weighted line will fall through the cavity to the target area beneath. Recover with a length of hooked fencing wire pushed through the hole from the back of your box. This job is easier with two but you can manage on your own, as Figure 4.112 shows.

Tie your cables to the nylon line and draw them in – again it is easier when working in pairs.

Thermal insulation

You must give due consideration to cables grouped together within a roof space or placed in a cavity wall which will have thermal insulation added. Where possible, avoid contact with insulation but, if direct contact is unavoidable, you must apply a rating factor to your cable. In practice, this will mean using a larger cable if your circuit is to run at maximum capacity. Please refer to earlier sections for details of how this works.

A word concerning 'boxing out'

If you box out before you wire, your job will be far easier to manage. Cutouts for accessory boxes must be reasonably shallow if you are to avoid using long machine screws to fit your accessory. Take into consideration the depth of the plaster line and add a couple of millimetres or so for good measure. Add this measurement to the depth of your steel accessory box and that will be the depth of your hole. Making it deeper will cause more work for you in the end. It is best if you can allow about 5 mm of the box to protrude from the face of the construction wall so the plaster line will be reasonably flush with the leading edge of your box, as Figure 4.113 illustrates.

Use two *pan* or *round headed* screws together with expansion plugs to secure your box to the

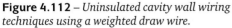

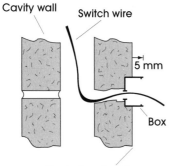

Figure 4.113 – *Allow your pressed steel accessory box to stick out about 5 mm from the face of the construction wall.*

wall of the building. If fixed with nails or one screw, a knock will throw your box out of square when plastering takes place. Once fitted, check the alignment of the box with a small 80 mm water level.

Boxing out with foam-filled blocks has its problems. To get around this either cement your box within the block work to secure a fixing or use two long 75 mm woodscrews to penetrate the insulating foam. Either way is not straightforward but Figure 4.114 will help to make this point a little clearer.

Avoid installing accessory boxes on damp walls in old houses. Dampness, general building dregs and rubble can often build up within an accessory box over a period and cause *nuisance tripping* if a residual current device (RCD) is in the circuit.

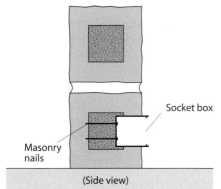

Figure 4.114 – *Very long screws or masonry nails will secure a steel accessory box in foam-filled thermally insulated blocks.*

Fitting your boxes back to back

Unless the wall you are chopping out is thick, it is best to avoid placing boxes back to back. It will cause a weakness to develop within the wall, which will stop you from fixing your boxes in the conventional way. If you have no other options but to fit them in this fashion, render them in using a four-to-one mix of sand and cement. Your best approach by far is to place them adjacent to each other on either side of the wall, as described in Figure 4.115.

Single accessory boxes are made with four tapped lugs; three are fixed and the fourth is adjustable. Fit your box with the adjustable lug horizontally. Check the level of your box and screw to the wall. Adjust for final alignment at the second-fix stage of your job.

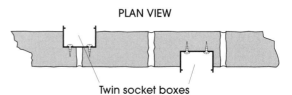

Figure 4.115 – *Back-to-back sockets are more secure when staggered.*

Wiring from the ground floor ceiling space

When the ground floor is solid there is no alternative but to wire the complete ground floor installation from the upstairs floor space. A three- or four-bedroom house will accommodate at lease three final ring circuits. These would serve the *kitchen, ground* and *first floor* areas. Please refer to Regulation 314.

Doing the job

First, drill a series of holes in the timbers to allow your cables to run throughout the ceiling void. Properly designed holes will not weaken the timbers but drilling anywhere you fancy will! Position your holes and slots in timber joists as illustrated in Figures 4.116 and 4.117.

A common mistake is trying to force as many cables as possible into one hole. Please do not do this. It will cause cable burn. It is far better to drill a few more holes – it is a lot safer that way.

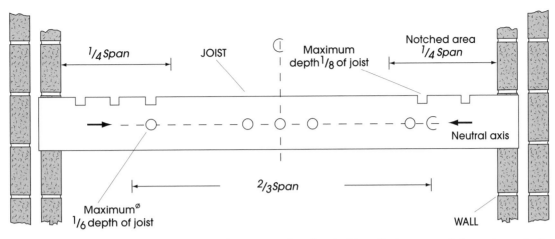

Figure 4.116 – *Holes and notches formed in timber as part of an electrical installation must only be cut in particular areas. Reference is made to the Building Regulations.*

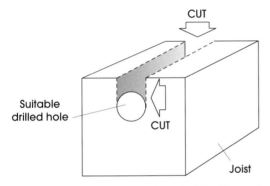

Figure 4.117 – *A cut-away section of a joist illustrating how a notch may be made to contain an electrical conduit.*

Summary so far...

- Holes no more than *one-sixth* the depth of the joist.

- Drill your holes along the *centre* of the neutral axis.

- Drill within the *middle two-thirds* span of the joist.

- You can cut notches for conduit providing the joist is greater than 250 mm in depth and carries a uniform load.

- Form your notches within the *first quarter* of the timber span measured from each supporting wall – but no more than *one-eighth* of the depth of the joist.

Floor traps

A quick and efficient way to form a trap is to cut across the width of your floorboard with a jigsaw at an angle of 45° whilst hugging the edge of the joist beneath. Repeat at the other end of your proposed trap and remove the tongues at the sides. Set the blade of the jigsaw shallow so it will not damage any services underneath in places where you are unable to see. Secure your trap with woodscrews as shown in Figure 4.118.

Where it is not possible to lift a traditional floorboard in the usual way, run a jigsaw parallel to a couple of nearby joists cutting the floorboard across its width. Set your jigsaw on a shallow cut to avoid unexpected runs of *cable, gas* or *water pipes*. Lift your newly formed trap.

As there will be no support to serve the trap, nail a suitable size timber onto the joists, under

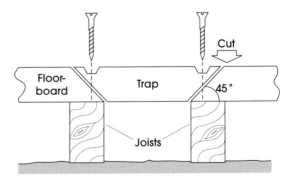

Figure 4.118 – *Cutting a small inspection hatch in a conventional floorboard.*

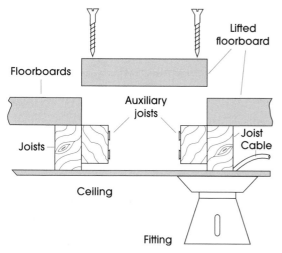

Figure 4.119 – *Support timbers secured to the side of the joists will prop up a section of lifted floorboard where fixing is unavailable.*

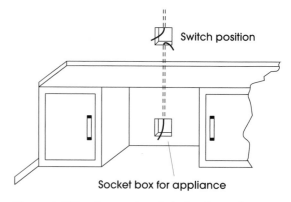

Figure 4.120 – *A remotely switched socket outlet.*

the floorboard at either end so that the section of flooring you have removed can be safely replaced. Figure 4.119 illustrates this.

Kitchen installations

When you prepare accessory boxes for a kitchen installation, always use a water or laser level to obtain a common height throughout the kitchen area. Your accessories must be uniform and level with any wall tiles installed later.

Kitchen component drawings show a detailed and planned arrangement of the finished kitchen. It is important to scale off your plan to target the exact position of your electrical accessory but be sure you are using the correct scale when measuring! This way you will not make any mistakes. Allow about 100 mm from the top of the worktop to the underneath side of your socket. This will allow enough space for plugs and flexible cables.

Control low-level *flex outlet plates* for refrigerators or waste disposal units from a position above the worktop. When this is required, wire your dedicated *final ring circuit* into a *switched fused connection unit*. From this position, route your load-bearing cable to a 20 amp flex outlet plate below the worktop level, as illustrated in Figure 4.120.

Remember to fit a fused connection unit near to a gas hob. This will provide a supply for an automatic ignition control system if one is required.

Fit a standard single accessory box to serve a telephone point. Set your box a few millimetres back into the wall, taking into account the depth of the plaster line and the thickness of the wall tiles. This way the leading edge of your accessory box will be flush with the tiles.

Please remember to wire all your equipotential bonding in accordance with Regulations 413-02-01 to 03.

Nearing completion of your first fix stage

In summary form, consider the following points:

- Label your cables – you may not complete the second fix stage!

- Trim back all cables to about 140 mm, tuck them into your socket and switch boxes before plastering.

- Check all channelling or oval conduit drops are secure.

- As an option, cover all accessory box lugs with a small section of insulation tape to stop them being contaminated with plaster.

Preparing for second fix

When the plaster is reasonably dry, remove any contamination from within the box and *re-tap* the threads serving the lugs if heavily soiled. Prepare your cables for connection using a sharp

128

knife, an adjustable cable stripper and a pair of side cutters. Fit rubber grommets to your steel accessory boxes to protect your sheathed cables and tailor-make all insulated conductors to suit your connection points. This will avoid cable pinching and scuffing.

Strip off about 10 mm of insulation around the conductor with an adjustable cable stripper. Pliers or side cutters will score the copper conductor, which will lead to the copper wire snapping off when pressured by way of the terminal screw. Place all your *common* conductors within the terminal housings and screw firmly home. Use a flat-bladed screwdriver, by hand. Never screw by means of a battery-operated drill. Add *green/yellow* oversleeving to your bare CPC for both protection and identification.

Fixing your accessory

If you need longer screws to fit your accessory, cut to length with a *threaded bolt shearer*: never use pliers as they can damage the threads. Screw your accessory to the *adjustable lug* first. It is far easier this way, especially if you have to use longer than normal screws, when boxes are further back into the wall than necessary.

Handy hints

- A battery-operated *rotary cutter* is a useful tool when working with installed *mini-trunking*, which has to be re-worked.
- Smear a little grease on bolts and screws serving outside agricultural installations. This will help prevent corrosion from setting in.
- Leaving a hammer hooked to the upper rungs of a ladder is asking for trouble.
- Keep a first aid kit on site – you never know when you might need it.
- Use the correct-size drilling machine when you cut 100 mm diameter holes in brickwork to serve a domestic extractor fan.
- Keep to the rules – it could save your life.

You must protect brass fittings from wall dampness or they will turn black around the edges where the brass is in contact with the wall. Fit moulded see-through plastic gaskets between the fitting and the wall. To avoid problems, always make sure these gaskets are in place. When the surface is completely dry, remove the plastic membranes.

Summary so far...

1 Final ring circuits and alternative lighting installation methods have shared much of this chapter. Although different, all have similar practical installation techniques when PVC insulated and sheathed cables are used to form an installation.

2 Popular methods of wiring a lighting installation include:
   (a) the joint box method
   (b) the loop-in or three-plate ceiling rose method
   (c) the central joint box system
   (d) the use of steel and plastic conduit.

3 Always install sufficient inspection boxes throughout your installation for ease of wiring.

4 Voltage drop will take place within lengthy cable runs when the current drawn is high or running at maximum. Use a larger cable or calculate your new size mathematically.

5 Apply a *rating factor* to cables in contact with thermal insulation or which are grouped together.

6 Do not drill or notch timber joists randomly as this could cause structural weakness. If in doubt, ask someone who knows.

7 Add floor traps when using the joint box method of wiring.

Separated extra-low-voltage (SELV) lighting

Halogen *extra-low-voltage* spotlights are an efficient way of providing high-intensity illumination for display and domestic applications. When applied to recessed lighting fittings, lamps have a clear, toughened glass cover to protect against humidity and general deterioration of the reflector. Figure 4.121 illustrates a typical extra-low-voltage halogen lamp.

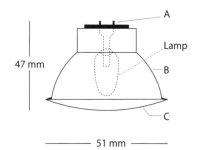

Figure 4.121 – *An extra-low-voltage halogen lamp. A, contact pins; B, reflector; C, toughened glass cover.*

There are two methods of wiring SELV lighting:

- the central transformer method
- the multi-transformer method.

The central transformer method

Figure 4.122 illustrates the basic wiring arrangements serving this type of installation. Keep in mind the following points when you are working with this method of wiring:

- The *volt amp* (VA) rating of your transformer must match or over-accommodate for the potential load in amps of your *secondary circuit;* the low voltage lamps. Remember that current flow will increase within the secondary circuit due to the extra-low voltage you are using.

- Your cable will be larger than normal due to the additional current.

- You might have to use *heatproof sleeving* over the ends of your conductors.

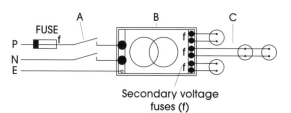

Figure 4.122 – *Extra-low-voltage lighting – single transformer method. A, double-pole control switch; B, step-down transformer served with secondary voltage fuses; C, low-voltage lights.*

As a practical example, consider the following. Six 12 volt, 50 watt halogen lamps are to be fitted in a shop window for display purposes. Calculate the current flow in the extra-low-voltage circuit. Make recommendations as to the rating of the transformer required for the proposed lighting installation.
Solution:

$$\text{Total current flowing in the extra-low-voltage circuit} = \frac{\text{total wattage}}{\text{voltage}} \quad (4.4)$$

Applying known values:

$$\text{Total current} = \frac{6 \times 50}{12}$$

Total current = 25 amps.

Calculating the size of the transformer required:

$$\text{Transformer rating} = \text{secondary voltage} \times \text{secondary current} \quad (4.5)$$

$$= 12 \times 25$$

$$= 300 \text{ volt-amp (VA)}$$

Thus a 400 VA transformer would be ideal.

- Wire a double-pole switch into the low-voltage (230 V) side of your lighting arrangement. This will avoid the use of a high-current switch on the extra-low-voltage (12 V) side of your circuit.

- Use standard cable to serve the 12 V lights unless your circuit can be completely kept apart from other 230 V cables. Regulation 411-02-06 confirms this.

- Do not connect exposed conductive parts serving a SELV system to earth. Please see

Regulations 411-02-05 to 07 for further details.

- Work out your current requirements for the 12 V side of your installation and select the size of your cable wisely.

- Do not install with metallic sheathed cable. Please refer to Regulation 411-02-06 (ii) for additional guidance.

- Hot spots will develop if you handle unprotected halogen bulbs. Be sure they are the correct voltage for your transformer as you can obtain these lamps for 6, 12 or 50 V supplies.

- Avoid *dimmer switches* as the reduced working temperature of the lamp has an effect on the halogen cycle. In time, they will blacken but to restore, the lamp should be burnt using the maximum working voltage for a short period. This will help.

The multi-transformer method

Figure 4.123 shows you the key wiring arrangements for this sort of installation. The biggest advantage is that the extra-low-voltage lights are wired in a similar way to an ordinary lighting circuit. The only difference is that each lighting point has its own *mini-transformer*. Another major advantage is that the size of the supply cable is the same as normal lighting cable.

Extra low voltage is defined as a potential difference not exceeding 50 V AC or 120 V DC when measured between *phase and neutral* or between the *phase* conductor and *earth*.

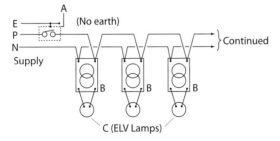

Figure 4.123 – *Extra-low-voltage lighting – the multi-transformer method. A, local switch; B, lighting transformer for one low-voltage lighting fitting; C, low-voltage light.*

Three-phase and neutral supply

Three-phase and neutral (TPN) supplies are used in industry and commerce. The system comprises three live phase conductors known as *P1, P2* and *P3* that are completely independent from each other. They are colour coded as RED, YELLOW and BLUE or *brown, black* and *grey* (EU colour harmonisation). The *neutral* conductor was colour coded *black* – but *blue* is the new colour.

Voltage measurements taken from any phase to neutral or earth will provide a value of 230 V AC. By measuring between any combinations of phases as Figure 4.124 illustrates, you will obtain a value of 400 V.

The electrical *earth conductor* is connected to the *star-point* of the local community transformer as it is with a single-phase supply. The consumer's main earth supply originates from the lead sheath of the supply cable.

Individual three-phase requirements for powering heavy motors and industrial machinery are wired from the load side of a power-rated protective device. In all, there will be *three* coloured phase conductors and a CPC and possibly a neutral, if for example, single phase is required. Figure 4.125 illustrates how a single- and a three-phase circuit are wired from a TPN distribution centre.

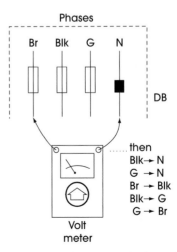

Figure 4.124 – *Testing the voltage of a three-phase and neutral supply at a distribution board.*

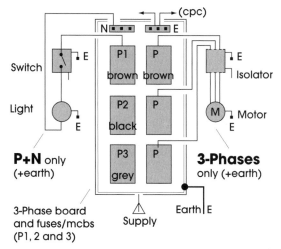

Figure 4.125 – *Wiring arrangements for single- and three-phase circuits.*

Checking whether a supply is present

It is easy to get an electric shock. Checking the circuit you are to work on will reduce this risk considerably. Figure 4.126 explains how you can do this with a simple flow chart and a light emitting diode voltage tester.

The risks associated when positioning and fixing electrical equipment

Briefly, these are the following:

- weight
- size, shape and centre of gravity
- lifting
- handling and balance, especially if you have undiagnosed diabetes
- fixing methods
- environmental concerns.

Weight

If the equipment is too heavy, get someone to help you or use mechanical means to do your job. Generally, if you have to handle a load of more than 20 kg, power-lifting equipment must be used.

Size, shape and centre of gravity

Get help if the item you are to install is large and of an odd shape. Decide between you who will provide instructions.

Lifting

Providing you are able to lift the load, please consider the following safe-lifting points:

- Stand close, feet either side of the load.
- Make sure your route is clear.
- Squat down, with knees bent and back straight, and hold your load firmly.
- Lift with your leg muscles – but keep your back straight.
- Keep your load close to your body whilst moving.
- Change direction with your feet; never twist your body.
- Avoiding lifting over shoulder height – use steps but never a chair.

Handling

Managing is easier with mechanical lifting aids but training is essential before you use them. Inspect your load for sharp or ragged edges and always kit yourself out with industrial gloves and footwear. Check there is plenty of room to position your goods before transportation takes place. If you are using mechanical means, keep a firm eye on balancing your cargo whilst on the move.

Fixing

Use suitable fixing devices for your appliance. Think about the type of building fabric you are fixing to. Examples are:

- Brickwork – wall plugs, expansion bolts.
- Concrete – wall plugs, expansion bolts, threaded stud and expansion bolts.
- Damp-proofed walls – adhesive and self-adhesive clips.
- Plaster board – spiral fixings, toggle bolts, compression fixings.

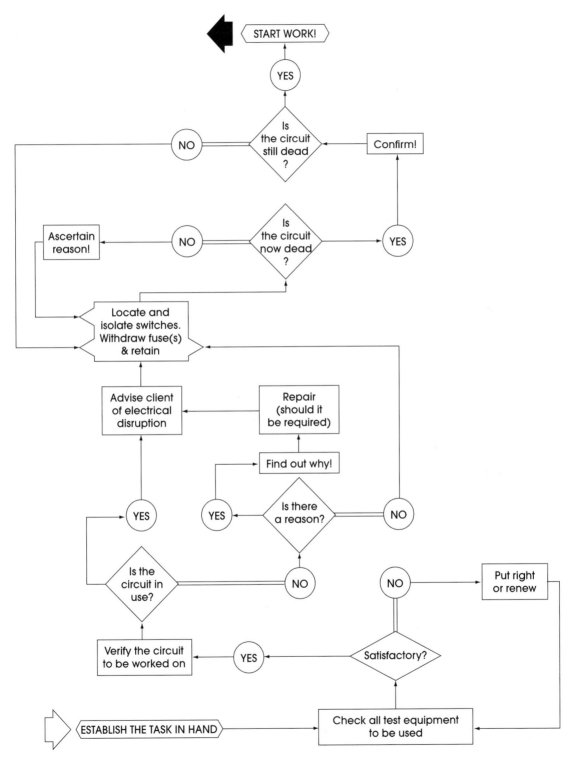

Figure 4.126 – *Disconnection procedure.*

- Steel – stud work, self-tapping screws, hit-clips®.
- Timber – wood screws, coach bolts.

Environmental concerns

You must take into consideration where you intend to place your electrical equipment. Regulations 512-06 and 522 will explain more fully.

Give special consideration when you fit apparatus in the following places:

- Airing cupboards – dampness/humidity and lack of space.
- Bathrooms and kitchens – dampness, gas and water.
- Farms – damage, animals, use of RCDs.
- Caravans – use of BS 4343 splash-proof sockets.
- Garden sheds – dampness, the use of a 30 mA RCD.
- Boiler houses – heat, vibration, use of special cables.

The effects of the following must also be looked at carefully:

- ionisation (a type of radiation)
- weather – hot, cold wind or storm
- corrosive atmosphere
- impact, stress and vibration
- animals, plants and mould growth
- the presence of foreign bodies which would harm the electrical equipment you install.

Portable tools

Building site portable hand tools, other than battery-operated tools, must be *portable appliance tested* every three months and a certificate issued.

Visual tests include the following:

1 The condition of the plug needs to be checked out.
2 The yellow service lead and the body of the appliance will need to be inspected.

Instrumentation tests include the following:

1 An insulation test (must be above 500 000 Ω) at 500 V DC.
2 Earth continuity test (ideally below 0.5Ω).
3 Flash test – but not electronic appliances (ideally under 2.5 mA).
4 Load test and fuse test.

If the appliance you are testing is OK, stick a PASSED sticky label on the appliance, as illustrated in Figure 4.127, and issue a formal certificate. Always attach a FAILED label to a faulty appliance.

Figure 4.127 – *Portable appliance test labels.*

Connecting your test instrument into a circuit

If damage is to be avoided it is important to connect instruments into a circuit correctly. Figure 4.128 illustrates seven commonly used test instruments and provides examples of their use.

Instrument	Method of testing	Comments	
Ammeter	Connect in series formation with the circuit. Measured in **amps**.	Disconnect the circuit at a convenient place. Ensure that all connections are sound.	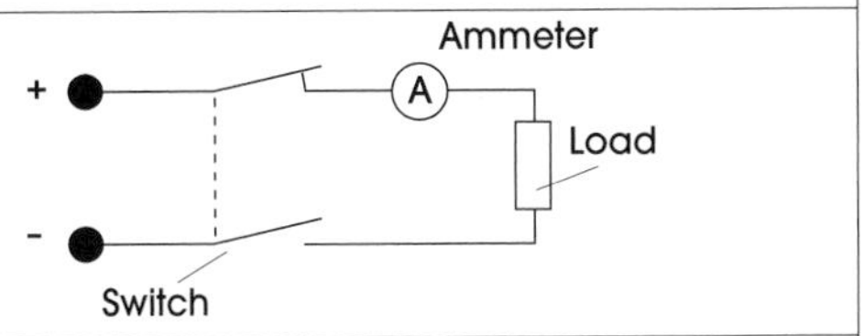
Voltmeter	Voltage measured in parallel with the circuit. Measured in **volts**.	Place the instrument probes across the incoming live and neutral supply.	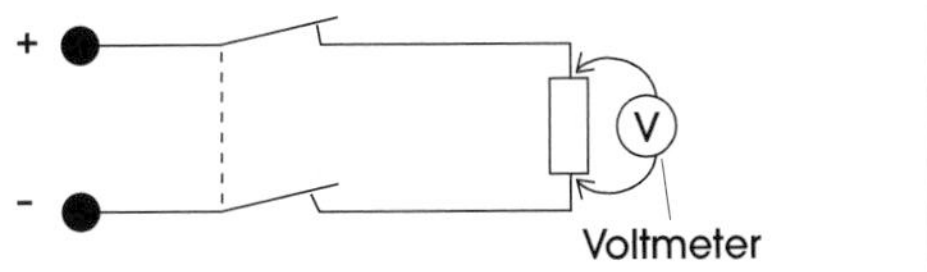
Continuity tester	Test probes are placed at either end of the conductor under test. Measured in **ohms** or **milliohms**.	Isolate the electrical supply and one end of the conductor under test.	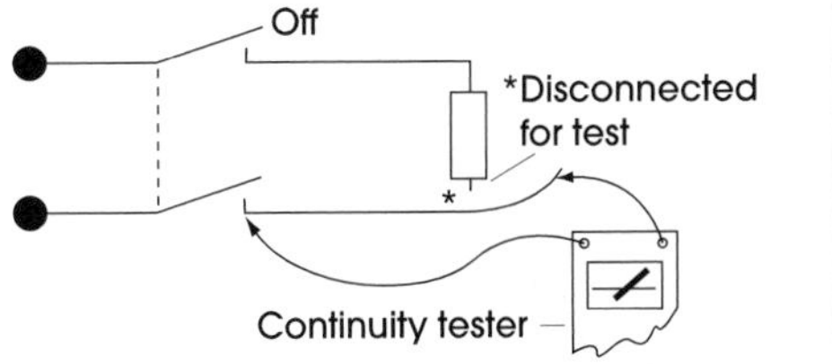
Insulation tester	Test in parallel with the circuit or with any conductor(s) and earth. Measured in **megohms** (10^6 ohms).	Isolate the electrical supply and main **neutral** when testing from a fuseboard. Remove the load from the circuit.	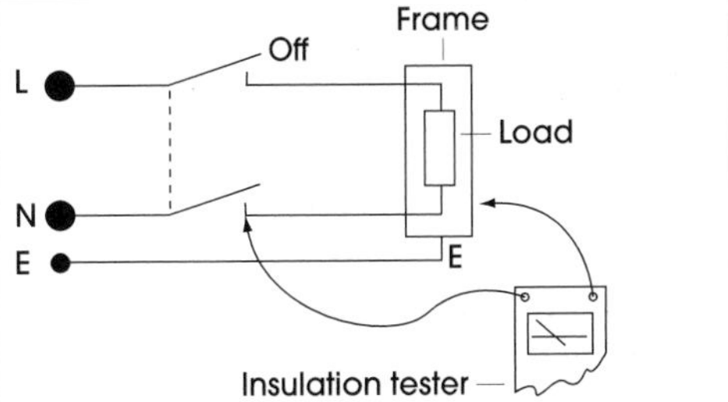
Kilowatt-hour meter	The windings in the meter are placed in series with the **live** and **neutral** supply conductors. Measured in **units** (1 Unit = 1000 **watts** × 1 **hour**).	Place securely in the correct terminals. Values are read directly from the display panel or dials.	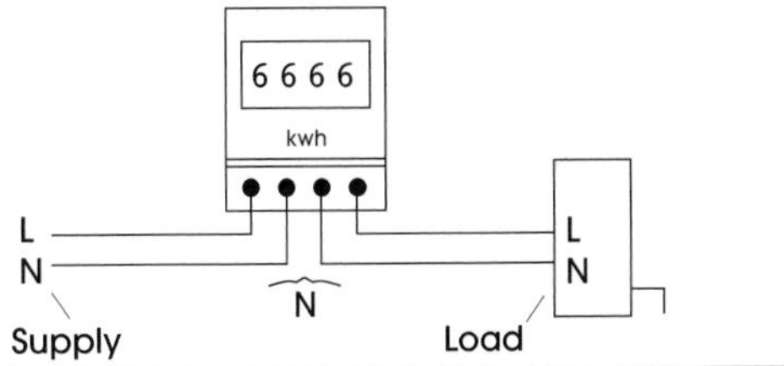
Ohm meter	The instrument test leads are placed in parallel with the component. Measured in **ohms** and **milliohms**.	Clean the leads of the component and place the test leads firmly on each end as shown.	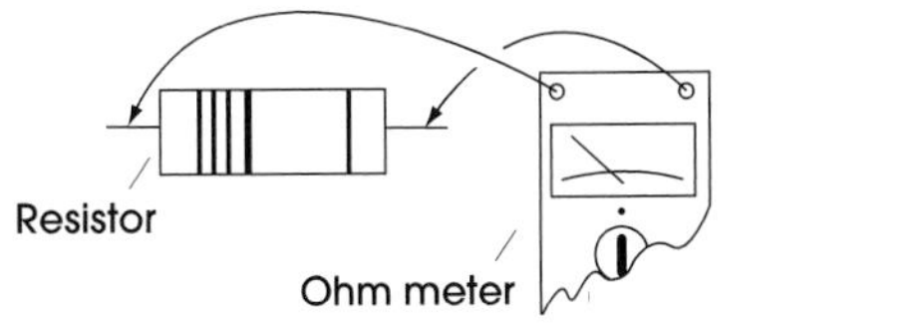
Watt meter	The instrument should be connected in circuit as illustrated. Measured in **watts** or **megawatts** (10^6 watts).	Break the circuit at convenient points and ensure that all connections are secure.	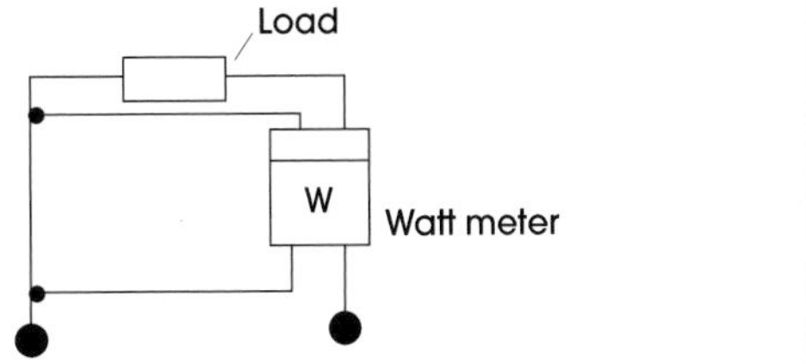

Figure 4.128 – *Connecting your test instrument into circuit.*

Summary

1 Methods of wiring extra-low-voltage lighting arrangements: (a) multi-transformer method, (b) central transformer method.

2 Do not connect exposed conductive parts serving a *separated extra-low-voltage system* to an electrical earth.

3 A three-phase and neutral system will supply the following voltages: between any phase and neutral, 230 V and between any combination of phases, 400 V.

4 Considerations associated with fixing electrical equipment are as follows: weight, size, shape, lifting and handling, your method of fixing and environmental concerns.

5 Give a little thought when equipment is placed in airing cupboards, bathrooms and kitchens, farms, caravans, garden sheds and boiler houses.

6 Other than battery-operated power tools, all site tools powered by 110 V have to be *portable appliance tested* every three months.

Review questions

1 Describe how lengths of cable basket are fitted together.

2 How would you prevent thermal buckling occurring within a PVC trunking installation?

3 Why are copper links bridged across each length of steel trunking?

4 State the space factor percentage for steel trunking installations.

5 Suggest a reason why underfloor trunking is used in industry.

6 What is meant by the term *handed* when applied to busbar trunking?

7 List three materials from which cable tray is made.

8 MI cables are available in a choice of three patterns – name two of them.

9 In your own words, briefly describe how steel wire armoured cables are prepared for termination.

10 Give four advantages of using steel conduit as a cable carrier.

11 How is PVCu conduit bent and shaped?

12 Explain how cable ducting is styled – and for what it is used.

13 Describe the type of switch best suited for an outside light but controlled from indoors.

14 What type of switching arrangement is required when three or more switches are wired to serve a single lighting point?

15 Which two values, when multiplied together, will give the size of transformer needed for a SELV lighting circuit?

Handy hints

- Clean out steel conduit thread-making dies regularly to maintain a good standard of workmanship.
- A power cable trailed on a flight of stairs spells *Danger*.
- Using a screwdriver as a chisel will cause damage to both the blade and the handle.
- Keep a small brush and a tin of touch-up paint to make good damaged steel conduit during the installation period.
- Tungsten is being constantly evaporated from the element of a domestic lamp (bulb) whilst switched 'ON'. When black appears on the inside of the glass envelope it is the beginning of the end of the lamp's useful life.
- Please remember these points when slicing through mild steel with a rotary cutting tool:
  - Replace your used wheel as intended. The centre hole and the diameter of the cutting wheel must be the same size as the original.
  - Check your cutting wheel frequently – look out for hairline cracks, etc.
  - Secure your workpiece firmly.
  - Wear eye and hand protection.
  - Keep the sparks away from combustible material – if possible work outside.
  - Keep a fire extinguisher at hand – just in case!

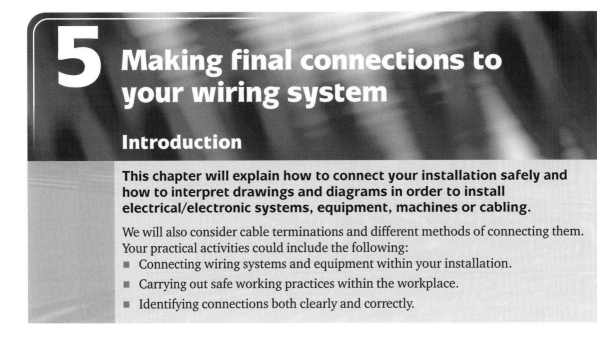

5 Making final connections to your wiring system

Introduction

This chapter will explain how to connect your installation safely and how to interpret drawings and diagrams in order to install electrical/electronic systems, equipment, machines or cabling.

We will also consider cable terminations and different methods of connecting them. Your practical activities could include the following:

- Connecting wiring systems and equipment within your installation.
- Carrying out safe working practices within the workplace.
- Identifying connections both clearly and correctly.

Cable terminations

There are many different types of cable terminations. Table 5.1 reviews a few that are common in electrical installation engineering today.

Table 5.1 – *Cable terminations.*

Type	Comment	Application/illustration
Busbar terminations	Tinned or bare copper. Sometimes bronze. Designed for twin rail busbars	Securing medium to heavy cables as illustrated in Figure 5.1
Cable lugs – crimped	Made from soft tinned copper. Various sizes	Cable terminations serving large switches, etc. Please see Figure 5.2
Pin and bullet terminations	Colour coded: RED up to 1.5 mm², BLUE up to 2.5 mm² and YELLOW up to 6 mm®	A male crimped termination is pushed into a female termination as illustrated in Figure 5.3
Mechanically screwed block terminations	Block connector strips made from polyethylene, nylon or rigid Bakelite²	For general use in electrical installation work, as shown in Figure 5.4
Crimped terminations – tag type	Insulated with hard PVC and colour coded RED, 0.75–1.5 mm², BLUE, 1.5–2.5 mm² and YELLOW, 4.0–6.0 mm² Maximum resistance between the conductor and the termination, 0.05 Ω	Various applications, e.g. motor terminals. Connected by crimping the body of the termination to the bare conductor. Many types (see Figure 5.5)
Soldered cable terminations	Made from tinned copper. Solder is melted into the top of the lug. The conductor is tinned and placed into the lug and topped up with solder. The lug is wiped clean of surplus solder and allowed to set	For terminating conductors serving heavy switchgear and busbar distribution systems (Figure 5.6)
Crimped tunnel terminations	Colour coded in three sizes and used similar to tag terminations. The uninsulated types are made from soft copper that has been split	The uninsulated type is used as part of a jointing kit for steel wire armoured cable, as in Figure 5.7

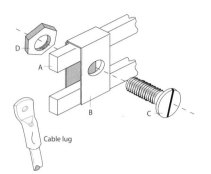

Cable lug

Figure 5.1 – *Busbar terminations.*

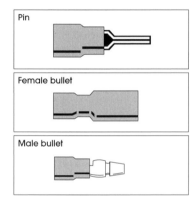

Pin

Female bullet

Male bullet

Figure 5.3 – *Pin and bullet terminations. (Reproduced by kind permission of Arena-Walsall Limited.)*

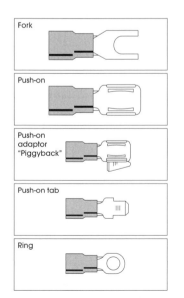

Fork

Push-on

Push-on adaptor "Piggyback"

Push-on tab

Ring

Figure 5.5 – *Hand crimped terminations. (Reproduced by kind permission of Arena-Walsall Limited.)*

Figure 5.2 – *Crimp terminations, loosely referred to as lugs. (Reproduced by kind permission of Arena-Walsall Limited.)*

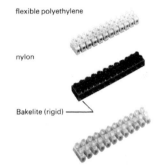

flexible polyethylene

nylon

Bakelite (rigid)

Figure 5.4 – *Mechanically screwed terminations – often called connector blocks. (Reproduced by kind permission of Arena-Walsall Limited.)*

Figure 5.6 – *Cable lug – soldered type. A, solder well; B, fixing hole.*

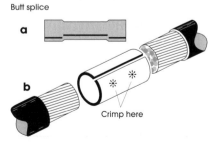

Butt splice

Crimp here

Figure 5.7 – *Tunnel terminations. (a) Insulated, hand crimped type; (b) non-insulated hand crimped type.*

Joint box terminations

The rules

1 Never use conductors that are too large for your terminal.

2 Figure 5.8 illustrates how to tailor-make your conductors to your point of termination.

3 Do not wire cable which is uncalled for into your joint box – it will hinder.

4 Place about 5 mm of cable sheath inside your joint box. Conductors must never be visible outside the joint box. See Figures 5.9 and 5.10.

5 Remove enough insulation from the conductor to fit snugly inside the terminal housing, but no more – or problems could arise.

6 Be sure all your terminals are secure. Loose terminals cause arcing – arcing generates heat and heat destroys!

7 All terminals must be sound and able to withstand the design current.

8 When you have finished, place a simple label on the lid of your joint box as guidance for those who follow you.

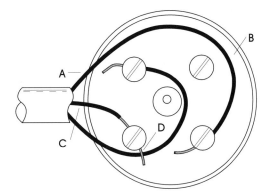

Figure 5.9 – *The insulation serving the conductor must not be visible outside a surface-mounted accessory.*

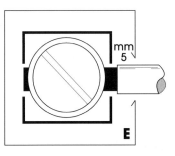

Figure 5.10 – *Place the outer sheath of the cable about 5 mm into the accessory to be connected.*

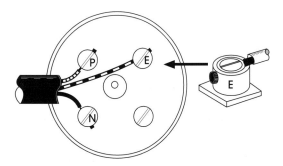

Figure 5.8 – *Cut your conductors to size. It is far more practical.*

Terminations – general guidelines

Generally, the size of your cable termination reflects its current carrying capacity. The requirement of our wiring regulations is that joints between flexible and non-flexible conductors must be easily reached for inspection. However, this does not apply to the following joints:

■ Jointed cables buried in the ground.

■ Joints enclosed in fireproof building material but not mechanically clamped.

■ Joints formed by welding, soldering and brazing.

■ Compression-type joints contained within a box made from fire-resistant material, as specified in BS 476 Part 5.

To avoid *over-current problems*, it is important that you know the current and voltage rating of your terminal.

Accessibility

You must be able to get to your joint box terminations easily – this is important. For example, it would be unwise to site a joint box under a tiled floor or in an area that would be difficult to get to when all building work had finished.

When opening a joint box, check the terminations are undamaged, electrically/mechanically sound and that the joint box is not broken or cracked.

The quality of a termination

A brief list follows, pointing out how careless work can have an effect on the quality of the termination:

- Too much exposed bare copper showing beyond the point of termination could cause future problems. See Figure 5.11.

- Under-tightening the terminal point will cause terminal damage through arcing when on load.

- Using the wrong size or a damaged screwdriver will cause physical harm to the head of the terminal screw, as shown in Figure 5.12.

- Tightening with a battery-operated screwdriver can cause the terminal screw to rotate within itself without tightening inside the terminal housing.

- Not securely fixing your joint box to a wooden joist or masonry block could mean that any physical movement associated with your cables will loosen conductors connected within your joint box. Clip all your cables!

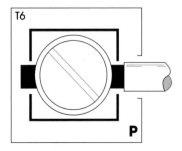

Figure 5.11 – *In this illustration, too much exposed bare copper conductor is showing beyond the point of termination.*

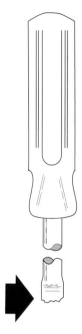

Figure 5.12 – *Using a blunt or damaged tool can affect the quality of the termination.*

Confirming the soundness of an electrical joint

This is a simple way to check you have the required level of continuity. It is ideal if you have a soldered joint.

You will need to use a recently calibrated milliohm meter that is both reliable and undamaged.

To test:

- Zero your meter by touching the two test leads together.

- Place your instrument probes either side of your joint.

- Press the test button. The value obtained must be near to zero but no greater than 0.05 Ω.

- If higher – remake your joint and retest.

- As a final check, touch your test leads together to verify that your instrument is working as intended.

Single- and multi-phase circuits

Domestic lighting circuits are installed using PVC sheathed cable and originate from a miniature circuit breaker distribution centre. Use either 1.0 or 1.5 mm² cable.

Wire industrial lighting arrangements with 1.5 mm² single cables drawn through steel conduit or trunking.

Figure 5.13 shows you how to wire a basic one-way lighting circuit – that is, switched from one position only. We will deal with the practical arrangements later.

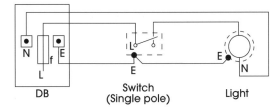

Figure 5.13 – *Wiring a one-way lighting arrangement in schematic form.*

Polarity of switches

The polarity of a conductor is whether that particular conductor is either *phase* or *neutral*. The phase conductor in the EU is BROWN whilst the neutral is BLUE. A brown *phase* conductor will always serve a switch controlling a lighting arrangement – never a neutral. If this were to

happen, the *phase* conductor would still be live at the lamp holder, even when the switch was in the OFF position. Figure 5.14 illustrates this.

Two-way switching

Figure 5.15 demonstrates how a two-way switch is wired to control a lighting circuit using the joint box method. For this, you must use twin- and three-core sheathed cables.

An alternative technique is to wire the circuit without the use of a six-terminal joint box. This is illustrated in Figure 5.16. This is the *conversion method* and has the advantage of having all cable terminations easily reached from one level. It is often easier to install.

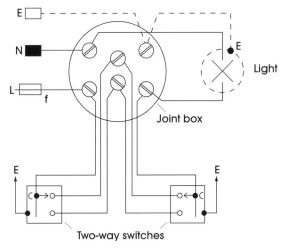

Figure 5.15 – *Wiring a two-way lighting arrangement by means of a joint box.*

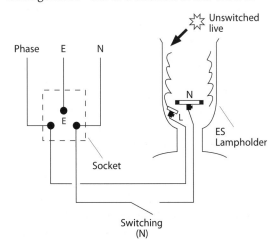

Figure 5.14 – *The phase conductor must always be connected to the live side of a switch. Never connect directly to the light.*

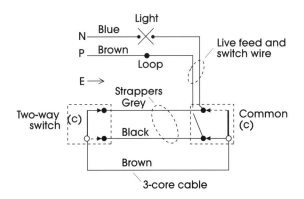

Figure 5.16 – *Wiring a two-way lighting arrangement without the use of a joint box.*

Intermediate switching

Use this style of switching within a two-way lighting arrangement where three or more switches are required as the means of control. Wire your new intermediate switch within an existing two-way switching arrangement as shown in Figure 5.17. You can have as many as you like – there are no restrictions.

Use only the *black* and *grey* core of the three-core cable. Cut the two *brown* core conductors and connect – see Figure 5.18.

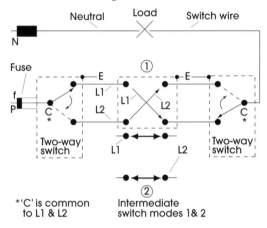

*'C' is common to L1 & L2

Intermediate switch modes 1 & 2

Figure 5.17 – *This illustration will show you how an intermediate switch is connected into a two-way lighting arrangement.*

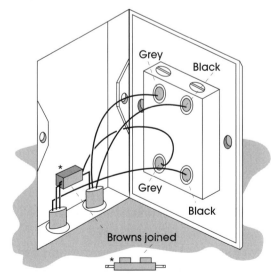

Figure 5.18 – *The two red conductors forming an intermediate switching arrangement are connected together within a connector.*

Types of switches

The design of switches follows in summary form:

1 Single gang (the name given to a stand-alone switch):
   - one-way (two terminals)
   - two-way (three terminals)
   - intermediate (four terminals)
   - double-pole (meaning that both phase and neutral conductors are switched as one – Figure 5.19)
   - dimmer (both one- and two-way)
   - sensi-touch (just a touch will switch your light on)
   - pull cord switches (both one- and two-way)
   - time lag (both mechanically operated and electronically styled)
   - passive infrared wall switches
   - audio switches (a handclap will trigger the switching device)
   - key switch (used for emergency lighting arrangements).

2 Double gang (the name given when two switches are side by side, as illustrated in Figure 5.20):
   - two-way
   - dimmer.

3 Three-, four- and six-gang lighting switches: all switches are identical and two-way.

4 Eight-, nine-, twelve-, eighteen- and twenty-four-gang switches. These are all modular switches supplied in kit form consisting of:
   - a steel accessory box
   - switches, indicating lamps, key switches and blanking off components
   - fuse units, push button switches and miniature flex outlet modules
   - switch mounting yokes, known also as grids
   - a multi-gang decorative switch face-plate

These are ideal for use in a large installation. Figure 5.21 shows a four-gang modular arrangement served with different accessories.

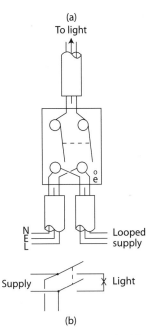

(a)
To light

N
E
L

Looped
supply

Supply ——— ✗ Light

(b)

Figure 5.19 – *Part (a) illustrates a double-pole switching arrangement where both the phase and neutral conductors are switched in one action. Part (b) shows this arrangement schematically.*

Figure 5.20 – *A domestic two-gang lighting switch. (Reproduced by kind permission of Walsall Conduits Limited.)*

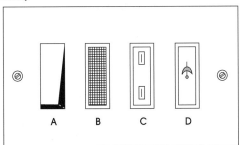

A   B   C   D

Figure 5.21 – *A modular switch can be fitted with different accessories – switches, dimmers, fuses, etc. A, lighting switch; B, indicator light; C, key switch for an emergency light; D, bell push.*

Final power circuits

Final ring circuit

It is possible to incorporate an unlimited number of sockets within a final ring circuit provided you meet certain conditions. Figure 5.22 illustrates such a circuit and summarises the regulations for this type of installation. Carry out your wiring in the usual way, clipping to timber joists or just hide within the fabric of the building, or conceal your cables under the plaster line, covered with steel or plastic channelling. Rewiring will then be less of a problem, if required.

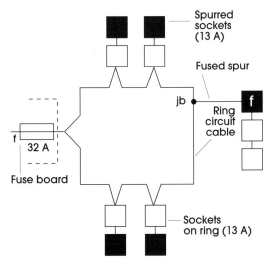

Figure 5.22 – *A final ring circuit to serve a maximum floor area of 100 m². You can use PVC, rubber or MI cables. Cross-sectional areas: aluminium, 4.0 mm²; copper, 2.5 mm² and MI, 1.5 mm².*

Spurred socket outlets

A spurred socket is a socket that is supplied from the final ring circuit as illustrated in Figure 5.23.

A spur may be supplied from one of the following:

- a mainline socket within the ring
- a joint box incorporated within the ring
- a fused connection unit.

Only one spurred socket is allowed per final ring circuit socket. If, for example, you had incorporated ten sockets within your ring circuit, then you can add a further ten, as spurs, using a twin and earth sheathed cable for each socket.

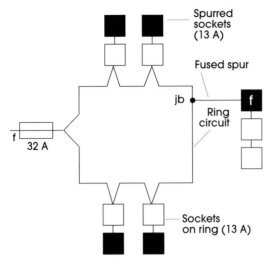

Figure 5.23 – *Spurred socket outlets wired from mainline final circuit sockets.*

An exception to this rule

You may install an unlimited number of sockets as a spur wired from your final ring circuit providing your source of power is from a *fused connection unit* within your final ring circuit. Figure 5.24 illustrates this point.

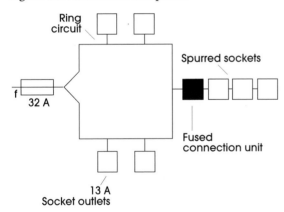

Figure 5.24 – *A fused connection unit included within a final ring circuit can supply an unlimited number of socket outlets.*

Wiring into your distribution centre

Figure 5.25 illustrates the basic components of a typical distribution centre. The *circuit protective conductors* are connected directly into the multi-way terminal bar, labelled 'A'. The BSEN symbol for *earth* is shown in Figure 5.26. This bar is

completely stand-alone and the sleeved conductors are colour coded *green/yellow*. The two heavy terminals, 'C', serve the incoming supply conductors and are usually 25 mm in cross-sectional area. The common distribution block, labelled 'B', serves all your out-going neutral conductors. Place these in the same numerical circuit order as your brown phase conductors connected from the top terminal of your over-current protection device, labelled 'D'.

Each circuit originates from its own over-current protection device – with heavier current consuming circuits nearest to the main switch. Remember to write up your circuit destination charts – this is important!

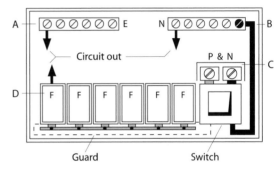

Figure 5.25 – *The basic sections of a typical fuse board or MCB distribution centre.*

Earth   BS EN 60617

Figure 5.26 – *The graphical symbol for an electrical earth.*

Radial circuits

Figure 5.27 illustrates the requirements for a standard radial circuit serving a floor area of up to 75 m^2, whereas Figure 5.28 shows the technical needs of a circuit when the area worked is up to 50 m^2. You then reduce your conductor from 4.0 mm^2 to 2.5 mm^2 when PVC insulated and sheathed cable is used.

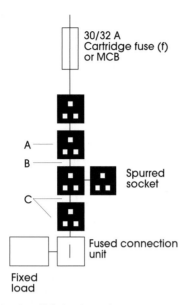

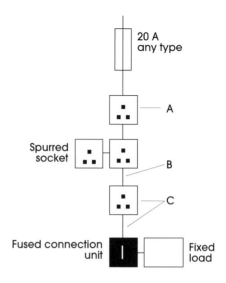

Figure 5.27 – *A radial circuit serving an area up to 75 m². A, unlimited number of 13 amp sockets; B, conductor sizes: PVC or rubber insulated, 4 mm²; C, radial sockets and one fused connection unit to serve a fixed load.*

Figure 5.28 – *Radial circuit serving a floor area up to 50 m². A, unlimited number of socket outlets; B, conductor sizes: PVC or rubber insulated 2.5 mm²; C, a fused connection unit supplied from a radial socket.*

Table 5.2 – *A selection of final circuits. Correction factors not applied.*

Circuit	Size of your conductor (mm²)	Rating of your protective device (amps)
Final ring circuit (using sheathed cables)	2 × 2.5	32
Domestic cooker	6.0, 10*	32 or 40*
Immersion heater (standard 3 kW)	2.5	16
Night storage heater (up to 3 kW)	2.5	16
Smoke detector/alarm	1.0	6
General lighting (1200 W per circuit)	1.0 or 1.5*	6 or 10*
Gas-fired central heating controls	1.0 or 1.5*	6 or 10*
Dedicated radial for a computer	2.5	20
Dedicated circuit serving a washing machine	2.5	20

Please note that figures accompanied with an asterisk (*) are connected. For an example, a 6 mm² conductor will be served with an over-current protection device of 32 amps but a 10 mm² conductor would be fitted to a 40 amp device.

Domestic final circuits

There are many and all wired in a similar way. Only the size of the conductor and the circuit protection device will vary.

Table 5.2 lists a few common circuits and recommends the size of cable to use, together with the rating of the over-current protection you must fit when PVC sheathed cable is laid under the following conditions:

- Routed away from thermal insulation.

- A stand-alone cable which is not grouped with others.

- In an ambient temperature of no more than 30°C.

- When your over-current protection device takes the form of a miniature circuit breaker (MCB).

Figure 5.29 shows the wiring for a typical domestic immersion heater circuit.

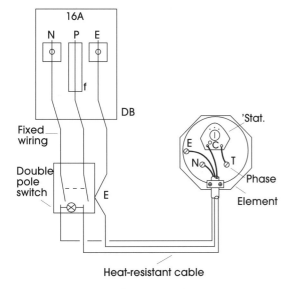

Figure 5.29 – *A typical immersion heater circuit (DB indicates distibution centre).*

Steel accessory boxes

Figure 5.30 illustrates a selection of these, which accommodate and protect the reverse of an accessory from mechanical damage or contamination. Cables must be neatly laid and capped with channelling, as shown in Figure

5.31, when your wiring is hidden beneath the plaster line. Allow the leading edge of your steel accessory box to stick out of the unplastered wall about 5 mm: it will then be reasonably flush with the finished plaster line. Figure 5.32 illustrates this.

Use *wood screws* and *expansion plugs* to fit your box into the recessed wall – never use nails! Now, level your box and fit rubber grommets in the holes to protect your cable from damage.

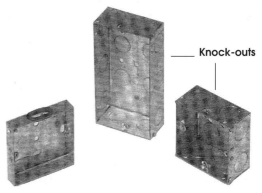

Figure 5.30 – *Pressed steel, first-fix accessory boxes – hole knock-out type. (Reproduced by kind permission of Arena-Walsall Limited.)*

Figure 5.31 – *Steel or PVCu channelling, sometimes referred to as capping. This product will help to protect your cables during the first fix and plastering stages of your job. Fitted with care, it will also provide a means of drawing cables in and out should alterations be needed during the course of the installation. (Reproduced by kind permission of Arena-Walsall Limited.)*

147

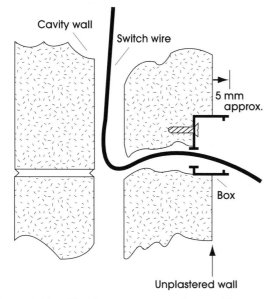

Figure 5.32 – *Allowing your accessory box to stick out slightly from the face of an unplastered wall will avoid using long machine screws during the second-fix period of your installation.*

After the plasterer has finished

When the plaster is dry, remove any contamination from inside your box and trim any plaster overhang from the edges. Retap the threaded lugs if they are full of dried plaster, then carry out the following tasks:

- Remove the sheath of the cable with a pair of sharp side cutters.

- Cut the conductors to suit the position of the terminals – leave sufficient slack.

- Remove about 10 mm of insulation from each conductor with wire strippers.

- Once prepared, place all common conductors into the correct terminal housing – the *brown* conductors within terminal 'L', and the *blue* neutral conductors in terminal 'N'. Use the common earth terminal to connect the bare circuit protective conductors, sleeved with *green/yellow* oversleeving. Make sure all your terminals are tight**!**

Planning your installation

There are many different circuits and Table 5.2 has provided us with some of them. Circuits such as these are included within the design stages of an installation but consider correction factors when selecting the size of the cables you require.

The majority of circuits you will install are classed as *radial circuits*, each consisting of one cable from your distribution centre, individually protected by an *over-current device* (mcb or fuse).

Immersion heater circuit

Figure 5.33 shows a typical 3 kW domestic water heater circuit. The total current drawn from this appliance is calculated by applying expression (5.1):

$$I = W/V \qquad\qquad (5.1)$$

where I is the total current in amps being drawn from the circuit, W is the power in watts generated and V is the nominal voltage of the supply.

Substituting figures, then $I = 3000/230 = 13$ amps.

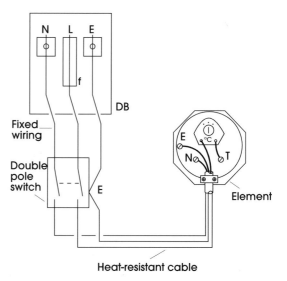

Figure 5.33 – *A good installation tip is to sleeve the plastic insulation serving the conductors to the heating element with coloured heatproof oversleeving. It gets very warm in the terminal housing! The flexible cable routed from a locally positioned double-pole switch must be of the heat-resistant type.*

It is usual to wire an immersion heater circuit with 2.5 mm² PVC sheathed cable for domestic use. Use this size cable for heaters up to 4 kW.

Central heating control circuit

Figure 5.34 outlines the basic wiring arrangements, in schematic form, for a central heating control supply. Take your supply from a final ring circuit, fused connection unit or serve directly from your local distribution centre terminating in a double pole switch as a means of isolation. Current drawn from the supply is low so you can use a lighting grade cable supplied from a 10 amp mcb.

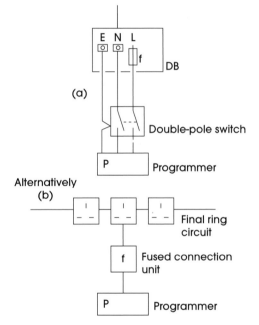

Figure 5.34 – *Alternative wiring arrangements for a central heating control supply.*

Domestic cooker circuit

It is important to match your cable size to the total kilowatt rating of the cooker you are wiring and any cable factors that might be applicable. A diversity factor is permitted and is explained by studying expressions 5.2 and 5.3. This will reduce the size of the conductor used to serve the circuit.

In general, the following expression is used:

$$I = 10 + (0.3It) \qquad (5.2)$$

If there is a socket incorporated within the cooker switch, then:

$$I = 15 + (0.3It) \qquad (5.3)$$

where I is the current in amps after an allowance for diversity has been made and It is the total current demand of the cooking appliance.

As a practical example, a domestic cooker is found to have a total load of 10.7 kW (10 700 W) and is connected to a 230 volt domestic supply. The cooker switch has a 13 amp socket incorporated within it. By using expressions (8.10) and (5.3), calculate the maximum current demand:

$$I = W/V$$

Substituting for known values: $I = 10\ 700/230 = 46.521$ amps.

Allowing for a diversity (5.3) then $I = 15 + (0.3It)$. Substituting figures, $I = 15 + (0.3 \times 46.5) = 28.95$ amps.

A 6 mm² PVC insulated and sheathed cable would be ideal but remember to check for correction factors. You may have to increase the size of your cable to meet these demands.

Provide means of isolation

See Regulation 476-03-04. Figure 5.35 illustrates the standard method of wiring a cooker and hob

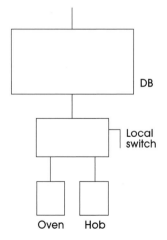

Figure 5.35 – *Basic wiring requirements for a split domestic cooker circuit.*

that are separate from one another. A 32 amp over-current device protects the two appliances. When a cooker hood is required, take your supply from the kitchen final ring circuit via a fused connection unit. It is easier than wiring from your local distribution centre.

Fixed wall heater circuit

Figure 5.36 illustrates how this type of circuit is wired – terminating within a double pole switch. If you are thinking about installing a wall heater in a bathroom, the control switch is best placed outside. Wiring is by use of 2.5 mm² PVC sheathed cable. Connect the flex from the accessory to a flexed outlet plate placed by the side of your wall heater. Regulation 476-03-04 confirms this.

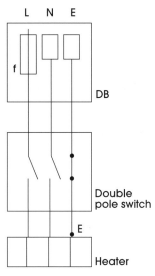

Figure 5.36 – *Basic wiring requirements for a fixed wall heater. When your heater is in a bathroom, the isolating switch will be placed outside the bathroom door and the flexible cable serving the heater will be connected to a flex-outlet plate.*

Electric shower circuit

First check out the current rating – use Expression (8.10) and then find out whether correction factors need apply to your circuit. Usually you will install either 6 or 10 mm² PVC sheathed cable, protected by a 32 or 40 amp circuit breaker. Figure 5.37 illustrates the basic circuit requirements. Connect to a permanent

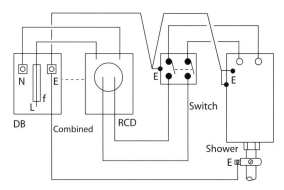

Figure 5.37 – *The basic wiring requirements for an electric shower when served by a residual current device, added for additional protection.*

electrical supply through a 30 or 40 amp double pole switch that has a mechanical switching movement separated by at least 3 mm. Clearly identify your switch and, if in the form of a wall switch, site outside the shower room. Your wiring must originate directly from the control switch without the use of a plug and socket arrangement. Remember to install an independent *circuit protective conductor* to serve as a supplementary, equipotential bond. This will link between simultaneously accessible exposed conductive parts of the equipment and extraneous metal forming part of the infrastructure of the shower room. In other words, if you can touch metal with both hands whilst standing in the shower room – bond it.

For additional safety, fit a 30 mA residual current device into your circuit. Regulations 554-05-02 and 03 confirm this.

Doorbell (transformer) circuit

Connect your transformer to the permanently live supply of your ground floor lighting circuit via a fused connection unit – fused at 2 amps. Figure 5.38 illustrates this. Alternatively, you can take a supply directly from the local distribution centre terminating at a high-level double pole switch or use the DIN rail within your distribution unit to mount your transformer. The mcb serving the transformer will provide a means of isolation if required.

When wiring the extra-low-voltage side in simple bell wire you must take into consideration

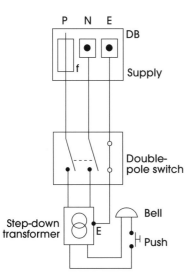

Figure 5.38 – *A simple doorbell circuit using a small step-down transformer as the means of power.*

the phenomenon of voltage drop. You will not have to worry if it is a house bell you are wiring but a bell within a warehouse is another thing! A practical example follows.

A 3 volt under-dome bell circuit recently installed to serve a warehouse sounded feeble even though the terminal voltage was correct. The current drawn from the circuit was 0.45 amps. The total resistance of the circuit was to be 3.2 Ω. Prove theoretically why the bell sounded so weak.

By applying expression (8.12):

voltage drop = IR

where I is the current within the circuit in amps and R is the total resistance of the circuit in ohms.

Substituting for known values, then voltage drop = $0.45 \times 3.2 = 1.44$ volts (and the answer why the bell sounded so feeble – any suggestions?)

Your garage installation

First, calculate your maximum current demand and choose a suitable cable. Let us assume that the garage is detached from the house. Route your supply cable either overhead or underground – the choice is yours, but if you decide on an underground installation then use

steel wire armoured cable. PVC sheathed cable fixed to a catenary wire is ideal for overhead delivery. Figure 5.39 describes this arrangement in schematic form. Allow a Type C or D miniature circuit breaker to protect your garage supply cable. This will be better if a freezer is placed in there.

Consider the following. The design of a recently built garage was to include the following circuits:

- one 3 kW immersion heater
- one 100 watt lighting point
- one fused connection unit to serve a fixed 3kW wall heater.

Calculate the total potential current demand on the garage installation (230 volt supply):

Total power = 6100 watts.

Current drawn (expression (8.10)) = watts/amps.

Substituting for figures then garage drawn = 6100/230 = 26.5 amps.

Choose the size of your supply cable by referring to the Wiring Regulations (BS 7671).

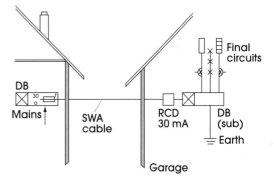

Figure 5.39 – *A garage installation using an overhead catenary cable.*

Off-peak (restricted use) installations

Outlined in Figure 5.40 are the general requirements for this type of installation. You will need a suitable size distribution centre as all your circuits will be radials terminating at a double pole switch. Final ring circuits play no role whatsoever in off-peak installation work.

151

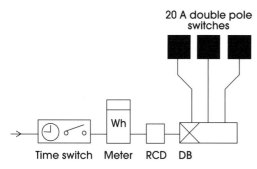

Figure 5.40 – *General requirements for the control of an off-peak installation. (The meter and the time switch, now usually a single unit, are provided by the supplier.)*

Domestic installations are for night storage heating loads whilst farms take advantage of this system by using off-peak electricity for cooling bulk milk tanks whilst most of us are in bed fast asleep. Protection for most appliances is by a 16 amp miniature circuit breaker but you may come across larger ones from time to time requiring at least 32 amps.

A brief look at industrial circuit arrangements

Figure 5.41 illustrates a typical wiring method used to control an industrial compressor motor serving a cold room installation. The wiring for each control switch is in *series formation* (one after the other) and provides a means of switching 'ON'/'OFF' an electromagnetic switching coil. Other than the main control switch, all other switching devices are automatic. They are triggered by outside forces such as temperature, high or low pressure or time clocks.

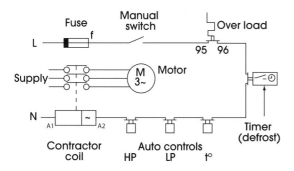

Figure 5.41 – *A basic control circuit serving a cold room installation.*

HP and *LP* represent the high and low-pressure switches and *t°* the control thermostat.

The coil is energised when all switching modes are *made* ('ON') and the machine will operate. Provide over-current protection for your control circuit separately as your motor circuit current will be high and will require a discrete higher rated breaker.

You can apply this type of idea to any manner of circuits requiring outside management.

Wire industrial circuits within trunking and steel conduit. MI cable is also an option – never use PVC sheathed cable.

Motor circuits with remote over-current warning facilities

Wire your motor circuit with a remote over-current warning mode as illustrated in Figure 5.42.

Find the rating of the motor, or the amount of current that is safe to draw from the circuit, on the manufacturer's nameplate. This value is a rough guide to your cable size – but do check elsewhere for guidance.

You can wire your remote warning indicator circuit with a lighting grade cable (1.0 or 1.5 mm²) as the current demand is very low but provide for over-current protection, independent from your motor circuit.

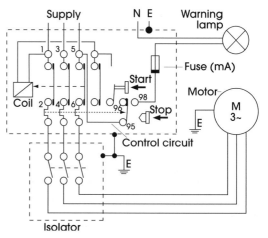

Figure 5.42 – *Direct-on-line (DOL) motor control circuit showing the wiring of a remote overload indicator-warning lamp.*

A question of voltage drop

BS 7671 Regulation 525-01-02 is satisfied when a voltage drop occurring between the supplier's terminals and a fixed current-using appliance or equipment does not exceed 4% of the nominal voltage (U_0) of the supply. Too much voltage drop will have an effect on other current-using equipment. Please consider the following – ignore correction factors for this exercise.

A 20 metre, 230 volt single-phase circuit is designed to supply 27.75 amps. The circuit wiring will be single copper PVC insulated cable drawn through steel conduit. Calculate your minimum size cable to act in accordance with our regulations governing voltage drop.

Given that:

maximum permitted voltage drop = 0.4 × voltage

Substituting for figures, the maximum voltage drop = 0.4 × 230 = 9.2 volts.

Given that:

actual voltage drop = mV/A/m × $I\,l$/1000

(5.4)

where mV/A/m is the millivolt drop per amp per metre, I is the current flowing in the conductor and l is the length of the cable in metres, then substituting for known values:

9.2 = mV/A/m × 27.75 × 20/1000

Now, cross-multiply:

9.2 × 1000 = mV/A/m × 555

and divide each side of your equation by 555:

mV/A/m = 9200/555 = 16.57 mV/A/m

Choosing the size of your cable

Check out Regulation Table 4D2B and look for a suitable cable having a voltage drop of less than 16.57 mV/A/m. Figure 5.43 has edited this data but if you want to be more exact, then give a little thought to the surrounding temperature of your installation.

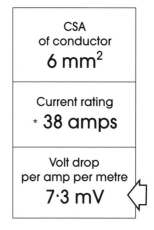

CSA of conductor
6 mm²
Current rating
* **38 amps**
Volt drop per amp per metre
7·3 mV

Figure 5.43 – *Voltage drop per amp per metre and the current-carrying capability for a 6 mm² copper conductor. (* Installed in conduit; two cables at single phase, AC.)*

Flying leads

Green/yellow insulated flying leads fitted from the back of a steel accessory box to the earth terminal serving an accessory need to fit in the following situations. Regulation 543-02-07 will provide you with further detail:

■ Where your installation is within steel trunking or conduit and the carrier acts as a protective conductor.

■ When your installation is wired using mineral insulated cable.

■ When the circuit has been wired using steel wire armoured cable.

■ When both threaded lugs serving your steel accessory box are adjustable.

The cross-sectional area of a flying lead must be at least equal to that of the CPC serving the accessory.

Multi-phase circuits
A brief description

Multi-phase circuits are reserved for the power requirements of certain types of electric motor. The three live phases, known as *P1, P2* and *P3*, respectively, are electrically separate from each other. The voltage produced has a displacement of 120° between each of the phases generated. This creates an automatic rotating magnetic field and, when applied to an electric motor, will cause the motor to rotate. There is no need for a neutral connection; only the three phases are used. Figure 5.44 illustrates this.

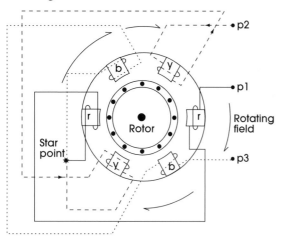

Figure 5.44 – *A three-phase squirrel cage motor. When served with 400 volts it produces a rotating magnetic field with the windings.*

Connecting a three-phase motor

The winding arrangement to serve this type of machine is either *star* or *delta,* as shown in Figure 5.45. Connect each of your external phase conductors to a terminal housing connection point labelled *U1, V1* and *W1* in that order, as illustrated in Figure 5.46. On very old motors, the markings will show *L1, L2* and *L3*, or sometimes the letters *A1, B2* and *C3* are used.

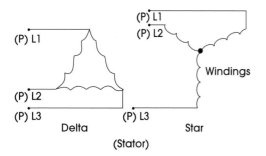

Figure 5.45 – *The windings of a three-phase motor are positioned in either star or delta arrangement.*

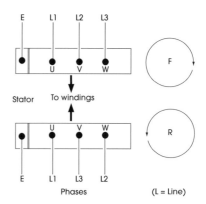

Figure 5.46 – *To reverse the spin of a three-phase motor, swap over any two phases.*

At the time of publication of this book, the colour codes given to the principal phases were as follows:

- Phase 1 (U1) – *BROWN*
- Phase 2 (V1) – *BLACK*
- Phase 3 (W1) – *GREY*

Reversing the spin of a three-phase motor

To do this just interchange any two-phase conductors as shown in the last illustration. It is good practice to swap over the two outer phase conductors.

Voltage values

A nominal (in name only) voltage of 400 volts is available between any combinations of two phases and a value of 230 volts between any phase conductor and earth.

Three-phase distribution centres

Distribution centres provide five separated sections to house the following:

- Phase 1 – Brown
- Phase 2 – Black
- Phase 3 – Grey
- Neutral – Blue
- Earth (the CPC) – Green/Yellow.

Each of the five supply conductors are securely connected to a separate distribution bar which houses termination screws for either outgoing conductors or provides the means to serve fuses or miniature circuit breakers with power. Figure 5.47 illustrates this. Terminate each coloured phase conductor within the top section of a miniature circuit breaker whose current rating will protect your circuit from over-current or short circuit conditions. Lighting circuits will require a 6 or 10 amp breaker, heating control circuitry 2 amps, washing machines and dishwashers need 16 amp protection whilst cookers and final ring circuits will both originate from a separate 32 amp breaker. Terminate your black neutral conductors within the neutral distribution bar in the same order as its accompanying phase conductor. This rule also applies to your CPCs when connected to the earth bar serving your distribution centre.

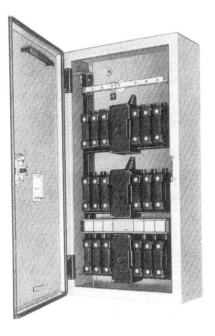

Figure 5.47 – *A three-phase distribution centre – High Rupturing Capacity (HRC) type. (Reproduced by kind permission of Arena-Walsall Limited.)*

Electrical drawings explained

There are five types of electrical drawings:

- block diagram
- circuit diagram
- general assembly diagram
- schematic diagram
- wiring diagram.

Block diagram

A useful way to forward an idea without the need for technical detail as it provides a means of focusing on potential problem areas and enables planning for a later stage. Figure 5.48 is an example of a block diagram for motor speed control.

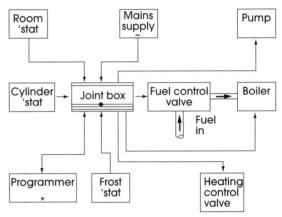

Figure 5.48 – *A block diagram will forward an idea without the need for technical detail. This illustration provides detail for a central heating control centre.*

Circuit diagram

This type of diagram uses simple graphical symbols from BSEN 60617 to represent components, accessories and appliances and shows the way they are interconnected. In Figure 5.49, vertical and horizontal lines represent your wiring and the graphical symbols are those published by British Standards. Do not use custom-made symbols – they cause confusion for those who follow.

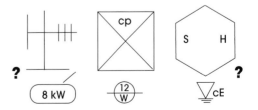

Figure 5.49 – *DIY location symbols cause confusion for others.*

General assembly diagram

This is a physical layout diagram and shows the exact detail of the location of components, accessories and appliances. Each component part is drawn, labelled and sometimes numbered in proportion to its size, as illustrated in Figure 5.50.

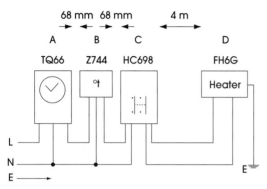

Figure 5.50 – *A general assembly diagram – also known as a physical layout diagram.*

Schematic diagram

Schematic diagrams use formal graphical symbols. They represent cabling drawn as one line, as shown in Figure 5.51.

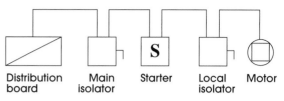

Figure 5.51 – *Schematic diagrams use formal BS or BS/EN symbols.*

Wiring diagram

Electrical wiring diagrams show point-to-point wiring interconnections to serve your installation. An ideal drawing for site or small works is illustrated in Figure 5.52.

▬▬▬▬▬▬▬

Are your connections mechanically sound?

Two methods for checking are generally accepted:

- By inspection/handling and knowledge of the size and type of connection required for your task.

- By using a milliohm meter and measuring the resistance across the joint.

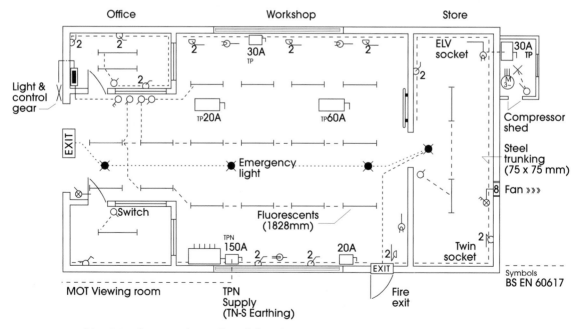

Figure 5.52 – *This wiring diagram of a small workshop shows point-to-point wiring to allow the installation to be carried out.*

Soldered joints

Your soldered joint must look bright and shiny but, if it appears dull and looks pitted, you must resolder, as it is most likely to be a dry joint. That means poor electrical continuity!

To prove your joint is sound, first check your milliohm test meter and then place the leads across either side of the joint and measure the resistance. If your joint is okay, the value you will obtain will be very near to zero but no more than 0.05Ω. A dry joint will produce a much higher value – probably nearer to 0.5Ω. After testing, retest your meter by touching the leads together.

Mechanical joints

To recap and bring together items from previous sections:

- Your joint must accommodate the conductors you are to join.
- Tailor-make and route your conductor to your chosen terminal.
- Tight terminals are essential.
- Terminals must be accessible and be able to withstand the design current.
- Loose terminals cause arcing – arcing creates heat and heat causes damage!
- Over-tightening can damage the thread serving the terminal screw.
- A blunt screwdriver will damage the head of the terminal screw.

Checking terminals are suitable

Terminals must be suitable for the purpose they are intended for. It would be stupid to use a PVC insulated block connector in the terminal housing of a heater as the high temperature generated would, over time, soften and melt the insulation.

To check, please consider these common-sense guidelines:

1 *By size*: Large terminal for large conductors – never remove strands to accommodate your terminal.

2 *By colour*: Crimped terminations are colour coded. For example, red is for 1.0 mm^2 and 1.5 mm^2 conductors whilst yellow will accommodate up to 6.0 mm^2.

3 *By the type of terminal insulation*: Moulded ceramic connectors and terminals are ideal for hot places. Other types will possibly melt, exposing live conductive terminals.

4 *By written information*: Obtainable from the paperwork accompanying some types of jointing kits. For example, when you are jointing steel wire armour cables together or connecting cabling to serve a central heating control system.

Preventing cable joint corrosion

Joint corrosion is harmful to a wiring system, as it is important that all terminations will allow the passage of a *fault current* to earth. If you are unable to avoid a corrosive atmosphere, then use a wiring system that will withstand the harsh conditions, for example a non-metallic cable carrier.

Materials that will cause corrosion to a wiring system include:

- A combination of aluminium and copper – especially in damp conditions as illustrated in Figure 5.53.
- Certain plaster undercoats containing corrosive salts.
- Materials used in the construction of floors and dadoes.
- Acidic types of timber, e.g. oak.
- Copper cables, lime and cement.
- Excessive soldering flux and copper.
- Dissimilar metals and dampness will create electrolytic activity.
- A saline (salty) atmosphere and bare copper or aluminium.

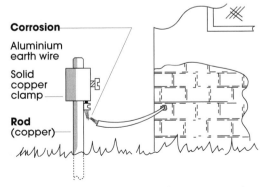

Figure 5.53 – *An aluminium conductor connected to a copper earth rod will sooner or later start to corrode.*

157

Allowing the passage of a fault current

You must check your terminations and connections to make sure they will allow a passage of fault current to earth. Consider these points:

- Is your conductor the correct size; will it be connected to a dissimilar metal?
- What is the material your conductors are made of? If you have used copper and aluminium, then corrosion will set in.
- Where have you placed the joint? A dry position is far better than a damp one.
- Have you removed all traces of flux from your soldered joint?
- Have you placed a cover over your outside joint? This is important, especially if it is in brackish/salty surroundings.

Why do I have to calibrate my test instruments?

If you use your test instruments regularly their reliability and accuracy gradually weakens. Make sure you regularly calibrate them to compensate for errors that have built up over the months. This will maintain their performance within the specification of the instrument and keep you within the law.

A professional engineer will calibrate your instruments in an environmentally controlled laboratory, as Figure 5.54 illustrates.

Figure 5.54 – *Professional calibration services are carried out in environmentally controlled laboratories. (Reproduced by kind permission of Robin Electronics Limited.)*

Installation test certificates

An installation test certificate (a completion certificate) is a formal way of confirming that your installation is free from fault and conforms with the requirements of BS 7671 – Part 7 (our Wiring Regulations).

Useful information in summary form follows:

- Use your certificate for a new installation or circuits added to an existing installation.
- It must not be used for periodic inspection work, as special forms are available for this.
- Do not log alterations or additions where no circuitry is involved on your completion certificate. Use a minor electrical works certificate instead.
- The completed certificate is usually handed to the builder – keep a copy for your records.
- Remember to sign and date your certificate. Be sure all appropriate boxes and columns are completed and that you have described the total scope of the testing, for example all the fixed wiring served by 230 volts AC.

A little help to complete your installation test certificate

Filling out is relatively straightforward but listed below are items that will point you in the right direction. Your *NVQ Level 3* syllabus will deal with all your testing and inspection techniques.

1. Details of client: their name and address.
2. Address of the installation: where the installation is situated.
3. The extent of testing: the areas you have inspected and tested.
4. The date of the next inspection: for a house, every 10 years.
5. Supply characteristics of the installation: type of earthing arrangements (TT, TN-S, TN-CS, etc.). Voltage, earth loop impedance, prospective short circuit, etc.
6. Particulars of the installation: maximum demand, means of earthing and earth electrode details.

Table 5.3 – *Personal protective equipment (PPE).*

Parts of your body protected	Protection offered	Illustration
Head	Hard hat	 **Figure 5.55** – *A construction site hard hat. (Reproduced by kind permission of Robin Electronics Limited.)*
Ears	Ear protection/industrial earplugs	 **Figure 5.56** – *Ear protection fitted to a hard hat. (Reproduced by kind permission of RS Components Limited.)*
Eyes	Goggles, safety spectacles	 **Figure 5.57** – *Lightweight safety eyeglasses. (Reproduced by kind permission of RS Components Limited.)*
Face	Visor or face shield	
Lungs	Dust mask, industrial respirator	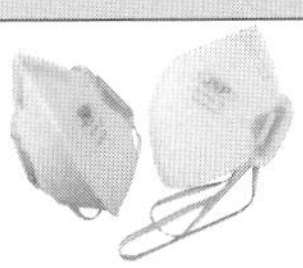 **Figure 5.58** – *Disposable dust mask. (Reproduced by kind permission of RS Components Limited.)*
Hands	Industrial gloves to suit and barrier cream	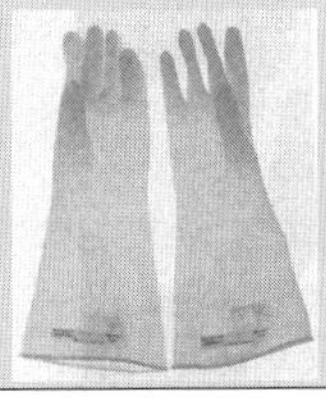 **Figure 5.59** – *Industrial gloves for electricians to BS 697 (1986). (Reproduced by kind permission of RS Components Limited.)*
Knees	Knee pads	
Elbows	Fitted elbow protection pads	
Feet	Steel-capped shoes/boots which meet with the requirements of *Directive 89/686/EEC*	
Your body	Safety overalls (preferably with zips)	
General requirements	The following: Protective clothing for special duties Hair nets when working near moving parts Harness belt for working at height High-visibility fluorescent waistcoat Life jacket when working near water Industrial apron and special gloves for use when working with battery acid Remember to use your seat belt when travelling in your company's transport. See also Chapter 3 for more PPE equipment	

7 Details of the main protective conductor: size, type of material and whether bonded to other services.

8 Comments on the existing installation: if your installation is new, write 'NONE'.

9 Inspection schedule: questions to answer and boxes to tick.

10 Test result schedule: circuit destinations, over-current devices used, size of your conductors, insulation values and earth loop values, etc.

Remember to add the serial numbers of all equipment used to test your installation.

Personal protective equipment

Preventing personal injury

Table 5.3 list random safety measures designed to prevent personal injury in your workplace. Your employer should always provide personal protective equipment (PPE) free of charge.

Using your tools safely

Take good care of your tools – they are your bread and butter and are easily lost or misplaced. Be careful if other trades borrow them. On a large site, it may be the last you will see of them! Use insulated tools when carrying out your electrical duties and for their intended purpose. Do not use on very high voltages that the moulded tool insulation cannot withstand.

Before starting a new job, check your tools for defects (fractured side cutters, cracked screwdriver handles, etc.) and replace as necessary. Regrind the blade of your screwdriver if you find it to be rough, lumpy or rounded.

Your test equipment must be in sound condition. Check out the casing, the state of your probes and the battery's energy level. Test instruments are important – you will not want to be let down by them.

A few do's and don'ts

■ *Don't* – use your screwdriver to lift floorboards or to chisel masonry; use the correct tool (Figure 5.60 illustrates this).

■ *Do* – check your test instrument leads are fused and have finger barriers as shown in Figure 5.61.

■ *Don't* – attempt to mend power tools unless you know what you are doing; report them to your supervisor.

■ *Don't* – bang hammers together; they will splinter.

■ *Do* – be careful where you place extension leads; they are easy to trip over!

■ *Do* – check your power tool has a clutch when working at height.

■ *Do* – show and supervise younger workmates how to use electrical power tools and cordless drills such as those shown in Figure 5.62.

Figure 5.60 – *Use the correct tool to lift floorboards – never a large screwdriver.*

Figure 5.61 – *Finger barriers on test probes are designed to prevent accidental contact with live conductive parts. (Reproduced by kind permission of Robin Electronics Limited.)*

Figure 5.62 – *Demonstrate to inexperienced workmates how to use electrical power tools within the workplace. (Reproduced by kind permission of RS Components Limited.)*

How to report a potentially dangerous situation

You must report dangerous situations in writing to an appropriate person. These circumstances or conditions might include one or more of the following:

- Deposits of dangerous waste or asbestos – any health hazard in general.
- Rotten flooring – torn and loose stair carpeting.
- Hidden/disused wells.
- Structural defects.
- Unsafe steps or ladders.
- Dangerous switchgear or electric cabling.

Treat situations with caution and seek expert advice if you are unsure what you are dealing with.

Deal with potential dangers and risks within the workplace using the following methods:

- elimination
- substitution
- enclosure
- guards
- a safe system of work
- supervision/training
- PPE.

Isolation procedures before disconnection

Minimise accidents involving electric shock by making a routine inspection of the circuit before you make the final connection. Carry out this type of inspection with the help of a simple flow chart as illustrated in Figure 5.63.

Testing for the presence of voltage

To test for the presence of voltage use one of the following approved methods:

- *The light emitting diode* or LED voltage tester as shown in Figure 5.64. (Some models incorporate a 'bleep' that is triggered when a voltage is detected above 50 volts.)
- *The multimeter* illustrated in Figure 5.65 is ideal for site work for the measurement of both AC and DC. Many models have auto-ranging facilities making values quicker and easier to read.

Never use a neon screwdriver under any condition – they are not an approved method for testing for voltage and can provide false readings.

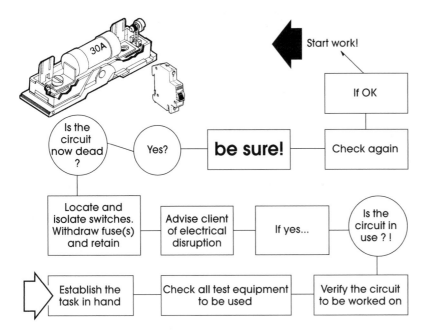

Figure 5.63 – *Procedure for making a final connection within an occupied workplace.*

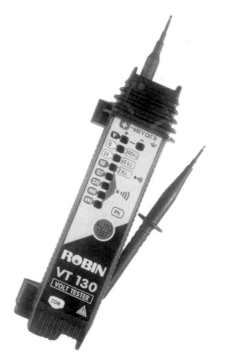

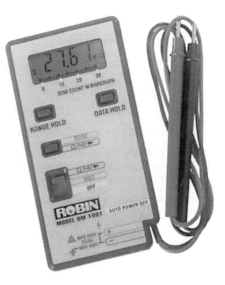

Figure 5.64 – *A light emitting diode (LED) voltage indicator (Reproduced by kind permission of Robin Electronics Limited.)*

Figure 5.65 – *A simple multimeter; an ideal test instrument for site work. The test leads and probes must meet the terms of the General Series Directive 38 [GS38]. The illustration shows a digital auto-range multimeter made by Fluke-Robin Limited. (Reproduced by kind permission of Robin Electronics Limited.)*

Summary

1 Aim for secure joints – loose ones will give you problems.

2 Wire radial final circuits in a similar fashion – only cable sizes and protective devices will differ.

3 Multi-phase circuits are reserved for power distribution and certain types of electric motor.

4 Use a milliohm meter to check the health of a jointed conductor.

5 Remember to calibrate your test instruments at least once a year.

6 The supply of all PPE is free of charge.

Handy hints

- Your paperwork can either make or break a job.

- Avoid discussing sensitive subjects and personal gossip.

- If you are taking an extended break, rub your tools over with a little light oil to stop them getting rusty.

- Introduce yourself to your customer when meeting them for the first time. Tell them when you are leaving your workplace and when work is completed.

- Reading glasses will damage in seconds if splashed with PVC adhesive. Be careful!

Review questions

1 Describe a use for large crimped cable lugs.

2 Explain the type of termination that is supplied with a steel wire armoured cable jointing kit.

3 Why should you make sure that all electrical terminations are sound?

4 How would you confirm the reliability of an electrical joint?

5 Name three different types of domestic switching arrangements.

6 What size cable would you use to install a 3 kW immersion heater? Please do not take into account the need for correction factors.

7 What are three-phased circuits used for in electrical work?

8 Briefly describe the use of block diagrams.

9 How would you check terminals are suitable for their intended use?

10 List two methods of protecting your ears from high noise levels.

11 Give two approved practices for detecting voltage.

12 How would you report dangerous situations within your workplace?

13 Describe what PPE you would use when working with battery acid.

14 Why is it not a good idea to bond aluminium with copper?

15 State the maximum recommended resistance between conductors which have been bonded together to form a joint.

6 Complementary knowledge

Introduction

This chapter will help to provide you with hands-on understanding and an introductory working knowledge of the following:

- The common transformer.
- The domestic immersion heater.
- Central heating control systems.
- Electrical supply systems.
- Bonding techniques.
- Resin-filled cable jointing.
- Intruder and fire alarm systems.
- Lightning protection.

Although one or two of the topics listed are not strictly an NVQ knowledge requirement, *City and Guilds of London* feel they will prove useful to you when you are a qualified electrician.

Basic transformers

The transformer is a simple device that has no mechanical moving parts, the principles of which were discovered by Michael Faraday way back in 1831. Made to any size to achieve any task, the transformer consists of two lightly insulated coils of wire called the *primary* and *secondary* windings. These windings are separately wound from each other on a common laminated iron core, illustrated in Figure 6.1.

The transformer works on the principle of the rise and fall of a *magnetic force field* produced by an *alternating voltage* applied to the *primary winding*. This in turn causes a fluctuating magnetic field within the primary coil and by *mutual induction* an alternating current is *induced* into the *secondary winding*. The frequency of the supply is unchanged – only the *secondary voltage* is increased, decreased or stays the same.

A similar effect can be demonstrated when a *single loop* of wire is rotated within a fixed

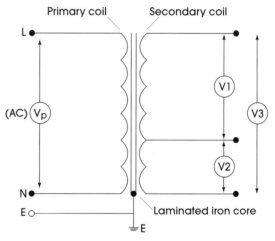

Figure 6.1 – *A simple transformer. V_p denotes the primary voltage; V1, V2 and V3 indicate various secondary output voltages.*

magnetic field. As the loops cut through the lines of magnetic flux at right angles, an electromotive force (voltage) is induced in the loop.

Types of transformers

If both primary and secondary windings have the same number of turns of wires, the voltage induced in the secondary would be equal to the applied primary voltage. If the turns forming both windings are not the same, then the voltage will be proportional, but different. Thus a transformer with a primary coil of *100 turns* and a secondary of *1000 turns* and *10 volts* applied across the primary windings will induce *100 volts* in the secondary coil.

A transformer will only function when an *alternating voltage* is applied to its primary windings. Connecting the primary winding to a *direct current, DC,* supply would cause the transformer to act as an electromagnet or possibly burn out.

If the transformer supplies a higher voltage than the voltage applied, it is called a *step-up transformer.* When the output voltage is lower, it is known as a *step-down transformer.* When the output voltage is the same as the input voltage, the device is known as an *isolating transformer.* Often a ratio is applied to a transformer, for example *1:4.* This means that for every one primary turn there are four secondary turns.

Transformers are efficient machines, having an average capability of about 96%.

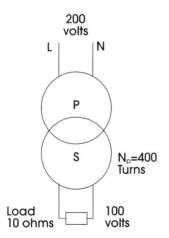

Figure 6.2 – *A schematic illustration of a 2:1 step-down transformer.*

Finding the current drawn from the circuit

Figure 6.2 illustrates a simple 2:1 step-down transformer. There are *400 turns* forming the primary winding which is served with a *200 volt AC supply*. The secondary winding generates *100 volts* whilst connected to a load of 10 Ω.

To find the current within the secondary winding, apply expression (8.6):

$$I = \frac{E}{R}$$

where I is the total current flow, E is the secondary (induced) voltage and R is the resistance in ohms.

Substituting figures, then

$$I = 100/10 = 10 \text{ amps.}$$

After finding the current flowing in the secondary winding, we must use the following expression to find the current drawn from the primary winding:

$$\frac{E_\text{p}}{E_\text{s}} = \frac{I_\text{s}}{I_\text{p}} \tag{6.1}$$

where E_s is the voltage applied to the primary winding, E_p is the voltage induced in the secondary winding, I_p is the current in amps within the primary winding and I_s is the current drawn from the secondary winding.

Substituting with figures:

$$200/100 = 10/I_\text{p}$$

Cross-multiplying and calculating in terms of I_p:

$$I_\text{p} = 1000/200 = 5 \text{ amps}$$

Calculating the power taken from the circuit

It looks as though we are getting something for nothing but by applying expressions (6.2) and (6.3) and finding the total power, measured in watts, in both primary and secondary windings it will clearly show that we are not!

$$\begin{aligned} \text{Primary power} &= I_\text{p}E_\text{p} \tag{6.2} \\ &= 5 \times 200 \\ &= 1000 \text{ watts.} \end{aligned}$$

Secondary power $= I_sE_s$ (6.3)
$$= 10 \times 100$$
$$= 1000 \text{ watts.}$$

This proves that the primary power equals the secondary power.

Finding by calculation the number of turns of wire

To calculate the number of turns of wire within the secondary winding, use the following expression:

$$\frac{E_p}{E_s} = \frac{N_p}{N_s} \qquad (6.4)$$

where N_p is the number of turns in the primary winding and N_s is the number of turns in the secondary winding (E represents the voltage).

As an example, return to Figure 6.2 where the primary coil has *400 turns* of wire. Substituting with figures gives

$$200/100 = 400/N_s$$

Cross-multiplying:

$$200N_s = 400 \times 100$$

Dividing both sides of your equation by 200, then

$$N_s = 40\,000/200$$

Thus, for the secondary winding, $N_s = 200$ turns. This transformer has a 4:2 (or 2:1) winding ratio.

A way you can check

Do this by expressing the ratio in terms of current drawn from both the primary and secondary windings and calculating the power (amps × volts) generated in both sets of windings. Applying the following expression:

$$\frac{N_p}{N_s} = \frac{I_s}{I_p} \qquad (6.5)$$

where I_p is the current flowing in the primary winding and I_s is the current drawn from the secondary winding (N represents the number of turns of wire).

Multivoltage transformer

Figure 6.3 schematically illustrates a multivoltage transformer. By studying the illustration, you will see the transformer has several voltage ranges – the type you might expect to find in a radio or television receiver. You will not find this type at site level.

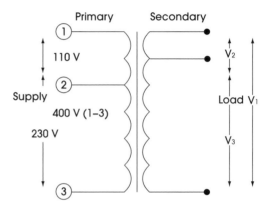

Figure 6.3 – *Schematic illustration of a multi-voltage transformer.*

Testing

Check the *voltage supplying* and the *voltage generated* by the transformer. Alternatively, measure the resistance of both sets of windings with the supply completely isolated from your transformer. If you are testing an *isolating transformer*, both sets of windings will produce similar values.

Open-circuit conditions within the windings are easy to detect but it is more difficult to check out *short-circuit* conditions unless you have prior knowledge of the resistance of the winding under test. Secondary voltage tests taken without a connected load will produce a slightly higher value than expected.

Summary so far...

1 The transformer is completely dependent on an alternating voltage.

2 There is no physical path between the primary and secondary windings.

3 Mutual *electromagnetic induction* provides for a secondary voltage.

4 Power generated in watts, in both sets of windings, is equal. You can never get something for nothing!

5 Testing is by use of a voltmeter – alternatively isolate the electrical supply and measure the *total resistance* of both sets of windings.

6 Isolating transformers have similar resistance values serving both sets of windings.

7 Direct current applied to a transformer will turn it into an electromagnet or burn it out.

8 Transformers can be made to any size.

9 Michael Faraday discovered the electrical science of the transformer in 1831.

Handy hints

Portable site transformers – your practical checklist:

- Check for damage; never use if broken.
- Your transformer's power rating is in kVA. At 110 volt, 1 kVA will provide up to 800 watts.
- Keep your transformer away from bottled gas or petroleum vapour.
- Some transformers are fitted with a *thermal cutout* as a means of protection from overheating.
- Clean both inside and out when considered necessary.
- Site transformers are either 5 or 10 kVA rating.
- Obtainable for *three-* or *single-phase* supplies.

Domestic immersion heaters

Cylinders clad in thermal foam insulation are obtainable in a variety of sizes and are fitted with immersion elements rated up to 3000 watts single phase. This topic is in accordance with the requirements of Regulations 554-05-01 to 03.

Designing your circuit

Figure 6.4 illustrates a typical dedicated immersion heater circuit terminating by means of a double pole switch served with a pilot light.

Install with heat-resistant 1.5 mm² flexible three-core cable from the control switch to the immersion element. Ordinary *PVC* or *rubber-insulated cable* will soon break down because of the heat generated.

Originate your circuit from the local distribution centre. Use 2.5 mm² PVC sheathed cable from a 16 amp breaker and terminate your run in a 20 amp, illuminated, double-pole switch within reach of the immersion cylinder. Keep your cable route away from any heat source or mechanical apparatus associated with the hot water or any central heating system.

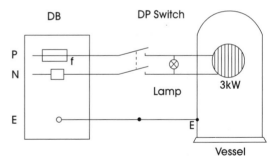

Figure 6.4 – *Wiring an immersion heater circuit: when taken from your distribution centre, use 2.5 mm² cable for elements up to 3000 watts.*

Fault finding

Lime scale will attack the sides of an immersion element in hard water areas. Microscopic pinholes will form, allowing the water access to live conductive parts of the element. If an RCD protects the installation, tripping will occur. The element will then have to be replaced.

An element can also become faulty with age. Test the element with a multimeter switched to the ohms scale with the supply completely isolated. If the element is okay, the value you obtain will match the mathematical assessment you would have carried out before your practical test ($R = V^2/W$ or $R = 230 \times 230$ divided by 3000). Check the *insulation value* of the element by measuring the resistance between both *current-carrying terminals* and *earth*. If you have a problem the value could lie between 0 and 0.4 MΩ (400 000 ohms).

To confirm an open circuit within the element, use a clamp meter and conduct your test at the distribution centre where conditions are less crowded. First make sure the immersion heater's thermostat is working as intended using a LED voltage tester and then check your over-current device is sound. Switch your clamp meter to a suitable scale (say 15 amp full-scale deflection), if not self-adjusting – then open the jaws to take in the phase conductor which serves the immersion heater circuit, Figure 6.5. A value of about 13 amps will be recorded on your instrument if your element is sound and working as intended.

Intermediate faults

Sometimes an intermediate fault condition will develop caused by thermal movements within the element. A higher test voltage will identify this problem but it is best to change the element for a new one.

Changing an immersion heater

Remove the contents of the airing cupboard and cover the floor with old newspapers to soak up any spilt water. Turn the stopcock off, isolate and disconnect the electrical supply cable to your immersion heater.

Only use a purpose-made box spanner to remove the element – anything else might cause damage. Fit your immersion box spanner to the flange of the element and place equal pressure on either side of the 'tommy-bar' whilst turning anticlockwise. Take care to keep the box spanner squarely aligned to the flange of the element since slipping could cause damage to the thin wall of the cylinder.

Figure 6.6 illustrates the basic design features incorporated into a modern hot water storage

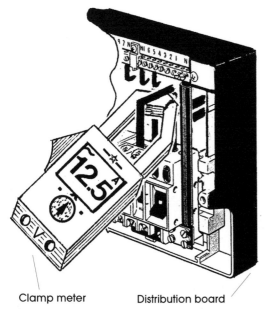

Clamp meter   Distribution board

Figure 6.5 – *Clamp meter method of testing an immersion heater element.*

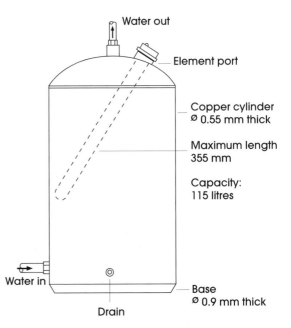

Water out

Element port

Copper cylinder
Ø 0.55 mm thick

Maximum length
355 mm

Capacity:
115 litres

Water in

Drain

Base
Ø 0.9 mm thick

Figure 6.6 – *Hot water storage vessel: design features.*

vessel. After you have removed the element from the cylinder, consider the following points:

- Clean off any lime scale deposited around the entry into the hot water cylinder.
- If bottom entry, remove any lime scale from the *bottom* of the cylinder.
- Remove the old fibre washer if stuck to the flange and discard.
- Clean out the threads of the port with a wire brush.
- Smear a little jointing compound onto the threads of the new element and new fibre washer. Remember to remove the old fibre gasket or the new element will leak.
- Insert your new element into the port serving the cylinder, making sure the element/cover lid is on. Turn clockwise by hand until tight.
- Finish off tightening with your box spanner but do not over-tighten as it could split the fibre washer and then it will leak!

Dealing with over-tight elements

Playing a gentle flame around the neck of the element will often weaken the bond between the element and the flange before withdrawing in the accepted manner. This method is not very practical if the vessel has been factory clad in thermal insulation but, with the use of a thermal barrier, the technique will be successful.

Problem stopcocks

If your stopcock (tap) is not holding the water back after you have removed the element, try siphoning a few litres out of the cylinder into a bucket. It's best, if you can, to use a couple of metres of hose pipe but if the worst comes to the worst, use large bore green/yellow oversleeving. It is far slower, but you will eventually get there! You will then have plenty of time to carry out the usual tasks before fitting the element.

Bottom entry cylinders

1 Isolate your supply and disconnect the flexible lead to your element.

2 With the cylinder still full of water, undo the element by one turn. Never try to release the

element when the tank is empty – you will cause damage by creasing the sides of the vessel.

3 Attach a hosepipe securely to the drain-off point and route the hosepipe outside.

4 Release the drain-off valve and allow the water to flow from the storage vessel.

5 Remove the old element and proceed in a similar way as though you were changing a top entry model.

Dealing with lime scale deposit

One of the advantages of choosing a bottom entry cylinder is you can remove accumulated lime scale with a prefabricated homemade scoop as shown in Figure 6.7. Alternatively, use a manageable section of wide mini-trunking. It is soft and flexible and will do the job just as well.

A severely contaminated tank can cause difficulties when you need to change the element. The deposited lime scale can completely swallow up the immersion element, making it impossible to remove. Under these conditions, seek the advice of a plumber.

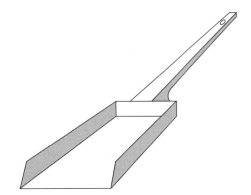

Figure 6.7 – *A simple home-made scoop for removing lime scale deposit from the bottom of storage vessels. Alternatively, use a section of wide mini-trunking; this will also do the job.*

Rewiring the flexible lead

Replacement flexible service cables must be of the heat-resistant type; 1.5 mm² three-core for a 3000 watt element. Figure 6.8 illustrates the relationship between the element, flexible

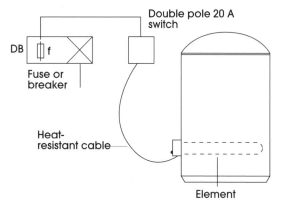

Figure 6.8 – *The basic wiring arrangements serving a domestic immersion heater circuit.*

service cable and the 20 amp double-pole switch served from the local distribution centre.

Over a period, copper heating element terminations will weaken and soften. Take care to support the terminal posts with a pair of pliers when you are rewiring. They can twist/snap off if too much pressure is applied!

Off-peak water heating installations

Figure 6.9 shows a typical dual-element hot water storage vessel. The *day tariff* heater

occupies the top section; the lower part is for the *off-peak* installation. Wire as a radial circuit from your off-peak (restricted) distribution centre to a 20 amp double-pole switch. Your over-current protection will take the form of a 16 amp miniature circuit breaker (MCB) of a 15 amp fuse. Wire from your 20 amp control switch to the terminals of the element in the manner described for top and bottom entry immersion heaters.

Automatic control

Figure 6.10 describes how both day and off-peak circuits can be controlled automatically. The de-energised contactor provides a supply to the day tariff heater. When the timed off-peak circuit comes into play, the contactor energises and provides switching from day to off-peak in one action. This system is popular in commercial installations.

Bonding

Regulation 554-05-02 calls for an *independent* CPC from the principal earthing terminal within the local distribution centre to the water pipe through which water flows to the cylinder.

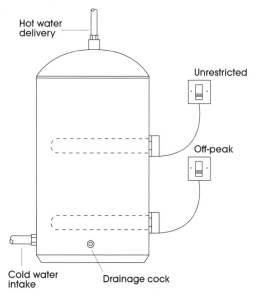

Figure 6.9 – *A hot water storage vessel incorporating both unrestricted (24-hour) and off-peak tariff heating elements.*

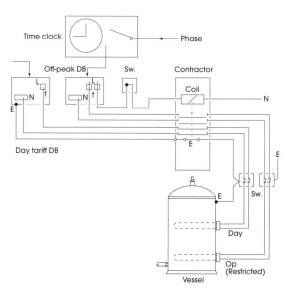

Figure 6.10 – *You can use a contactor to control both 'on-' and 'off-' peak tariffs automatically.*

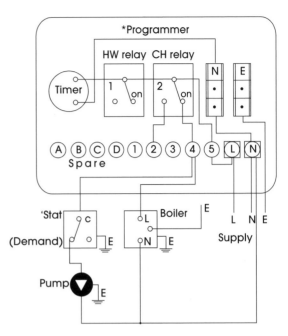

- A smear of petroleum jelly or grease over the threads of a PVC solvent tin will prevent the lid from sticking.
- To avoid PVC solvent spillages always return the lid to the container after use. Knocking over could prove costly!

Figure 6.11 – *Basic central heating control – gravity system.*

Domestic central heating controls

Take care when making your connections to central heating control circuitry – just one misplaced wire will cause a great deal of trouble for you. Two methods are used:

1   Direct wiring connected to a central programmer.

2   The central joint box method of wiring.

The direct wiring method

Programmers take the form of an *electronic timing device*, backed up with a rechargeable battery. This controls two or more relays and will serve, either automatically or manually, the heating controls and all current-consuming equipment such as *diverter valves* and *circulation pumps*, all of which are supplied from the central programmer.

Interconnections within the programmer's terminal housing must be in strict agreement with the manufacturer's wiring instructions.

Figure 6.11 illustrates a basic central heating gravity system. The programmer controls the boiler, circulating pump and room thermostat.

Wiring techniques

It is best to use 1 mm^2 PVC insulated and sheathed cable – larger sizes might be too bulky to fit into the terminals serving the programmer. You can take your 10 amp supply either from your distribution centre or from a fused connection unit forming part of a final ring circuit. Terminate your circuit within a 20 amp double-pole switch.

Choose carefully where you position your programmer. Many surface models have top fixing screws – leave plenty of headroom for final assembly. Site your room thermostat on a north-facing wall away from any heat source or direct sunlight at about 1.5 metres above the finished floor level. Figure 6.12 shows a typical

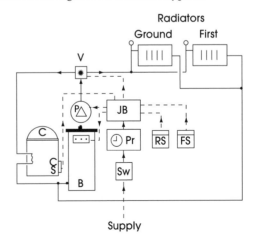

Figure 6.12 – *A typical central heating control system. B, boiler; C, cylinder; CS, cylinder stat; FS, frost stat; JB central joint box; P, pump; Pr, programmer; RS, room stat; Sw, double-pole switch; V, valve.*

171

arrangement controlling a fully pumped system. Remember to bond the central heating system in accordance with Regulation 413-02-02.

A little help during your installation

Try to use a wiring technique that will stop you making silly mistakes. Consider the following:

- Do not become distracted, and work at a pace that suits you.

- Write the role of each cable on the outer sheath using a permanent gel-pen or marker. Example: 'Feed' – 'Room 'stat' – 'Cable A valve' – 'To boiler'.

- Connect as intended and in accordance with the wiring diagram. One wrongly terminated conductor could produce a huge number of faults.

- Keep checking your wiring/connections as your installation progresses.

- Prepare one cable at a time and screw the conductors firmly home. Loose conductors will cause problems and lead to terminal arcing when on load.

- Add cable identification markers to each conductor to correspond to the terminal occupied. Regulation 712-01-03 (ii) confirms this.

Some programmers have spare terminals incorporated within the terminal housing. These are for interconnection purposes. The terminals have letters of the alphabet printed next to them in order to distinguish them from the functional terminals (see Figure 6.11).

Fault finding

Always use a good quality multimeter – never test using a neon screwdriver as they can give false readings and lead you on a wild goose chase! Wrongly placed conductors can easily lead to long-lasting, head-scratching fault conditions. If you have a problem, recheck your connections in relation to the manufacturer's wiring layout and the destination of your cables. Make sure you have a healthy power supply, your breaker or fuse is sound and all your connections are tight.

As with all test procedures, remember to check your instrument both before and after you have looked into your problem.

The central joint box method

You will receive a purpose-made joint box, housing a row of numbered electrical terminals, from the plumber. This will form part of his central heating control kit that also includes a three-way valve, a cylinder thermostat, a room thermostat and a wall-mounted programmer. Figure 6.13 illustrates the form your joint box/enclosure might take. Make your connections in a similar fashion to the direct wiring method but it is useful to keep pencil-written destinations on the outer sheath of the cable until after you have commissioned the heating installation. This way it is easier to make good should faultfinding become necessary.

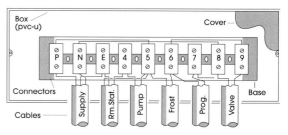

Figure 6.13 – *Central heating controls: central joint box method.*

Wiring from your central joint box

Supplied with the central heating control kit is a basic '*dot-to-dot*' block circuit diagram. This will give you guidance and help to provide a trouble-free installation. Figure 6.14 illustrates this. Each installation conductor shown on the diagram is numbered. Terminate your hardwiring within a matching numbered connector block or accessory, as shown in the illustration. Prepare *one conductor at a time* and attach a numbered identification tag to the conductor.

The advantage of this method is that it reduces the number of cables entering the programmer. This way all conductors are easily terminated.

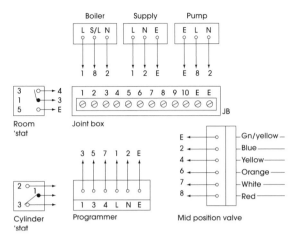

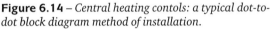

Figure 6.14 – *Central heating contols: a typical dot-to-dot block diagram method of installation.*

Summary so far...

1 Approach your task in a logical manner and take your time.

2 Place your box spanner squarely onto the flange of the immersion element – turn firmly.

3 Always use heat-resistant flexible cable if a replacement is necessary.

4 Remember the following:
- Take care when removing and fitting a new element.
- Clean off lime scale contamination.
- Secure by means of jointing paste.
- Use the correct tools.

5 Choose a suitably sized enclosure to place your wiring connector block.

6 Wire your installation using a lighting grade cable.

7 Label each cable on the cable sheath.

8 Place a numerical cable marker on each conductor to correspond to the terminal it occupies.

9 Take care when you connect.

10 Avoid site distractions.

11 Check your progress frequently.

12 Test with a good quality multimeter; never use a neon test screwdriver.

Review questions

1 What are the names given to the two insulated windings in a transformer?

2 Describe the difference between a *step-up* and *step-down* transformer.

3 Describe a method of testing a transformer.

4 Voltage tests on a transformer without a connected load will produce one of the following:
- a lower than expected voltage
- a higher than expected voltage
- the voltage will not alter in any way
- there will be no voltage output from the transformer.

5 Describe the construction of an isolating transformer.

6 What type of cable must you use when making a final connection to an immersion heater?

7 State a method of testing for an *open-circuit* condition within an immersion heater.

8 Briefly describe how you would remove an immersion element from a cylinder.

9 What would happen if you left the old fibre washer/gasket attached to the neck of the element port?

10 If your copper cylinder is fitted with both *peak* and *off-peak* immersion elements, please state where the off-peak element is fitted.

11 What are the two accepted methods of wiring control circuitry to serve a domestic central heating system?

12 What cable size would be best to use to wire your central heating controls?

13 Where is it best to fit your room thermostat?

14 What means would you provide to isolate your central heating control system?

15 Describe one advantage of choosing the central joint box method of wiring central heating control circuitry.

Handy hints

- Damage can be caused to electronic lighting transformers forming part of an inductive circuit when 'spikes' are generated within the supply.
- A 6 volt bell or buzzer will make an emergency continuity tester.
- PVC electrical tape will become hard and brittle during the winter months but, if you keep it in your trouser pocket, it will soak up enough warmth to keep it in a soft and workable condition.

Electrical supply systems and earthing arrangements

Regulation 312-03-01 provides for the following groups:

- TT system
- TN-S system
- TN-CS system
- IT system
- IT system (not used for public supplies).

The first letter indicates the *earthing arrangements* at the supply source. This refers to the local distribution transformer. The second letter advises of the *installation earthing arrangements* and the third letter points to the *earthed supply conductor* arrangements.

Reviewing the initials

The first letter

T: At least one point of the supply is earthed. Figure 6.15 illustrates this.

The second letter

This points to the relationship between the *exposed conductive parts* and *earth.* Figures 6.16 and 6.17 will explain this.

- T: The conductive parts are connected directly to earth and are independent of the supply earth.
- N: The conductive parts are connected directly to earth at the source of supply.

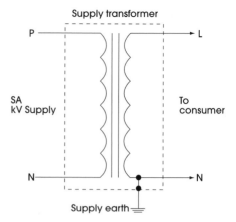

Figure 6.15 – *In a TT earthing arrangement the neutral of the supply is connected directly to earth at the community transformer.*

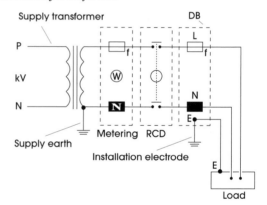

Figure 6.16 – *In a TT system, the neutral conductor is connected directly to earth at the transformer. The installation electrode is independent of the earth created at the transformer.*

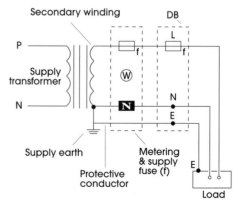

Figure 6.17 – *In a TN-S earthing arrangement the neutral conductor is connected directly to an earth point at the supply transformer.*

The third letter

This indicates the physical arrangement of the protective and neutral conductors serving a TN supply system.

S: Both the protective and neutral conductors are separate from each other.

CS: Both the protective and neutral conductors are combined together in one cable. This is known as a PEN cable which comes from a *Phase-Earth/Neutral* combination cable.

A quick look at the types of supply systems

TT systems

The delivery of electricity to rural Britain is by means of overhead cables from a neighbouring transformer. This method of power distribution is called a TT system. It will provide a phase and neutral supply to your customer but *not* an earth. The home occupier is responsible for providing a suitable earthing arrangement for their installation.

When water came to our homes in cast iron or copper pipes, earthing could be easily be

achieved by clamping a protective conductor to the supply side of the stopcock, as illustrated in Figure 6.18. Blue polyethylene water pipes have now replaced these old ones but, unfortunately, for us, polyethylene will not conduct electricity – so we have to find other means of protecting our installation! Protection comes in the form of an *RCD*. In older properties, you might find a *voltage-operated earth leakage circuit breaker* but this type is far less reliable than the current type. To bring an installation up to date, a current-operated breaker should always replace a voltage type.

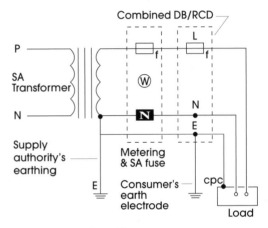

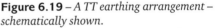

Figure 6.19 – *A TT earthing arrangement – schematically shown.*

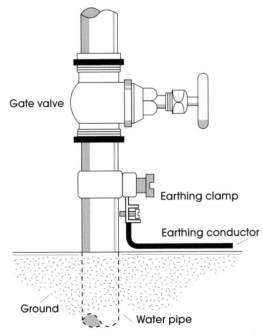

Figure 6.18 – *An old way of providing an installation earth that can no longer be relied upon.*

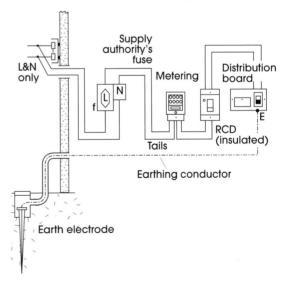

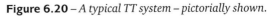

Figure 6.20 – *A typical TT system – pictorially shown.*

Figure 6.19 illustrates a typical TT distribution system in schematic form and brings into focus the association between the current-carrying conductors and the earthing arrangements provided. To explain this graphically, Figure 6.20 shows the relationship between the incoming supply cables and the provisions the consumer has made for earthing their installation.

TN-S systems

You will find this type of supply system in urban areas where the delivery of power is by means of

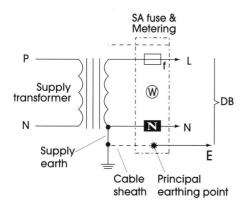

Figure 6.21 – *In a TN-S earthing arrangement the incoming supply cable sheath provides for an independent earth which is also connected to the neutral conductor at the transformer (see also Figure 6.17).*

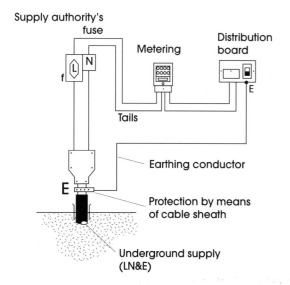

Figure 6.22 – *A pictorial view of a TN-S system.*

underground cables. Your earth is obtained by simply clamping your protective conductor onto the lead sheath of the supply cable, which in turn is routed to your distribution centre's earthing terminal. This provides a direct route to the star-point of your local transformer. It is earthed at this point to guarantee your fuses and breakers will operate as intended under a fault condition to earth.

Figures 6.21 and 6.22 illustrate the association between the supplier's terminals and the earthing arrangements serving a TN-S system.

For additional protection, install an RCD. Regulation 413-02-06 applies in this case.

TN-CS systems

The use of a *combined* neutral and protective conductor to serve an installation is known as a TN-C system. If the system is connected to an installation that has an independent protective and neutral conductor (the way a house would normally be wired) then the combination is known as a TN-CS system (suppliers refer to it as PME).

Figure 6.23 shows the schematic arrangement for this type of system. In practice, the combined neutral/protective conductor is grounded many times throughout the supplier's distribution network. A fault condition from phase to earth is really a fault between the *phase* and *neutral* conductors because of the combination of the

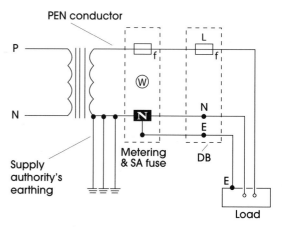

Figure 6.23 – *General wiring schedule for a TN-CS earthing arrangement.*

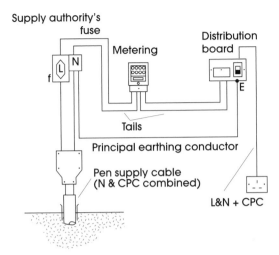

Figure 6.24 – *A typical TN-CS earthing arrangement shown in graphical form.*

neutral and protective conductors. Figure 6.24 illustrates this graphically.

TN-C system

When a consumer's installation originates from a privately owned isolating transformer supplied by a PEN cable and all wiring throughout the installation is in *copper-sheathed* PEN cables the system is referred to as a TN-C system. To remind you – a PEN cable is a cable where the *neutral/protective cable* is as one or a Phase-Earth/Neutral combination cable.

Wired throughout with MI cable, a special gland pot is fitted with a flexible copper lead that serves as a combined neutral and protective conductor. Figures 6.25 and 6.26 illustrate this point graphically.

This type of installation is not in general use but you may come across it – especially if you have to work in a certain department store in Southampton, England. Figure 6.27 shows the relationship between the source of the supply, subcircuit over-current protection device and the connected load. It is impossible to use an RCD with this type of installation as both neutral and earth conductors are combined as one. Figure 6.28 illustrates this graphically.

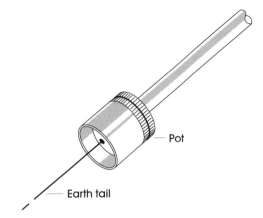

Figure 6.25 – *This special gland pot is fitted with a flexible lead embedded within the brass pot. It is used to form a neutral/earth point, which in turn forms part of a PEN cable to be used within the TN-C installation.*

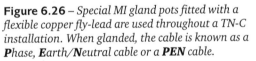

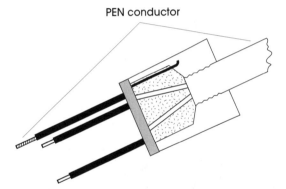

Figure 6.26 – *Special MI gland pots fitted with a flexible copper fly-lead are used throughout a TN-C installation. When glanded, the cable is known as a **P**hase, **E**arth/**N**eutral cable or a **PEN** cable.*

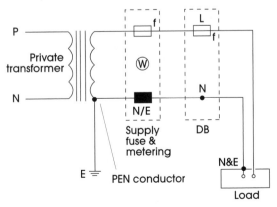

Figure 6.27 – *A TN-C earthing arrangement using a private transformer. Earth concentric wiring using PEN cables is used throughout the consumer's installation.*

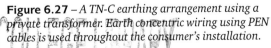

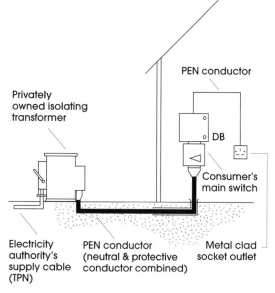

Figure 6.28 – *A typical TN-C installation shown in picture form.*

Electrical bonding techniques

There are many areas where bonding is very important but is sometimes overlooked, including bathrooms, kitchens, utility rooms, milking parlours, dairies and petrol stations.

Contact with water will lower your body's resistance and produce lethal currents even when a lower voltage is present. An average body resistance measures about 6500 Ω. If you are wet, your body's resistance drops by 75%. A combination of stray electrical currents and water can be a one-way ticket to your local mortuary – carry out bonding in all areas of high risk where water or condensation are, or could be present. This applies irrespective of whether an area has an electrical installation or not.

To sum up: *bonding minimises the potential difference* which, under fault conditions, could appear between conductive parts (for example, phase to earth) and ensures that all unrelated metalwork is electrically placed at *zero volts*. (The term we use for *unrelated metalwork* in electrical engineering is *extraneous metalwork*. This term will be used again in this book.)

Bonding methods and procedures

There are two types of bonding:

- Main equipotential bonding (Regulations 413-02 and 471-08).

- Supplementary bonding (Regulation 547-03).

Main equipotential bonding

This requires all extraneous conductive parts (that is, metalwork not forming part of your electrical installation) and all exposed conductive parts (for example, pressed steel enclosures serving a connected load) to be bonded together to an electrical earth. Figure 6.29 illustrates this point using radial protective conductors (cpc) from a common earthing bar. If you wish to link the parts you have to bond, please keep your protective conductor *whole* (do not cut it).

The term *extraneous parts* can include the following. Refer to BS 7671 Regulation 413-02-02. There are many – these are just some of them:

- Main gas, water and oil services.

- Compressed air supply.

- Central heating pipe work and air conditioning ducting.

- Exposed steel joists, metal stairs and exposed metal infrastructure.
- Steel guard rails and the infrastructure serving dairies and milking parlours.
- Metal cladding forming doors and walls.
- Lightning protection systems.

Wire separate protective bonding conductors to each extraneous part; the size being not less than 50% of the main bonding conductor (often 10 mm^2) or a minimum of 6 mm in cross-sectional area. Alternatively, as mentioned in a previous paragraph, your bonding connector can be *looped* from one extraneous part to another, providing your cable is *continuous* and not broken whenever making a bonding connection.

The best way to do this is to slice about 20 mm of insulation from your green/yellow conductor, fold the bare copper in half and place it within a compression terminal as shown in Figure 6.30 and crimp. Please refer to Regulation 547-02-01 for further details.

Position your bonding terminations so they are accessible for testing – a requirement of Regulation 526-04-01.

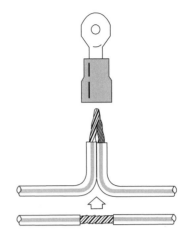

Figure 6.30 – *An unbroken bonding conductor designed to serve various exposed and extraneous conductive parts.*

Agricultural situations

Cattle are very sensitive to electric shock and, if subjected to voltages even as low as 50 volts AC, can, under defined conditions, die. Bond well and check your bonding clamps are well out of reach of the livestock. This will prevent the animals from nibbling the conductors and generally disturbing the bonding clamps.

Gas and water services

Bond your main gas and water services within 600 mm from the individual meters and on the consumer's side of the installation. It is wise to shunt the gas meter to prevent damage caused by fault currents flowing through the mechanical mechanism. Figure 6.31 illustrates this. If a

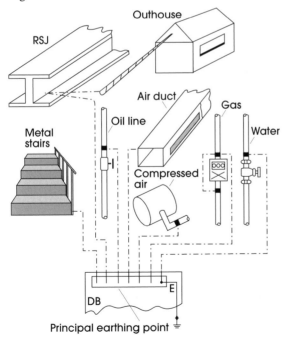

Figure 6.29 – *An example of equipotential bonding arrangements.*

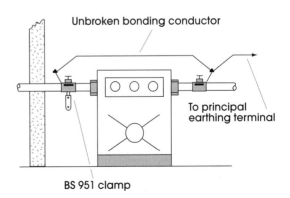

Figure 6.31 – *Equipotential bonding techniques: shunting gas and, if appropriate, water meters.*

179

water meter is absent from the installation electrically bond the service pipe as near to the stopcock as practical on the *consumer's* side of the pipe work.

It is best to check with your gas and water people before bonding to their equipment just in case they insist on certain requirements. Regulation 547-02-02 confirms this.

Special requirements for bathrooms

This requires installing an accompanying bonding conductor from the principal earthing terminal to both hot and cold water pipes serving the bath or shower and to all *extraneous* and *exposed* conductive parts. The term we use for an accompanying bonding conductor in electrical engineering is *supplementary bonding* and this term will be applied again in this book.

Alternatively, a supplementary bonding conductor can link all *exposed* and *extraneous* conductive parts but your green/yellow conductor must be *continuous* as described in an earlier paragraph. Figure 6.32 illustrates this point graphically.

If you require additional safety, your bathroom can be fitted with a high sensitivity RCD serving a small MCB distribution centre, as shown in Figure 6.33. Regulation 471-08-01 confirms this.

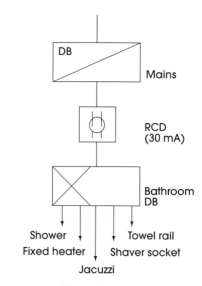

Figure 6.33 – *For additional protection, install a high-sensitivity RCD into a bathroom installation.*

Supplementary bonding

This requires all *exposed* and *extraneous* conductive parts to be electrically common with each other, as illustrated in Figure 6.34. Bonding will maintain a common potential zone of zero volts. To meet this regulation a supplementary bonding conductor is required to have a minimum cross-sectional area of 2.5 mm when mechanically protected by mini-trunking, channelling or conduit or placed in an unreachable position. If unprotected, you may

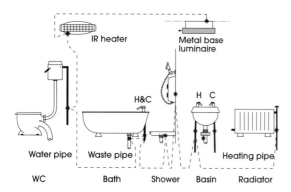

Figure 6.32 – *Bond bathroom installations well in order to reduce the risk of electric shock.*

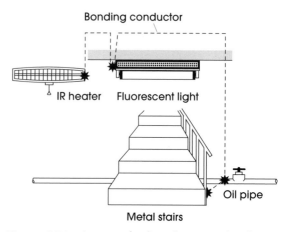

Figure 6.34 – *An example of supplementary bonding arrangements.*

use 4 mm² bonding cable. Please refer to Regulation 547-03 for details.

Special bonding requirements for protective multiple earthing (PME) supplies

The use of a *combined* neutral and earth distribution system requires approval from the Department of Energy. This not only enforces legal requirements on the people who supply our electricity but on the people who use it as well. For the consumer, this requires that special bonding arrangements be implemented within the installation. Previous paragraphs have already reviewed this topic.

The principal PME earthing conductor

The cross-sectional area of the double-insulated tails from the supplier's service fuse to the meter influences the size of *your* main earthing conductor forming part of a PME system. If the neutral is either 16, 25 or 35 mm² then the consumer's neutral will be the same and the principal earthing conductor linking the *supply neutral block* with the *earthing bar* within the distribution centre will be 16 mm² in cross-

sectional area. The size of the main equipotential bonding conductor from the earthing bar within the distribution centre to the principal gas and water or oil supply will then be 10 mm². Refer to Figure 6.35 for graphical detail. A word of warning – if the service fuse is 100 amps you *must* install 25 mm² double-insulated service tails.

If the supply neutral conductor is 50 mm² in cross-sectional area then the size of the principal earthing conductor will rise to 25 mm². You must then increase the cross-sectional area of your main equipotential bonding conductor to 16 mm². For further information, check out Table 54H of BS 7671.

Additional protection

Use a *RCD* for additional protection if required. You must not use *fault voltage circuit breakers* (FVCB) in combination with a PME installation. The low neutral/earth impedance path developed by this system will make the device completely unworkable by actually short-circuiting the operating coil.

Where PME is not permitted

This usually arises from the difficulty in satisfying the PME bonding requirements. The following types of installations apply:

- Caravans and mobile homes or when a building has been constructed using a metal structure – a RCD is recommended.

- Milking parlours and dairies – a RCD is recommended.

- Mines and quarries. Special earth leakage measures are required to act in accordance with the Mines and Quarries Electrical Regulations (1956).

- Construction sites where a 30 milliamp RCD is required.

- Petrol filling stations and swimming pools. Employ 'area to area' RCDs as a means of protection against direct contact from live conductive parts.

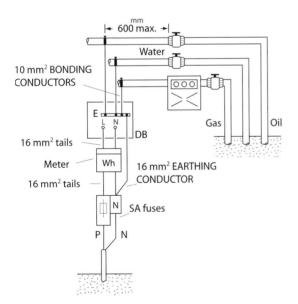

Figure 6.35 – *An example of protective multiple earthing (PME) requirements.*

Circuit protective conductors

Protective conductors appear in many different forms depending on the design of the installation they are serving. Solid drawn steel conduit provides a very suitable protective conductor *as long as all joints are secure and installed correctly.* The nominal cross-sectional area of 25 mm diameter steel conduit is about 130 mm² – this is more than enough for the majority of installations. Steel cable trunking can offer an even greater cross-sectional area. An installation built from 150 × 150 mm diameter trunking will provide a protective conductor area of approximately 750 mm². Take care throughout your first-fix stage to maintain *electrical and mechanical continuity.* Firmly assemble and bridge with a copper earthing link each section of trunking, as illustrated in Figure 6.36. Keep in mind it only requires one badly made set of joints to produce a high level of impedance and this, coupled with a phase to earth fault condition, would be sufficient to create a very dangerous and unreliable installation.

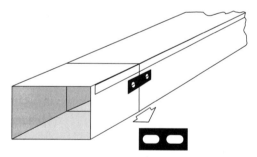

Figure 6.36 – *Each section of your steel trunking installation must be bridged with a copper earth/bonding link and secured by means of shake-proof fixing screws.*

Your choice of protective conductors

The choice is limited to the design of the installation. Listed are a selection that are in general use – Regulation 543-02-02 confirms this.

- The steel wire protecting armoured cables.
- The sheath of lead- or copper-insulated cables.
- Steel cable trunking.
- Welded or solid drawn steel conduit that has been properly installed. Regulation 543-02-01 confirms this.
- Single green/yellow cable insulated with PVC.
- The integral conductor that forms part of a PVC insulated and sheathed cable. Please remember to sleeve the bare CPC using *green/yellow* oversleeving. Plain *green* coloured insulated cable is no longer acceptable.
- Copper tape.
- Continuously formed extraneous conductive parts – for example, long reinforcing steel joists, steel ducting, cable basket and tray work.

Disconnection times: protection against electric shock

To offer a practical degree of protection against electric shock, Regulation 413-02-09 and Table 41A require the earth-fault loop impedance (see Figure 6.37) to be sufficiently low at each socket outlet to allow for automatic disconnection (by way of an MCB or fuse) to take place within 0.4 s. If the installation is serving an agricultural, horticultural or temporary installation, the disconnection time is 0.2 s. Disconnection times are successful when the voltage is between 220

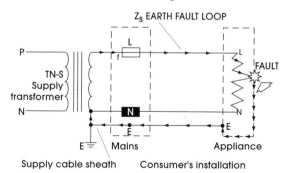

Figure 6.37 – *The total value of Z_s, the earth loop impedance within the installation, will vary depending on the length and size of cable used. The external impedance, Z_e, will also vary and this will depend on the length of service cable from the intake position of your installation to the supply transformer.*

and 227 volts AC and is from a TN supply system. Check out your *earth loop impedance* with a digital earth-fault loop impedance tester set to a suitable scale. Use a *digital earth leakage circuit breaker timing tester* to obtain the value, in milliseconds, for the speed of disconnection but take the time to set your instrument correctly before making your test.

If your earth loop impedance tests are very high – say over 1.2 Ω when served by a B-type 32 amp MCB, check your earthing connections at each accessory for tightness and add a supplementary protective conductor to your circuit to lower the impedance value.

Generally, for fixed equipment such as lights, storage heaters and fans, etc., the disconnection time must not exceed 5 s.

Automatic disconnection

Automatic disconnection due to a phase fault to earth or an over-current condition is operated by means of the following:

1 Over-current protection:
   - miniature circuit breakers (MCB)
   - mould case circuit breakers (MCCB)
   - fuses
   - overload relays (found in starters in electric motor circuits)
   - thermal cut-outs (serving instant hot water heaters)
   - button current disruptors (attached to the frames of electric motors).

2 Earth leakage protection:
   - residual current devices (RCD)
   - fault voltage circuit breakers (FVCB).

Stand-alone RCDs respond to a leakage of current either from *phase* or from *neutral* to *earth* and therefore are very unsuited as a means of protection against over-current. For this type of protection, you must use a combined MCB/RCD, which is a device specially designed to mount into a DIN-rail designed distribution centre.

Earth-free local equipotential bonding

This is a very specialised arrangement often found in research centres which, for practical purposes, bonds all extraneous conductive parts together, but not to earth.

An electrical engineer, but only when certain conditions are met, can specify this type of installation. To find out more, look up BS 7671 Regulations 413-05 and 471-11-01.

Summary so far...

1 The four principal methods of power distribution, where the source of supply (for example the local transformer) is earthed at one point are TT, TN-S, TN-CS and TN-C.

2 TT systems are found in rural areas and the consumer is required to provide the means of controlling potential earth leakage problems.

3 TN-S systems are found in urban districts and the lead sheath of the underground supply cable acts as a CPC. This type of distribution is rare in rural areas.

4 A TN-CS arrangement provides a combined *phase, neutral/earth cable* (called a PEN cable) and this serves an installation having both *separate* and *independent* CPCs. This type of distribution is installed in both urban and rural areas.

5 TN-C systems are generally in decline and are only used in conjunction with privately owned isolating transformers. MI cables are used, the copper sheath acting as both *neutral* and *CPC*.

6 Bonding minimises the potential difference appearing between extraneous and exposed conductive parts and produces a common potential of zero volts.

Summary so far...

7 Methods of bonding:
- main equipotential bonding
- supplementary bonding
- earth-free equipotential bonding.

8 Main equipotential bonding connects all extraneous conductive metalwork (gas and water pipes) to the principal electrical earthing point in your distribution centre.

9 Supplementary bonding links all exposed conductive parts with all extraneous conductive parts. Example: pipe work to hand basins and baths linked with fixed electrical equipment.

10 There are special bonding requirements when installing a PME supply.

11 A PME supplied installation should not serve the following: milking parlours and dairies, mines and quarries, temporary installations serving a construction site and swimming pools.

12 Circuit protective conductors include:
- the outer sheath of metal clad and steel wire armoured cables
- steel conduit
- steel trunking, cable tray and cable basket systems
- copper tape
- single green/yellow PVC insulated copper/aluminium cable
- continuously joined extraneous conductive parts.

13 In the event of a fault condition to earth, electrical disconnection must take place within 0.4 s for domestic and industrial installations served with socket outlets and 5 s for fixed electrical equipment such as lights and hand driers, etc. Sockets serving farm and temporary installations must auto-disconnect within 0.2 s.

14 An electrical engineer can only authorize earth-free equipotential bonding.

Review questions

1 Name four different types of UK power distribution systems.

2 A TT power supply consists of one of the following:
- Phase, neutral and a supplier's earthing terminal.
- Phase and neutral conductors only.
- Phase and a combined neutral/earth conductor.
- Phase and neutral conductor supplied from a private isolating transformer.

3 In your own words, describe the construction of a PEN cable.

4 Where would you be most likely to find a TT power distribution system?

5 What type of installation cable would we use for a TN-C distribution system?

6 Name two types of bonding used in electrical installation work.

7 Name four extraneous conductive parts where separate protective bonding could be required.

8 The main gas service must be bonded within one of the following distances from the supplier's meter:
- 600 m
- 500 mm
- 450 mm
- 600 mm.

Review questions

9 Suggest an additional safety factor, other than bonding, which we can incorporate within a bathroom installation.

10 State the size of conductor needed for a principal earth wire when the metering tails (from the service fuse to the meter) are both 16 mm in cross-sectional area and the supply is from a TN-CS system.

11 Why is it not possible to use a RCD on an installation served by a TN-C supply system?

12 Where would you bond on the main water pipe serving a small bungalow?

13 When mechanically protected, state the minimum size conductor recommended for supplementary bonding.

14 Why is a fault voltage circuit breaker prohibited within a PME installation?

15 Under a phase-to-earth fault condition, state the disconnection time demanded if the installation is within an agricultural location – for example, a pig farm.

Handy hints

- It is easier to attach bonding conductors to earthing clamps during the *first fix period* of your installation when conditions are not so cramped but they must be easy to get to for testing purposes.
- Corrosion will set in if you connect an *aluminium circuit protective conductor* onto a copper earthing rod.
- Where a room contains a fixed bath or shower cubicle, a socket outlet must be at least 2.5 metres away from the cubicle.
- Never rely on the service side of a water main (that is, from the stopcock to the floor) to provide a first-rate earth. Much of our original cast iron plumbing has been replaced with plastic or polythene.
- The term SELV now means, Separated Extra-Low Voltage.
- The thermistor, an electronic semiconductor component made from a compound of oxides of manganese and nickel, will rapidly decrease in resistance from about $0.1 \text{ M}\Omega$ at 20°C to a mere $10 \text{ }\Omega$ at 373 K. The thermistor can be used as a sensitive thermometer.
- The thyristor is a semiconductor used in circuits for the control of mercury arc rectifiers.
- Do keep to *site protective clothing dress rules* – these regulations will save you from harm.

Over-current protection – a brief summary

The requirements for an over-current device depend on the following:

- The current rating must be related to the design of the circuit.
- The *type* (B, C, D, etc.) must be well suited to the circuit's earth impedance value – measured in ohms.
- It will need to operate automatically on over-current.
- It must be able to disconnect your circuit in the time required.
- It must have good breaking capacity.
- The device must be easily identified as an *over-current device*.
- The rated short-circuit capacity must be well matched with your *prospective short-circuit* at that point. For example: a 'B' rated mcb has a short-circuit capacity of 6 kA whilst a BS 1361 supplier's fuse is rated at 33 kA and a semi-enclosed, BS 3036 fuse is rated at just 1 kA. These are all OK when your prospective short-circuit is above 1.2 kA.

Miniature circuit breakers

This type of over-current protection is dependent on the following:

- The prospective short-circuit current at the source of the supply.

185

- The load your circuit is carrying.
- The type of load – for example you might require a type 'D' MCB to serve a large site transformer whereas a type 'B' would satisfy a lighting circuit.
- The short-circuit capacity of the device.

Electric motors

How they work – AC induction motor

Figure 6.38 illustrates a typical AC induction motor. This type of motor is known as a *squirrel cage* motor as the rotor (the part that rotates) (Figure 6.39) resembles the type of cage squirrels were once kept in as pets in the early 1800s. This induction motor is designed for use on either *single-* or *three-phase* systems.

Figure 6.40 shows you how the windings are placed within the *stator* of a three-phase motor – this is the part that does not rotate. It also shows the winding's relationship with the supply

voltage. These are buried into soft laminated iron slots contained in a rolled steel housing.

When a three-phase supply is connected to the windings, a rotating magnetic field is automatically produced. It is important to understand that the rotor is not connected in any way to the supply voltage. It takes the form of a cylindrical, soft iron, laminated component, as described in Figure 6.39. The rotor is mounted on a shaft that travels through its centre (Figure 6.39), allowing it to spin unhindered within the stator. Bearings housed in the two end shields support the rotor shaft – Figure 6.41 illustrates this. Copper bars, drawn into hollowed slots, run at measured distances throughout the length of the rotor. These are all joined together (made common) at both ends by means of a brass ring brazed to the ends of the copper bars – refer back to Figure 6.39.

When a coil of wire cuts through a magnetic field at right angles to it, an electromotive force (emf) is induced in the coil. The same electrical

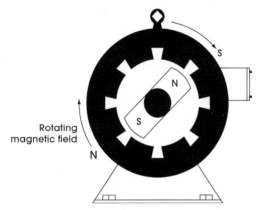

Figure 6.38 – *A simple synchronous electric motor.*

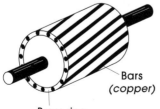

Figure 6.39 – *The squirrel cage rotor. The copper bars are joined together by means of brass rings fitted at either end of the rotor.*

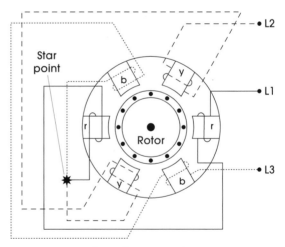

Figure 6.40 – *A three-phase squirrel cage motor showing the windings and wiring arrangements.*

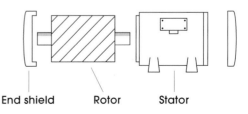

Figure 6.41 – *The three main parts of an electric motor.*

principle enables a squirrel cage motor to operate by working on the principle that a rotating magnetic field produced in the stator windings induces an emf in the copper rotor bars by 'transformer action', often referred to as mutual induction.

Since the windings are short-circuited by brass rings positioned at either end of the rotor, currents will be able to flow through the rotor circuit. They too will set up their own magnetic fields and, in doing so, will interact with the magnetic field produced within the stator windings.

The stator's rotating magnetic field, known as the *synchronous speed* of the motor, has the effect of dragging the rotor around with it. The current produced in the closed loop of copper bars serving the rotor opposes the very current producing it. The only way to oppose this change is for the closed loop within the rotor to spin in the same direction as the rotating magnetic field generated within the stator windings.

In practice, the rotor speed will be slightly less than the synchronous speed. The difference between the two speeds is known as the '*slip*'. It can vary from 2.5 to 5.5% at normal loads.

The basic theory of DC motors

A coil of wire with slip rings attached to the open ends, illustrated in Figure 6.42, is positioned between two opposite poles of a permanent

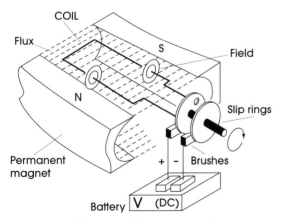

Figure 6.42 – *The way a DC motor responds to a magnetic field coupled with a DC current supplying the winding(s).*

magnet. Applying a DC voltage to the slip rings will *shift* the position of the coil. There will be movement. One side of the loop will be *pushed up* whilst the other side will be *forced down*. Rotation is gained by increasing the number of turns on each coil and adding more coils to our original design. Once turning and cutting through the invisible lines of magnetic flux, a secondary voltage will be induced into the coil. This generated electromotive force *opposes* the applied voltage. Sometimes this induced voltage is referred to as the *back emf*.

This is the basic principle applied to direct current electric motors.

Electromagnetic relay

The form an electromagnetic relay takes is a soft, laminated projecting iron core with many turns of lightly insulated wire wound around it. This is called the solenoid which, when served with a suitable voltage, becomes an electromagnet. Energizing the relay circuit will cause the sprung switching arrangement that is attached to the solenoid, and called the armature, to be attracted to the magnetic solenoid. This movement provides a positive mechanical switching action for a second circuit.

Some applications are in:

- Control panels.
- Switching of large heating loads which are controlled by thermostat.
- Modern cars to control electrical circuits.
- Some older telephone exchanges.
- Passenger lift control centres.
- Electric motor control (these relays are known as contactors).

The root mean square (RMS) value of an alternating voltage

The *mean*, or average, value of an AC voltage, illustrated in Figure 6.43, indicates the square root of the average sum of the squares of the individual voltage values taken during a period of one-half cycle.

187

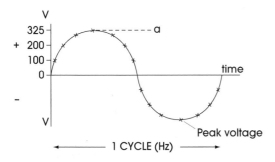

Figure 6.43 – *The peak value of an AC voltage is always greater than its RMS value.*

Mathematically, the RMS value will be as follows:

$$\text{RMS} = \frac{\sqrt{V_1^2 + V_2^2 + V_3^2 + \ldots}}{\text{number of values}} \qquad (6.6)$$

On the other hand, you can add the square of the instantaneous values, and then divide your answer by the number of values taken over one-half cycle and finally take the square root of this solution.

The RMS value, or *effective value* as it is sometimes known, is an important factor in an alternating voltage as it manages the heating effect (IR^2) formed within the conductor. It corresponds closely in value to a stable DC voltage that produces the equivalent heating and lighting effect.

The largest voltage or *peak voltage* is shown as 'a' in Figure 6.43. With this in mind you can now express the RMS value as

$$\text{RMS} = \frac{a}{\sqrt{2}} \qquad (6.7)$$

where a is the peak voltage and $\sqrt{2}$ is the square root of 2 (1.4142).

Transposing expression (6.7) in terms of a, the peak voltage is then

$a = \text{RMS voltage} \times \sqrt{2}$.

The RMS value of current is 0.707 × the peak value obtained whereas the average voltage is 0.637 × the peak value.

An interesting point in passing: the peak value of a 240 volt AC RMS supply is a staggering 339.4 volts!

All AC measuring instruments used in our work are in RMS values.

The distribution of electrical power to the consumer

Most of our electricity is generated between 11 000 and 33 000 volts by a machine known as an alternator, driven at high speed by a steam turbine. The turbine is fuelled by coal, nuclear energy or gas. Wind and wave power also have their role to play in the direct generation of electricity to supply our National Grid. The generated electricity from many different power stations is then transformed in value to 132 000, 275 000 or 400 000 volts and fed into the Grid. Substations, built in principal locations, provide the means by which power is taken from the National Grid and reduced to 11 000 volts.

In rural areas, distribution is by means of insulated conductors carried on high-quality insulators attached to wooden poles painted with a preservative (Figure 6.44). These are

Figure 6.44 – *The distribution of power to rural communities from local substations is by wooden poles supporting high-quality insulators and insulated conductors. The voltage carried is 11 000 volts AC.*

routed from local substations to community transformers supported safely out of reach between two sizeable wooden poles – Figure 6.45 illustrates this. These transformers are rated (measured) in kilovolt-amps (that is, apparent power) but not kiloamps. At this point, the voltage is reduced again to 400 volts. A network of overhead (but sometimes underground) triple-phase and neutral conductors then distributes power to the consumers. Each house requiring a single-phase 230 volt supply is tapped off alternate phases along the route in order to balance the load. In urban areas, power distribution is connected in a series of rings. This helps to decrease voltage drop and the cross-sectional area of the distribution conductor.

Figure 6.45 – *Transformers, suspended on wooden poles, reduce the incoming voltage to 400 volts (three-phase and neutral) for distribution to rural homes and businesses throughout the community. Earthing arrangements are usually TT.*

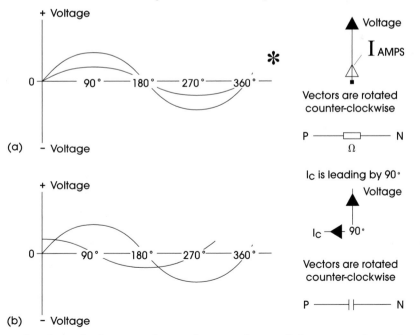

Figure 6.46 – *(a) The relationship between voltage and current when applied to a pure resistance in an AC circuit. (b) The relationship between voltage and capacitance when applied to an AC circuit.*

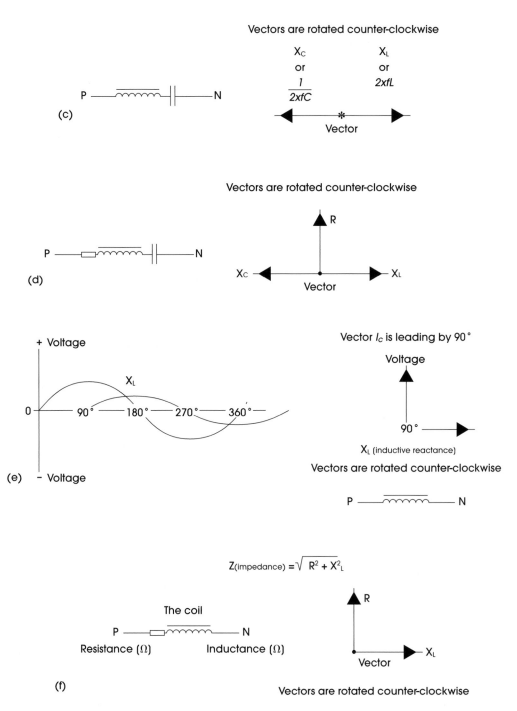

Vectors are rotated counter-clockwise

X_C
or
$\dfrac{1}{2xfC}$

X_L
or
$2xfL$

Vector

(c)

Vectors are rotated counter-clockwise

R

X_C

X_L

Vector

(d)

+ Voltage

X_L

0   90°   180°   270°   360°

(e)   – Voltage

Vector I_C is leading by 90°

Voltage

90°

X_L (inductive reactance)

Vectors are rotated counter-clockwise

P   N

$Z_{(impedance)} = \sqrt{R^2 + X^2_L}$

The coil

P   N

Resistance (Ω)   Inductance (Ω)

R

X_L

Vector

(f)

Vectors are rotated counter-clockwise

Figure 6.46 continued – *(c) The relationship between pure inductance and capacitance in series when applied to an AC circuit. (d) The relationship between pure resistance, inductance and capacitance in series when applied to an AC circuit. (e) The relationship between voltage and pure inductance when applied to an AC circuit. (f) Finding the impedance of a simple coil or solenoid.*

Practical activities

You might be asked, as part of your electrical course, to draw circuit waveforms and phasor diagrams for AC circuits containing the following, of which some are in series formation:

- Pure resistance.
- Pure capacitance.
- Pure inductance and capacitance.
- Resistance, inductance and capacitance.
- Pure inductance.
- Finding the impedance (Z) of a coil.

Please refer to Figure 6.46 for technical details.

Resin-filled cable joints

There are many different types of jointing kits available to suit every application. We will review the popular straight-through joint – a three-core 6 mm^2 SWA/PVC cable.

Scope and limitations

- All standard steel wire armoured cables.
- PVC (XLPE) – SWA/PVC cables.
- Special cables – example: mines and quarries cables and cables up to 3.3 kV.
- Armoured control and telephone cables.

Making sure you understand what you are doing

If you have never attempted to make a *resin-filled cable joint* by yourself, please read the instructions accompanying your jointing kit – this is most important, as sometimes, you will *not* have a second opportunity to make the joint!

Useful guidelines

- Your cables must be 'dead'.
- Do not smoke whilst making the joint.
- Make sure your joint is made in a well ventilated area.
- Do not breathe in the fumes created by the liquid resin.

- Wear protective gloves when handling/pouring the liquid resin.
- Avoid getting the liquid resin on your skin – it will stain and is difficult to remove once dried.
- Wipe up liquid resin spillages immediately they happen – wear your gloves!
- Place all waste material (boxes, pieces of moulded plastic, strands of steel wire armouring and PVC off-cuts) in the site skip.
- Do not make your joint in the rain.
- Your liquid resin/hardener package must be mixed in a warm environment so it will set properly – this is important.

Putting your resin-filled joint together

This is a step-by-step approach to make things easier for you. To demonstrate, we will be jointing a 3-core 6 mm^2 steel wire armoured cable – my apologies for the long list!

- Place the bottom section of your joint on a flat, dry surface and saw off part of the ends to allow your cable to snugly fit into the 'half-cups' provided for cable entry.
- Remove sufficient armouring and inner cable bedding to expose your coloured conductors. Range your conductors so that their ends are just past the centre position of the bottom section of your joint.
- Leave about 10 mm of inner PVC bedding past the point where you have cut the steel wire armouring. To maintain your bonding and continuity, you must expose about 10 mm of armouring, as illustrated in Figure 6.47.
- Repeat your preparation routine with the other cable, making sure you range the end of your conductors a little past the mid-point position of the base section of your joint.
- Place each cable into the half cups provided so they are facing each other. Check that the *outer* PVC sheath of your cable is about 15 mm past the cable entry point into the joint.
- Cut your conductors where they are to be jointed. Remove a few millimetres of the

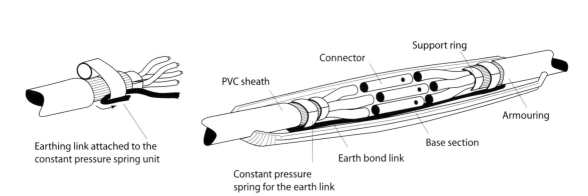

Figure 6.47 – *Cable core arrangement serving a resin through joint.*

coloured insulation and join colour to colour with the joining devices provided. If they are uninsulated, you might prefer to sleeve them if you are concerned that they could touch each other or rub against the earth continuity strap, which also may be uninsulated.

■ After successfully jointing your conductors, fit the earth bonding/continuity strap from each side of the exposed steel wire armouring by tucking the strap firmly under the constant pressure spring and winding this spring around the galvanised armouring as shown in Figure 6.47. Take time to do this properly – *the circuit protective conductor is very important!*

■ Finally, wrap a layer of tape around the two cables where they enter the plastic joint to prevent resin leakage when filled. Sometimes the manufacturer will add soft foam seals to the kit instead of insulating tape.

■ Saw off the ends of the top section of your joint so that your cable will fit snugly around the 'half-cups' allowed for cable entry into the plastic joint.

■ Place the top section of the joint onto the bottom section and 'click together'. If your joint has no built-in automatic fixing lugs, then you will find plastic or metal spring-clips to slide onto the side of the joint in order to obtain a good seal.

■ Use a mastic sealer or an adhesive strip/ insulation tape to seal your external cable ends. This will help to prevent resin leakage.

Preparing the industrial resin filler for your plastic joint housing

■ Put on the plastic gloves provided in your jointing kit.

■ Take out the flexible inner plastic bag from the stiff outer protective bag.

■ Remove the rigid plastic divider that separates the resin from the hardener.

■ Push the contents of the bag together for about two minutes by squeezing, rolling and manipulating to produce an even coloured mix. If it is very cold, then mix in a warm location. This will help make the resin mix set quicker when poured into the joint.

■ Push the mixed contents of the bag to one corner and slice off about 10 mm of the opposite corner (free from liquid) to form a pouring hole.

■ Empty the contents of your bag into the top of your joint to a level that is 2 or 3 mm from the top of the opening. Do this within ten minutes, as after that time the resin will start to set – especially during warm weather. If you overfill, the resin will spill over the sides of the plastic housing when placing the lid and your joint will appear unprofessional.

■ Click on the lid provided – your joint is complete!

It is best to leave your freshly completed joint in a safe position until it has hardened. Once set, place your joint in the ground and back fill. Make sure there are no sharp flint stones or other objects around your joint when packing the soil to reinstate your trench. If it is practical, bed your joint on about 100 mm of sand and add the same depth on top to form protection. Finally, remember to place a plastic yellow 'Danger – electrical power cable below' strip about 300 mm above the top of your newly formed joint.

Fire detection and alarm systems

Requirements

The requirements you must follow to install fire detection and alarm systems must comply with the demands of BS 5839, Part 1:1998. It would be wise to obtain a photocopy of these requirements, called the Code of Practice for Systems, Design Installation and Servicing from your college library or, if they are unable to help, from your local public library. There is usually a small charge attached to this service. BS 7671: 1992 (our Wiring Regulations) will not apply to this type of installation.

What type of cable may I use?

You can wire using MI cable or a suitable fire-resistant/flame-retardant cable such as Pirelli FP200®. Other makes, such as Fire Tuff®, are available from your electrical wholesaler.

Segregating the cables you use in fire detection and alarm circuits from other installations, by at least 300 mm, will meet with the requirements of

Regulations 528-01-03 to 04. However, separation is not required when your fire alarm system is installed using MI cable.

It is wise to leave the wiring of your fire alarm until most of the construction work is finished. This will help to avoid accidental damage to the cables and panel.

Wiring your fire alarm

Please read the manufacturer's technical instructions before starting work. Wiring methods do vary from manufacturer to manufacturer so it is best to become familiar with the task ahead before you start your installation.

Wire fire detectors and call points in a continuous parallel formation arrangement as illustrated in Figure 6.48. You may install up to 30 current-consuming smoke detectors from one zone – wire as shown in Figure 6.49. Call points are not current-consuming, so supply any number you like from one zone. Never spur off from your circuit as spurring would make it very difficult to monitor for breaks and other problems that can occur. Wire your circuits or zones as short as possible. For your sounders, wire in parallel formation and serve with *two* circuits. If there are four sounders sited in a long passageway, wire the first on circuit 'A', the

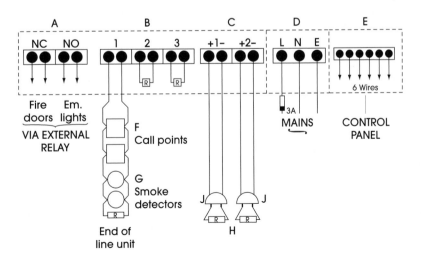

Figure 6.48 – *Fire alarm panel termination block. A, auxiliary contacts; B, fire detection zones; C, sounder circuits; D, low-voltage mains supply; E, connections to a remote indicator panel; F, call points; G, smoke detectors; H, end-of-line resistor; J, sounders; N/C, normally closed contacts; N/O normally open contacts.*

second on circuit 'B', the third on circuit 'A' and the fourth controlled from circuit 'B'. Your last smoke detector, manual call point or sounder *must* be fitted with an end of line resistor – these are with your fire alarm package as shown in Figure 6.50.

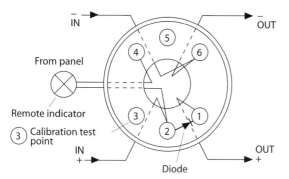

Figure 6.49 – *Wiring arrangement for a typical smoke detector base.*

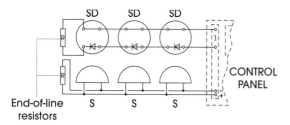

Figure 6.50 – *Wire your sounders and smoke detectors as a continuous radial, terminating with an end-of-line resistor as illustrated. SD, smoke detectors; S, polarised sounders.*

Intruder alarm systems

Our regulations do not apply to extra-low-voltage intruder alarm systems. BS 7671 classifies an intruder alarm system as a Category 2 installation (see Regulation 528-01-03 and BS 6701). Wire in separate PVCu conduit or mini-trunking and keep your circuits away from large current-consuming electric motors, contactors and other low-voltage mains services.

Modern systems

As with fire detection and alarm circuits, the designs of intruder alarm systems vary from manufacturer to manufacturer. It is important to read and digest the instructions before you start your installation.

Contemporary systems are very refined and can use a wide range of devices to trigger an alarm condition. Here are just some of them:

- Infrared barriers.
- Extra-low-voltage passive infrared detectors.
- Glass breakage detectors.
- Pressure mat (connects usually open).
- Magnetic door contacts.
- Body temperature detector.
- Ultrasound motion detection.

Others include Doppler devices, active microwave motion detectors and personal attack buttons.

Type of wiring

It is best to use three-pair, multi-colour stranded wire, of about 0.25 mm^2 in cross-sectional area. Please resist using telephone cable for your intruder alarm installation – proper three-pair/stranded cabling is far better for this type of work.

A typical system would operate from an independent direct current source of between 10 and 18 volts originating from a central control panel from which all wires serving the installation are connected. Some intruder and alarm systems have incorporated a small key pad where the operator has to log in a personalised PIN in order to activate or deactivate a protected 'walk-in area'. Other keypad options are available – these vary from manufacturer to manufacturer.

Connecting from your panel to your movement detectors and triggering devices

Figure 6.51 illustrates in broad terms a typical termination layout serving an intruder alarm panel in which both extra-low and low-voltage circuits are connected. Provide separation in order to segregate the two systems if you are building the control panel yourself – Regulation 528-01-07 will confirm this. When purchasing your intruder alarm panel over the counter, your electrical separation requirement is inbuilt.

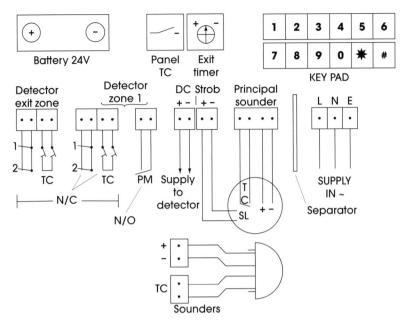

Figure 6.51 – *Termination arrangements serving a typical intruder alarm panel. TC, tamper circuit; N/C, normally closed contacts; N/O, normally open contacts; SL, strobe light; PM, pressure mat.*

Terminating your movement detector

A typical PIR movement detector (Figure 6.52) will accommodate up to three circuits. A small connector block provides two terminals for a permanent DC extra-low-voltage supply and a further two for the alarm circuit. The last pair of terminals is reserved for the series wired tamper circuit. It is necessary to connect each coloured wire into the small terminal block correctly since damage could result from wiring the wrong way. Always read your instructions.

Lightning protection

Lightning protection is a highly specialised skill and generally does not fall within the scope of our electrical regulations, other than the general requirement of providing a main equipotential bonding conductor from the lightning protection system to your main earthing terminal. On a tall commercial building, an earthing terminal will take the form of a purpose-made copper earthing bar often some 30 mm wide by 8 mm thick, mounted on spacers near to the source of the electrical supply. A suitable size earthing conductor originating from the supplier's earthing point (the size will depend on the type of earthing arrangements and the cross-sectional area of the 'tails' serving the installation) will be cable lugged and bolted to this bar. Make your earth/bond connection for the lightning protection circuit at this point.

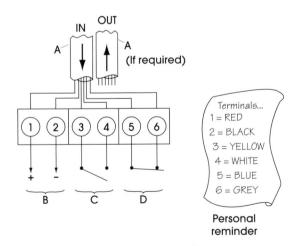

Figure 6.52 – *Termination arrangement serving a typical movement detector. A, six-core installation cable; B, extra-low-voltage supply serving the detector; C, alarm circuit; D, tamper circuit.*

195

Useful guidance notes

- BS 6651, Codes of Practice for Protection of Structures against Lightning. Section 9 provides guidance on lightning protection of structures with a built-in explosive risk.

- BS 7430: 1998, Code of Practice for Earthing Lightning Protection. Section 23 provides guidance on lightning protection.

- Hazardous area classification web site at www.hazardousareas.com

7 Basic electronics

Introduction

Electronics is the name given to a branch of electrical work that makes use of various devices such as resistors, semiconductors, etc., where current flow is not necessarily through a continuous conductor, as in the case of electrical installation work, but through a vacuum, gas or semiconductor, such as a transistor.

This chapter will provide you with a basic knowledge of electronics and act as a stepping stone to more advanced levels. The topics within this chapter form part of an introductory aid to help you in your everyday working activities. The knowledge gained will enable you to build on basic skills and gain more confidence within the workplace.

Soldering techniques

Soldering is a heating process of melting a soft lead–tin alloy metal over and between two wires or between one wire and a printed circuit board to form an electro-mechanical joint, as illustrated in Figure 7.1.

Just twisting bare copper wires together will lead to a chemical process known as *oxidation*. The oxide formed over the wires creates an electrical barrier (a resistance) between the two twisted conductors and reduces the current flow within the circuit. Keep in mind that the voltages applied to electronic circuits are very small compared with the voltages you have to deal with in your installation work and soldering will prevent this problem.

A few safety precautions to keep in mind

Please take a little time to read the following points:

- Check the condition of your soldering iron, flexible lead and plug and choose the right solder for your task.
- Place your iron in a spiral rest when you are not using it and keep the hot iron away from flammable materials and liquids.
- Lead is poisonous – avoid breathing in the fumes from the hot iron.
- Keep the hot tip away from your flexible supply cable, as shown in Figure 7.2.
- Heat shunts (a tool that allows soldering of delicate parts without damaging the component) can become very hot: take care when handling!
- A damp sponge is useful to remove *overloaded solder* from the tip of the soldering iron.
- Use *safety glasses* to protect your eyes when you are desoldering.

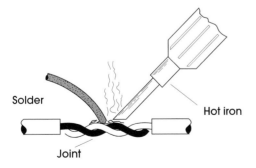

Figure 7.1 – *Soldering: a process of melting a soft lead–tin alloy over and between two wires that are to be bonded together.*

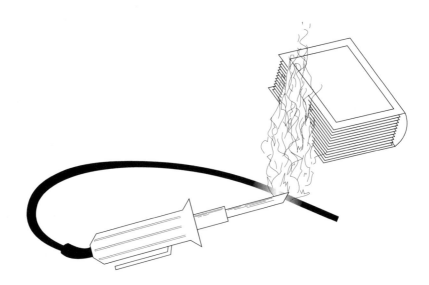

Figure 7.2 – *Place the hot tip away from the lead and from burnable materials when in immediate use.*

- It is not good practice to file *copper plated* steel soldering iron bits; always replace if damage occurs.

Soldering a conductor

A step-by-step approach follows:

1 Clean the conductors with cleaning fluid and position on thermal insulation.

2 Choose the correct type and gauge of solder (22 gauge with built-in flux – a wetting agent) for lightweight electrical connections, illustrated in Figure 7.3, and select the appropriate tip to do your job. Adjust your temperature control to about 250°C. Switch on.

3 When your iron has reached the required temperature, clean the tip using a tip cleaning pot as illustrated in Figure 7.4 then *tin* your bare conductors by offering the solder wire to the hot tip of the iron and transferring a blob of solder to the base of the copper conductors. Both conductors will now look bright and shiny.

4 Twist the tinned conductors together; apply a splash of solder to the tip of your soldering iron, Figure 7.5, and place the twisted conductors on top of the hot soldering iron. Distribute the heat evenly – *do not over-heat* and, if additional flux is used, then use sparingly.

5 The hot solder will unite with your joint. It will appear bright and shiny, as illustrated in Figure 7.6 part (a), but avoid 'spiky joints' as shown in part (b). Now clean your soldering iron tip with a damp sponge and switch off.

6 Place a heat-shrink insulator that will comfortably fit over the soldered joint and warm with a hot air blower. The heat-shrink insulation will get smaller and fit snugly around your joint.

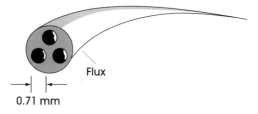

Flux

0.71 mm

Figure 7.3 – *Three-core non-corrosive flux incorporated within 22 standard wire gauge (SWG) solder wire.*

Figure 7.4 – *Tip cleaner/tinner pot for bench top use. (Reproduced by kind permission of RS Components Limited.)*

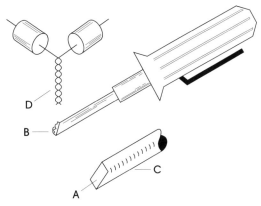

Figure 7.5 – *A, solder applied to the working area of the iron; B, solder blob; C, soldering bit; D, twisted and tinned conductors to be soldered.*

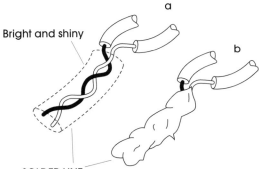

Figure 7.6 – *The right and the wrong way to make a soldered joint. (a) Satisfactory; (b) too much solder and spiky.*

Additional points

There are a few more points that I feel you should keep in mind:

- Dull and pitted joints need to be re-soldered.

- Always keep the heated iron under the workpiece.

- Keep your solder in a constant fluid state.

- Use a heat shunt when necessary.

- When soldering a component to a printed circuit board, first bend the leads as shown in Figure 7.7. This will stop the component from falling out when the board is turned over for soldering.

- Leave a small gap between the joint and the insulation to prevent the insulation from melting when heat is applied.

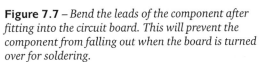

Leads bent

Figure 7.7 – *Bend the leads of the component after fitting into the circuit board. This will prevent the component from falling out when the board is turned over for soldering.*

Types of solder

Solder is an *alloy* (a mixture of two or more metals) made from about 80% tin and 20% lead. Soft solder, used for electrical and electronic work, will melt between 200 and 300°C. Hard solder, often known as *silver solder,* contains quantities of silver mixed with the alloy. Brazing solder is a mixture of zinc and copper. It will join copper surfaces together permanently. Many solder wires used in electronics are *rosin cored* and an additional wetting agent (flux) is not necessary. This type of solder consists of 60% tin and 40% lead and is ideal for general electrical jobs that need careful handling. Rosin core solder wire is obtainable as a reel, stick or on a dispenser, as illustrated in Figure 7.8.

At the manufacturing stage, by adding small amounts of sulfur, arsenic or bismuth, the characteristics of solder can be changed. This type of solder is for special use and is not for general use.

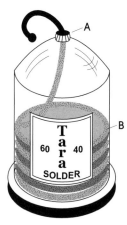

Figure 7.8 – *Rosin core solder wire from a dispenser. A, dispenser port; B, solder coil.*

Why do we use flux in soldering?

Soldering flux is an efficient way to remove the unwanted oxide. It allows the molten solder to bond with the copper wires. Flux is a wetting agent – it helps maintain the solder in liquid form when heated. Use your flux sparingly and choose the thickness of your solder to allow you to make your joint within about 2 or 3 seconds.

Standard wire gauges

You can find flexible solder wire in five different standard wire gauges (SWG): 14, 16, 18 and 24 SWG.

- For small components, use 18 SWG.
- Use 22 or 24 SWG solder for medium size tasks such as connecting large power transistors.
- One of the largest diameter solder wires, 16 SWG, is ideal for electrical installation engineering tasks.

Types of soldering irons and their use

Find different kinds and styles of soldering irons in Table 7.1. As a rule of thumb, the thickness of the solder wire we use will be in proportion to the size of the soldering iron bit.

Voltages

The four most common voltages at which soldering irons operate are as follows:

- 230 volt AC for workshop use.
- 110 volt AC for site work.
- 50 volt AC for production work and motor vehicle repair workshops.
- 12–24 volt DC for field tasks (where there is no mains electricity).

Table 7.1 – *Soldering irons used in electrical work.*

Type of soldering iron	Use and comments
Auto feed	Used in continuous process work. Solder wire is automatically fed onto a heated soldering tip where it is applied to the work piece (110 or 230 volts).
Cordless	Gas operated or heated by a rechargeable battery. Used by field engineers where there is no access to mains electricity.
Hobbyist	Low wattage 'throw-away' type. Okay for occasional tasks – 230 volt.
Miniature	Used in the workshop to solder *surface mounted devices* by hand. Low wattage only and 230 volt.
Soldering station	Used by professionals. Temperature controlled and replacement parts available. Suitable for most applications providing the soldering bit is changed. Soldering stations can be expensive (110 and 230 volts).
Soldering gun	Used for fast heat applications. Reaches the maximum tip temperature in less than ten seconds. The gun provides intermittent power – used on 230 volt mains supply.
Variable temperature	Ideal when a soldering station is impractical and temperature control is required.

Power ratings

Power ratings vary but are not always proportional to the size of the iron:

Miniature mains soldering irons	15 watt
Hobbyist irons	25 watt
Professional soldering irons	35–40 watt
Large heavy-duty soldering irons	100 watt

A *watt* is a unit of power or energy. Multiply the value of the current in *amps* flowing in the circuit by the applied *voltage* to obtain the power rating in watts.

Plugs, sockets and connectors: definitions

Plug

A hand-held device with electrical contact pins designed to be slotted into a socket.

Electronic plugs are either insulated or screened and are attached to a flexible cable. Figure 7.9 illustrates two such plugs.

Socket

This is a device with internal contacts, formed into a stretched hollow or slot. These female contacts hold a plug to serve an electronic circuit as shown in Figure 7.10.

Connector

These come in all shapes and sizes. They act as a flexible mechanical coupler for joining cables/conductors together. Table 7.2 lists five common plugs or connecting devices used in electronics and explains their use.

Electronic components
How to identify

The following can identify electronic components:

- Colour coding – *resistors, capacitors, wires, etc.*
- Component leads – *capacitors, integrated circuits and transistors.*

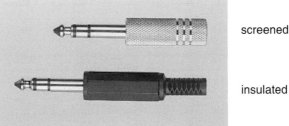

screened

insulated

Figure 7.9 – *Electronic three-pole plug. (Reproduced by kind permission of RS Components Limited.)*

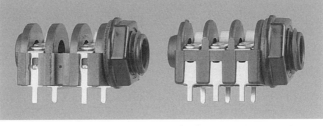

2-pole mono   3-pole stereo

Figure 7.10 – *Two- and three-pole printed circuit board mounting sockets. (Reproduced by kind permission of RS Components Limited.)*

Table 7.2 – *Common plugs and connecting devices used in electronics.*

Accessory	Comments	Illustration
DIN connector	DIN stands for *Deutsche Industrie Norm*. Use these plugs for television, CD players, videos, audio equipment, computers and digital radios. They are available with 3, 4, 5 and 7 pins. The wire connection points are the soldered type and the connection pins are often silver-plated. Suitable up to 100 volts AC or 150 volts DC at 2 amps	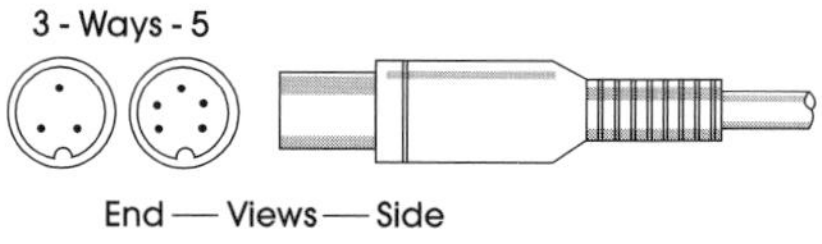 3 - Ways - 5 End — Views — Side **Figure 7.11** – *DIN connector.*
Speaker plug	This is a two-pinned plug. Often one pin is flat whilst the other is round so the plug is connected correctly. Used in audio speaker circuits	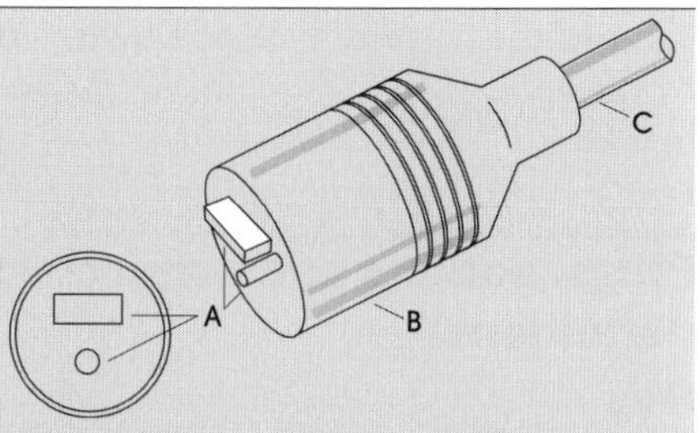 **Figure 7.12** – *Speaker plug. A, connection pins; B, moulded case; C, service cable.*
Phono connector	A squat type of plug often with a coloured insulated mounded body. Used in audio equipment. One insulated wire is connected to each connection point. Obtainable as a moulded metal case type for heavier use	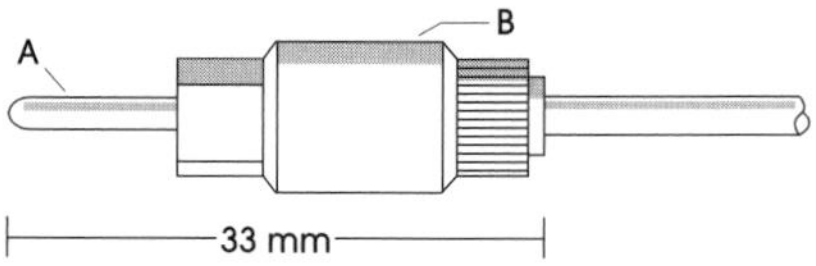 33 mm **Figure 7.13** – *Phono connectors. A, connection pins; B, moulded case.*
Insulation Deformity Connector, known as IDC connectors	Similar to a telephone outlet connector. The insulation ruptures when forced into the connector with an IDC connector tool. Often used to terminate *ribbon cable*	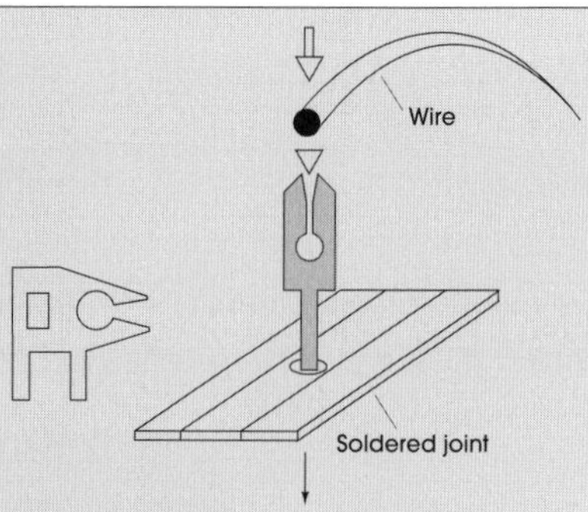 Wire Soldered joint **Figure 7.14** – *Insulated deformity connectors.*
Banana plug	Quite chubby and has a small spring attached to the conductive parts as illustrated. Will accept one soldered connection only. Often used to serve certain types of instrument leads	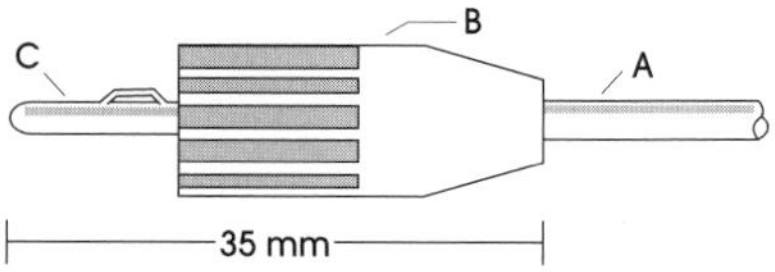 35 mm **Figure 7.15** – *Banana plug. A, single conductor; B, moulded case; C, connection pin.*

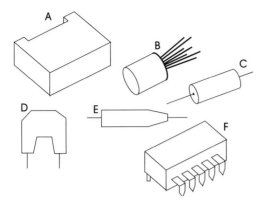

Figure 7.16 – *Many electronic components can be recognised by their shape. A, flat pack; B, metal can relay; C, resistor; D, capacitor; E, diode; F, integrated circuit.*

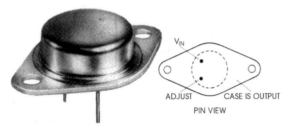

Figure 7.16a – *A three-terminal, variable voltage regulator. (Reproduced by kind permission of RS Components Limited.)*

- Shape of component – *flat pack, metal can relays, resistors, capacitors, semiconductors and integrated circuits (Figure 7.16).*
- Arrangement of the leads – *diodes, relay bases and TTL devices.*
- The material from which the component's outer case is made – *variable voltage regulators (Figure 7.16a), metal relay cans, plastic used for TTL devices, coloured see-through plastic used for light emitting diodes and tubular glass fuses.*
- Letters and numbers (summarised by the word *alphanumerical*, which will be used again in this book) – *resistors and capacitors.*

Resistors

Table 7.3 describes four different types of resistors used in electronic work. A brief description of their make-up and an illustration

of their BSEN 60617 location symbol are available.

Other types of resistors

Many other types of resistor are available including the following:

- Wire wound.
- Top adjusting (the value of your resistance may be slightly altered).
- Conductive plastic.
- Sub miniature.
- Open (skeleton type) – preset.
- Thick film resistor network.

Finding the value of a resistor

Resistor values are represented by a series of coloured bands around the body of the resistor or are coded using a mixture of letters and numbers (alphanumerical coding). Resistors do not represent their stated value so a *tolerance factor* is provided to balance this situation. The tolerance factor of a resistor is a plus/minus percentage of the stated value. This is obtained from the last coloured band when reading from left to right. As an example, if a 100 Ω carbon resistor has a tolerance of 10%, the true value will lie between 90 and 110 Ω.

How to work out the value

Each colour corresponds to a number to enable you to work out the value, as Figure 7.21 illustrates.

- *Band 1 (from left to right)* represents the first number.
- *Band 2* is the second number.
- *Band 3* is the multiplier.
- *Band 4 (far right and slightly separated from the others)* is the tolerance of the resistor.

When five bands are used, the first three represent the first three numbers. The fourth band then becomes the multiplier and the fifth and last band is the percentage tolerance to expect.

Table 7.4 will help you work out the value of an unknown resistor. For example, a four-band

203

Table 7.3 – *Resistors used in electronic work.*

Type	Description or use	BSEN 60617 symbol and figure number
Fixed resistor	Made from carbon, metal oxide, metal film or glaze. Values from 10 Ω to 1 MΩ. Power rating from 0.125 to 300 watt housed within an aluminium heat sink *A, resistance element; B, body of the resistor; C, connection leads.*	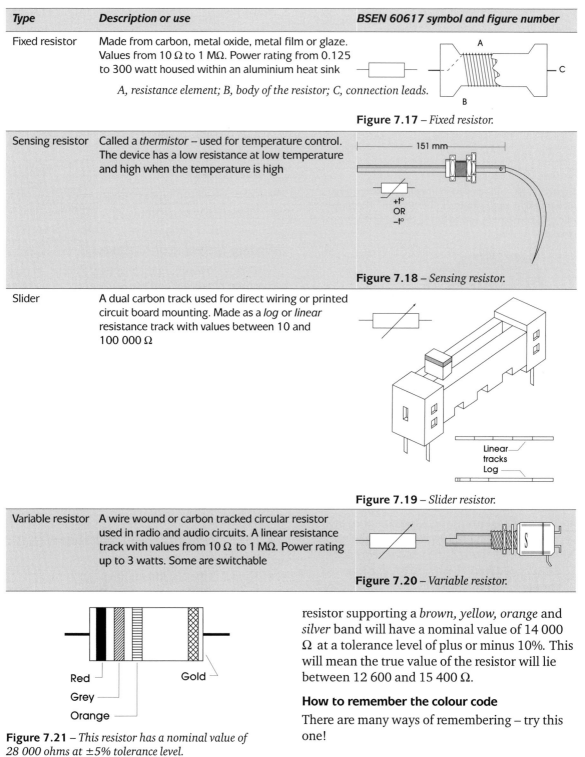 **Figure 7.17** – *Fixed resistor.*
Sensing resistor	Called a *thermistor* – used for temperature control. The device has a low resistance at low temperature and high when the temperature is high	**Figure 7.18** – *Sensing resistor.*
Slider	A dual carbon track used for direct wiring or printed circuit board mounting. Made as a *log* or *linear* resistance track with values between 10 and 100 000 Ω	**Figure 7.19** – *Slider resistor.*
Variable resistor	A wire wound or carbon tracked circular resistor used in radio and audio circuits. A linear resistance track with values from 10 Ω to 1 MΩ. Power rating up to 3 watts. Some are switchable	**Figure 7.20** – *Variable resistor.*

Figure 7.21 – *This resistor has a nominal value of 28 000 ohms at ±5% tolerance level.*

resistor supporting a *brown, yellow, orange* and *silver* band will have a nominal value of 14 000 Ω at a tolerance level of plus or minus 10%. This will mean the true value of the resistor will lie between 12 600 and 15 400 Ω.

How to remember the colour code

There are many ways of remembering – try this one!

Table 7.4 – *Resistor colour coding.*

Colour of bands (1–3)	Number	Multiplier (band 3)	Tolerance as a percentage
Black	0	1	–
Brown	1	10	1
Red	2	100	2
Orange	3	1000	–
Yellow	4	10 000	–
Green	5	100 000	–
Blue	6	1000 000	–
Violet	7		–
Grey	8		–
White	9		–
Gold (last band)			5
Silver			10
No colour (where the last colour would have been)			20

Bleached **Br**ead **R**arely **O**ffends **Y**oung **Gree**dy **Blue**bottles **V**andalising **Grey** **Wh**eat meal

The bold-type letters stand for the colour or the first letters of the colour in numerical order. For **Bl**eached, read *black* (0) and for **Br**ead, translate as *brown* (1) and so on.

Resistor coding using both numbers and letters

Figure 7.22 illustrates this method of coding. The first letter, reading from left to right, indicates the multiplier – or the position of the decimal point (please refer to Table 7.5 for details) whilst the second letter identifies the percentage tolerance of the resistor.

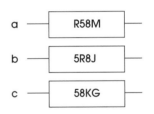

Figure 7.22 – *Resistors coded with both numbers and letters. a, 0.58 Ω; b, –5.8 Ω; c, 58 000 Ω, with a tolerance of 2%.*

As an example:
R 58 M translates as **0.58** Ω at 20% tolerance, whilst **5 R 8 J** means that the resistor is **5.8** Ω at 5% tolerance.

Table 7.5 – *Finding the value of resistors using a code of both letters and numbers.*

First letter	Multiplier (Ω)	Term	Second letter indicating tolerance	As a percentage
R	1	ohms	F	1
K	1000	kilo	G	2
M	1000 000	mega	J	5
G	1000 000 000	giga	K	10
T	1000 000 000 000	tera	M	20

205

Capacitors

A capacitor is an electronic device that will allow an electric charge to be stored when both plates are at opposite potentials (one positively charged, the other negatively charged). This is *capacitance.*

A thin section of insulating material such as mica (the *dielectric*) and two matching size tin foil plates placed either side of the dielectric will make a very simple capacitor. Figure 7.23 illustrates this. Applying a direct current voltage of opposite potentials (one *positive,* one *negative*) across the plates will give the illusion that current is flowing. This will quickly decrease when the capacitor is fully charged.

If you now remove your DC supply, the plates will hold their charge of electricity. To discharge, link the leads of the capacitor together by means of an insulated test resistor. Current will 'flow' but this time in the reverse direction.

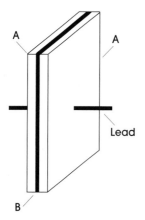

Figure 7.23 – *A simple capacitor. A, plates; B, dielectric insulating material.*

The unit of capacitance

The unit of capacitance is the *farad,* whose symbol is F. This is a very large unit to use, so for practical purposes it is subdivided into smaller units call *microfarads.* This represents a millionth part of one farad and is given the symbol μF. The *picofarad* is smaller still, which is equivalent to one-millionth part of one microfarad – identified by the symbol pF.

Graphical symbols (capacitors)

Figure 7.24 illustrates the BSEN 60617 symbol for a capacitor. Electrolytic capacitors (capacitors that must have the correct direct current polarity across their terminals) have a similar symbol but a small plus (+) sign is added to indicate the positive terminal.

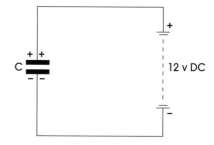

Figure 7.24 – *A BSEN 60617 graphical symbol for an electrolytic capacitor. The capacitor is connected across a 12 volt battery.*

Types of capacitors

A few of the many types of capacitor are:

- solid tantalum
- high capacity – paper insulated
- computer grade – high ripple
- ceramic.

Table 7.6 describes four different types of capacitor commonly used in electronics.

Capacitor value coding

This can vary slightly, but most manufacturers will follow the same coding as laid down for resistors.

Large cylinder-type capacitors used in electrical engineering have their values printed on the side of their protective containers. Smaller varieties are colour coded – read as picofarads.

The *tolerance colour code* is slightly different from those of resistors and this will be clear to you when checking through Table 7.7. When reading colour-coded resistors, you must take the first band of colour to be the one from the point of connection.

Table 7.6 – *Commonly used capacitors.*

Capacitor type	Description/use	Illustration
Fixed non-polarised	Housed in a plastic or metal can. Various shapes. Various values from 2.2 pF to several microfarads. General use in electronic and electric motor circuits	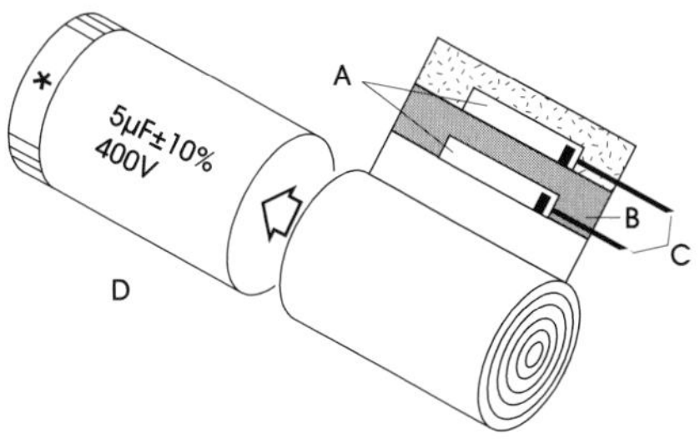 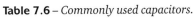 **Figure 7.25** – *An open view of a non-polarised capacitor.*
Polarised	Often housed in single or double-ended cans. Sub miniature types are about 7 x 4 mm in size. Used in radio and television circuitry. Essential to connect correctly	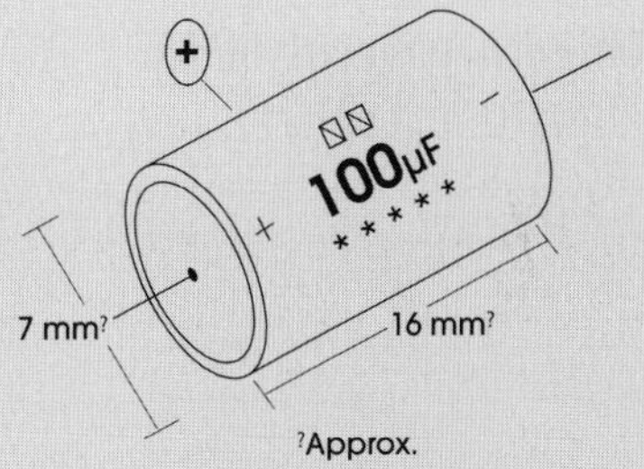 **Figure 7.26** – *Polarised capacitor (it has positive and negative terminals).*
Trimmer	Used when final adjustment to a circuit is needed. Usually made with a mica dielectric and ceramic base	 **Figure 7.27** – *Trimmer capacitor (can be varied in value). (Reproduced by kind permission of RS Components Limited.)*
Variable (air type)	Consists of two metal plates. One plate is rotated by means of a central spindle to intermingle with the second plate that is fixed. Both plates are insulated from each other – the dielectric is air. Used as a radio tuner	 **Figure 7.28** – *Variable air-type capacitor.*

Table 7.7 – *Capacitor tolerance colour coding.*

Colour of tolerance band	Percentage tolerance
Brown	1
Red	2
Orange	2.5
Green	5
White	10
Black	20

Other types of electronic components

Complementary metal oxide semiconductors (C-MOS)

Handle these devices with care. *Static electricity –* an electrical charge that is stationary – can harm them.

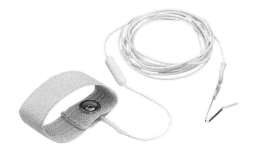

Figure 7.29 – *An anti-static wrist strap. (Reproduced by kind permission of RS Components Limited.)*

C-MOS semiconductors include the following:

- operational amplifiers
- general integrated circuits
- programmable clock/timer integrated circuits
- memory integrated circuits.

Use *anti-static handling devices* to prevent your fingers touching the conductors serving the device. It is advisable to wear an electrically earthed wrist strap, as illustrated in Figure 7.29.

Discrete semiconductor devices

This is the name given to diodes, thyristors, triacs and AC mains power regulators (see Figure 7.30). It also describes any stand-alone electronic device that is not part of an *integrated circuit.* This type of circuit is a circuit consisting of many devices that, together, form a single appliance where sub-dividing would destroy it, for example, a video phone or a DVD player.

Transistor–transistor logic devices (TTL)

These components belong to a group that also contains the *complementary metal oxide semiconductor.* Each group member provides the same basic logic functions. They all have different supply voltages, circuit layouts, switching speeds and logic levels. You will have to obtain data sheets that provide details of pin connections. These are available from your retail/wholesale outlet. A TTL circuit is illustrated in Figure 7.31.

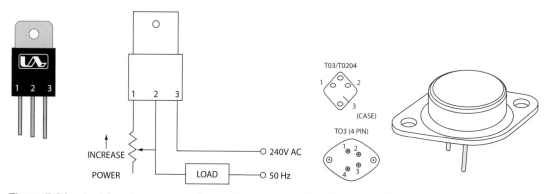

Figure 7.30 – *An AC mains power regulator, left; transistor, right. (Reproduced by kind permissioin of RS Components Limited.)*

Figure 7.31 – *Transistor–transistor, logic circuit – TTL. (Reproduced by kind permission of RS Components Limited.)*

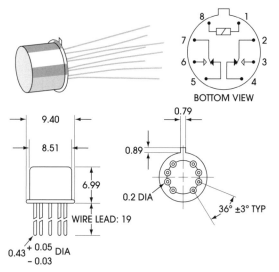

BOTTOM VIEW

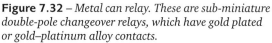

WIRE LEAD: 19

$0.43^{+0.05}_{-0.03}$ DIA

Figure 7.32 – *Metal can relay. These are sub-miniature double-pole changeover relays, which have gold plated or gold–platinum alloy contacts.*

Metal can relay

This component is a sealed, airtight relay (a switch operated by a coil of wire around a soft iron core which, when energized, becomes a magnet and attracts a switching action that either opens or closes electrical contacts) as shown in Figure 7.32.

Flat pack

Similar to a metal can relay but constructed as a *double-pole change-over switch* for very low current use (typically 2–4 amps AC or DC). The movement is similar to a two-way switch. The relay contacts are silver-plated. Figure 7.33 illustrates the internal wiring arrangements.

Plastic dual-in-line plugs (DIL)

This component is designed to terminate ribbon cable or single conductors and can be fitted within standard integrated circuit sockets.

Insulation displacement connectors (reviewed earlier) placed within the bottom of the plug allow for termination of the ribbon cable. This is used for computer and printer circuitry, etc. This component is also available for soldering directly onto a printed circuit board as Figure 7.34 illustrates.

'D' type connectors

Use this type of connector, looking like a tall letter 'D', to terminate a ribbon cable. Figure 7.35 illustrates this.

BOTTOM VIEW

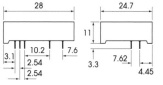

Figure 7.33 – *Flat pack. This double-pole changeover relay has gold-flashed silver contacts. (Reproduced by kind permission of RS Components Limited.)*

Figure 7.34 – *Dual-in-line socket. (Reproduced by kind permission of RS Components Limited.)*

Figure 7.35 – *'D' type connectors. (Reproduced by kind permission of RS Components Limited.)*

There are three ways to do this:

- By the insulation displacement method, providing a four-point contact.
- By soldering.
- By crimp, snap-in contacts aided by an insertion/extraction tool. Ask your tutor to show you one and to demonstrate how to use it.

Computers and printers use this type of connector. They are available with between 9 and 50 terminating points called '*ways*'.

Graphical symbols – electronics

Symbols illustrate and provide details of electronic circuitry. Each symbol follows each other in the same order as the circuit is wired. Imagine it as an electronic road map as Figure 7.36 will illustrate. If practical, draw your symbols in similar proportions to each other.

Table 7.8 lists a selection of graphical symbols used in electronic wiring diagrams. Others are available by looking through BSEN 61607, which larger public reference libraries will provide for you on request.

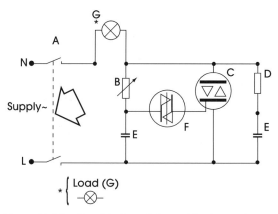

Figure 7.36 – *Graphical symbols used in electronic wiring diagrams. A, double-pole switch; B, variable resistor; C, varistor; D, resistor; E, capacitor; F, thyristors; G, lighting load. The circuit is for a domestic dimmer switch.*

Do not make up your own graphical symbols when designing a circuit. People who follow you will be confused – mistakes will then happen.

Strip board

Strip board is a board on which electronic components are soldered to form a circuit. Made from glass fibre-reinforced plastic, the board has

Table 7.8 – *Graphical symbols used for electronic drawings.*

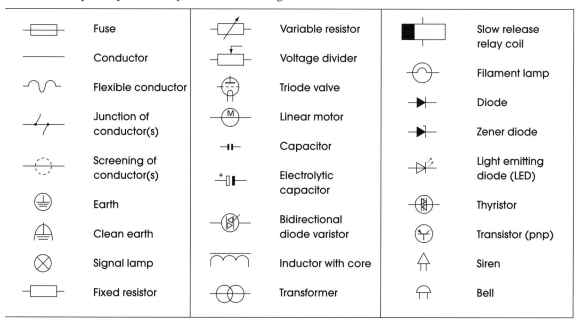

	Fuse		Variable resistor		Slow release relay coil
	Conductor		Voltage divider		Filament lamp
	Flexible conductor		Triode valve		Diode
	Junction of conductor(s)		Linear motor		Zener diode
	Screening of conductor(s)		Capacitor		Light emitting diode (LED)
	Earth		Electrolytic capacitor		Thyristor
	Clean earth		Bidirectional diode varistor		Transistor (pnp)
	Signal lamp		Inductor with core		Siren
	Fixed resistor		Transformer		Bell

strips of copper running its entire length. Each strip of copper has been insulated from the next. These are known as tracks and each track has tiny holes that are equally placed along its length. The holes provide an *anchorage point* for the electronic components to be soldered onto the copper track. The other side of the board has an insulated surface on which the components rest. The copper leads serving the components are threaded through the factory-made holes onto the copper track from the insulated side. This is the way to permanently solder the component to the copper strip.

A letter of the alphabet serves each copper track whilst the holes in the track are labelled with numbers. This provides a helpful wiring aid.

Track management – a way to isolate your components

When it is required to isolate components from one another, make a physical break within the copper track. To do this, just cut away the track with a suitable diameter drill bit or sharp electricians' knife within your chosen hole. This will electrically separate the two newly formed halves of the track from each other.

Strip boards are sometimes used for production work – but normally this type of work is favoured for prototype assembly schemes within a research and development department. For you, it is an ideal way to practice your soldering skills and getting the feel of both handling and mounting electronic components.

Other types of insulated component board

Printed circuit board

This is a board where the complete circuit is 'copper etched' onto the surface of the insulating board. The mounted components appear on the plain side of the board. You will have to drill tiny holes through the printed copper track (a sharp drill is essential or the copper track will tear) before your components can solder/be mounted. Avoid distractions – or you will make mistakes.

Printed component values on the copper trackside of the board provide helpful construction guidance.

Surface mount technology

Very similar to a printed circuit board except that the manufacturer has made tiny holes within the printed circuit board to accommodate your electronic components. The finished product is referred to as a PCB – surface mount board.

Breadboard

This technology is often used in the experimental/development and proving stages of a project. Breadboarding has several advantages over other methods of producing a working circuit. These are:

- Components are quicker and easier to install.
- No soldering is required.
- Far fewer connections are required between the components.
- All components are reusable.
- Design changes are easier to make.
- Few tools and little equipment are required.

Breadboard construction

Figure 7.37 illustrates a typical basic breadboard. Components and connecting wires are pushed into small holes that have sprung retaining contacts. Some holes, such as Row 5 of the illustration, are joined together internally

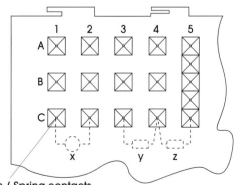

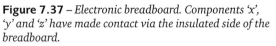

Holes / Spring contacts

Figure 7.37 – *Electronic breadboard. Components 'x', 'y' and 'z' have made contact via the insulated side of the breadboard.*

providing a means for a common connection. As a wiring aid, all holes are labelled with *numbers* and *letters*. This helps to avoid making silly mistakes.

Preparation – component mounting and soldering

Handle your components carefully with clean hands and plenty of patience. Take trouble to use your heat shunt whenever necessary – especially when mounting semiconductor components or damage will occur.

Listed are a few practical tips that you will find useful:

- Remove any dirt from your wire/cable and strip the insulation using wire strippers adjusted to the correct depth (see Figure 7.38). Avoid using wirecutters or pliers as the pressure-dent you make on the copper conductor will cause a weakness and your wire will snap off when bent.

- Snipe-nose pliers will be useful for the following jobs:
  - as a heat shunt
  - to bend and shape your conductors
  - to mount conductors into circuit boards
  - to hold a component whilst soldering.

- Mount your component as intended. Check the polarity – positive to the positive terminal and negative to the negative terminal. Examples include batteries, diodes and polarised capacitors.

Figure 7.38 – *Automatic wire stripper. (Reproduced by kind permission of RS Components Limited.)*

- Once you have placed your component's lead within the tiny hole serving a printed circuit board, bend the lead at right angles to stop your component from falling out when you turn the board over for soldering.

- Check the temperature of your iron before tinning the leads of your component – if too hot, damage could result!

- Your component *must* rest on the all-insulated side of the circuit board. Offer your pre-tinned soldering iron to the copper strip/component-lead junction until it is hot enough to melt the rosin core solder. Avoid solder splashes from one track to another when making your joint.

- Snip off the unwanted section of your component lead after the joint has cooled. Aim to shear off towards the floor – never upwards, as you could easily target your eye!

You have now finished your joint and it will have just the right amount of solder, appear bright and smooth and without spikes. If your joint appears to be dull or spiked, have too much flux or be peppered with minute holes over its surface, it is best to resolder. The resistance of your failed joint could be greater than 0.05 Ω between the two joining conductors – and that would be too much.

As a final check, make sure you have not splashed solder onto your circuit board causing a short-circuit between tracks, that there are no strands of loose wire and all your joints are sound. Remove solder splashes with a *desoldering tool*. Ask your course instructor to show you how to use this tool. Remove solder spikes by reheating the affected joint. You can easily remove loose strands of wire with a sharp pair of side cutters, whilst reheating until molten will take care of any unsound joints.

Why do components break down?
Resistors

Resistors will do one of two things. Either they will break down in an *open circuit* mode or they will greatly increase in value.

The following reasons will cause high value failure:

- Movement of carbon granules.
- An outside heat source.
- Moisture, causing the resistor to become bloated.
- Too much voltage or current.

The following conditions will cause an open circuit failure:

- Mechanical stress.
- Broken connections or a dry joint.
- Too much internal heat caused by load.
- Too much external heat leading to soldered joints melting.
- Broken wire in a wire wound resistor or badly made component.
- Electrolytic reaction (the chemical effect of two different metals after moisture has been absorbed).
- Impurities, causing *crystallisation* (the formation of crystals) inside a wire wound resistor.
- Physical and chemical changes within, due to the age of the component.

Capacitor

Common faults include the following:

- Capacitor plates shorting out due to the movement of silver in moist conditions. For example, a mica capacitor.
- Swollen body, due to moisture or high temperature.
- Short-circuit (plates touching each other) due to mechanical impact, rupture or too high a voltage.
- Intermediate open circuit due to mechanical damage.
- A fault condition between the dielectric (the material insulation between the plates) and one of the capacitor plates can produce changeable values.
- Broken lead.

A practical exercise – constructing a light-operated transistor switch

Figure 7.39a shows a point-to-point schematic wiring diagram for a light-operated transistor switch. Figure 7.39b will provide you with a practical layout. With knowledge gained from this book and experience you have built up within and outside your lecture room, try to construct this light-operated transistor switch. If you have a problem, ask your course instructor for guidance. Good luck with your project!

You will need:

- A small section of strip board.
- One variable resistor (100 000 Ω).
- One light-dependent resistor (reference ORP 12).
- One carbon resistor (2200 Ω, which is 2.2 kΩ).
- One transistor (reference 2N 3053).
- One 6 volt lamp at 60 milliamps.
- A matching lamp holder for your 6 volt lamp.
- A reliable 9 volt battery or a 9 volt DC supply source.
- About 300 mm of insulating connecting wire (0.25 mm² or less will be fine).
- Two terminal posts to allow DC power to your circuit board.

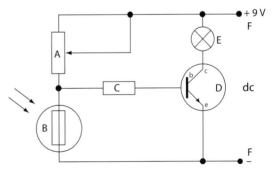

Figure 7.39a – *Constructing a light-operated switch. A, variable resistor (100 Ω max); B, light-dependent resistor (ORP 12); C, resistor (2.2 kΩ); D, transistor (2N 3053); E, lamp (6 volt/60 mA); F, direct current supply (9 volts).*

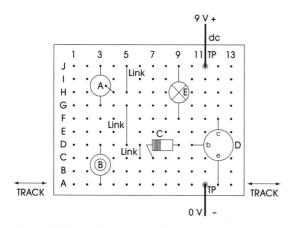

Figure 7.39b – *The circuit applied to an electronic strip board. TP, terminal posts to connect your 9 volt battery. Cut your copper track between reference points D6 and D7.*

Your light-dependent resistor (LDR)

This type of resistor is expensive. It is wise to solder flexible wire to the component's leads before connecting to your circuit. By *not* bending your leads too close to the body of the LDR you can avoid possible mistakes.

Figure 7.40 illustrates the preferred way to bend and prepare transistor leads for soldering. Bend your lead once only – this will reduce the risk of them snapping in half. If you use flexible wire to mount your LDR, always add insulation to the leads of your component in the form of small-bore electrical oversleeving.

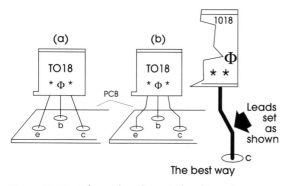

Figure 7.40 – *The preferred way to bend transistor leads for soldering. (a) the wrong way, (b) the preferred way. Transistor connections: b –base, c – collector, e – emitter.*

Terminal posts

Use tapered terminal posts in electronic assembly work as power input/output points. The tapered part of the structure occupies a hole within the copper track – the positioning is your choice. Soldering onto the circuit board copper track forms a permanent connection for an incoming or outgoing supply source, as illustrated in Figure 7.41.

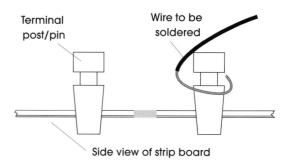

Figure 7.41 – *Tapered terminal posts are used for power input/output terminals, soldered in securely.*

How your transistor works

Imagine your transistor as a workshop 13 amp switched socket outlet. A small flick of the control will allow a large amount of current to flow through the connected load.

With this in mind, it is easy to design a simple circuit to warn of too much moisture in the soil. Monitoring is by means of two soil-bound probes. When unwanted moisture is present, a tiny current of a few milliamps flows from one probe to the other and along the wire leading to the base terminal of the transistor, as illustrated in Figure 7.42. This small amount of current is enough to open the transistor's gate, which allows a far greater current flow from the collector terminal (c) to the emitter terminal (e). The circuit is complete – the warning light is 'ON'.

If ever you decide to make this device, it is wise to add a resistor in series formation (the way Christmas tree lighting is connected) with the probe leading to the base (b) of the transistor. This will protect your circuit if the two

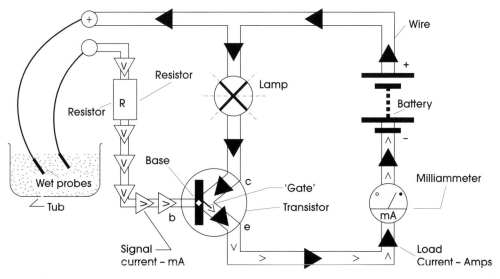

Figure 7.42 – *How a transistor operates using a simple moisture detector circuit as an example. b, base; c, collector; e, emitter; R, resistor.*

probes accidentally touch each other. Add a milliamp meter in series with your battery if you require additional data for your project. You can obtain probe sensitivity by means of a slider resistor wired in series with the positive (+) probe.

Summary

- Twisting bare wires together will cause *oxidation,* which creates an electrical resistance.
- Use soldering guns for fast heat application.
- Thermistors are used for sensing temperature differences.
- A capacitor enables an electrical charge to be stored. Both plates are at opposite potentials.
- We have reviewed four different types of circuit board:
  - Strip board, an insulated board with copper tracks.
  - Printed circuit board, an insulated board where the circuit-track is printed in copper.
  - Surface mount technology, comparable to a printed circuit board but accompanied by tiny holes on which to solder/mount components.
  - Breadboarding, a wiring system using spring retaining contacts.
- Terminal posts are used for power input or output points to serve an insulated circuit board.

Review questions

- Why is it unwise to twist untinned copper wires together to form a joint?
- Describe the purpose of a heat shunt.
- Why do we use soldering flux when making a joint?
- State four common voltages used for soldering irons.
- Insulation deformity connectors are described as one of the following:
  - a soldered type of connector
  - an electronically clamped connector
  - a connector where the insulation is ruptured
  - a twisted wire connection suspended in epoxy resin.
- How do you find the value of a resistor?
- Name the part of a capacitor that is sandwiched between its plates.
- Describe a use for a variable air-type capacitor.
- Why handle C-MOS electronic devices with care?

- Apply a 'group-name' (generic) to components such as diodes, thyristors and triacs.
- Describe the function of a *flat pack*.
- Draw the following BSEN graphical symbols used in point-to-point wiring diagrams: (a) a fixed resistor, (b) a fuse, (c) an electrolytic capacitor.
- A circuit board that has spring retaining clips to hold your component leads and connecting wires is called a:
  - printed circuit board
  - breadboard
  - surface mount technology board
  - strip board.
- State two uses for snipe-nose pliers in electronic assembly work.
- What is the role played by *tapered terminal posts?*

Handy hints

New technologies include the following devices:

- A multi-laser, hand-held temperature measurer that can provide digital readings without contact (Figure 7.43).
- A two-way personal communicator that is usable up to 310 metres. An ideal tool for large construction sites.
- An integrated laser measurer that offers an exact digital read-out up to 15 metres.
- A portable laser levelling system. Perfect for the alignment of pressed steel kitchen accessory boxes.
- It is possible to activate a passive infrared (PIR) detector by VHF radio transmissions or thermal currents escaping from a heating extract vent.
- High-frequency fluorescent fittings have an earthed capacitor in circuit. This will cause nuisance tripping if connected to a circuit protected by a 30 milliamp RCD.
- Never use a high-voltage test when portable appliance testing (PAT) electronic equipment. Damage to internal components will result.

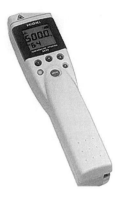

Figure 7.43 – *A multi-laser, handheld temperature measurer. (Reproduced by kind permission of RS Components Limited.)*

Introduction

In this chapter we go from the very nature of electricity to the more practical side of our work. I hope that the topics listed will be of interest and provide a deeper understanding of electrical installation engineering.

The electrical science contained in this chapter borders on the more practical aspects of our work and I trust will provide further interest coupled with a fuller understanding of your chosen career.

Atoms are the basic building blocks of our Universe. To understand the nature of electricity we must first have a working knowledge of the atom, an understanding of how it is constructed and its relationship with other atoms. Under clear and certain conditions, the movement of electrons will lead to a condition we know as electricity – this is what we will be dealing with first. The mechanical science will provide a clearer understanding of the role that components play and their relationship with one another in electrical engineering.

A quick look at the atom

Let us first take a close look at an atom of hydrogen, made up of three principal parts as shown in Figure 8.1. The *proton*, a positively charged particle, together with the *neutron*, a particle that carries no charge at all, form the nucleus of the atom. A single negatively charged particle called an *electron* completes our trio by tracking around the nucleus as our Moon orbits the Earth. The positively charged particle forming part of the nucleus continually attracts the electron but the orbit is firm.

Generally, an electron is about three times larger than the proton it orbits. Surprisingly, protons are *1840* times heavier than their orbiting cousins are. Whether we are studying an atom of copper or aluminium, gold or silver, the basic atomic building blocks remain the same – only their quantities vary from element to element. *Hydrogen* is the lightest element known to science – *lawrencium* is one of the heaviest. An element is a pure substance that cannot be resolved into simpler substances by normal chemical means.

The atomic nucleus is 10 000th the size of the complete atom and can be compared, by rule of thumb, to a large marble 10 millimetres in diameter, centrally suspended within a spherical bubble some 215 millimetres in width. Clearly, the majority of the volume taken up by an atom is just space, as Figure 8.2 illustrates.

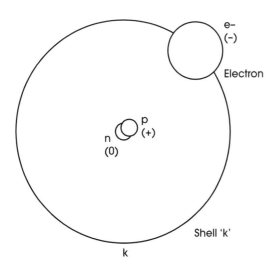

Figure 8.1 – *An atom of hydrogen.*

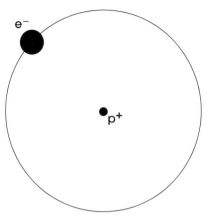

Figure 8.2 – *The vast majority of an atom of hydrogen is space.*

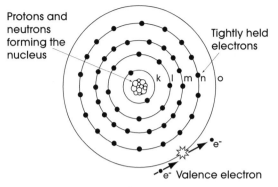

Figure 8.4 – *An atom of silver in schematic form.*

An atom of silver

An atom of silver, illustrated in Figure 8.3, is formed from 47 protons and 61 neutrons, composing the central nucleus. To electrically balance the atom so that it is neither positively nor negatively charged 47 orbiting electrons accompany the nucleus. The electrons are placed in orbits, or shells, which do not overlap each other. A lower case letter of the alphabet identifies each orbit or *shell*. The orbit nearest the central mass is known as the '*k*' shell and contains two electrons. The one furthest from the nucleus, called the '*o*' shell, has just one

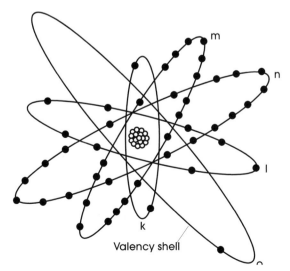

Figure 8.3 – *An atom of silver.*

orbiting electron. Figure 8.4 illustrates the arrangement in a simple schematic form.

All about the valency shell

The valency shell is the most important shell, as far as electrical current flow within a conductor is concerned. It is in this shell that loosely held electrons are able to flow from one atom to another, moved by an *electromotive force* – an energy source in the form of a voltage.

Silver is a good conductor of electricity – it has large atoms and many orbits as the last illustration shows and because of this the valence electron is very much further away from the centre of the atom and therefore there is far less hold. A shifted electron freed from its regular orbit by an electromotive force stands a good chance of striking another valence electron around a neighbouring atom. The electron under attack flies off to hit another valence electron and so on. This is the start of electron flow, the process we call *current flow*.

If an atom has two valence electrons in its outer shell, say nickel or mercury, the striking energy level will be halved and the conductivity within the conductor will be poorer. Whatever the element, there are never any more than *eight* electrons located in its outer shell. Mica, rubber and plastic are *insulators* of electricity and have many electrons located within their outer shell.

Practical thoughts

Problems will develop when the flow of valence electrons is top-heavy when compared to the size of the conductor used. Released energy, in the form of heat, builds up whenever an electron knocks another from its orbit. If the flow is too much the conductor will increase in temperature and any over-current protection serving your circuit will snap into play.

How many electrons are there per shell?

There is a maximum number of electrons any atom can have in one shell and this number can be calculated by use of the following expression:

$$2N^2 \qquad (8.1)$$

where N represents the shell number of the atom. As an example, consider an atom of mercury (Hg):

Orbit number	Shell	Maximum number of electrons	Actual number of electrons
1	k	2	2
2	l	8	8
3	m	18	18
4	n	32	32
5	o	50	18
6	p	8	2

'p' becomes the valency shell.

As you can see from this example, there are only two electrons within the valency shell, making mercury a reasonable conductor of electricity. Liquid mercury is used in 'tilt-switches' and certain types of relays.

Electromotive force and current flow

A simple generator also has the ability to knock loosely held electrons from their orbit to create current flow within a conductor. To demonstrate this principle in rock-bottom terms, two permanent magnets with opposite poles are placed opposite to each other as shown in Figure 8.5. A single, stationary coil of wire is added to this arrangement and positioned at right angles to the magnetic flux. At this point, no electromotive force (emf) is induced in the single coil of wire. If we rotate the coil so that it is seen to be cutting through the invisible magnetic lines

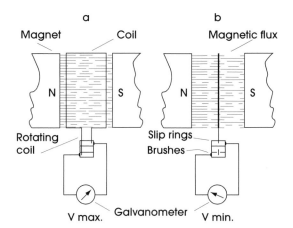

Figure 8.5 – *The principle of a simple generator.*

of flux, a voltage is immediately induced in the coil. This is referred to as the *emf* and the amount of voltage it will supply will depend on the *speed* the coil is rotated and the *density* of the magnetic flux. A strong magnet would be responsible for the generation of a higher voltage compared to a weaker one.

Other ways of producing electricity

■ Chemically – where two metal electrodes are immersed within an electrolyte (this is a liquid that conducts electricity due to the presence of both positive and negative ions). Level 3 will deal with the chemical interaction between the electrodes and the electrolyte which produces an emf from within the cell.

■ Magnetically – see the paragraph above.

■ By thermal means – by use of a thermocouple. This is a device which consists of two *dissimilar* metallic wires that have been twisted and welded together at one end. This end is the *hot* junction. The other end that supports two free ends is the *cold* junction. When both end sections of the wire are kept at different temperatures, an emf is produced. Measure the emf generated with a suitable milliamp meter.

The electron, the amp and the coulomb

The unit of current is the *ampere* and is directly related to electron flow. Electrons are negatively charged particles and flow from the negative to the positive terminal – the exact opposite of what was thought in those very early pioneering days, many years ago. Somebody had it wrong! But then we do say *the Sun is rising* when what we really mean is *the Earth is turning*.

Figure 8.6 shows a simple circuit of three 2 ohm resistors wired in series formation and served by a 6 volt supply from a battery. The term *ohm* (symbol Ω) is a unit of *electrical resistance* defined as *the resistance between two points of a conductor when 1 volt is applied between these two points and which produces a current of 1 amp.*

We calculate the total resistance of the circuit by adding the individual values together. Hence

$2 + 2 + 2 = 6\,\Omega.$

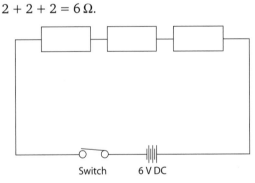

Switch   6 V DC

Figure 8.6 – *Resistors connected in series formation.*

Ohm's law

Ohm's law states that the current flowing in a circuit is *proportional* to the voltage applied and *inversely proportional* to the resistance – the temperature must be constant. Thus

$$\text{current in amps} = \frac{\text{voltage}}{\text{resistance}} \qquad (8.2)$$

or

$$I = \frac{V}{R}$$

Substituting for figures, $I = 6/6 = 1$ amp.

By definition, an amp is 624×10^{16} electrons flowing past a given point in one second. We call this quantity of electrons passing a fixed point every second a *coulomb,* symbol (Q). We calculate the value in coulombs for any given circuit by the following expression:

$$Q = I \times t \qquad (8.3)$$

where Q is the value in coulombs, I is the current in amps and t is the time in seconds.

Resistance and power

Resistance

The ohm is the unit of resistance and is the opposition offered to current flow within a conductor, as outlined in Figure 8.7. It is the mathematical ratio of the electrical potential (the voltage) to the current flow through your conductor. To describe resistance in real terms, imagine running up hill in a muddy cable tunnel littered with rubbish. Electrons would meet a similar opposition as this when getting past an electrical resistance.

To find the total resistance of your circuit, divide the current into the applied voltage. For an example, glance back to Figure 8.7.

A carbon resistor of unknown value completes a simple circuit. By instrumentation, the voltage registered was 10 volts and the current 0.5 amps. Calculate the value of the resistor:

$$\text{resistance} = \text{voltage/current}. \qquad (8.4)$$

Substituting for known values, then

$$\text{resistance} = 10/0.5$$

Thus the value of the resistor = 20 ohms (Ω).

Power

The unit of power, named after James Watt (1736–1819), is defined as *the energy spent by a current of one amp flowing through a conductor, the ends of which are maintained at a potential difference of one volt.*

Multiply the current by the voltage to obtain the power generated within your circuit. If you wish to express the power in kilowatts (kW), then divide your answer by 1000. Return to

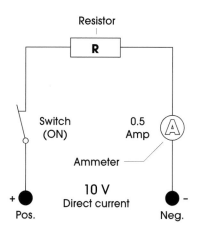

Figure 8.7 – *By dividing the applied voltage by the current, the value of an unknown resistor can be found.*

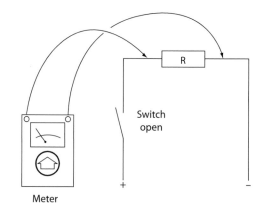

Figure 8.9 – *Measuring the value of an unknown resistor.*

Figure 8.7 and calculate the total power within the example circuit.

Given that

watts (W) = current (I) × voltage (V)   (8.5)

and substituting figures, then

watts = 0.5 × 10

Therefore

W = 5 watts (0.005 kW).

Figure 8.8 shows the practical steps to take when measuring voltage, current and power. The illustration shows a DC arrangement which could equally be used on an AC mains circuit. Measure resistance with an ohmmeter as illustrated in Figure 8.9 but *isolate* the power before proceeding to test.

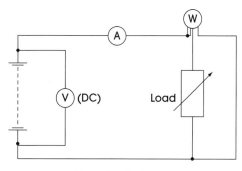

Figure 8.8 – *Finding values by instrumentation.*

Summary so far...

1 The raw material of an atom is the same no matter what the element is. Only the quantities are different.

2 Electricity is a flow of *negative particles* called electrons.

3 Silver is a good conductor of electricity.

4 The outer shell of an atom is called the *valency shell* – in conductors the valency electrons are free to move from one atom to another.

5 To find the power within a circuit, multiply the current within the circuit by the voltage applied to the circuit.

Ohm's law

In 1827, Georg Simon Ohm put together an electrical principle that has been with us ever since. His law is one of the cornerstones of electrical science and is of prime importance to every one of us who work in the electrical industry.

Ohm's law states that *the current flowing in a circuit is directly proportional to the voltage applied and inversely proportional to the resistance at a constant temperature.* Mathematically, this is written as

$$I = \frac{E}{R} \qquad (8.5)$$

where E is the electromotive force (the applied voltage) in AC circuits, I is the current in amps and R the resistance in ohms. V often replaces E when applied to DC systems.

Practical problems involving Ohm's law

There are several different ways to calculate the value of current flow, resistance, power generated and the voltage applied. Figure 8.10 shows some of them. As a practical example, consider the following problem:

A 230 volt heating element of unknown power is to be replaced during a planned maintenance programme. Only the voltage and the element's resistance is measurable, as other forms of instrumentation are not available. Calculate the power generated in watts.

Assume the total resistance measured was 26.45 ohms and the known voltage 230 volts. By referring to Figure 8.10:

$$\text{power in watts} = V^2/R \qquad (8.6)$$

where V is the applied voltage and R is the total resistance in ohms.

Substituting with figures:

power in watts $= 230^2/26.45 = 52\,900/26.45$

$W = 2000$ watts (2 kW).

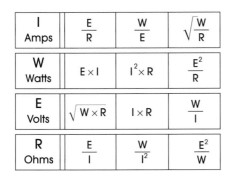

I Amps	$\dfrac{E}{R}$	$\dfrac{W}{E}$	$\sqrt{\dfrac{W}{R}}$
W Watts	$E \times I$	$I^2 \times R$	$\dfrac{E^2}{R}$
E Volts	$\sqrt{W \times R}$	$I \times R$	$\dfrac{W}{I}$
R Ohms	$\dfrac{E}{I}$	$\dfrac{W}{I^2}$	$\dfrac{E^2}{W}$

Figure 8.10 – *Other ways to evaluate current, power, voltage and resistance.*

Current and switching problems

Difficulty can arise after an installation has been finished when a standard 10 amp switch has been installed to control a large inductive lighting load. Within a short period a switching problem will occur – resulting in damage to the switch. Imagine our circuit to have eight 120 watt twin fluorescent light fittings served from a 230 volt distribution centre. Providing the power factor is less than 0.85, the current drawn from the supply would be

$$I = \text{total power in watts} \times 1.8/\text{volts} \qquad (8.7)$$

Substituting for known figures:

$I = (120 \times 2) \times 7 \times 1.8/230$

$I = 15$ amp (this is overloading the switch by 50%)

The practical solution would be to change your 10 amp lighting switch for a 20 amp one.

Assessing demand

Figure 8.10 has shown that the power in watts equals the current in amps multiplied by the applied voltage. By transposing this expression in terms of I by dividing each side of the equation by V, we can obtain the current within the circuit in terms of W and V.
Hence

$$\text{current } (I) = W/V \qquad (8.8)$$

By adding together the total power that might be consumed throughout the circuit and dividing by the applied voltage, the maximum current is calculated.

Problems relating to installation faults in series

A fault to earth within an installation served with steel conduit where a section of the conduit is badly connected can cause a serious problem.

If, for example, a brass bush had been poorly installed within steel conduit serving a 30 amp socket it would create an unacceptably high resistance within the circuit's protective steel conduit – illustrated in Figure 8.11. A section of

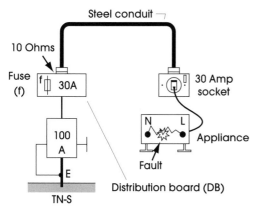

Figure 8.11 – *Loosely installed steel conduit can cause problems should a fault to earth occur.*

conduit would become live to touch in the event of a phase to earth fault occurring.

Let us assume the carelessly installed bush has a resistance of 10 Ω measured between the metal-clad distribution centre and the conduit. If a phase to earth fault occurred within the appliance, on the side of higher potential, the appliance, socket outlet and conduit as far as the loose bush would become very uncomfortable to touch – it would be electrically live! Figure 8.12 shows this in schematic form. By applying Ohm's law (expression (8.1)), you will see that the current within the CPC, which in this case is the steel conduit, is

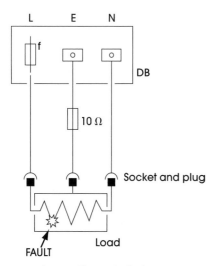

Figure 8.12 – *The installation fault shown schematically.*

current in amps = volts/resistance

Substituting figures:

current in amps = 230/10 = 23 amps

The fault current, calculated to be 23 amps, would provide sufficient power to cause a lot of damage to the installation. The power generated within the fault ($I \times V$) would be 23 amps × 230 volts, which equals 5290 watts (5.29 kW). This is sufficient to cause a lot of damage to the installation!

The moral to this real life example is to make sure all your conduit accessories are nice and tight. Please bear in mind, a semi-enclosed fuse (rewirable type) will maintain nearly twice its rated current before the fuse element blows. If in doubt, include a supplementary CPC within the steel conduit. Please refer to Regulation 547-03.

The way to calculate resistances in series formation

Series formation wiring is the way you would wire Christmas tree lighting, one light after the other. It is as though all lights on the tree are just one large lamp.

A fault where two resistances are in series formation, where one is the product of the fault condition, is calculated by the following expression:

$$R_T = R_1 + R_2 + R_3 + R_4 \ldots \qquad (8.9)$$

where R_T is the total resistance in ohms (Ω) and R_1, etc., are the individual resistance values. Consider the following example. Figure 8.13 illustrates a simple circuit made up of three 2 Ω and one 10 Ω resistor placed in series formation and supplied with a potential (voltage) of 32 volts. Find out more about the properties of this circuit.

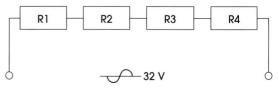

Figure 8.13 – *Resistances wired in series formation, similar to Christmas tree lights.*

First, replace symbols with known figures:

$R_T = 2+2+2+10$

Total resistance (R_T) = 16 ohms.

Apply Ohm's law (expression (8.5)) to find the current within the circuit:

$I = E/R = 32/16 = 2$ amp

As all the components are in series with one another, it makes sense that the current flow is the same throughout the circuit. Imagine the resistors as an electric fire element.

Finding the voltage drop across each resistor

The individual resistors (which we will refer to as *loads*) will produce a voltage drop (VD) that is in direct proportion to the resistance offered and the voltage applied. To find this value within a series circuit, the following expression is used:

voltage drop (VD) = current in amps × individual resistance in ohms   (8.10)

Cast your eye back to Figure 8.13 and apply expression (8.10):

voltage drop across $R_1 = 2 \times 2 = 4$ volts

voltage drop across $R_2 = 2 \times 2 = 4$ volts

voltage drop across $R_3 = 2 \times 2 = 4$ volts

voltgae drop across $R_4 = 2 \times 10 = 20$ volts.

By adding the individual voltage drops together, the total applied voltage is calculated. Hence

applied voltage = $VD_1 + VD_2 + VD_3 + VD_4$.   (8.11)

Substituting by figures then

applied voltage (V) = 4+4+4+20 = 32 volts.

Calculate the power generated in watts in a similar way by using this expression:

power in watts (W) = I^2R (8.12)

where I is the current in amps and R is the individual resistances in ohms.

Consider a practical example of this expression:

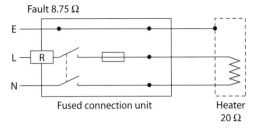

Fault 8.75 Ω

E

L — R

N

Fused connection unit

Heater 20 Ω

Figure 8.14 – *An electric heater served by a poorly connected fused connection unit.*

Let us suppose a 230 volt electric fire, offering a resistance of 20 ohms, is supplied through a badly connected terminal serving a fused connection unit. The fault, illustrated in Figure 8.14, has a measured resistance of 8.75 Ω between the incoming and outgoing phase conductor.

Referring back to expression (8.9):

$R_T = R_1 + R_2$

and suiting the needs of our problem

$R_T = Rf(fault) + R(resistance of the load)$.   (8.13)

Substituting by figures:

$R_T = 8.75 + 20 = 28.75$ ohms.

This figure reduces the power output by nearly a third. Calculate the total current within the faulty circuit by use of expression (8.5) (Ohm's law):

current in amps (I) = 230 volts/(20+8.75) = 8 amps.

The voltage drop across the faulty connection may also be found using expression (8.10) *(IR)*.

Providing figures for this voltage drop:

VD = 8 amps × 8.75 Ω = 70 volts.

Similarly, the voltage drop across the load is

VD(load) = 8 amps × 20 ohms (the resistance of the element) = 160 volts.

Check your arithmetic by adding the two voltage drops together (160 V + 70 V). Your answer must be the same as the voltage applied to your circuit.

The power generated within the faulty connection

By checking back to Figure 8.10 or expression (8.12), you will see that the power generated within a circuit is *the square of the current multiplied by the resistance.* Substituting for known values:

> power in watts (W) generated by the fault condition = $8^2 \times 8.75 = 560$ watts

This is sufficient to do a lot of damage to the fused connection unit, so always make sure your terminals are tight and electrically sound! Refer to Regulation 526.

Schematically Figure 8.15 shows the relationship between the current flow and the impedance (resistance within an AC circuit) offered by the *load* and *series* fault condition.

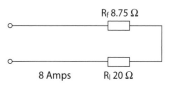

Figure 8.15 – *Schematic relationship between current flow and the impedance offered by the load and fault condition.*

Ohm's law – primary to secondary cells

Problems involving secondary cells (rechargeable batteries) are often the result of *large internal resistances* building up within the cell. This is due to *chemical* and *plate sediment* offering a suitable passage to the internal current from one plate to another. In practice, the sediment lies as a heap at the bottom of the cell!

If the internal resistance, r, is low in value, a rapid discharge of the cell will follow without any external load connected across its terminals. This will affect the total voltage output of the battery – which could lead to unforeseen costs; for example, if connected to a group that was serving a fire alarm or emergency lighting system. Reference is made to Regulation 313–02–01.

Figure 8.16 represents a faulty 24 volt lead-acid accumulator connected across an external

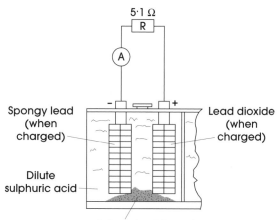

Figure 8.16 – *A faulty cell serving a 24 volt lead acid accumulator.*

load of 5.1 ohms. When measuring the current taken from the battery, 4 amps were registered. Calculation shows this to be incorrect, as Ohm's law states that the current is a ratio of voltage and resistance or $I = V/R$.

Substituting by figures:

> current drawn from the battery = 24 volts/5.1 ohms = 4.705 amps.

The current reading of 4 amps, Figure 8.17, must be the direct result of the internal resistance of the cell. This makes sense, as both the internal and external are in *series* with each other and therefore will affect the current flow through the circuit.

Use the following expression to find the value of the internal resistance, r:

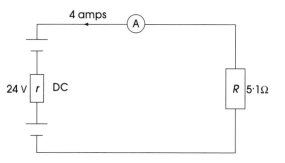

Figure 8.17 – *Schematic relationship between load, current and the internal resistance of a faulty cell.*

$$I = \frac{V}{R+r} \qquad (8.14)$$

where I is the current in amps, V is the terminal voltage of the battery, R is the external load in ohms and r is the internal resistance of the cell.

Arranging expression (8.14) in terms of r, the internal resistance

First, cross-multiply the expression and present it in terms of V:

$$V = I(R+r)$$

and then in terms of r:

$$r = \frac{V}{I} - R.$$

Now substitute for known values:

$$r = (24/4) - 5.1$$

Thus the internal resistance, $r = 0.9$ ohms.

When the power source is a portable generator, calculate the internal resistance using the following expression:

$$r = \frac{E-V}{I} \qquad (8.15)$$

where E is the voltage generated, V is the value of the terminal voltage under load and I is the value of the current drawn in amps.

Compound internal resistance within batteries

Several batteries, each with a similar internal resistance and wired together in series formation, will cause a *compound resistance* to develop within the cells. Figure 8.18 shows six healthy batteries in schematic form connected together in series formation and developing an output of 12 volts DC.

Suppose you place an external resistance, R, of 6 Ω across the output terminals. By applying Ohm's law (expression (8.5)), you will find the current flow (V/R) will be 2 amps and the power generated ($I \times V$) will be just 24 watts. If your six healthy cells were to be replaced with cells each with an internal resistance of 1 Ω (Figure 8.19), your current flow would be calculated using the following expression:

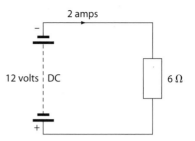

Figure 8.18 – *Six healthy 2 volt cells wired in series formation will develop an output of 12 volts.*

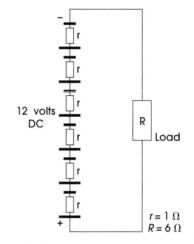

Figure 8.19 – *Six cells each with an internal resistance of 1 ohm wired in series formation.*

$$\text{current in amps } (I) = \frac{V}{R + r_1 + r_2 + r_3 + r_4 + r_5 + r_6}$$
$$(8.16)$$

where V represents the terminal voltage, R the external resistance and r_1 to r_6 the internal resistances of the batteries.

Substituting with figures:

$$\text{current in amps } (I) = \frac{12}{6+1+1+1+1+1+1} = 1 \text{ amp}$$

Calculate the power generated by using expression (8.5) ($W = IV$). Substituting figures for known quantities, then

power in watts generated (W) = 12 watts.

This is half of the original value from figures drawn from the healthier circuit. A similar set of batteries serving an intruder alarm or an emergency lighting arrangement would be condemned and replaced immediately.

Internal cell resistance in parallel formation

Figure 8.20 illustrates *two one-celled batteries* with similar internal resistances that are in parallel formation. When connected to an external resistance, *R*, use the following expression to calculate the current drawn from the circuit:

$$I = \frac{V}{R + r/2} \qquad (8.17)$$

where *I* is the current drawn from the circuit, *R* is the external resistance and *r* is the internal resistance of the battery. (This is when both batteries have similar internal resistance values.)

Replace any cell that has sludge at the bottom of its container. Its condition will be 'terminal'. Replace with new ones. The internal resistance provides a vital path for electrons to reduce the efficiency of the battery as Figure 8.21 clearly shows. If you are unable to see the bottom of your battery, run a health check by measuring the cell voltage with a reliable DC voltmeter and calculate the *specific gravity* of the acid with a good hydrometer. Read and understand the instructions first before using the hydrometer.

Installation problems involving Ohm's law

A DIY greenhouse supply

Take a situation that would arise if your customer insisted on supplying his own appliances to serve an old 5 amp electrical mains supply (yes, people still have them!). Imagine his equipment is to serve a small greenhouse which, although not entirely past its useful life, is old and reference to loading has long gone. The equipment provided included the following:

- one halogen floodlight of unknown wattage
- one small bank of tubular heaters.

Checking the continuity measurements showed the floodlight had a resistance of 57.6 Ω and the small bank of tubular heaters 19.2 Ω.

Since the wiring for both the light and heater bank are in *parallel* formation with the electrical mains, the total resistance of the load serving the installation must be checked out to calculate the maximum current demand required for the greenhouse. Figure 8.22 provides a detailed schematic form of the proposed installation.

To find the total resistance of the load theoretically, use the following expression:

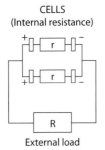

CELLS
(Internal resistance)

External load

Figure 8.20 – *Two single cells wired in parallel formation each with a similar internal resistance.*

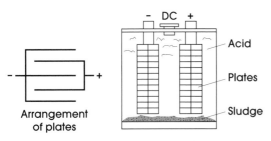

Arrangement of plates

Figure 8.21 – *A cell with an internal resistance will quickly run down.*

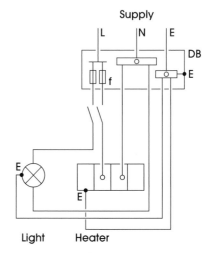

Figure 8.22 – *Both the lighting and heating circuits are wired parallel with each other.*

$$\frac{1}{R_T} = \frac{1}{R_1} + \frac{1}{R_2} \tag{8.18}$$

where R_T is the total resistance in ohms and R_1 and R_2 are the individual resistances of the two loads.

Now, substitute the known values:

$$\frac{1}{R_T} = \frac{1}{57.6} + \frac{1}{19.2}$$

Now, select a common multiple (1105.92) and work through:

$$\frac{1}{R_T} = \frac{19.2 + 57.6}{1105.92} = \frac{76.8}{1105.92}$$

Cross-multiply and bring the expression into terms of R_T (the total resistance of the two loads):

$$R_T = 1105.92/76.8 = 14.4 \text{ ohms}$$

By applying Ohm's law (expression (8.5)), the maximum current demand will be found:

$$I = V/R.$$

Now put in your known values:

$$I = 230/14.4 = 15.9 \text{ amps}$$

The loading would be too much for this installation but, providing the service mains supplying the greenhouse with electricity is 1.5 mm² or greater, then the current protective device (miniature circuit breaker (mcb) or semi-enclosed fuse) can be up-graded to a higher value. The value of course would depend on the cross-sectional area of the mains conductors.

A quick way to calculate the resistance of just two known resistances in parallel is to use the following expression:

$$R_T = \frac{R_1 R_2}{R_1 + R_2} \tag{8.19}$$

If you have any more than two resistances, then use expression (8.18).

Multiple faults in RCD-protected installations

An RCD will automatically isolate the supply when, for example, there are three installation faults but will remain stable with two problems.

To understand this, we will return to our theory and consider the following practical dilemma.

Figure 8.23 outlines a typical example where faulty appliances in the form of a single-phase electric motor, a wall light and a water heater element are all leaking small quantities of electricity from their neutral conductors to earth. Our problem follows.

A periodic installation test on a smallholding indicated three independent neutral-to-earth faults. The three fault paths to earth were 5000, 4000 and 20 000 Ω, respectively. The installation, served with a 230 volt, single-phase supply (and because socket outlets were not required) was protected with the help of an RCD tripping-rated at 100 milliamps (mA).

Independently, neither of the fault conditions would activate the RCD. The smallest recorded value of 4000 Ω would only draw 57.5 mA from the supply. Since all three faulty circuits are in parallel formation to earth, their total combined resistance will always be *less* than the smallest fault value. Use expression (8.18) to find the total resistance of the parallel fault paths to earth:

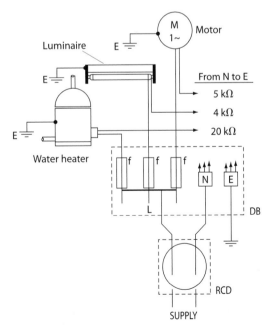

Figure 8.23 – *Parallel paths between the neutral and the protective conductor will produce a low impedance value.*

$$\frac{1}{R_T} = \frac{1}{R_1} + \frac{1}{R_2} + \frac{1}{R_3}$$

Substituting figures:

$$\frac{1}{R_T} = \frac{1}{5000} + \frac{1}{4000} + \frac{1}{20000}$$

Selecting a common multiple (20 000) we get

$$\frac{1}{R_T} = \frac{4+5+1}{20000} = \frac{10}{20000}$$

Bring the expression into terms of R_T by cross-multiplying:

$$RT = 20\,000/10$$

Thus the total resistance of the three fault-circuits (R_T) = 2000 ohms. By applying Ohm's law (expression (8.5)), the total earth leakage current to earth is calculated:

$$I = V/R = 230 \text{ volts}/2000 \text{ ohms} = 0.115 \text{ ohms}$$

By multiplying by 1000 the current in amps is expressed in terms of milliamps (1000 mA = 1 amp):

$$0.115 \text{ amps} \times 1000 = 115 \text{ milliamps.}$$

In practical terms, this figure means the 100 mA RCD would trip out – it is 15 mA over its working range.

Useful knowledge concerning neutral earth faults and a RCD

If you find yourself in a situation where you have a *neutral-to-earth fault* within an installation, please remember that *any* circuit that is drawing current is capable of knocking your trip out – whether it has a faulty neutral or not.

All neutral conductors are common with each other (they all share the same neutral distribution bar), as illustrated in Figure 8.24. Therefore, any healthy circuit drawing current would experience a divided neutral path on the current's return journey to the supply transformer. The majority of current within the neutral conductor would return via the common connection point at the distribution centre but a small amount would leak away to earth at the *fault-point* within the installation.

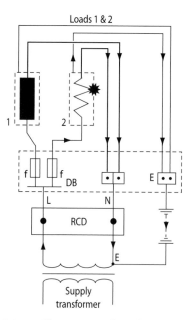

Figure 8.24 – *All your neutral conductors are common with each other. A fault-to-earth with any neutral would experience a divided path to the supply transformer.*

Current entering the RCD must be the same in value as the current departing from the device. If not, an imbalance will occur and the RCD will detect a fault condition and auto-trip.

Locate your fault first

It is best to remove all the black or blue neutral conductors from the common distribution bar and switch off all the MCBs before you test each neutral to earth with a 500 volt insulation tester. When you have discovered your defective conductor, stick a temporary piece of green/yellow tape on it as a marker, to identify it from the other healthy conductors. Fault-finding can be a little easier with a good quality *digital* meter switched to the milliohm or ohm scale. The nearer you are to your fault, the *lower* the value that will appear on your meter – a useful point to remember!

The installation of an RCD must meet the demands of BS 7671 – Regulation 531-02-01 to 531-05-01.

Summary so far...

1 There are many ways to express Ohm's law – see Figure 8.10.

2 Check you have the correct size of lighting switch when second fixing inductive circuits.

3 It is important that steel conduit installations are mechanically secure when you are using the conduit as a protective conductor.

4 Add resistances, wired in *series* formation, to obtain the total resistance of a circuit.

5 Resistances in parallel are calculated differently – see expression (8.18).

6 Calculate the voltage drop across a component by multiplying the current within the circuit by the resistance of the component (*IR*).

7 Sludge within a secondary cell will create an internal resistance and destroy the battery.

8 If you are not sure of the current rating of an appliance check out the resistance and apply Ohm's law (expression (8.5)). Note: this is not always possible, especially if the appliance has an electronic element within its circuitry.

9 Tackle *neutral-to-earth faults* from the distribution centre by disconnecting all of your neutral conductors and isolating each MCB – then find your problem conductor first.

10 A good digital continuity meter is a very useful tool when fault-finding.

The residual current device

Figure 8.25 shows a simple scene where a 13 amp plug serves an electric fire. The CPC has been carelessly disconnected. Under normal healthy working conditions, such a break would probably be unnoticed. However, if a *phase fault to earth* occurred within the appliance, there would be a serious problem. Without an RCD in

circuit – and if supplied from a TT earthing arrangement – there would be no safeguard against direct contact with electricity. An unfortunate victim who, at the same time touched the faulty appliance and, say, a metal radiator, could suffer a lethal electric shock.

Figure 8.26 shows the basic internal wiring arrangements serving a typical RCD. An RCD, serving a complete installation, is often found in rural areas where overhead cables supply our electricity and where an earth point from the supplier is not available.

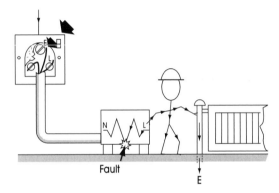

Figure 8.25 – *A fault path taken in the absence of a protective conductor.*

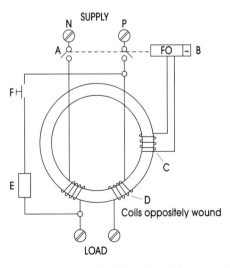

Figure 8.26 – *RCD. A, double-pole switch; B, tripping relay; C, fault sensing coil; D, circular transformer with induction coils; E, test resistor; F, test button.*

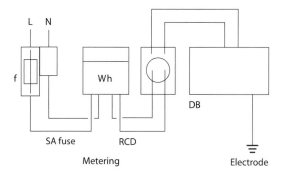

Figure 8.27 – *Incorporating an RCD within a circuit.*

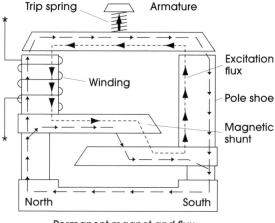

Permanent magnet and flux

Figure 8.28 – *The field weakening or polarised relay.*

Start by planning the controls serving your installation around your RCD as illustrated in Figure 8.27 – Regulation 412-06 applies.

Current flowing both in and out of the device is completely *balanced* under a no-fault condition. The way this works is by the use of a ring-like transformer in which the electrical load travels through two opposing coils wound around the ring. In a healthy circuit, the opposing coils would produce an equal and opposite magnetic flux and there would be no current to induce in the supplementary sensing coil 'C' of Figure 8.26. Under a fault condition, from either a phase or neutral leaking current to earth, the RCD is electrically thrown out of balance. This induces a very small current into the fault-sensing coil, 'B', and it is this output that provides a special polarised magnetic tripping relay with an input signal. The signal allows the device to activate. This operates by cancelling the permanent magnetic flux by the excitation flux generated in the windings of the polarised magnetic relay.

Sensitivities

The type of toroidal transformer and sensing relay used controls the sensitivity of your RCD. Figure 8.28 outlines the basic requirements for a polarised or weakening trip relay. The RCD ranges from 2.5 to 1000 milliamps tripping rating but the way they work can be very different. Some electronically amplify their output whilst others use magnetic methods to trigger the tripping mechanism. Generally, an electronic amplified RCD is far slower than a

polarised type and has the added disadvantage that it is voltage-dependent.

Nuisance tripping

Unlike the voltage operated earth leakage circuit breaker, the RCD is independent and unaffected by parallel earth paths that can cause so much trouble when voltage operated breakers are used. Parallel earth paths can be unintentionally created – Figure 8.29 illustrates a few of them. RCDs will also trip for no apparent cause. A few of the more general reasons why tripping occurs are:

■ Long runs of MI cable can act as a mini-capacitor and activate the device.

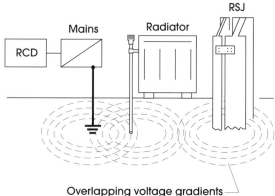

Figure 8.29 – *Examples of parallel earth paths.*

- Switching on or off rows of fluorescent lights can sometimes mislead the RCD into thinking there is a fault.
- Sometimes if large current-consuming electric motors are isolated.
- Spikes in the supply voltage.
- Unrelated mechanical vibration near to the RCD.
- Lightning striking the high-voltage power cables.
- Using the wrong type of *radio frequency interference* (RFI) filter as many designs incorporate capacitors connected directly to earth.

A noisy RCD is a good sign that there is trouble ahead – a point to remember. If you think you have a problem with your RCD, switch it off together with all your breakers or remove fuses – then disconnect all your outgoing neutral conductors serving the installation. Switch back on your RCD and, if the device still trips out, there is a fault within the device itself.

The voltage-operated earth leakage circuit breaker

Where earth leakage protection has not been upgraded, this type of circuit breaker is still in demand in many rural homes today. The device will respond to about 50 fault-volts entering the sensing coil and this is enough to trigger the switching moment. Figure 8.30 illustrates the internal wiring arrangements and the relationship with the installation it is protecting. We have stopped using this type of device now in favour of the current-operated circuit breaker because of its disadvantages:

- The unintentional shorting out of the voltage sensitive coil.
- The soil around the earth electrode must be kept moist during dry weather.
- The electrode has to be placed *outside* the resistance area of any other unrelated metalwork that is electrically earthed. If overlooked it will short out the voltage sensitive coil – the device will be useless. Figure 8.31 will illustrate this clearly.
- If two independent systems stake their electrodes close to each other with their earth resistance areas overlapping (see Figure 8.32), a fault current crossing the resistance area will find a conductive path to the tripping coil serving the fault-free installation. At this point, any stray current will return through a convenient path that is not within the resistance area of the electrodes and activate the healthy trip.

Figure 8.33 shows a typical wiring arrangement for an RCD and a voltage-operated circuit breaker. Both have electrodes – but for different

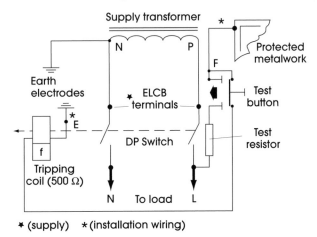

★ (supply) ★ (installation wiring)

Figure 8.30 – *Voltage-operated earth leakage circuit breaker. Terminal E is connected to an earth electrode, whilst an insulated conductor to the earthing point of the protective metalwork connects terminal F.*

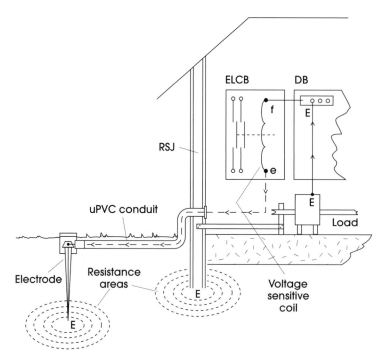

Figure 8.31 – *The earth electrode must be placed outside the resistance area of any other unconnected metalwork to avoid short-circuiting the voltage-sensitive coil.*

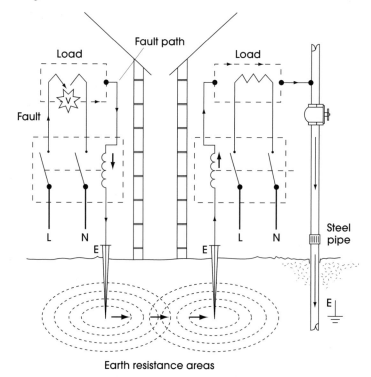

Figure 8.32 – *Troublesome tripping can occur when two or more earth resistance areas overlap each other.*

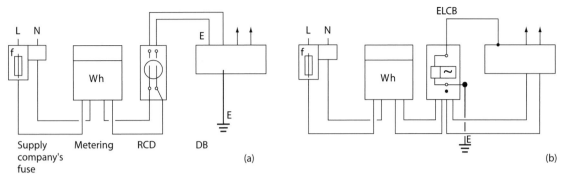

Supply company's fuse   Metering   RCD   DB   (a)   (b)

Figure 8.33 – *Incorporating current (a) or voltage-operated (b) circuit breakers into an installation.*

reasons. The voltage-operated breaker allows the fault current to complete its journey back to the transformer to complete the coil circuit. An electrode accompanies the current-operated breaker so the fault current can drain to the general mass of the earth and minimise any voltage occurring between exposed conductive paths. This will unbalance the toroidal transformer and the system will trip.

Fault-finding made easier

A phase or neutral conductor leaking electricity to earth will cause your RCD to trip out. If you have a *neutral-to-earth fault* within your installation, *any* heavy current-consuming appliance on *any* circuit will trigger the RCD's 'auto-switch-off' sequence. This is because all neutral conductors are common within the neutral block. Current from a healthy circuit will travel back through the neutral to the common neutral block on its way home to the local transformer but some of the current will take another route and travel along the faulty neutral to meet your earth fault. It can be frustrating, especially when you switch on your kettle and the trip pops out when the fault is located elsewhere!

A practical example

Figure 8.34 illustrates a typical *neutral-to-earth fault* within a circuit serving an electric motor. When the motor was first connected, the neutral conductor had been wedged against the wall of the metal-clad terminal housing. Constant vibration over the years had worn the insulation

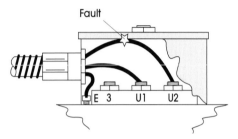

Figure 8.34 – *A neutral-to-earth fault found within the terminal housing of an electric motor.*

protecting the conductor and caused a fault condition. To locate the problem, consider the following steps:

- Switch *off* your main switch and circuit breakers (fuses must be removed).

- Disconnect the *black or blue neutral* conductors – then switch back *on* your RCD. If your trip is healthy your RCD will remain 'ON'.

- Remove any lamps within the installation.

- Switch back *off* your RCD and test all your outgoing phase and neutral conductors to earth with a 500 volt insulation tester. Ignore values above 0.5 MΩ (500 000 ohms).

- The insulation value of your faulty conductor will appear as either zero or near to zero. Find the destination of this circuit from the circuit chart and follow the circuit through to your fault.

- Find and repair the problem then test again. The value you obtain must not be less than 0.5 MΩ. BS 7671 Regulation 713-04-04 confirms this.

Sometimes it is an advantage to divide the faulty conductor at a midway point if your fault has very low impedance to earth. Cutting the conductor will help you to find out in which half the error lies. If you decide to do it this way, use a good *digital* ohm/milliohm meter. The closer to the fault you get, the lower the value you will obtain. Once found, remember to reconnect your conductors! This is a good way to find a problem within a final ring circuit when cable runs are longer than usual between sockets.

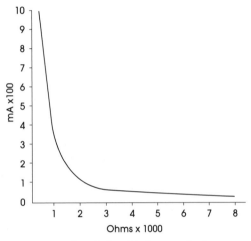

Figure 8.35 – *The relationship between fault current and impedance.*

Summary so far...

1 A current-operated RCD is completely independent of voltage.

2 A voltage operated circuit breaker has many disadvantages and should be avoided.

3 RCD tripping currents range from 2.5 mA to 1000 mA at various load ratings.

4 Nuisance tripping can occur with both types of automatic circuit breaker.

5 A noisy RCD often indicates a fault condition which is about to happen.

6 A neutral to earth fault will trigger the isolating mechanism within an RCD when heavy current flows from any circuit protected by an RCD.

- The phase colours serving all EU Member States are as follows:

  BROWN, BLACK and GREY with BLUE for neutral. Flexible cables are colour coded BROWN (phase), BLUE (neutral) and GREEN/YELLOW (c.p.c.).

- Don't dive into muddy waters – if you are not sure, ask someone!

Figure 8.35 illustrates the relationship between fault current and impedance when the supply voltage to earth is 230 volts AC.

Capacitors

By placing two similarly shaped metal plates squarely together, separated by a special type of insulating material called a *dielectric*, you are well on your way to constructing a simple capacitor – see Figure 8.36.

Farads or subdivisions of farads are the measurement of *capacitance*. Three factors are responsible for this value:

- the surface area

- the distance between the plates

- the type of dielectric used.

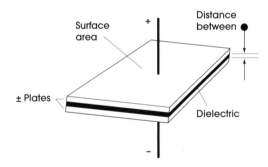

Figure 8.36 – *A simple capacitor.*

Dielectric strength

Many different materials are processed and formed into dielectrics. However, it is important that the voltage applied to the plates is not responsible for breaking down this special insulating material separating them for this will destroy the capacitor.

The voltage per unit thickness of dielectric is the principal value that provides the working efficiency of the capacitor. This term is called the *dielectric strength* and is the maximum electric field strength the insulating material is able to withstand before breaking down with heat.

Listed is a selection of examples that you will find in general use. Values are in kilovolts (thousands of volts) per millimetre thickness:

- Mica (used in high frequencies): 40–200
- Waxed paper (used in low frequencies): 40–60
- Glass (used in high frequencies): 5–30
- Paper (used in low frequencies): 4–10
- Air (used for radio tuning): 3–6.

Figure 8.37 shows the terminals of a 12 volt battery connected to a simple capacitor. Keep in mind that *electron flow is a stream of negatively charged sub-atomic particles*. By applying an electrical pressure across the two plates, the positive plate will continuously attract an electron flow from the negative plate. This will continue until the voltage across the capacitor is equal to that of the battery. Disconnecting will leave the capacitor fully charged.

At this stage, negative electrons serving the material forming the dielectric are repelled from the fully charged negative plate and attracted to the positive plate. Like magnets, *'like poles repel – unlike attract'*. The electrical pressure between the two opposing plates produces an elliptical

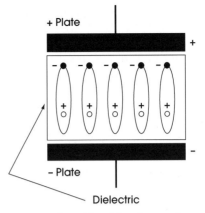

Figure 8.38 – *The orbits of the electrons become elongated. This distortion is known as dielectric stress.*

deformity within the orbits of the electrons forming the sandwiched dielectric, as illustrated in Figure 8.38. This atomic distortion is known as *dielectric stress* and is directly proportional to the voltage applied. Too much voltage and breakdown will occur in the form of a burnt hole through the dielectric from one plate to another.

Handy hints

- Capacitor aided motors are attended by 400 volt working range capacitors.
- Capacitors, which provide a means of starting an electric motor, are of the 230 volt type. Never mix the two up to avoid a breakdown.

Releasing dielectric energy

A quick and simple way to demonstrate the release of this energy is to short-circuit the two disconnected leads serving a *charged* capacitor. The expanded orbits of the negatively charged dielectric electrons then cease to be under any stress and the electrons stored in the capacitor's negative plate travel towards the positive plate at enormous speed. This results in the familiar 'crack' and spark display when the leads are placed together. Be very careful if you do this.

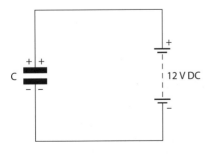

Figure 8.37 – *A 12 volt battery connected to a capacitor.*

Capacitors and alternating current

Unlike direct current (DC), alternating current (AC) is constantly reversing in polarity many times a second. Alternating current travels in a wave-like cycle. It is one complete change of electrical polarity in a given time period, often referred to as the *periodic time*. Generating companies within the UK develop a voltage waveform of 50 cycles per second, written as 50 Hz (50 hertz, pronounced 'hurts', and named after Heinrich Hertz (1857–1894)). To generate a basic periodic waveform, a single loop of wire has to be rotated within a uniform magnetic field. The resultant theoretical waveform will be *sinusoidal* in shape. Please see Chapter 7 for details.

An AC voltage applied to a capacitor, Figure 8.39, will cause the plates to charge and discharge many times a second until fully charged, when the voltage stored will equal the applied voltage.

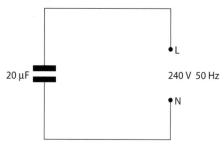

Figure 8.39 – *An alternating voltage applied to a capacitor.*

Reactance

As the potential across the capacitor increases, it offers a resistance to current flow. Since the flow of current is dependent on this 'opposed voltage' or *capacitive voltage*, the phenomena is known as *capacitive reactance*, symbol X_c.

Expression (8.20) shows that the capacitive reactance is the mathematical reciprocal of twice the value of π (Greek letter pi) multiplied by the frequency of the supply in hertz and the value in farads of the capacitor under review. Hence

$$X_c = 1/2\pi fC \qquad (8.20)$$

where π is 3.142, f is the frequency in hertz and C represents the value of the capacitor in farads.

Explaining the unit of capacitance

The value of a capacitor is expressed in *farads*. This unit of measurement is far too large for practical purposes so *microfarads* are used. A microfarad is one-millionth of a farad and its electrical symbol is μF. Take as an example a small capacitor whose measured value is 0.000 02 farads. To convert to microfarads, just multiply by 1 million:

> 0.000 02 farads $\times$ 1000 000 = 20 microfarads (μF).

To convert back to farads, divide the value in microfarads by 1 million or move the decimal place six places to the left. The *picofarad*, generally found in electronic circuits, is equivalent to one-millionth of a microfarad and the symbol is *pF*.

Evaluating the current drawn

Figure 8.39 illustrates a simple circuit consisting of a 20 μF capacitor connected to a 230 volt, 50 Hz supply. The capacitive reactance, X_c, must first be found to calculate the current drawn from this circuit. First, refer back to expression (8.20):

$$X_c = 1/2\pi fC$$

Substituting figures:

$$X_c = 1/2 \times 3.142 \times 50 \times 0.000\ 02 = 1/0.006\ 284 = 159.134$$

When you have calculated the capacitive reactance, it is then an easy step to find the current flowing in your simple circuit using the following expression:

$$\text{current } (I) = V/X_c$$

Substituting figures for symbols:

$$\text{current} = 230/159.134 = 1.4 \text{ amps}$$

For a less precise method consider the following expression:

$$\text{microfarads } (\mu F) = 3182.6801 \times \text{current in amps/applied voltage} \qquad (8.21)$$

where 3182.6801 is a common factor. This expression is only okay for 50 Hz per second generated supplies. For 60 Hz supplies, the factor 2650 should be applied. To illustrate (and remember it is not as precise as expression (8.20)), please refer back to Figure 8.39:

$\mu F = 3182.6801/230 = 19.99$ (greater accuracy to the seventh decimal place!)

Variations of this expression

current = microfarads × voltage/3182.6801 (8.22)

or

voltage = 3182.6801 × current in amps/microfarads (8.23)

The current flow in a pure capacitive circuit will seem to travel from one plate to another. This is an illusion, as both surfaces are completely isolated from each other by the dielectric sandwiched between the plates. When you connect an AC supply to your capacitor, it is constantly charging and discharging every electrical cycle and it is a phenomenon that creates this false impression.

Capacitor connected in series

Figure 8.40 shows how a 10 and 20 μF capacitor are connected in *series* formation (you connect them as you would Christmas tree lights). To find the total capacitance within the circuit, the following expression is used:

$$\frac{1}{C_T} = \frac{1}{C_1} + \frac{1}{C_2} + \frac{1}{C_3} \dots$$ (8.24)

where C_T is the total capacitance in microfarads and C_1 to C_3 are the values of the individual capacitors measured in farads or microfarads.

To evaluate, first find the lowest common multiple (LCM) which, for this example, is 20.

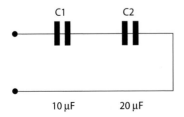

C1   C2

10 µF   20 µF

Figure 8.40 – *Capacitors connected in series formation.*

Now substitute your known figures for the symbols used:

$$\frac{1}{C_T} = \frac{1}{10} + \frac{1}{20} = \frac{2+1}{20}$$

Now cross-multiply your expression:

$3C_T = 20$

and dividing both sides of the equation by 3:

$C_T = 20/3 = 6.66 \, \mu F$

A quicker way is to apply the following expression – but only for *two* capacitors in series formation:

$$C_T = \frac{C_1 C_2}{C_1 + C_2}$$ (8.25)

By working it out yourself, you will find both the answers are the same.

Capacitors connected in parallel formation

Figure 8.41 illustrates how a 10 and 20 μF capacitor are wired in *parallel* formation. The total capacitance of the circuit is calculated with the following expression:

$$C_T = C_1 + C_2$$ (8.26)

where C_T represents the total capacitance of the combination and C_1 and C_2 are the individual values for each capacitor.

Substituting figures for symbols:

$C_T = 10 + 20.$

Thus

total capacitance $(C_T) = 30 \, \mu F$

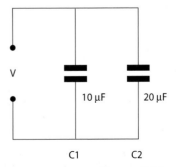

V

10 µF   20 µF

C1   C2

Figure 8.41 – *Capacitors wired in parallel formation.*

Capacitors connected in a combination of series and parallel wiring

If you study Figure 8.42, you will see that the capacitors are arranged in both *series* and in *parallel* formation. To calculate the total value of this circuit you must first target the *series leg* of this arrangement and find the total capacitance (see expression (8.24)). Next, re-introduce the value you have calculated into the original circuit as a single item. By applying expression (8.26), you can work out the capacitance of the parallel section to a single value. Finally use expression (8.24) for the two remaining capacitors in series formation.

Let us calculate, first, the series leg of the arrangement:

$$C_\mathrm{T} = \frac{C_1 C_2}{C_1 + C_2} \qquad \text{(this is expression (8.24))}$$

$$C_\mathrm{T} = \frac{10 \times 20}{10 + 20} = \frac{200}{30} = 6.66 \ \mu\mathrm{F}$$

Next, the total parallel section of the circuit is:

$$C_\mathrm{T} = C_1 + C_2$$

$$C_\mathrm{T} = 10 + 20 = 30 \ \mu\mathrm{F}$$

Finally the total capacitance of the two remaining components are connected together in series formation expression (8.24):

$$C_\mathrm{T} = \frac{6.66 \times 30}{6.66 + 30}$$

Thus the total capacitance of the series/parallel combination = 5.45 μF.

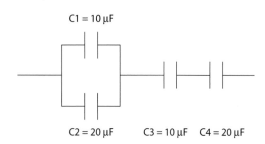

C1 = 10 μF

C2 = 20 μF   C3 = 10 μF   C4 = 20 μF

Figure 8.42 – *Capacitors wired in parallel (left) and series formation (right).*

If the precise size of capacitor is unavailable to use as a replacement, design an equivalent value with two or more and use it as a stopgap.

As a practical example, consider a small electric motor served by a faulty 4 μF oil-filled capacitor. One of many capacitors we have available is valued at 20 μF – but by connecting this one and an unknown in *series* formation, we can obtain the correct value required.

Calculate theoretically using the following expression:

$$\frac{1}{C_\mathrm{T}} = \frac{1}{C_1} + \frac{1}{C_x}$$

where C_T is the total capacitance required (in this case 4 μF, C_1 is the value of the capacitor available (we have chosen a value of 20 μF) and C_x is the unknown value of the accompanying capacitor.

Substituting with figures:

$$\frac{1}{4} = \frac{1}{20} + \frac{1}{C_x}$$

Expressing this in terms of C_x:

$$\frac{1}{C_x} = \frac{1}{4} - \frac{1}{20}$$

Finding the common multiple (20) then

$$\frac{1}{C_x} = \frac{4}{20}$$

Now, cross-multiply, bringing in terms of C_x:

$$C_x = 5 \ \mu\mathrm{F}$$

By calculation, therefore, to produce a temporary replacement value of 4 μF we have to connect a 5 and a 20 μF capacitor in series formation. I hope that we will have a spare 20 μF capacitor 'in the box' – if not, it will be a journey to the wholesaler to collect a proper one!

Circuits containing both capacitance and resistance

In the pure capacitive circuit, power is not consumed. Both current and voltage are out of phase with each other by 90°. At the end of each half-cycle, the energy stored within the capacitor returns to the supply.

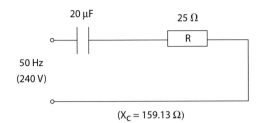
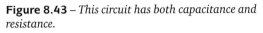

Figure 8.43 – *This circuit has both capacitance and resistance.*

If you place a resistance in series formation within a pure capacitive circuit as shown in Figure 8.43 a new electrical factor will emerge. The current that flows in a circuit of this type is limited to the *capacitive reactance, X_c*, of the capacitor and the resistor, R_1, in ohms. These two components form the *impedance* of the circuit. The symbol for impedance is Z; it is calculated by applying the following expression:

$$Z = \sqrt{(R^2 + X_c^2)} \qquad (8.27)$$

where R is the resistance of the resistor in ohms and X_c is the capacitive reactance in ohms (remember that X_c also appears in expression (8.20)).

Substituting with figures gives

$Z = \sqrt{(25^2 + 159.13^2)} = \sqrt{(625 + 25\ 322.35)} = 161.0\ \Omega$ the impedance of the circuit.

Inductive circuits

A pure *inductive* AC circuit uses a coil of wire in much the same way as a resistor – that is, to limit current flow within a circuit. Figures 8.44 and 8.45 illustrate two examples of an inductive circuit: an air coiled *solenoid* and a small step-down transformer. Practical applications include autotransformers, electric bells, electromagnets and electric motors.

An electromagnetic field surrounds a load-bearing conductor – if you could see it, it would be similar to the pattern formed on the surface of a pond when throwing a stone into it: the ripples become symbols of the magnetic flux surrounding our conductor (Figure 8.46). When applied to an inductor, it has the effect of

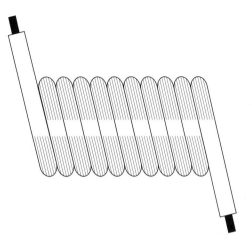

Figure 8.44 – *A simple air-core solenoid.*

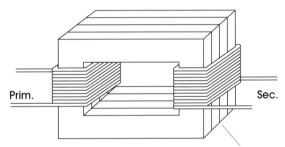
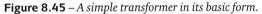

Figure 8.45 – *A simple transformer in its basic form.*

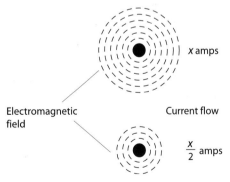

Figure 8.46 – *The electromagnetic field surrounding a load-bearing conductor is directly proportional to current flow.*

introducing a *secondary* voltage into the windings, directly opposite to the polarity (i.e. positive/negative) of the voltage creating it. By examining Figure 8.47, you will be able to see this idea more clearly.

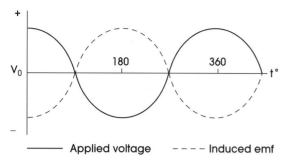

Figure 8.47 – *A secondary voltage induced into a conductor directly opposes the polarity of the voltage creating it.*

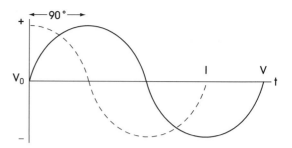

Figure 8.48 – *In an inductive circuit, the current lags behind the voltage by 90°, whereas in a pure capacitive circuit the current leads the voltage by 90°.*

Since the *secondary* or *induced emf* (electromotive force – voltage) is 180° out of phase with the applied voltage it will act as a current limiter. (This is why a *choke* is fitted within a fluorescent fitting.) Although acting very similar to a typical resistor, it is *not* a resistor but operates by means of the phenomenon of inductance and is identified as an inductive reactance. The *Henry (H)* is the unit of inductance.

Calculate the value in ohms of an inductive circuit by using this expression:

$$X_L = 2\pi f L \qquad (8.28)$$

where π is 3.142, f is the frequency in hertz, L is the value of the inductor in henries and X_L is the value of the inductive reactance in ohms.

Lagging current

In a pure inductive circuit the current lags behind the voltage by 90° as Figure 8.48 shows. The stored energy is within the electromagnetic field surrounding the inductor. Each time the magnetic field collapses energy is returned to the circuit. Not all the energy travels back – a small percentage filters off in the form of heat to overcome the natural resistance of the coil winding. Inductors, as we know them, are not pure inductors because of the element of natural resistance within the windings. Maybe one day superconductivity will provide us with an answer to this problem!

When you have found the value of your circuit's inductive reactance, the next step will be to calculate the current in amps flowing in the circuit. Do this by using the following expression:

$$\text{current in amps } (I) = \text{voltage}/X_L \qquad (8.29)$$

where X_L is the value of the inductive reactance in ohms.

You can also express this equation (8.29) as

$$I = \text{voltage}/2\pi f L \qquad (8.30)$$

Impedance triangle

A way to find the *total impedance* of a circuit containing both *resistance (R)* and *inductive reactance (X_L)* within, for example, a coil is to form a *right-angled impedance triangle*. You can then obtain your value either through measurement or calculation. Resistance and inductive reactance are not addable as they are *out of phase* with each other by 90°. Figure 8.48a illustrates a simple impedance triangle in which the perpendicular (R) represents a 2 Ω resistance whilst the horizontal side represents a coil of 3 Ω inductive reactance. To find the impedance of this circuit (Z), just measure the total length of the hypotenuse. This is by no means accurate but if it is essential to be so, then use the following expression:

$$\text{impedance } (Z) = \sqrt{(R^2 + X_L^2)} \qquad (8.31)$$

or

$$\text{impedance} = \sqrt{(4+9)} = \sqrt{13} = 3.6\,\Omega$$
$$\text{(the total impedance of the circuit).}$$

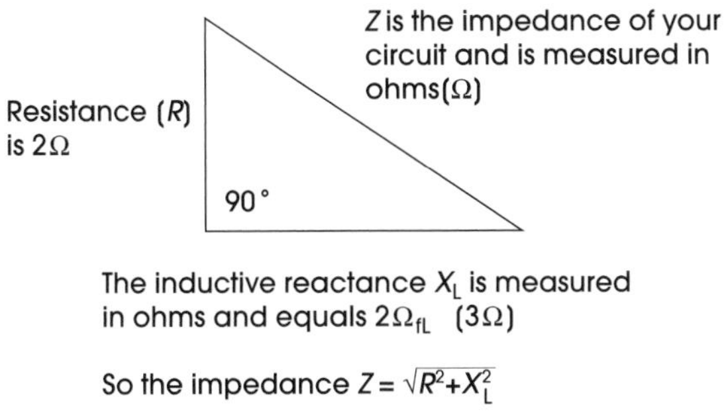

Z is the impedance of your circuit and is measured in ohms(Ω)

Resistance (R) is 2Ω

90°

The inductive reactance X_L is measured in ohms and equals $2\Omega_{fL}$ (3Ω)

So the impedance $Z = \sqrt{R^2 + X_L^2}$

Figure 8.48a – *An impedance triangle.*

A practical example highlighting both current and inductive reactance

Calculate the value of the inductive reactance and the current consumed in amps when a 0.382 henry locking solenoid is connected to a 230 volt, 50 Hz supply.

First, calculate the inductive reactance X_L:

$$X_L = 2\pi fL \tag{8.32}$$

Substituting figures:

$$X_L = 2 \times 3.142 \times 50 \times 0.382 = 120.024\ \Omega$$

Now find the amount of current consumed:

$$I = \text{voltage}/X_L \tag{8.33}$$

Replacing with known values:

$$I = 230\ \text{volts}/120.024 = 1.916\ \text{amps}$$

Series circuit containing resistance, capacitance and inductance

Figure 8.49 illustrates a simple series formation circuit containing one 10 μF capacitor, a 0.382 henry solenoid and a 10 Ω resistor connected to a 230 volt, 50 Hz supply.

Calculate the total impedance, Z, of a series circuit consisting of all three components by using the following expression:

$$Z = \sqrt{[R^2 + (X_L - X_C)^2]} \tag{8.34}$$

where R is the total resistance in ohms, X_L is the value of the inductive reactance in ohms and X_C is the value of the capacitive reactance in ohms.

To find the total impedance of this circuit we must first calculate the inductive reactance (X_L):

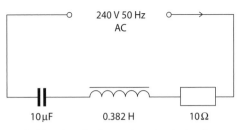

240 V 50 Hz AC

10 μF   0.382 H   10 Ω

Figure 8.49 – *A series formation circuit that has capacitance, inductance and resistance.*

$$X_L = 2\pi fL \tag{8.32}$$

$$X_L = 2 \times 3.142 \times 50 \times 0.382 = 120.024\ \text{ohms}$$

Next the capacitive reactance (X_C):

$$X_C = 1/2\pi fC$$

$$X_C = \frac{1}{2 \times 3.142 \times 50 \times 0.00001} = 318.268\ \text{ohms}$$

Now the values of all three components have been found: R = 10 ohms (taken from Figure 8.49), X_L = 120.024 ohms inductive reactance and X_C = 318.2 ohms capacitive reactance. Returning to expression (8.31) and substituting figures:

$$Z = \sqrt{[10^2 + (120 - 318.2)]^2} = \sqrt{[100 + (-198.2)^2]} = \sqrt{39\,383.24}.$$

Therefore Z = 194.4 Ω impedance.

To find the current flowing in your circuit, apply the following expression:

current (I) in amps = voltage/impedance or $I = V/Z$. $\tag{8.35}$

$$I = 230/198.4 = 1.15\ \text{amps}$$

A curious characteristic of this type of problem is the *collective voltage drop* across all three components is not determined arithmetically as, for example, when measurements are calculated with DC circuits served by resistors. We have dealt with this in previous paragraphs.

Calculating the power generated within the circuit

To find the power generated within our circuit expression (8.12) is used:

power in watts (W) = I^2R

As energy levels created by the capacitor and inductor are returned to the circuit during every cycle, it makes sense to say that no power is used within these two components. All we have to consider is the resistive element of the circuit – the one 10 Ω resistor:

$$\text{power in watts (W)} = 1.15^2 \times 10 = 13.2$$

Types of capacitors

Six commonly used capacitors are as follows:

- *Air capacitor* – This type of capacitor has movable plates, using the air as a dielectric and is applied to radio circuits for tuning purposes.
- *Paper capacitor* – Constructed with two long strips of thin aluminium foil and waxed paper as a dielectric which, once sandwiched between the two plates, are rolled up like a long turf of grass. After housing the assembly in a suitable container, a termination point is added to each plate. Used in motor circuits and supply problems relating to power factor correction.
- *Ceramic capacitor* – Used for high frequency work in television and radar and takes the form of a ceramic disc or tube sandwiched between two silver foil plates.
- *Electrolytic capacitor* – Two strips of aluminium foil, together with gauze containing ammonium borate, are rolled to form a cylindrical component and placed in a suitable container. An oxide insulating film is deposited on one of the plates and acts as a dielectric. The electrolytic capacitor is a polarized device, having both *positive* and *negative* terminals and is applied to DC smoothing circuits.
- *Mica capacitor* – Mica, acting as a dielectric, has a thin film of silver deposited directly on its surface. The arrangements of plates are in parallel formation. Because of its low loss, high dielectric strength and reliability, mica capacitors are applied to television and other high-frequency circuits. Values vary from a few picofarads to about 0.01 μF.

- *Oil-impregnated capacitor* – An oil-impregnated paper, used as a dielectric material, is sandwiched between two strips of aluminium foil. It is similar in design to the waxed paper capacitor but usually takes the form of a rolled or oval assembly. Values vary from 40 pF to many microfarads. Used mainly for low-frequency work.

Summary so far...

1. You can make a simple capacitor from two similar shaped conductive plates that are sandwiched between a special insulating material called a dielectric.

2. The voltage per unit thickness of the dielectric is the principal value that determines the working efficiency of the capacitor.

3. Reactance is AC resistance and is calculated by applying the following expression: $2\pi f L$.

4. Examples of inductance are air-cooled solenoids, transformers, electric bells, electromagnets and electric motors.

5. There are many types of capacitors and they are applied in many different ways. Paper capacitors are widely used in the electrical installation industry.

Handy hints

- Handle capacitors with care – they could be fully charged.
- Every capacitor has a safe working voltage. To double the working voltage, connect two or more in *series* formation.
- High temperatures are often the cause of bloated capacitors.
- Metal glaze resistors are expensive but very reliable.
- Resistors, which produce very high values, may have been exposed to heat, excess voltage or moisture.

Review questions

1 Describe why the *valency shell* of an atom is important.

2 Which is a better conductor of electricity, copper or silver?

3 Briefly describe *electrical resistance* using your own words.

4 State two ways of calculating the *power generated in watts* within a circuit.

5 Calculate the total resistance of three 10 ohm resistors connected together in series formation and the current flow if 80 volts were to be applied to it.

6 How would you evaluate voltage drop?

7 Why do batteries run down when *not* connected to a load?

8 Write down the expression you would use to calculate the resistance of *resistors wired in parallel*.

9 Where would you find a *toroidal transformer*?

10 Describe the term *dielectric stress*.

11 What is the total capacitance of three $20\,\mu F$ capacitors wired in *series* formation?

12 Find the value of three $20\,\mu F$ capacitors wired in parallel formation.

13 Explain why power is not consumed within a pure capacitive circuit.

14 How would you calculate the value of an inductive circuit?

15 Draw a simple circuit comprising the following:
- a resistor
- a solenoid
- a capacitor.

Values need not be included in your sketch.

The resistance of a conductor and the effects of voltage drop and temperature variations within a circuit

All conductors other than superconductors have a built-in resistance to electricity. Calculate the natural resistance of any cable by using the following expression:

$$R = \frac{\rho \times L}{a} \tag{8.36}$$

where ρ (pronounced 'rho') is the resistivity of the conducting material measured in ohms per metre (Ω/m). The resistivity for copper at 20°C is 1.8×10^{-8} and for aluminium it is 2.8×10^{-8}. L is the length of the cable in metres, a is the cross-sectional area in metres squared (m^2) and R is the total natural resistance of the conductor in ohms.

Natural resistance within a conductor will cause a *voltage drop* to occur and this is *directly* proportional to the current flow within the circuit. To calculate the voltage drop within a circuit use the following expression:

voltage drop (V) = current flow × the natural resistance of the conductor (8.37)

Consider Figure 8.50 as an example and the following problem:

A 200 metre circuit of 2.5 mm² copper cable is installed to serve a single-phase, 230 volt induction motor that draws 23 amps from the supply. Assume an ambient temperature of 20°C and ignore the practicalities of this problem.

Given that the resistivity of copper is $1.8 \times 10^{-8}\,\Omega/m$, calculate the potential voltage drop within the conductors.

First, apply a combination formula of expressions (8.33) and (8.34):

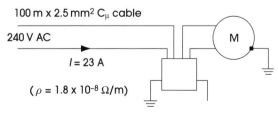

Figure 8.50 – *A 230 volt induction motor drawing 23 amps from the supply is served with a 100 metre run of 2.5 mm² copper cable. This is a study exercise only.*

voltage drop $= I(\rho L/a)$ (8.38)

Remember to express all terms in metres so the expression is calculated in standard units. For example:

$1\text{ m}^2 = 1000 \times 1000\text{ mm} = 1\,000\,000\text{ mm}^2$
or $1\text{ mm}^2 = 1 \times 10^{-6}\text{ m}^2$

Returning to expression (8.35):

$$\text{voltage drop} = 23\left(\frac{1.8\times10^{-8}\times200}{2.5\times10^{-6}}\right)$$

Therefore

voltage drop $= 23 \times 1.44 = 33.12$ volts.

Current flow and resistance

Had the load in the last example been replaced with a 500 watt halogen lamp, drawing 2.173 amps from the supply, the voltage drop would have been reduced to 3.12 volts. This would represent a voltage drop of 1.35%, clearly showing the relationship between current flow and the resistance within the conductor (intrinsic resistance). Figure 8.51 illustrates the association between a variable current, voltage drop and the built-in resistance of the conductor.

In practical terms, an electric motor experiencing such a large drop in voltage would automatically stop, triggered by the thermal overload circuit within the starter. If the protection was set too high or the machine had no overload device, the motor would most probably burn out. The moral to this example is not only to select the *correct size cable* but also to think about the *physical length* of the circuit from the distribution centre to the appliance or independent motor.

Factors affecting the resistance of a conductor

There are four factors affecting the resistance of a conductor:

1 The material from which the conductor is made (copper, aluminium, steel).

2 The cross-sectional area of the conductor.

3 The temperature of the conductor (for example, when it is very cold the resistance is less).

4 The length of the conductor.

Material composition

Electrical conductivity is very dependent on the size of the atom and the number of free electrons in its outer shell. Copper, which is very good, follows silver. These elements/conductors have large atoms and just one loosely held valence electron.

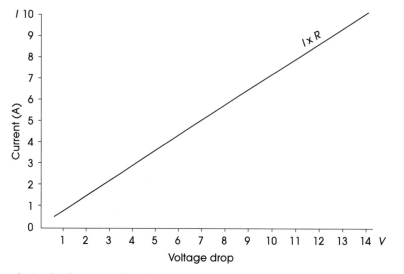

Figure 8.51 – *The relationship between voltage drop and current. Given that the total resistance of the cable is 1.44 Ω, a voltage drop of 5.76 volts would be experienced when a current of 4 amps is flowing in the circuit.*

Resistivity

Different materials have different electrical resistivity factors. The term *resistivity* indicates the resistance between two opposite faces of a metre cube of the material under examination. The *unit of resistivity* is the ohm/metre, indicated by the Greek letter ρ (rho).

Cross-sectional area

The resistance of a conductor is inversely proportional to its cross-sectional area (csa). To illustrate, take two water pipes, one large and one small, as illustrated in Figure 8.52. Let the water pressure in the tank stand for the voltage and the flow of water through the pipes the current within the circuit. The natural resistance of the conductor is comparable to the diameter of the water pipes. It is obvious the larger of the pipes offers less resistance than the smaller one. The bigger pipe allows a greater volume of water to flow – and so it is with electricity. The larger the cross-section of the conductor, the smaller the resistance will be when you compare with a smaller-sized conductor.

In practical terms, if the current is very high and the conductor is too small for your connected load then expect trouble, for your conductor will either be warm to the touch or so hot that the insulation serving your cable will start to blister, leading to a total burn out!

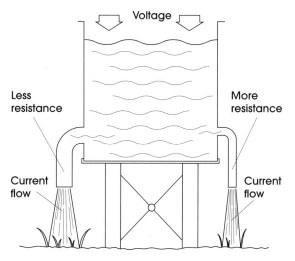

Figure 8.52 – *Less resistance is experienced in the larger water pipe compared to the smaller one.*

Temperature

Generally, a *rise* in temperature will produce a *rise* in resistance in most conductors. Two exceptions to this rule are the conductor/elements carbon and silicon and they both have a *negative* coefficient of resistance. They will respond with a *decrease* in resistance on the temperature rising.

To calculate the changed resistance of a conductor due to an increase in ambient temperature, use the following expression:

$$\frac{R_1}{R_2} = \frac{1 + \alpha t_1}{1 + \alpha t_2} \tag{8.39}$$

where R_1 is the original resistance of the conductor, R_2 is the final resistance of the conductor, t_1 is the initial temperature in degrees Celsius (°C), t_2 is the final temperature in degrees Celsius and α (the Greek letter alpha) is the temperature of the conductor.

For copper, α is calculated at 0.0043 ohms for each degree Celsius rise whereas tungsten has a temperature coefficient of 0.0045 Ω/°C. This factor is often written as 45×10^{-4} Ω/°C.

Converting to degrees Celsius

From Fahrenheit, use this expression:

$$°C = \frac{\left(°F - 32\right) \times 5}{9} \tag{8.40}$$

If your temperature is expressed in degrees *Kelvin* (K), where 0 K is absolute zero, then

$$°C = K{-}273.15$$

As a practical example, to show the influence temperature has on the resistance of a conductor, please consider the following:

A 230 volt single-phase circuit, wired throughout in 2.5 mm² MI copper cable, is found to be drawing 4.31 amps from the supply at 5°C. The installation is placed where the surrounding temperature varies from 5 to 30°C over a 24-hour period. At 5°C, the resistance of the conductor is 1.276 Ω.. Calculate both the resistance and the voltage drop within the conductor at 30°C.

Assume the temperature coefficient of copper to be 0.0043 ohms per degree Celsius.

First, refer to expression (8.35):

$$\frac{R_1}{R_2} = \frac{1 + \alpha t_1}{1 + \alpha t_2}$$

Substituting figures:

$$\frac{1.276}{R_2} = \frac{1 + (0.0043 \times 5)}{1 + (0.0043 \times 30)}$$

Cross-multiplying and dividing throughout by 1.0215:

$$1.0215 \times R_2 = 1.276 \times 1.129$$

$$R_2 = \frac{1.276 \times 1.129}{1.0215} = 1.41 \text{ ohms}$$

Thus the increase due to temperature rise = 1.41–1.276 ohms = 0.134 ohms.

Now to calculate the voltage drop within the conductor. Regulation 525-01-02 requires the voltage drop between the incoming supply terminals and a fixed current-using appliance should not exceed 4% of the nominal voltage (U_0) of the supply. In a 230 volt supply, 4% of the nominal voltage is 9.2 volts. The following expression will determine this figure mathematically:

permissible voltage drop = $U_0 \times 0.04$ (8.41)

where 0.04 is the percentage voltage drop permitted.

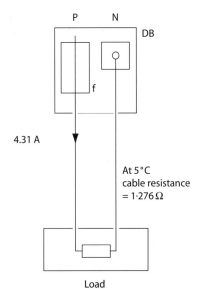

Figure 8.53 – *A single-phase circuit where the ambient temperature varies from 5 to 30°C.*

Voltage drop at 5°C = current flow × resistance of the conductor

(as illustrated in Figure 8.53). Thus

voltage drop at 5°C = 4.31 amps × 1.276 ohms = 5.49 volts

voltage drop at 30°C = 4.31 amps × 1.41 ohms = 6.077 volts.

The second voltage drop due to temperature rise is not sufficiently high enough to breach the electrical regulations. This was a theoretical exercise, but it will provide you with an insight into problems involving conductors that are subjected to temperature variations.

Length

The last factor affecting the resistance of a conductor is *length*. Since the resistivity of a conducting material is a constant throughout the complete conductor, it makes sense that the resistance is in direct proportion to length, as Figure 8.54 illustrates. By using expression (8.33) the resistance of a conductor can be found when the resistivity (ρ) of the material is known. Resistivity is determined by accurately measuring across two opposite sides of a metre cube of the material under test. To repeat, for copper, this figure is 1.8×10^{-8} Ω/m.

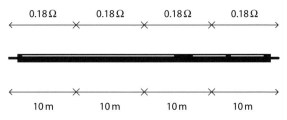

Figure 8.54 – *The resistance of a conductor is directly proportional to its length.*

Theoretical wiring systems

Domestic lighting circuits start from a distribution centre, wired in either 1.0 or 1.5 mm² PVC insulated and sheathed cable. Industrial circuits use steel conduit or trunking installations as a cable carrier and single insulated conductors replace the sheathed cables used in domestic work.

One-way switching

Figure 8.55 illustrates the basic circuitry required to install a one-way lighting circuit. One-way means the lighting arrangement is only operational at one position.

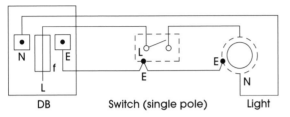

Figure 8.55 – A one-way switching arrangement serving a lighting circuit.

Two-way switching

Two-way switching arrangements are completely different. There are several ways to wire and Figure 8.56 shows how to connect using a six-terminal joint box. In practice, the switching arrangement uses two- and three-core PVC insulated and sheathed cables for domestic purposes. One of the alternative ways you can use to wire a two-way switch is the *conversion method*. Figure 8.57 illustrates this method. Advantages include having all the connections on one level without having to add in a joint box.

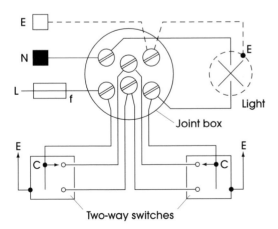

Figure 8.56 – A two-way lighting arrangement wired using a six-terminal joint box.

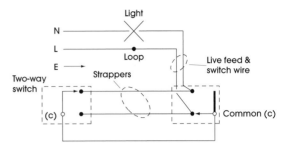

Figure 8.57 – A one-way lighting arrangement converted to a two-way circuit.

Intermediate switching

Figure 8.58 illustrates the method used to incorporate *intermediate switching* into a two-way lighting circuit. There is no such 'animal' as a stand-alone intermediate switch. To include this type of switch you must first have a two-way switching arrangement – then you can incorporate as many intermediate switches as you like within your circuit.

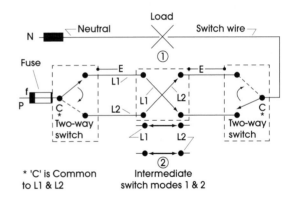

Figure 8.58 – A two-way and intermediate switching arrangement.

Power circuit arrangements

The best known of all power circuit arrangements is the *final ring circuit*. Unlike a single 5 or 15 amp socket method, Figure 8.59, a final ring circuit can serve an *unlimited* number of sockets, provided you are able to provide certain conditions within your circuit. These conditions are:

■ the size and type of cable used for the final ring circuit

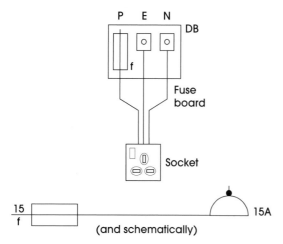

Figure 8.59 – *A 15 amp radial circuit.*

providing power to remote areas where it might not be practical to extend the cables forming the ring. Wire just one spur from any socket that forms part of the final ring circuit. This means if ten socket outlets form the ring, then you may install ten additional in the form of *spurred sockets*. Figure 8.61 will make this point easier to understand.

- the size of the area the installation has to provide for
- the size of the over-current protection device (fuse, MCB or MCCB).

Construct your installation in a similar way to Figure 8.60. Refer to BS 7671 Regulation 314, Chapters 43, 46 and 55 for additional guidance.

Spurred sockets from a final ring circuit

A stand-alone spurred socket from a ring circuit (top right side of Figure 8.60) is a useful way of

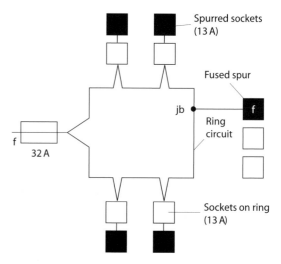

Figure 8.61 – *One socket, spurred from a mainline socket, can be wired to serve a remote location.*

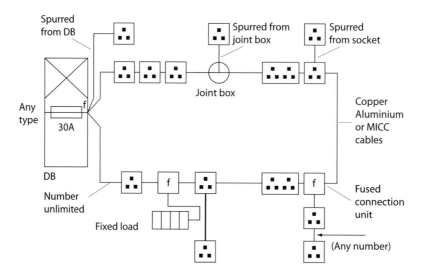

Figure 8.60 – *A final ring circuit recommended for floor areas of 100 m². Use rubber insulated PVC sheath or MI cables to wire your circuit. Conductor csa: Copper –2.5 mm², aluminium – 4.0 mm² and MI – 1.5 mm².*

An exception to this rule

It is possible to supply an unlimited number of socket outlets as a spur from a final ring circuit as long as the service cable comes from a *fused connection unit* and has the protection of a 13 amp fuse. Figure 8.62 illustrates this point and shows that only 13 amps can be drawn, no matter how many sockets are installed!

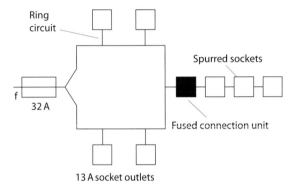

Figure 8.62 – *An unlimited number of 13 amp sockets can be served from a fused connection unit.*

Appliances

Permanently connected appliances, such as fridge freezers, washing machines, etc., can be hard-wired into a final ring circuit but they have to be protected with a switched fused connection unit, sensibly rated. See Figure 8.60, bottom centre, for a fixed and permanent load served from a ring circuit fused connection unit.

Over-current protection

Please bear in mind that the size of the over-current protection device (fuse or breaker) that attends your final ring circuit will either be rated at 30 or 32 amps, so it would be foolish to include any heavy current-consuming appliances such as an immersion heater or tumble drier, etc., as fixed wiring. These two items alone will draw about 20 amps from the supply – then you will only have around 10 amps left to serve your final ring circuit. It is best to wire a dedicated appliance ring.

Testing your final ring circuit

Once installed, remove all final ring circuit conductors from their connection points within your distribution centre and test your circuit for continuity to establish that all *three* conductors (phase, neutral and the CPC) are a *complete* ring and *not* two radial circuits connected at your distribution centre (Figure 8.63 explains this). Typically, your ohmmeter values will be about 0.25 to 0.9 ohms when measuring the phase conductor and neutral conductor from end to end. The CPC will be about 1.67 times the value of one of the current-carrying conductors. See Figures 8.64 and 8.65 for graphical details.

To continue, our leading body recommends the following procedure. I feel that this method is unnecessarily drawn out, as there are other quicker ways to obtain the figures required for an *Inspection Certificate*. With this in mind, we will continue with the recommended test procedure.

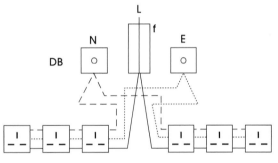

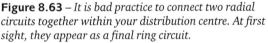

Figure 8.63 – *It is bad practice to connect two radial circuits together within your distribution centre. At first sight, they appear as a final ring circuit.*

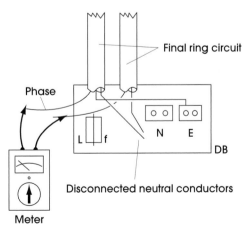

Figure 8.64 – *Testing for continuity within your final ring circuit. Step one, measure the resistance of your phase conductor and then, neutral conductor from end to end.*

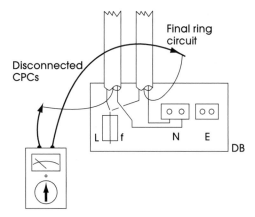

Figure 8.65 – *Testing for continuity within your final ring circuit. Step two, measure the resistance of your CPC from end to end.*

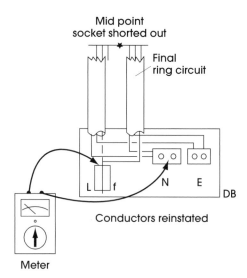

Figure 8.67 – *The value you record should be about half of the value noted at the start of your test.*

At a midpoint position within the circuit make all three conductors common with each other (join them together). Do this by linking all conductors serving the socket outlet via a 13 amp plug as shown in Figure 8.66 and switch 'ON' the socket.

Now take a value with your ohmmeter between the *phase* and *neutral* conductors. This should be about *half* the value you recorded at the start of your test when you measured the phase conductor from end to end – Figure 8.67 illustrates this. To finish off your test take an ohmic value between your phase conductor and

the CPC, as shown graphically in Figure 8.68. The value you obtain should be approximately a *quarter* of the first reading you gained measuring the phase conductor from end to end *plus* a quarter of the original value you acquired from the two open ends of the CPC.

Put back all *six* ring circuit distribution centre conductors and remove your linked-out 13 amp plug from the midpoint socket outlet position.

Figure 8.66 – *Link out the phase, neutral and protective conductor but short-circuiting a 13 amp plug.*

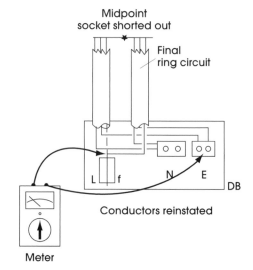

Figure 8.68 – *Test finally between the phase and the CPC.*

In practice, it is very difficult to select a mid-point position – socket outlets are never so obliging, so the figures you obtain are only approximate.

A practical example

Consider the following – a final ring circuit comprising five twin 13 amp sockets installed over an area of 90 m².

The first step. After disconnecting the appropriate conductors from the distribution centre, a value between the open ends of the phase conductor is 0.4 Ω. The neutral conductor also displays the same 'end-to-end' value of 0.4 Ω.

The second step. Switch your test to the open ends of the CPC. The value you will meter will be about 0.66 Ω.

The third step. Short-circuit the *midpoint* of your final ring circuit as described in Figure 8.66 and record the resistance offered in ohms between the phase and neutral conductors.

Expect the following value:

$$\frac{\text{approximately half the value of the first step}}{1} \tag{8.42}$$

Substituting figures, we get

approximate resistance $R = 0.4/2 = 0.2$ ohms.

The fourth step. To end the test, take a final value from between the phase conductor and the CPC. Your expected value in ohms will be approximately

$$\frac{\text{first step reading}}{4} + \frac{\text{second step reading}}{4} \tag{8.43}$$

Substituting your figures

resistance R approximately $\dfrac{0.4}{4} + \dfrac{0.66}{4} = 0.1 + 0.165 = 0.265$ ohms

If your figures are okay then you have continuity within your ring circuit and all is fine. High values could mean you have loose terminals so do check and get your figures to the value they should be.

Insulation testing your circuit

After you have completed your final ring circuit, it must be insulation tested. To do this, measure the resistance of the insulation serving the conductors with a 500 volt insulation tester. Take a value between both the phase and neutral conductors and between each current-carrying conductor and the CPC – Figure 8.69 illustrates this. The value you record must not be less than 500 000 ohms (0.5 MΩ). If less, then you must check for possible reasons – check Regulation 713-04-04. Finally, check all your conductors are where they should be within the distribution centre.

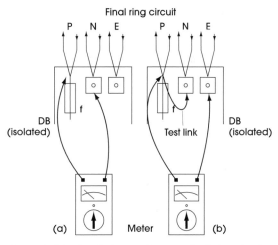

Figure 8.69 – *Insulation testing your final ring circuit.*

Thirteen amp radial circuits

When the demand for current is small, the *radial circuit* is a suitable alternative to a final ring circuit – it is also cheaper to install.

Figure 8.70 illustrates the basic requirements for a circuit serving a floor area of about 75 m². As with a ring circuit, you can have permanently connected equipment and an unlimited number of 13 amp sockets providing you meet certain conditions (see BS 7671 Chapters 43, 46 and 52).

There are two types – the first type of radial is designed to serve a floor area of up to 75 m², protected by an over-current device rated at 32 amps and wired in 4.0 mm² cable. The second type provides for floor areas up to 50 m². When a copper conductor is used, you are able to use

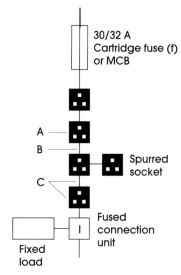

Figure 8.70 – *13 amp radial circuit: A, unlimited number of 13 amp socket outlets; B, cable sizes: rubber insulated or PVC sheathed copper cables at 4 mm², aluminium at 6 mm² and MI at 2.5 mm². Your maximum floor area will be 75 m².*

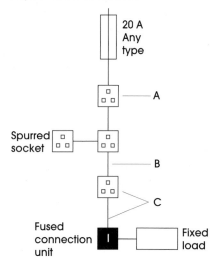

Figure 8.71 – *13 amp radial circuits for smaller floor areas: A, unlimited number of socket outlets; B, rubber or PVC sheath copper cables may be used at 2.5 mm², aluminium conductors at 4 mm² and MI at 2.5 mm². Your maximum floor area will be 50 m².*

2.5 mm² cables but you must use a 20 amp protective device and this could be any type of fuse, MCB or MCCB.

Figure 8.71 summarises the conditions laid down for this type of radial circuit. Additional information is obtainable from the IEE's On-Site Guide.

Other radial circuits

Other domestic radial circuits include the following:

- Immersion heater – use 2.5 mm² cable (16 amp breaker).

- Central heating controls – use 1.0 or 1.5 mm² cable (6 or 10 amp breaker).

- Cooker – use 6.0 or 10 mm² cable (32 or 40 amp breaker).

- Fixed wall heater – use 2.5 mm² cable (16 amp breaker).

- Electric shower – use 6.0 or 10 mm² (32 or 40 amp breaker).

- Door bell (230 volt side) – use 1.0 mm² cable (6 amp breaker).

- Garage distribution centre – use 4.0 mm² cable (20 amp breaker).

- Off-peak heating – use 2.5 mm² cable up to 3 kW and 6.0 mm² for higher ratings (16 or 32 amp breaker).

- Dedicated computer supply – use 2.5 mm² cable (16 amp breaker).

Fibre optics: a brief insight

Use optical-fibre communication cable for the transmission of data, telephone conversations and television channels. Surprisingly, you will discover the diameter of the glass fibre core is only some 0.125 mm, as illustrated in Figure 8.72. This is very small when compared to many of our smallest conductors. The bulk of the cable supports a thin glass core which, compared to the surrounding cladding, has a higher *refractive index*. (A refractive index (*n*) is defined as *the sine of the angle of incidence to that of the subsequent angle of refraction when the light source passes from one medium to another.*) Check out this ratio in your old GCSE physics examination notes. Glass, you will find, has a refractive index of between about 1.5 and 1.7 (there are no units to remember!).

Either an *infrared* light source operating just below the level you are able to see or a low-

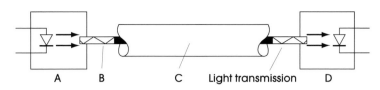

Figure 8.72 – *A fibre optic cable. A, guided light transmitter; B, glass core; C, protective cladding; D, guided light receiver.*

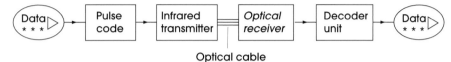

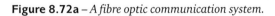

Figure 8.72a – *A fibre optic communication system.*

powered laser is used for an *optical* transmitter. An optical transmitter is an invisible light source; the light, which is retained within the glass core, then rebounds off the junction of the core and cladding by internal reflection. This process allows the infrared light to go through the glass core at great speed. Visible light is *absorbed* within the glass core. It is not used for transmission purposes.

Figure 8.72a is a block diagram describing a typical fibre-optic telecommunication system. In summary, speech, converted into electrical signals, is *pulse code modulated* in a *coder* and then fed into an optical transmitter where signals, converted into a light source, are projected through the glass core of the fibre-optic cable. When the light source arrives at the other end an optical receiver changes the light source back into electrical pulses and decodes it into speech or data.

The advantages of using a fibre-optic communication system

There are many – the main ones are:

- Free from electrical interference.
- Far lighter and easier to handle than copper cable.
- User security greatly improved.
- Voltage drop is not relevant.
- The system can span far greater distances than conventional wiring methods.
- Fibre optic networks are able to carry far more information.

Handy hints

- Draping a halogen hand lamp over the top of a door could cause a fire hazard or badly scorched paintwork.

- Change your contactor coils with care. Internal springs serving the laminated armature can catapult from sight if awkwardly disturbed.

- Avoid overloading a portable generator. The voltage drop brought about could easily damage the field coils (windings) of your portable drill.

- It is best to handle *Category 2* lighting diffusers wearing industrial cotton gloves. This way, body grease from your fingers will not be in contact with the reflective coating. The coating is very thin and rubbing it too much will destroy the reflective surface.

- Before you switch off a distribution centre, make sure there are no computers on-line. Lost work causes loud and raised voices!

- Unforeseen problems can quickly appear if you blunder into a new job as though there were no tomorrow. It might be a little wearisome but think the job through before you start work. Remember the acronym 'STRAW' – **S**top, **T**hink, **R**eview **A**nd **W**ork. Your job will be better for it!

Review questions

1 To calculate the intrinsic resistance of a conductor, what expression would you use?
2 Name four factors that affect the resistance of a conductor.
3 What expression would you use to find the changed resistance of a conductor due to a rise in temperature?
4 Name one element that has a *negative* coefficient of resistance.
5 Which expression would you use to convert degrees Fahrenheit to degrees Celsius?
6 Calculate 273.15 Kelvin in terms of degrees Celsius.
7 BS 7671 Regulation 525-01-02 instructs that the voltage drop between the incoming supply terminals and a fixed current-using appliance should not exceed one of the following values:
   (a)   5% of the nominal voltage
   (b)   6% of the nominal voltage
   (c)   4% of the nominal voltage
   (d)   8% of the nominal voltage.

8 How many *intermediate switches* are permitted within a two-way switching arrangement?
9 Explain the consequences should a 2.2 kW motor experience a large voltage drop.
10 When is it allowable to spur off an unlimited number of socket outlets from a final ring circuit?
11 State the size of cable required to install a radial circuit serving an area of 75 m².
12 What is the maximum floor area that may be used when wiring a radial circuit using 2.5 mm² PVC insulated and sheathed cable?
13 Suggest two uses for fibre-optic cable.
14 List three advantages of using fibre-optic cables.
15 State the size of over-current protection required for a final ring circuit when installed using 2.5 mm² PVC insulated and sheathed cable and designed to serve an area of 100 m².

Summary so far...

1 All cables have a built-in (intrinsic) resistance to electricity.
2 Intrinsic resistance will cause voltage drop to occur within the conductor and is directly proportional to current flow. The greater the current the greater the voltage drop.
3 The four factors affecting the resistance of a conductor are the material the conductor is made from, the cross-sectional area of the conductor, the temperature and the length of the conductor.
4 The voltage drop between the incoming supply terminals and a fixed current-using appliance must not go beyond 4% of the nominal voltage of the supply. Nominal, in this case, means 'supposed', 'in name only' or 'declared voltage'.
5 There are several ways of wiring a two-way switching arrangement. The *conversion method* is far the easiest.
6 You can include as many *intermediate switches* as you require within a two-way switching arrangement.
7 Final ring circuits are wired in 2.5 mm² cable in the form of a ring. Include as many as you need within a 100 m² area. Protect your circuit by means of a 30 amp fuse or 32 amp 'B'-Type breaker.
8 Install an unlimited number of 13 amp sockets as a spur providing your spur originates from a fused connection unit served with a 13 amp fuse.
9 You must test your final ring circuit for both continuity and insulation resistance.
10 There are many advantages gained from using fibre-optic cable for telecommunications, data and television communications. Security and a system free from electrical interference are just two of them.

Mechanical science

The simmerstat

Use a simmerstat to regulate heating loads. Every home that has an electric cooker is equipped with at least four or five of them that provide temperature control to individual radiant or halogen plates and possibly one or two grill elements as illustrated in Figure 8.73.

A domestic simmerstat's industrial counterpart, known as a *power controller* or *burst firing module*, can switch far heavier loads. They operate in a similar fashion to their domestic cousins although some apply electronics within their circuits in order to operate. Industry uses this type of simmerstat for various applications of temperature control.

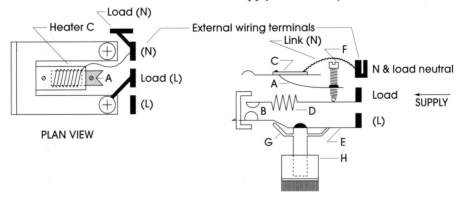

Figure 8.73 – *Simmerstats serving a domestic cooker.*

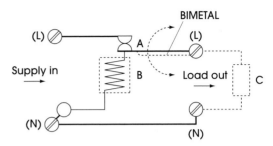

Figure 8.74 – *An internal line diagram for a domestic simmerstat. A, switching contacts; B, internal heating element; C, external heating load.*

Figure 8.74 illustrates the internal wiring arrangements of a typical simmerstat whereas Figure 8.75 graphically shows the internal structure of the device.

Function

A simmerstat will prevent *thermal over-run* by a combination of manual control and automation and so passively monitors the temperature of the connected load.

Inside the device there is a tiny heating element mounted on a small length of thermal insulation attached to a bimetal strip (Figure 8.76). Its function is to gently warm the bimetal component to cause linear movement. The heating element assembly is supported on a supporting cradle, lever arm and adjustable pivot which, when thermally moved, provides movement for a snap sprung-loaded switching action to occur. Once the load contacts are opened, the small heating element loses its supply of electricity and cools. The reduction in

Figure 8.75 – *Graphic details of a domestic simmerstat. A, bimetal strip; B, switching contacts; C, internal heating element; D, control spring; E, sprung metal delivery arm for the phase conductor; F, adjustment screw; G, cam; H, manual control knob.*

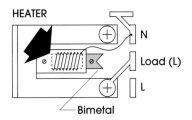

HEATER

N

Load (L)

L

Bimetal

Figure 8.76 – *A heating element within the simmerstat (shown as an arrow) is mounted on a bimetal strip.*

temperature produces a displacement in the bimetal strip away from the midpoint of the simmerstat. This allows a reduction of pressure on the switching arm originated by the adjustable pivot attached to the bimetal strip. When sufficiently cooled, the switching contacts will snap closed providing a path for current serving both external load and the tiny integral heating element. The procedure is then repeated.

Bimetal thermostat

Application

The role of the thermostat is as a *thermomechanical* device for maintaining a steady temperature. One of the most common methods is the bimetal strip type so adapted that, when heated or cooled, its movement will automatically open or close electrical terminals.

Test the bimetal principle by using two equal lengths of dissimilar metal such as brass and iron riveted together to form a single component. As both pieces of metal have different rates of expansion, the brass section will become longer than the iron when heated and this will cause the bimetal strip to bend as shown in Figure 8.77. This represents the bimetal principle in its most basic form.

At 18°C — BRASS

At 70°C — IRON

Figure 8.77 – *The principle of the bimetal strip. A, before heat is applied; B, after heat is applied. The coefficient of linear expansion of iron is 0.000 012/K whereas for brass it is 0.000 019/K.*

The bimetal thermostat is used for various applications. Here are some of them:

- Electrical controls and central heating radiator valves.
- Frost protection and controlling electrical trace heating.
- Industrial space heating arrangements.
- Electric motor overload controls.
- Portable electrical heating controls.
- Solar powered heating controls.
- Ventilation and air conditioning controls.

Figure 8.78 demonstrates in schematic form how a simple thermostat is included within the wiring arrangements serving a basic ventilation system.

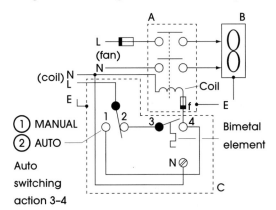

Figure 8.78 – *A thermostat used to control a basic ventilation system. A, contactor; B, electric fan; C, thermostat.*

Function

The role of a thermostat is to prevent thermal over-run by means of automatic control. Figure 8.79 schematically shows the internal wiring arrangements serving the domestic frost stat. When connected to a load of less than 13 amps it is advisable to provide a neutral conductor to terminal four. Doing this will complete the *heat anticipator circuit,* the internal load taking the form of a small resistor located near the bend in the bimetal strip as shown in the last illustration. The resistor, valued between about 0.3 and 0.4 MΩ, gently preheats the bimetal strip to prevent over-run of the connected heating load. An adjustable heat anticipator circuit is

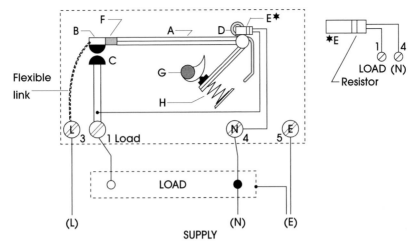

Figure 8.79 – *A domestic thermostat: A, flexible bimetal strip; B, phase supply contact often aided with a permanent magnet; C, fixed contact serving the load; D, sprung heat sink; E, heat anticipator resistor about 0.43 MΩ; F, insulator; G, control spring and cam; H, cam spring.*

incorporated within many up-market industrial thermostats. This is ideal when precision is called for.

Operation

First, choose your working temperature and adjust the control knob to suit. The knob is push-fitted onto a spindle that is fixed firmly onto a cam wheel. When a drop in the room temperature is experienced, the built-in bimetal strip unwillingly bends inwards – look back at Figure 8.79. A small permanent magnet fitted to the underside of the free moving 'phase' contact provides a snap-on action for the approaching load contacts. This thermo-magnetic principle operates well in reverse when a rise in ambient temperature is experienced. The magnet helps to prevent unnecessary arcing from occurring on the load terminals.

Working problems

Open-type thermostats are fitted with ventilation grills and these can become polluted in dirty conditions or when fitted in agricultural surroundings. Often they just get full of dirt and are unable to do their job properly. In damp or humid conditions, the pollution within causes RCD tripping problems. The thing to do would be to isolate your circuit and remove all dampness and contamination from inside the thermostat.

Fit a fine mesh guard around the body of the thermostat to keep out unwanted contamination if this is a practical option.

Capillary thermostat

The *capillary* or *line voltage thermostat* is widely used where conditions are hostile or in situations where it would be impractical to use a conventional temperature sensing device, for example within an ice bank serving a bulk milk tank or in a high-temperature oven.

This type of thermostat is fully adjustable and the switching contacts are heavy enough to allow for direct switching without the need for an in-line contactor or relay.

The way it is made

Both the capillary and sensing bulb are hollow and they are interlinked. Gas is added within the bulb during the manufacturing stage. This gas expands and contracts proportionally to the rise and fall in temperature. An increase in temperature gives rise to an increase in pressure within the sensing bulb and expands the bellows proportionally. Upon reaching the required working temperature, the bellows will automatically switch 'ON' a spring-loaded micro-switch. This switch either opens or closes the circuit it is controlling – Figure 8.80 illustrates the basic principles.

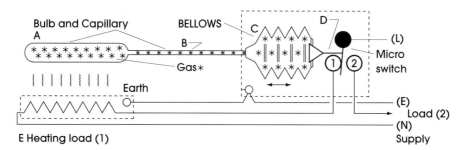

Figure 8.80 – *The capillary thermostat, shown pictorially. A, sensing bulb; B, capillary tube; C, bellows; D, micro switch; E, external heating load.*

Capillary thermostats can be used for a variety of applications:

- under-floor heating arrangements
- air conditioning units
- all types of ovens
- cold rooms
- ice control within bulk milk tanks
- industrial unit heaters (factory warm air units with an electric fan).

Mercury bulb thermostat

You can see this type of thermostat in industrial and commercial installations – sometimes controlling refrigeration equipment.

A small sealed glass or plastic tube houses a small quantity of liquid mercury. The mercury acts as a switching medium bridging the

switching terminals fitted within the glass tube. The glass mercury tilt switch is attached to one end of a bimetal spiral arrangement whilst the other end is free to rock as in a see-saw, pivoted at the centre of the glass tube as shown in Figure 8.81. An increase or decrease in temperature will nudge the bimetal spiral to turn. In doing so the glass tube will tilt and the mercury will bridge the two *switching conductors* – current will flow.

Switching action

There are generally two types you will come across: one- or two-way switching arrangements as Figure 8.82 shows.

The two-way switch has a set of *three post contacts* fitted within the glass container. The *common* terminal is in the centre with the *normally open* and *normally closed* contacts on either side of it. When tilted *anticlockwise* the conductive pool of mercury makes contact with the *common* and *normally closed* switching posts. Reversing the movement creates a conductive path from the *common* terminal to the *normally open* terminal. Mercury is heavy (13.6 times the

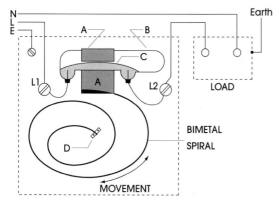

Figure 8.81 – *The mercury tilt thermostat, shown pictorially. A, switching cradle; B, glass or plastic mercury switch; C, liquid mercury; D, bimetal spiral, centrally fixed.*

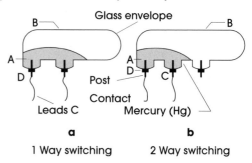
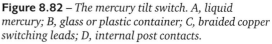

Figure 8.82 – *The mercury tilt switch. A, liquid mercury; B, glass or plastic container; C, braided copper switching leads; D, internal post contacts.*

weight of clean water) and provides instant contact with the switching posts in the glass tube. Electrical arcing is minimised and the weight of the mercury counter-balances the action of the bimetal spiral and prevents any spring action from reversing the switching mode until a suitable temperature degree of difference has been reached. This is called the *temperature differential*.

Thermometers

It is easy to confuse *temperature* with *heat energy*, but the two terms are completely different. The temperature of a body is a measurement of its energy level or 'hotness' and can be expressed in Kelvin (K), or degrees Celsius (°C), Fahrenheit (°F) or Réaumur (°R). For example, a large cylinder filled with hot water contains far more energy than the electric immersion element providing it.

Summary of types

There are many types – some are based on the expansion and contraction of liquids such as dyed alcohol or mercury. Others are dependent on the movement of a spiral bimetal strip or spring arrangement whilst work of a precise nature often requires a *platinum resistance thermometer* that converts the change in electrical resistance (caused by temperature variations) into Kelvin or degrees Celsius.

Thermoelectric thermometers are often used in industry where to use other types of thermometer would be impractical. This variety of thermometer uses two *dissimilar metals* such as iron and constantan and records the microscopic electrical current generated when they are heated.

Finally, the gas thermometer is often favoured in the refrigeration industry. This type operates by means of *gas pressure* changes brought about by temperature changes.

We will review just four of these.

Clinical thermometer

This specially designed instrument enables you to record your body temperature. Because your temperature is about 37°C (98.4°F), the scale is shortened to read only a few degrees either side of normal body temperature.

First aid boxes supplied to building and construction sites have this type of instrument as part of their kit.

Construction – A clinical thermometer consist of a small elongated, round glass phial, in which mercury has been added and which can flow into a slim glass tube. During the production stages, the capillary is formed into a miniature 'humpback bridge'. Called the *constriction,* this odd shape stops the column of expanded mercury sliding back into the glass bulb at the very time you need to read the recorded temperature – Figure 8.83 illustrates this. (To rejoin the separated column of mercury, just flick the instrument.)

After removing the air from the inside of the thermometer, the instrument is sealed and packaged into a familiar glass sleeve and graduated in divisions of 0.1°C from 35 to 43°C, as illustrated in Figure 8.84.

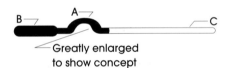

Figure 8.83 – *The clinical thermometer is designed with a constriction (that is, the hump within the capillary) which allows the body temperature to be read at leisure. A, constriction; B, glass phial; C, fine capillary. The more modern electronic type is rapidly replacing this type of thermometer.*

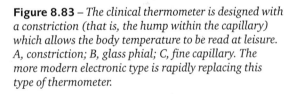

Figure 8.84 – *The clinical thermometer. A, point of constriction; Hg, liquid mercury.*

Spiral bimetal thermometer

This style of thermometer works with the aid of a bimetal spiral-shaped cylinder constructed from two dissimilar metals such as invar and brass – invar is an alloy that has a low rate of linear expansion. The outer end of the spiral cylinder is fixed as shown in Figure 8.85 – labelled C –

leaving the other end free to move. The free-to-move end of the spiral cylinder has a small spindle attached to it on which a pointer is mounted. An increase in temperature will affect the bimetal spiral and cause it to turn in a clockwise direction. As the pointer and spindle are parts of the spiral assembly, the pointer will be seen to magnify any displacement resulting from thermal expansion. Figure 8.86 illustrates

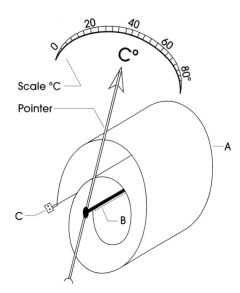

Figure 8.85 – *The basic working principles of the spiral bimetal thermometer. A, bimetal spiral made from invar and brass; B, the spindle fitted to the bimetal section of the thermometer; C, bimetal fixing point.*

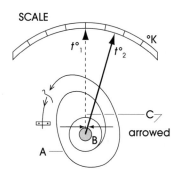

Figure 8.86 – *The spiral bimetal thermometer is set in motion when the long pointer magnifies a slight displacement caused by an increase or decrease in temperature. A, the bimetal spiral (also illustrated as 'A' in Figure 8.85); B, the spindle on which the pointer is supported; C, illustrating how a slight displacement is magnified.*

this graphically. Similarly, a *decrease* in temperature will cause the bimetal to unwind or advance in an *anticlockwise* direction.

Thermoelectric thermometer

In 1821, it was discovered that a tiny current could be produced when two wires of equal length, made from dissimilar metals such as copper and iron, were twisted together at one end. It was noticed that, when heat was applied at the twisted end, while a degree of difference was maintained at the other end, a minute current could be recorded when the two unattached ends were connected to a sensitive galvanometer – see Figure 8.87.

Construction – Modern thermoelectric thermometers consist of a series of two dissimilar metals such as antimony and bismuth. Each dissimilar section of metal is physically bonded to the next at a common junction. Each metal component, other than the join, has a strip of heatproof insulation positioned between them

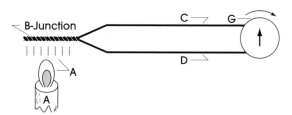

Figure 8.87 – *How a thermoelectric thermometer works – basic principles. A, heat source; C, copper; D, iron; G, galvanometer.*

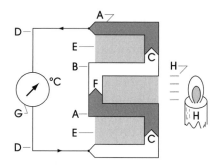

Figure 8.88 – *The principle of a thermopile. A, antimony (a bluish-white metal); B, bismuth (a white crystalline metal with a pinkish tinge); C, the hot junction; D, heat-resistant insulated conductors; E, insulation; F, the cold junction; G, galvanometer graduated in °C; H, heat source.*

as illustrated in Figure 8.88 – see note E. A set of high-temperature leads connect the two dissimilar metal ends of the instrument and a final connection is made to a sensitive galvanometer graduated in degrees Celsius. Thermometers of this standard are found in heavy industry and in laboratories in the form of hand-held instruments.

Gas thermometers

A gas thermometer consists of a small cylindrical lightweight metal reservoir some 150 mm long by about 11 mm wide to which nitrogen gas has been added – this is the business end of the instrument. The reservoir is connected to a long capillary tube. The hardened copper capillary is joined to a flexible sensitive *hollow* 'horse-shoe' type loop made from copper and housed within the main body of the thermometer – see Figure 8.89a.

Variations in pressure within the sensing cylinder caused by a rise and fall in temperature are transferred through the capillary to the copper sensing loop. This causes a slight

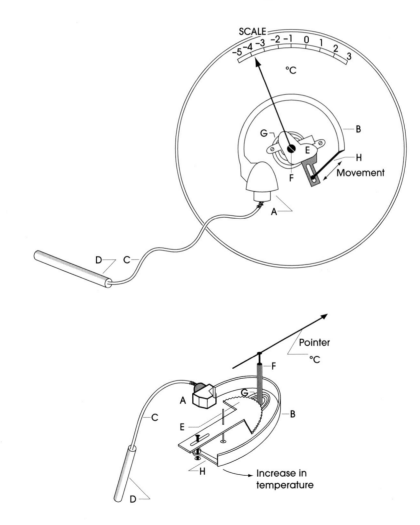

Figure 8.89 – *The capillary thermometer explained. A, pressure junction; B, copper sensing loop; C, capillary tube; D, gas reservoir; E, ratchet; F, cogwheel spindle supporting the indicating movement; G, hairspring controlling movement; H, movement lever.*

263

movement to occur. The end of the sensing loop is connected to an arrangement of levers, cog-spindles and a semicircular ratchet. The structure of the ratchet transfers thermolinear movement into an amplified semicircular motion. This amplified movement will allow you to take the temperature – see Figure 8.89b.

This is a reliable thermometer found within the refrigeration industry but it requires a small quantity of penetrating oil on the moving parts from time to time if misleading values are to be avoided.

Constant volume gas thermometer

You will not find this type of thermometer on site – it is more suited to the laboratory! The constant volume gas thermometer is *extremely* accurate. Briefly, it consists of a gas bulb in which the air has been taken out and nitrogen added. The bulb is connected to a vertically positioned cylindrical glass mercury reservoir (illustration note A in Figure 8.90).

How it works – Variations in temperature permit the nitrogen gas to increase or decrease in volume, allowing the mercury column to rise or fall in harmony with both pressure and temperature. Temperature is read from a scale adjacent to the column of mercury. The enlarged glass reservoir (A) shown in Figure 8.90 is illustrated for clarity and details of this

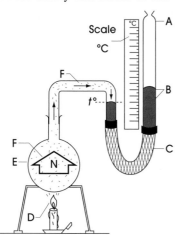

Figure 8.90 – *The constant volume gas thermometer explained. A, glass reservoir; B, liquid mercury inside the reservoir; C, flexible rubber connecting tube; D, heat source; E, bulbous gas tank bottle; F [N], gas pressure.*

thermometer have been added to provide you with a brief insight and practical awareness of the types of thermometers that are available.

Linear expansion

Expansion can cause many problems to an electrical installation. Hot weather can cause plastic conduit and trunking to warp or buckle under the stress caused by expansion.

Fortunately, this is avoidable. A well-planned installation would demand the use of *expansion couplers* throughout the system to reduce problems of this nature – Figure 8.91 illustrates this.

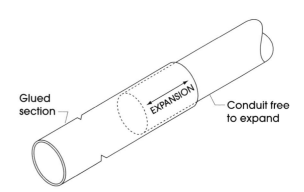

Figure 8.91 – *A PVCu expansion coupler used in plastic conduit installations.*

The advantages of linear expansion

Expansion in industry also has its advantages:

- Hot rivets burred into shape will bring two work pieces tightly together.
- Thermometers rely on the expansion (and contraction) of liquids.
- Bimetal strips used in over-current devices need expansion to function.
- Fluorescent starter switches require expansion to operate.
- Car directional indicators are dependent on expansion to work as intended.

Rates of expansion

Materials have different rates of linear expansion for each degree of temperature rise. Table 8.1 summarises in listed form several of the more

Table 8.1 – *Temperature coefficients for linear expansion for different materials for Kelvin and degrees Celsius (0 Kelvin = absolute zero).*

Compound or element	Temperature coefficient per Kelvin or °C (α)
Aluminium	0.000 026
Brass	0.000 026
Copper	0.000 016
Glass (regular)	0.000 009
Invar alloy	0.000 000 9
Iron	0.000 012
Platinum	0.000 008 9
Silica	0. 000 000 42

common materials we use in electrical work, together with their rates of linear expansion.

The increase in length of a given substance per Kelvin (Kelvin is measured in units – not degrees) or degree Celsius is called the *coefficient of linear expansion*. We express this as a numerical factor or multiplier for any given substance. The symbol representing this coefficient is the Greek lower case letter alpha, written α.

To provide an example, the coefficient of linear expansion for aluminium is 0.000 026/K. This means the linear expansivity for this metal is the fraction of its original length by which it expends per Kelvin rise in temperature.

Use the following expression to calculate problems involving linear expansion (α):

$$\alpha = \frac{\text{increase in length}}{\text{original length} \times \text{rise in temperature}} \quad (8.44)$$

As an example, consider the following: an aluminium conductor 200 cm in length has a measured temperature of 20°C. The conductor was placed into an industrial oven operating at a constant temperature of 100°C. After a period of one hour, the conductor was removed from the oven. Measured with a laboratory micrometer, the sample was 200.416 cm in length. From the data provided, calculate the coefficient of linear expansion for aluminium.

Your solution – Refer back to expression (8.41) and the data provided within the example:

increase in length = 200.416 cm–200 cm = 0.416 cm

original length = 200 cm

rise in temperature = 100°C–20°C = 80°C

So, substituting for known values:

$$\alpha = \frac{200.416 - 200}{200 \times (100 - 20)} = \frac{0.416}{16000} = 0.000026 /°C$$

which is the coefficient of linear expansion for aluminium.

By transposing expression (8.41), other unknown values are calculable in terms of known data. For example, you can determine the *original length* of the sample with respect to the other values.

Referring back to the expression:

$$\alpha = \frac{\text{increase in length}}{\text{original length} \times \text{rise in temperature}}$$

First, cross-multiply:

$$L_i = \alpha \times L_0 \times {}^\circ t \quad (8.45)$$

Next, dividing each side by $\alpha \times {}^\circ t$ you get

$$\text{original length } L_0 = \frac{\text{increase in length } L_i}{\alpha \times \text{rise in temperature } {}^\circ t} \quad (8.46)$$

This one you can work out for yourself!

Principle of moments

Definitions

SI units and symbols – The SI unit derived from force is the *newton*. It is defined as *the force required to produce an acceleration of 1 metre per second in a mass of 1 kilogram*. It has the symbol N and is named after Sir Isaac Newton (1642–1727).

The moment of a force about a point is calculated in *newton metre* (N m). Described as the *'turning effect'* of the force, it can also be stated that a moment is *equal to the product of the force (N) and the perpendicular distance (d) from the line of action of the force to the fulcrum (pivot)*.

Hence

$$\text{moment of a force about a point} = N \times d$$
(8.47)

This will become simpler by studying Figure 8.92, where F is the fulcrum, d is the distance from the turning point to the fulcrum and N is the applied *clockwise* force in newtons. A balanced force, illustrated in Figure 8.93, means that a force applied in one direction must equal a force applied in the opposite direction. Imagine the fulcrum as the middle of a seesaw. This will help you decide which moment is clockwise and which is an anticlockwise moment. A practical application of this would be two children of equal weight sat at either end of a seesaw. This is the *principle of moments* which is defined simply as:

the sum of all clockwise moments = the sum of all anticlockwise moments (8.48)

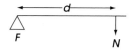

Figure 8.92 – *The moment of a force about a point is equal to the product of the force, N, and the perpendicular distance from the force to the fulcrum, F.*

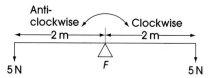

Figure 8.93 – *The sum of the clockwise moments will equal the sum of the anticlockwise moments when in a state of balance.*

Positive and negative moments

Traditionally, clockwise moments are *negative* while anticlockwise moments are *positive*. With this in mind, it can be said that the sum of all

moments is zero. Take as a simple example the previous illustration, Figure 8.93.

anticlockwise moments: $+(5 \times 2) = +10$ N m
clockwise moments: $-(5 \times 2) = -10$ N m.
Therefore: $+10$ N m-10 N m $= 0$

To confirm expression (8.45), balance a strong metric rule of uniform mass on a suitable balancing point (fulcrum). Add metric weights of known value by suspending them either side of the midpoint position with nylon thread. Adjust them until the metre rule is completely balanced. When *balanced* they will observe the principle of moments no matter how many 'moments' are operating at the same time, as Figure 8.94 clearly shows.

Clockwise moments (N_1): $20 \times 100 = -2000$.
Clockwise moment (N_2): $40 \times 25 = -1000$.
Thus, total clockwise moments (N_1) and (N_2): $-2000+(-1000) = -3000$.

Anticlockwise moment (N_3): $10 \times 50 = +500$
Anticlockwise moments (N_4): $25 \times 100 = +2500$
Thus total anticlockwise moments (N_3) and (N_4): $+500+(+2500) = +3000$

Therefore, algebraic sum of the moments: $3000-3000 = 0$.

Finding the magnitude of an unknown force

Figure 8.95 illustrates a simple arrangement in which a uniform rod is balanced at its midpoint position by means of a suspended thread. Two forces of known magnitude (N_1) and (N_3) are suspended 2 metres either side of the point of balance, F. A third and unknown weight (N_2) is placed 1 metre to the left of the fulcrum, F, and a equilibrium balance is gained.

Calculate the mass of the unknown force by algebraic means using expression (8.47) and referring to the previous illustration:

$$(N_2 \times d_2)+(N_1 \times d_1) = N_3 \times d_3$$
$$N_2 \times d_2 = (N_3 \times d_3)-(N_1 \times d_1)$$

Thus

$$N_2 = \frac{(N_3 \times d_3)-(N_1 \times d_1)}{d_2}$$

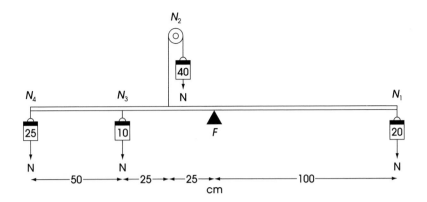

Figure 8.94 – *The principle of moments remains true no matter how many moments are operating at the same time.*

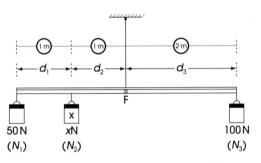

Figure 8.95 – *Finding the magnitude of an unknown force.*

Substituting for known values:

$$N_2 = \frac{(100 \times 2) - (50 \times 2)}{1} = \frac{200 - 100}{1}$$

$$= 100 \text{ N (the unknown force)}$$

To find the point of balance, reformulate this expression using:

$$d_3 = \frac{(N_2 \times d_2) + (N_1 \times d_1)}{N_3}$$

Again, substituting for known values:

$$d_3 = \frac{(100 \times 1) + (50 \times 2)}{100} = 2 \text{ metres}$$

When a problem has to be solved involving several moments acting at various points, it will be easier for you to sketch and label the problem with the data you have available. By adopting this method you will make your task clearer and easier to solve.

Centre of gravity

Figure 8.96 illustrates in pictorial form an irregularly shaped sheet of glass. All matter consists of a vast number of tiny molecules, each possessing its own weight factor and each attracted to the centre of the earth by the force of gravity. (By the way – a molecule is the smallest portion into which a substance can be divided, which is capable of an independent existence, yet still maintaining the properties of the original substance.)

For practical purposes, let us take for granted that all forces acting upon these tiny molecules are both parallel and vertical to each other, as the pull exerted by our planet is such a long way away. The result is that the total weight of the body (this time a piece of glass) acts through a single point that corresponds to the body's *centre of mass* – the centre of mass being the balancing point as illustrated in Figures 8.96 and 8.97.

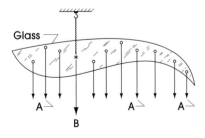

Figure 8.96 – *The way the force of gravity acts through an irregular shaped sheet of glass. A, gravity acting on individual molecules of glass; B, the centre of gravity.*

The centre of gravity of a body is defined as a fixed point at which the sum of all molecular weights acts and through which the force of gravity always passes.

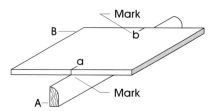

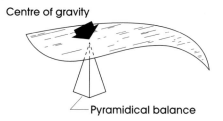

Centre of gravity

Pyramidical balance

Figure 8.97 – *The centre of gravity is found by placing the shaped glass on the pyramidal balance to obtain a state of balance.*

Figure 8.98 – *An alternative method of finding the centre of gravity by first marking a–b. A, skirting board; B, your workpiece.*

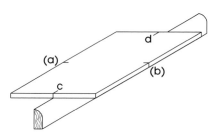

Figure 8.99 – *Next, rotate your workpiece through 90° and mark again, c–d.*

Practical methods of locating the centre of gravity

There are two well-tried methods of locating the centre of gravity of a flat body such as a sheet of electrical insulating material or a small steel side panel serving a site-built assembly. They are summarised as:

1 the balancing method

2 the plumb line method.

The *balancing method* – A straight section of bevelled skirting board would be an ideal way to demonstrate how we can use it to find the centre of gravity of a flat rectangular section of timber.

- Fix the side of the bevelled skirting board at 90° to the finished floor.

- Place and balance the work piece on top of the sloping edge and mark at the positions shown ('a' and 'b') in Figure 8.98.

- Rotate your work piece through 90°; balance and mark again ('c'–'d'), see Figure 8.99.

- As a way of checking, repeat, placing your work piece diagonally ('e'–'f').

- Join all your marked balance points, a–b, c–d and e–f, with a pencil line as shown in Figure 8.100.

- The exact centre of gravity will lie at the point where all three lines meet.

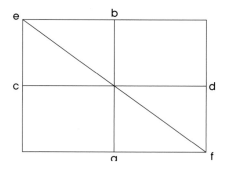

Figure 8.100 – *Join the marked balance points a–b, c–d, e–f (should you feel the need) with a pencil line.*

The *plumb line method* – This procedure is great if, for example, the centre of gravity has to be found for an irregularly shaped plywood template used for a special electrical project.

- First drill a few holes around the edge of the shape as described in Figure 8.101.

- Hammer a *slim nail* into a suitable timber overhang and place the template over the nail at A1, allowing it to swing freely.

- When the template is rested its centre of gravity will be at a point *directly below the nail*.

- Hook the end of the plumb line's nylon cord around the nail and allow it to swing freely, without brushing the template.
- When your plumb line has come to rest, mark the template very carefully at the top and bottom point where the nylon cord crosses the edge of your template, as illustrated in Figure 8.102.

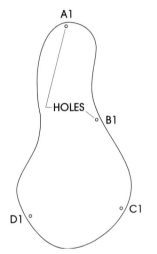

Figure 8.101 – *Use a template of the shape you wish to find the centre of gravity of and drill a series of holes around its edge – A1, B1, C1 and D1.*

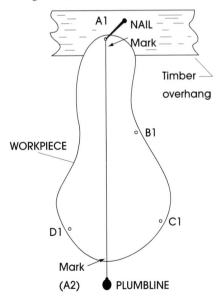

Figure 8.102 – *Mark the template carefully where the string of your plumb line passes the edge of your cutout shape.*

- Repeat the test from positions B1, C1 and D1.
- Remove your template and place it on a flat surface. Join all reference points A1–A2, B1–B2, C1–C2 and D1–D2 with a pencil line.
- The centre of gravity will lie at the point where all four lines intersect, as illustrated in Figure 8.103.

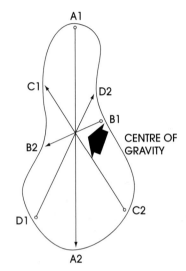

Figure 8.103 – *The centre of gravity lies at the point where all lines intersect.*

Conditions of equilibrium

Stable equilibrium

Equilibrium means stability or balance. When a body such as a factory-made electrical cabinet is tilted, then released to return to its original position, its centre of gravity *rises* during this period of displacement. This condition, *stable equilibrium*, can be seen in Figure 8.104.

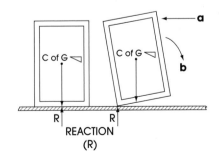

Figure 8.104 – *If a body is displaced (a), released (b) and returns to its original position, it is in a condition of equilibrium.*

269

Unstable equilibrium

If a body is slightly displaced the centre of gravity will *fall* during this short period of displacement. We call this condition *unstable equilibrium* and Figure 8.105 illustrates this idea using a pyramid-shaped body balanced on its tip.

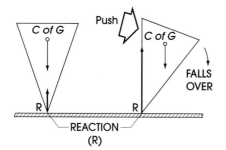

Figure 8.105 – *Unstable equilibrium (balance/stability).*

Neutral equilibrium

When a body is moved but settles in the same position when released, the centre of gravity will remain at a constant height during the period of displacement. This condition is known as *neutral equilibrium* and a football is an easy way of describing this idea. Figure 8.106 illustrates this.

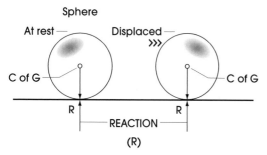

Figure 8.106 – *Neutral equilibrium (balance/stability).*

Principle of levers

A lever is a strong rigid bar that is able to turn freely at one point, as illustrated in Figure 8.107. You can use it to help displace or move a load, such as an electric motor.

Used properly, a lever will provide an excellent *mechanical advantage (MA)* for the user. You will

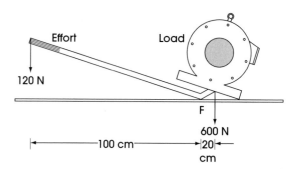

Figure 8.107 – *The principle of a lever. F, fulcrum; N, newtons.*

probably know that it is far easier to displace a heavy load using a lever with a long *effort arm* than a short one. Think of when you have to remove a car tyre from an alloy wheel.

Mechanical advantage

The mechanical advantage of a lever is defined as follows: *the ratio of the* horizontal *length of the arm from the fulcrum to the load to the* horizontal *length of the effort arm to the fulcrum.*

Figure 8.108 will make this clear to you. Hence:

$$\text{MA} = \frac{\text{effort arm length to fulcrum}}{\text{load arm length to fulcrum}} \tag{8.49}$$

You can also work it out by applying the principle of moments in relation to the load and the effort.

Let us recap: the moment of a force about a point is the product of the force and the perpendicular distance from the fulcrum (refer to Figure 8.107).

Load (which is 600 N) × 20 cm (the horizontal length of the load arm)

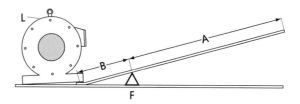

Figure 8.108 – *Use this lever to move or tilt a heavy electric motor. A, effort arm; B, load arm; F, fulcrum; L, the load.*

= effort (120 N) × 100 (the horizontal length of the effort arm)

or

Load × 20 = effort × 100

Dividing each side of the equation by (effort × 20):

load/effort = 100/20

Substituting for known values:

600/120 = 100/20 or 5 = 5.

Therefore the mechanical advantage = 5

The MA will increase by using a lever with a longer effort arm. This will make your task easier.

Classes of lever

You might be forgiven for thinking all levers work in the same way – but this is not so, as Figure 8.109 demonstrates. Levers are divided and classified into three groups, each group applying different operational principles.

Category 1 – Levers in this category operate, when the fulcrum is between the load and effort, as illustrated in Figure 8.109a. Examples include using a crowbar to shift a heavy electrical load and trimming a conductor with a pair of insulated wire cutters.

Category 2 – The second category of lever operates by positioning the fulcrum at, or towards, the end of the lever with the load situated between the fulcrum and effort (Figure 8.109b). Examples include undoing a bottle of beer using a bottle opener, pushing a loaded wheelbarrow and cracking open walnuts with a pair of nutcrackers.

Category 3 – The last category of lever has a mechanical disadvantage over other types as the fulcrum appears near or at the end of the lever while the effort is concentrated at a midpoint position between the load and the fulcrum (Figure 8.109c). An example is when an angler lands his catch using rod and tackle. A twin formation of this type of lever is when using site first-aid tweezers to remove a splinter.

The meaning of 'work done'

Work is done when a force produces movement in the direction of the force. For example, when a diesel tank engine pulls a freight train or whenever an apprentice climbs a ladder to carry out a task.

SI units

The *SI unit* of *work* is the *joule* (J) and is *the work done when a force of 1 newton (N) moves through a distance of 1 metre in the direction of the force.*
    Larger units are:

- the kilojoule (kJ) = 1000 J
- the megajoule (MJ) = 1000 000 J.

As work is said to be done when a force produces movement in the direction of the force, we can then say

work = force × distance moved in the direction of the force.   (8.50)

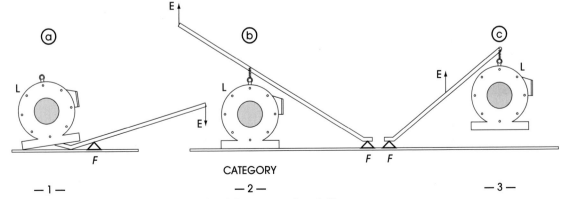

Figure 8.109 – *Categories of levers. L, load; F, fulcrum; E, point of effort.*

Alternatively, you can write it as

$$W = F \times S$$

where W is the work done in joules (J), F is the force applied in newtons (N) and S is the distance moved in metres (m) (remember 'S' for space).

Now, consider the following problem. *Calculate the work done* in kilojoules by a small diesel forklift truck applying a force of 1000 newtons over a distance of 80 metres.

Solution – First, refer back to expression (8.47):

$$\text{work done} = F \times S$$

Substituting known values:

$$W = 1000 \times 80 = 80\,000 \text{ J}$$

To convert to kilojoules, divide your answer by 1000; hence

$$kJ = 80\,000/1000.$$

Therefore the work done over a distance of 80 metres = 80 kJ.

Mass, weight and force

Mass

The *mass* of a body is the quantity of matter it contains. It is unaffected by changes of gravity. For example, a reel of 6-mm² cable will keep its same mass whether used on Earth or taken to the Moon – only its *weight* will alter. The mass of an object will depend on its *density* (ρ) (the Greek letter rho). Technically, the density of an object is in kilograms per cubic metre but it is easier to speak about it as a number. A column of liquid mercury would have a mass approximately 13.6 times greater than a similar column of clean water at 4°C, as Figure 8.110 illustrates.

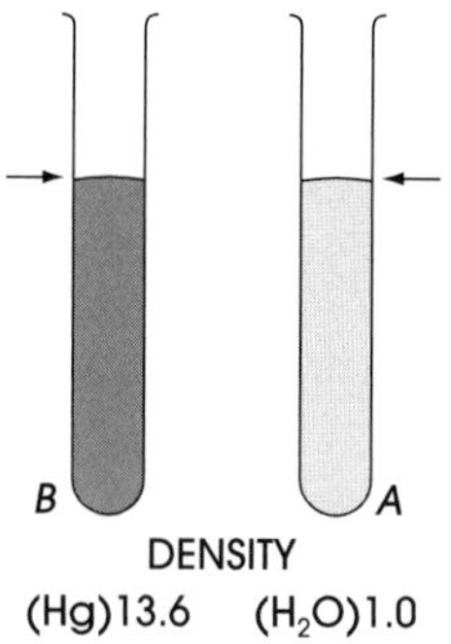

DENSITY

(Hg)13.6   (H₂O)1.0

Figure 8.110 – *A column of mercury has a mass 13.6 times greater than a similar column of water at 4°C. A, water; B, mercury.*

Find the mass of an object using the expression:

$$m = \rho \times V$$

where m is the mass of the object in kilograms, ρ is the density of the object and V is the volume of the object in cubic metres.

Mass is measured using a beam or top-pan balance but never a conventional spring balance that relies on gravity to provide a value. The basic unit of mass is the kilogram. Use this in various forms of multiples and submultiples – Table 8.2 illustrates this.

Weight

The force of gravity determines the *weight* of a body – its value is measured in newtons (N).

The weight of an object varies depending on where it is measured. You would weigh heavier within a coalmine than you would if you were to fly supersonically. An electrical appliance weighing 1 N on the surface of the Earth would, when weighed on the Moon, register a mere 0.166 N whereas if taken on a journey to the giant gas planet Jupiter, it would weigh an impressive 2.64 N.

Table 8.2 – *SI units of mass.*

Unit	Symbol	Subunit and equal to	Symbol
1 metric tonne	t	1000 kilograms	kg
1 kilogram	kg	1000 grams	g
1 gram	g	1000 milligrams	mg
1 milligram	mg	1000 micrograms	µg

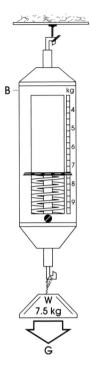

Figure 8.111 – *The weight of a body is defined as the force in newtons (N) acting on a mass upholding it. B, spring balance; G, the force of gravity; W, a 7.5 kg weight.*

In summary, the weight of a body is described as the force in newtons acting on a mass and upholding it, as Figure 8.111 illustrates.

Force

Measured in newtons, you can describe force as an influence that alters or tends to change the state of rest or motion of a body – formally defined as *the force needed to produce an acceleration of 1 metre per second on a mass of 1 kg.*

The acceleration experienced by a free-falling mass of 1 kg placed in a vacuum averages 9.8 metres per second^2 or 32 feet per second^2 if you prefer imperial measurements. This is g, the gravitational constant. It is logical to assume that the gravitational force acting on this mass must be 9.8 N in order to produce an acceleration of 1 metre per second^2 on a mass of 1 kg.

With these figures fresh in your mind, we can say that *the weight of a 1 kg mass is 9.8 newtons.*

Put another way, a body of mass m kg experiences a force of N newtons when allowed to fall freely within our gravitational field.

The value of the force F (expressed in newtons), is calculated by the following expression:

Force in newtons = mass in kilograms × g (the gravitational constant)

As a practical example, taking on board the gravitational constant, consider the following: calculate the work done in joules by an electrician of 70 kg mass climbing a vertical service ladder 7 metres high, given that the average value of 'g' is 9.81 m/s^2.

Solution – First, refer back to expression (8.47):

work done in joules (J) = force × distance moved in metres

or

work done in joules opposing gravity = (mass in kg × g) × distance

Substituting with known values:

work done = (70 × 9.81) × 7 = 4806.9 J

Efficiency of a machine

A machine is a device for overcoming physical resistance at one point by the application of a force elsewhere. Wire cutters, crimping tools and pulley wheels are classed as machines. Unfortunately, for us, they will always operate at less than their full potential as they are in opposition to internal losses such as gravity, air resistance and friction.

We are unable to design a machine with an efficiency of 100% – if we could, the useful work output would always equal the work input.

Expressed as a percentage

The efficiency of a machine (symbol, η, the Greek letter eta) is a percentage and defined as the ratio of the useful work output to the applied work input. Hence:

$$\text{efficiency } (\eta) = \frac{\text{work done by load}}{\text{work done by effort}} \times \frac{100}{1}$$

$$(8.51)$$

As an example, consider first a theoretically perfect machine taking the form of a workshop block and tackle, illustrated in Figure 8.112.

First, refer back to expression (8.50):

work done in joules = force in newtons × distance moved in metres

Figure 8.112 shows the work done by the load is 2 m × 100 N = 200 J, whereas the work done by the effort is 25 N × 8 m = 200 J.

To find the efficiency, look back to expression (8.51):

$$\text{efficiency } (\eta) = \frac{\text{work done by load}}{\text{work done by effort}} \times \frac{100}{1}$$

Thus

$$\eta = \frac{200}{200} \times \frac{100}{1}$$

Therefore the efficiency $(\eta) = 100\%$. This is not possible, as the following example will help to confirm.

Figure 8.113 provides a picture of an electric motor weighing 100 newtons raised through a vertical distance of 2 metres by a poorly maintained block and tackle. The effort required to lift up the load is 40 newtons moved through a distance of 8 metres.

To calculate the efficiency of this machine, the work done by both load and effort must first be calculated:

work done in joules = mass × distance moved

$$(8.52)$$

Work done by load $= 100 \times 2 = 200$ J
Work done by effort $= 40 \times 8 = 320$ J

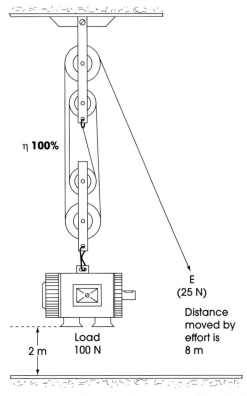

Figure 8.112 – *A theoretically perfect machine. E, the distance moved by the effort, 8 metres. The distance moved by the load was 2 metres.*

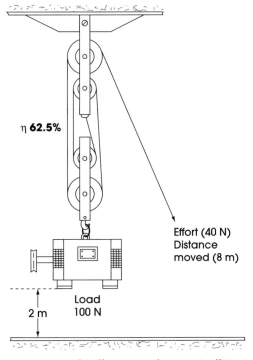

Figure 8.113 – *This illustration shows an inefficient machine. It has an inefficiency factor of 62.5%.*

Using expression (8.51):

$$\eta = \frac{200}{320} \times \frac{100}{1} = 62.5\%$$

This is clearly a very inefficient machine – but they do exist whenever maintenance is overlooked.

Velocity ratio and mechanical advantage

Velocity ratio

The *velocity ratio* (VR) of a machine is the ratio of the distance moved by the applied *effort* to the distance moved by the *load* in the same time. When the applied effort is *smaller* than the load, the VR is always greater than unity, so heavy loads are moved slowly with ease by moving the effort quickly.

You can also find out the velocity ratio by counting the number of *effective strings* serving the *lower* pulley arrangement. The block and tackle illustrated in Figure 8.112 has a velocity ratio of four. Alternatively, VR is found using the following expression:

$$VR = \frac{\text{distance moved by effort}}{\text{distance moved by load}} \quad (8.53)$$

Reflecting back to Figure 8.112:

$$VR = 8/2 = 4$$

The velocity ratio of a machine is expressed as a number – there are no units.

Mechanical advantage

The *mechanical advantage* (MA) of a machine is expressed as a number. It is the ratio of the load raised to the effort required to lift the load. It can be calculated using the following expression:

$$MA = \frac{\text{load raised in newtons}}{\text{effort required in newtons}} \quad (8.54)$$

Efficiency in terms of VA and MA

The efficiency of a machine (η) can be calculated in terms of the velocity ratio and mechanical advantage using the following expression:

$$\eta = \frac{MA}{VR} \times \frac{100}{1} \quad (8.55)$$

Referring back to Figure 8.113, expressions (8.50) and (8.51) and recapping:

- load = 100 N
- effort = 40 N
- distance moved by load = 2 m
- distance moved by effort = 8 m

Therefore

MA = 100/40 = 2.5
VR = 8/2 = 4

Hence

$$\eta = \frac{2.5}{4} \times \frac{100}{1} = 62.5\%$$

Wasted energy – The percentage of wasted energy can be evaluated by subtracting the efficiency factor obtained from 100%. Hence:

$$\text{wasted energy} = 100 - \eta.$$

Referring back to Figure 8.113:

$$\text{wasted energy} = 100 - 62.5 = 37.5\%$$

(If a perfect machine were to exist, the velocity ratio would be equal to the mechanical advantage.)

The efficiency of a tungsten filament lamp

This is calculated using this expression:

$$\eta = \frac{\text{power consumed in watts (W)}}{\text{illuminating power in lux (lx)}} \quad (8.56)$$

The efficiency of an electric motor

The efficiency of an electric motor will depend on the following conditions:

1 iron losses
2 magnetic losses
3 gravity
4 friction
5 air resistance
6 the condition of the bearings
7 to some extent, extremes in temperature.

Calculate the efficiency with the following expression:

$$\eta \text{ (motor)} = \frac{\text{power out}}{\text{power in}} \times \frac{100}{1}$$

Summary

1 A simmerstat is a device to regulate heating loads and to prevent thermal over-run.

2 Temperature is a measurement of a body's *energy level* or '*hotness*' and is expressed in Kelvin or degrees Celsius.

3 When a body is in a state of *equal balance*, the total sum of all *clockwise* moments will equal the sum of all *anticlockwise* moments.

4 Find the centre of gravity of a flat object with the use of a *plumb line* or by *balancing*. The three states of equilibrium are *stable, unstable* and *neutral*.

5 Express the efficiency of a machine as a *percentage* – it is the ratio of useful work output to applied work input.

6 Different materials expand at different rates when placed in the same temperature.

Review questions

1 Briefly describe the role of a simmerstat.

2 Suggest two metals which, when riveted together, will demonstrate the bimetal (bending by heat) principle.

3 Describe a problem that can affect an open type of thermostat.

4 Suggest a practical problem that can affect plastic conduit concerning *linear expansion*.

5 State briefly the principle of moments.

6 What is meant by the term '*centre of gravity*'?

7 How is the *mechanical advantage* of a lever defined?

8 Describe a method of calculating the *weight* of an object.

9 List the three conditions of *equilibrium*.

10 How is the velocity ratio of a machine measured?

11 List the two active components of a thermoelectric thermometer.

12 The mechanical advantage of a lever can be increased by one of the following:
   (a) by using a longer load arm
   (b) by using a longer effort arm
   (c) by increasing the pressure on the effort arm
   (d) by physically increasing the size of the fulcrum.

13 Bear out the following statement: one newton is approximately equal to the weight of 90 grams. True or false?

14 List three reasons that will affect the efficiency of an electric motor.

15 Why is it not possible for a machine to be 100% efficient?

The benefits of using an AC voltage compared to DC

The nominal (this means, in name only) voltage throughout the EC is 230 volts. The frequency of this supply is 50 cycles per second, which means it will take 1/50 of one second to complete one cycle.

The advantage of using an AC supply is that it can be transformed to a higher voltage for transmission across country with very little loss of power. If we were *unable* to do this, we would have to send the generated power using domestic voltages. This would cause a great deal of power loss (I^2R) throughout the network and much heat would be produced throughout the transmission lines caused by the natural resistance of the cable.

- Halogen lamps will eventually blacken when controlled by a dimmer switch set to a reduced voltage.
- The efficiency of an immersion heater cylinder may, as a guide, be taken as
  - unlagged – from 77 to 85%
  - lagged with a loose cover – 90 to 95%
  - factory moulded lagged – from 95 to 98%.
- The *efficacy* (effectiveness) of a lamp is the ratio of light in lux to the lamp power in watts.
- Misalignment between a motor and the load it serves is often to blame for vibration problems. Other reasons are:
  - an unbalanced rotor due to careless servicing
  - badly worn bearings
  - loose motor mounting bolts.
- EU manufactured electric motors are designed for 4% voltage variation.
- Domestic nylon carpets and other products have low melting points. Take care not to allow a hot masonry drill-bit to come into direct contact with nylon furnishings.
- Take time to do your job properly – rushed jobs are seldom good jobs.

Unfortunately, we are unable to transform direct current (DC) to a higher voltage so no advantage is gained from using this system. This discovery became apparent many years ago when the first custom-built public low-voltage DC power cable became operational in 1881.

Short-circuit capacities of protective devices

A protective device, such as a fuse or circuit breaker, will only function safely and as intended if it has a rated value that is greater than the prospective fault current at the point installed. As an example – imagine what would happen if you placed an old semi-enclosed ceramic fuse (rewirable type) into a faulty circuit given that the rated short-circuit capacity of this type of fuse is only 1 kA and your installation had a prospective fault current of 4.35 kA! It would be extremely dangerous to say the least. Table 8.3 provides you with a small selection of protective devices and their manufacturer's short-circuit capacities in kiloamps (kA).

Why we need fuses/protective devices in electrical installation work

We need protective devices within our circuits to defend our appliances and apparatus from harm should a fault condition arise. Protective devices such as fuses and circuit breakers will also shield our fixed wiring circuits from serious damage should a path of low impedance leak current from the phase conductor to earth or directly from phase to neutral.

Under such conditions, the fuse (a low melting point metal alloy wire) will *warm up, glow, blacken and melt*. Once ruptured, the circuit becomes completely isolated from the source of the supply. The circuit is now safe.

Table 8.3 – *Short-circuit capacities of protective devices.*

Quick Reference Type of protective device used (example: fuse, circuit breaker, cartridge, etc,) Description or title of device Maker's short-circuit capacity (kA)
A Cartridge fuses to BS 1361 Type1 Type 1 16.5
B Cartridge fuses to BS 1361 Type 2 (S.A. fuses) Type 2 33.0
C Semi-enclosed fuse (the rewirable type) Type S1A 1
D Semi-enclosed fuse (BS 3036) Type S2A 2
E Semi-enclosed fuse (BS 3036) Type S4A 4
F Cartridge fuse to BS 88 Part 2.1 (general use) (at 400 volt) 50
G Cartridge fuse to BS 88 Part 6 (general use) (at 230 volt) 16.5
H Cartridge fuse to BS 88 Part 6 (general use) (at 400 volt) 80
I Circuit breakers to BSEN 60898* M 1 1
J Circuit breakers to BSEN 60898* M 1.5 1.5
K Circuit breakers to BSEN 60898* M 3 3
L Circuit breakers to BSEN 60898* M 4.5 4.5
M Circuit breakers to BSEN 60689* M 6 6
N Circuit breakers to BSEN 60898* M 9 9

MCBs are divided into types. Each type has its own function and a selection of them are listed in Table 8.4.

Table 8.4 – *MCB types and the circuits they serve.*

Quick reference	MCB type	Recommended use or application of the MCB
i	1 and B	Small switching surges – commercial and domestic installations
ii	2 and 3	General use in industrial and commercial installations. Fluorescent lighting installations. Small motor circuits. Any circuit which produces a surge when switching on other than transformers
iii	C	Highly inductive circuits – large electric motors and groups of fluorescent lighting which are switched together
iv	4 and D	Ideal for electric welders and site transformers where a high surge current is expected. Some medical appliances may require a Type 'D' MCB such as x-ray machines, etc.

Answers

Chapter 1 (page 7)

1. Rotten/unstable flooring holes and pits, disused wells, structural defects, tripping hazards, sudden changes in the direction of stairways and chemical spillage, etc.

2. A personal health and safety risk. It is possible to connect faded-multi-coloured conductors wrongly, especially in diminishing light.

3. You must seek help and advice from an appropriate person.

4. You must put on a life jacket.

5. Check, your workforce and that any visitors who have evacuated the building are safe.

6. 112 is an alternative number to use.

7. The following – an accident leading to death or two or more days taken off work, hospitalisation or where faulty plant/equipment is blamed.

7. A mishap, an unforeseen event, a misfortune – a fluke.

9. Fire, explosion, toxic atmosphere or terrorist activity.

10. Your safety representative, a senior member of your management team or if all else fails, your local Health and Safety office.

11. Misjudgement, (c).

12. Before any site work commences, (b).

13. Your Health and Safety officer.

14. An unexpected happening, a crisis, an unexpected tight spot or an unexpected urgency.

15. The Health and Safety at Work Act -The Electricity at Work Regulations and BS 7671 [The Wiring Regulations].

Chapter 1 (page 23)

1. Carelessness, lack of knowledge, human limitation, weariness and horseplay.

2. For power tools and lighting arrangements, use a 110-volt system. For temporary site-accommodation, use a 230-volt power source.

3. This deed is against UK law. The material burnt produces toxic fumes and smoke. It also damages the environment.

4. These items could snag on live conductive parts and cause burns to the skin, electric shock or even death.

5. Secretary of State for Energy.

6. To protect farm workers and live stock from lethal voltages.

7. A Leclanché dry cell will produce 1.45 volts.

8. The hydrogen gas released during charging is inflammable.

9. Frost burn to your hands will occur when the temperature of the conduit is below freezing point.

10. Sound the alarm!
    - Try to extinguish the flames
    - Do not put your self in danger
    - If the fire can not be put out – escape by using the safest route out of the building.
11. 20 kg (this is about 44 imperial pounds).
12. Apply a cold-water bandage firmly around the affected joint.
13. Use something that is dry: a wooden handled brush, a plastic chair, a length of dry hosepipe, etc.
14. Place the casualty on his/her back on a flat surface
    - Open the airway by placing one hand on his/her forehead and tilting back the head.
    - Remove anything in their mouth which should not be there
15. Every three minutes.

Chapter 2 (page 45)

1. Rotten flooring, biological hazards [dead animals, rat's droppings, etc.], unstable steps/staircases, hazardous substances, hot surfaces, trip hazards, holes, disused wells, structural defects and safety of the existing electrical installation, etc.
2. In a locked, windowless building or container.
3. Traditional scaffolding, access tower, steps, ladder, trestles, hydraulic scissor platform, or hoist.
4. It is true.
5. Grain storage silo – item (c).
6. Hard hat, ear plugs, eye protection, visor, dust mask, industrial gloves, barrier creams, knee pads, steel capped boots/shoes, hair net, harness belt, high visibility clothing, life jacket (for working around swimming pools and open water), battery acid apron, etc.
7. Gas, water, electricity, telephone/fax, fuel oil, steam and air.
8. Removal of potential fire hazards, improved efficiency, accident reduction, improved

morale, good impression created, reduces complaints and produces a happier workforce, etc.

9. Items soiled with industrial contamination, chipped ceiling tiles, ladder damage, dirty hands and shoes, floor covering damage, damage to pipes and cables, chipped paintwork, burning/scorching etc.
10. Corrosive – item (b).
11. Substances causing death, or damage to health, etc.
12. Please see the illustrative answers grouped with these pages (p.287).
13. The paint will cover any defects or structural problems.
14. Scaffold plank, thick plywood or waterproof MDF products, etc.
15. Fencing/barriers automatically operated lighting arrangements, intruder alarm, warning notices, a night watchman, a security company to patrol on a regular basis.

Chapter 3 (page 67)

1. Personal protective equipment – loosely referred to as PPE.
2. Silver, platinum and gold. As a practical answer, copper must be accepted.
3. Steel wire armoured cable – sometimes-double steel wire armouring is used.
4. This is an abbreviation for, *Control of Substances Hazardous to Health.*
5. Safety footwear, suitable gloves, ear protection, eye protection, hardhat, overalls, and high visibility clothing, etc.
6. Within areas of extreme heat, emergency lighting served by a central battery system, fire detection and alarm systems, corrosive and radioactive atmospheres, where electrical screening is required.
7. C_g [cable grouping], C_a [ambient temperature], C_i [thermal insulation] and C_f [BS 3036 semi enclosed fuse].

8. No more than 4 per cent of the nominal voltage (U_0)

9. The spiral fixing devices will dislodge themselves from the ceiling aided by the weight of the fitting/luminaire.

10. Expansion bolts, large wall plugs [e.g. *Rawlplugs*®], and screws, threaded studding with nuts and washers to suit.

11. By providing a plywood backing above the ceiling tile – it is best if the backing is the same size as the soft ceiling tile.

12. Mark the wall where the hole or holes are to be drilled. Draw a right-angled cross with its centre over the mark [+]. If the cutting edge wanders from its target, it can be promptly corrected.

13. The person will be aware that English is spoken but people who are technically unacquainted with electrical jargon will not understand what is being said.

14. They provide operatives and management with details of variations to work that is to be carried out.

15. Paper work enclosures can be photocopied, processed and used to build a customer instruction manual. At site level, they are very useful to extract information, data and facts regarding assembly, fitting and the final connection of conductors to an appliance. They are also ideal to keep as a personal reference to be used if and when.

Chapter 4 (page 136)

1. A purpose made cable basket coupler – often supplied with a continuity-bonding link.

2. Fit an internal expansion coupler after every third length of trunking installed. Elongated holes [one above the other] should be formed at the end of the trunking to allow for thermal expansion. It is wiser to use pan-headed screws and washers that must not be over-tightened.

3. Used for electrical continuity when steel trunking serves as a circuit protective conductor.

4. A 45 % space factor must be observed.

5. Used in industrial installations as a means of distributing electrical power.

6. This means lengths of trunking can only be fitted one way in order to maintain the integrity of the polarity of the installation.

7. Glass reinforced polyester, low smoke and zero halogen [LSZH], mild steel, PVCu and stainless steel.

8. Bare copper, PVC covered, low smoke and fumes [LSF].

9. (a) Calculate the amount of armouring to be removed
   (b) Score around the protective sheath and the armouring
   (c) Remove the plastic protective sheath by cutting
   (d) Snap off the galvanised steel wire armouring
   (e) Slide on the plastic shroud, which protects the brass gland
   (f) Slide on the brass gland-nut and park below the plastic shroud
   (g) Remove about 25 mm of plastic outer sheath from the start of the steel wire armouring in order to accommodate the conical section of the gland
   (h) Splay out in conical fashion the 25 mm of prepared armouring as outlined in item (g)
   (i) Place the conical section of the gland below the splayed armouring
   (j) Push the conical section of the gland into the splayed armouring and reunite the two sections of the gland and tighten
   (k) Remove the inner bedding sheath up to about 10 mm from the bottom of the gland
   (l) Place the plastic shroud over the gland and fit, secured with a steel lock nut and brass earthing tag

10. May be rewired, can be added to, is an excellent protective conductor, galvanised

conduit is ideal for external use, can be installed using mixed sizes of conduit and can be wired using mixed cable sizes.

11. Bend by means of a bending spring made from steel.

12. A site built or manufactured enclosure in which cables are enclosed after it has been fitted along the chosen route. Made from metal, but not conduit or trunking, or alternatively can be constructed from timber or ridged (sp.?) plastic.

13. A 10-amp double pole switch is ideal as it isolates the live phase and neutral conductors from an outside luminaire.

14. A two way and intermediate switching arrangement using three-core and earth sheathed cable when applied to a domestic installation.

15. The value of the extra low voltage *current* in *amps* and the value of the extra low *voltage* applied. Transformers are rated in kVA [0.01 and 0.1 kVA etc.].

lighting arrangements, electric motors, and industrial heater banks, etc.

8. A way to forward an idea without the need for technical detail. It provides a means of focusing on potential problem areas. It enables planning to be carried out at a later stage.

9. Large terminations for large conductors.

10. Ear protectors and industrial earplugs.

11. A multi-meter set to the correct scale or an approved LED voltage indicator.

12. In writing to your safety officer, site supervisor or works manager. Both sign and date this document and keep a copy for reference.

13. Latex chemical gloves, eye protection and a battery-acid resistant apron.

14. Corrosion will develop – especially in damp conditions.

15. No more than 0.05 Ω – check using a milliohm meter.

Chapter 5 (page 163)

1. Terminated to conductors serving circuits from a main distribution bus-bar chamber. It is also a means to terminate large switch-fuses and isolators. Also used to terminate electrical equipment within heavy industry.

2. Tunnel terminations [crimped type].

3. Loose terminations will arc when on load. Arcing produces heat, leading to a breakdown of the insulation and the integrity of the copper conductor.

4. Use a milliohm meter.

5. One way, two way and intermediate switches. The use of double pole switches, PIR switches, time lag switches and time clock switching.

6. Use 2.5-mm^2 size cable. Domestic immersion heaters are 3 kW.

7. Transformer for 110 volt site power and

Chapter 6 (page 173)

1. Primary and secondary windings.

2. Step down reduces the applied voltage and step up increases the applied voltage.

3. A voltage meter accompanied with a suitable load, a continuity meter and an insulation tester.

4. A higher than expected voltage, (b).

5. Both sets of windings have the same number of turns of wire.

6. Heat resisting flexible three-core cable at 2.5 mm^2 in CSA.

7. A clamp meter set to about 20-amp full-scale deflection or by testing with a continuity meter.

8. Guidelines to be followed:turn off water and switch off the electricity serving the immersion heater. Disconnect the flexible supply cable. Unscrew the immersion

element with a box spanner. Using a 'tommy-bar', turn the failed element *anticlockwise*, maintaining equal pressure on both sides of the bar. Keep the box spanner squarely aligned to the flange of the element. Once removed displace any lime scale deposits that can be seen.

9. It will cause the neck of the cylinder to leak.

10. At the bottom of the cylinder.

11. Direct wiring method to a central programmer or alternatively, the central joint box method.

12. Usually 1.0 mm² PVC insulated and sheathed cable but if preferred use 1.5 mm².

13. Best positioned on a north-facing wall at 1.5 metre from the finished floor.

14. Either a double pole switch when the system is served from a dedicated breaker at the distribution centre or a fused connection unit fused at 3 amps.

15. It reduces the number of cables/conductors entering the programmer for final connection. It is easier to work on and will prevent cable crowding.

Chapter 6 (page 184)

1. TT, TN-S, TN-CS, IT.

2. Phase and neutral conductors only, (b).

3. PEN cable: a phase conductor, accompanied with a combined neutral and earth in the form of a copper stranded conductor wrapped around the insulated phase component. A black PVC insulated sheath provides protection for the combined neutral/earth element of this cable.

4. To serve rural communities and farms.

5. Mineral insulated cable. The gland pots used are accompanied by a flexible copper fly lead. Use this type of termination throughout the installation.

6. Main equipotential bonding and supplementary bonding.

7. Gas and water supplies, compressed air, oil and central heating pipes, exposed steel joists and air-conditioning ducting. Uncovered metal infrastructure, metal staircases, hand or guard rails. Open type steel work forming a dairy or milking parlour, etc. Metal cladding, forming doors and walls, etc.

8. 600 mm, (d).

9. A residual current device rated at 30 mA.

10. 16 mm².

11. Because the cable used represents both earth and neutral any residual current device placed in the circuit would trip out. The device would not stay 'ON'.

12. Within 600 mm from the supplier's meter.

13. Where mechanically protected, 2.5-mm² cable may be used.

14. The low neutral/earth impedance path developed by this system will render the device inoperative by effectively short-circuiting the operating coil.

15. Agricultural premises: 0.2 second.

Chapter 7 (page 216)

1. It will lead to a chemical process known as oxidation, which forms an electrical resistance between the two twisted conductors.

2. A tool designed to absorb heat and to allow delicate components to be soldered without thermal damage occurring.

3. Removes unwanted oxide and allows molten solder to bond with the copper wires. It also acts as a 'wetting' agent as it assists the liquidity of the solder.

4. Common voltages are 230 v [AC], 110 v [AC], 50 v [AC], 12–24 volts, [DC].

5. A connector where the *insulation* of the conductor is ruptured (c).

6. By reading the colour or *alphanumerical* code displayed.

7. The dielectric.

8. Used as a tuning circuit for a radio.

9. To prevent static electricity from damaging the component.

10. Discrete semi-conductor device.

11. It is a switch in the form of a double pole changeover relay designed for very low current use.

12. Please see the illustrative answers section of these papers (p.287).

13. Bread board, (b).

14. As a heat shunt, for bending conductors, to set or mount component leads into a circuit board. To gently hold components whilst soldering is taking place.

15. As power *input* or *output* points.

Chapter 8 (page 245)

1. Electrons within the valency shell are loosely held and are allowed to flow from one atom to another under the pressure of a voltage.

2. Silver.

3. Resistance is the opposition offered to an electron flow within a circuit and is measured [quantified] in ohms.

4. Power generated: Volts × Amps or Amps² × Resistance or the following,

$$\frac{\text{volts}^2}{\text{resistance}}$$

5. 30 ohms, 2.66 amp.

6. Volt drop = Current flow in amps × Resistance in ohms.

7. Often attributed to the physical breakdown of the cell.

8. $\frac{1}{R_T} = \frac{1}{R_1} + \frac{1}{R_2} + \frac{1}{R_3} + \frac{1}{R_4}$ ... and so on.

9. Within a residual current device [RCD] or a transformer.

10. The electrical pressure between the two plates of a capacitor causes an *elliptical deformity* within the orbits of the electrons. This deformity is *dielectric stress*.

11. 6.66 μF

12. 60 μF

13. Both the current and voltage are out of phase with each other by 90 degrees and the energy stored in the capacitor is returned to the supply at the end of every half cycle.

14. $X_L = 2\pi f L$

15. Please refer to the illustrative section of these pages (p.287).

Chapter 8 (page 256)

1. Volts   Watts   Volts²
   Amps   Amps²   Watts [either of these three]

2. Length, cross sectional area, temperature of a conductor and the material from which the conductor is made

3. $\frac{R_1}{R_2} = \frac{1 + (\alpha\, t_1)}{1 + (\alpha\, t_2)}$

4. Carbon (C).

5. $^\circ C = \frac{(^\circ F - 32) \times 5}{9}$

6. 0°C (zero degrees Celsius).

7. 4 per cent of the nominal voltage (c).

8. The number is unlimited.

9. The overload/current circuit would come into play.

10. When served via a fused connection unit.

11. 2.5 mm².

12. 75 m².

13. Data, television channels, telephone channels.

14. The following are correct:
    - Free from electrical interference
    - Easier to handle
    - User security greatly increased
    - Able to span greater distances
    - Able to carry far more data and information than conventional means.

15. Either 30 amp when a semi enclosed fuse is used or a 32-amp MCCB or MCB.

Chapter 8 (page 276)

1. To regulate heating loads and prevent thermal over run.

2. Brass and iron.

3. Accumulated grime, dust, humidity and atmospheric pollutants – this concoction will congest the ventilation grills.

4. Buckling plastic conduit, warping PVCu cable trunking systems.

5. The sum of all clockwise moments will equal the sum of all *anticlockwise* moments.

6. A fixed point at which the sum of all molecular weights acts and through which the force of gravity *always* passes.

7. The ratio of the length of arm from the *fulcrum* to the *effort*, to the length of arm from the *fulcrum* to the load.

8. A spring balance or any device dependent on the force of gravity.

9. Stable, unstable and neutral equilibrium.

10. VR = distance moved by the *effort* divided by the distance moved by the load.

11. Antimony, a bluish-white metal (Sb). Bismuth, a white crystalline metal with a pinkish shade (Bi).

12. By using a longer effort arm (b).

13. FALSE.

14. The following losses:
    - Iron losses
    - The effects of gravity
    - Frictional losses
    - Air resistance

15. There are practical efficiency losses such as gravity, air resistance, moreover, frictional losses.

    The useful work *output* can never equal the useful work *input*.

    Electric motors are also subjected to other losses such as:
    - Magnetic losses
    - Iron losses

Chapter 2 Qu. 12

DANGER OF DEATH

KEEP OFF
Danger of Death
if interfered with

Chapter 7 Qu. 12

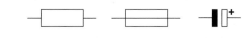

Chapter 8 Qu. 15

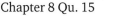

ac

Index